Everything,
All the Time, Everywhere:
How We Became
Post-modern

Everything, All the Time, Everywhere

How We Became Post-modern

Stuart Jeffries

VERSO

London • New York

First published by Verso 2021
© Stuart Jeffries 2021

1 3 5 7 9 10 8 6 4 2

Verso
UK: 6 Meard Street, London W1F 0EG
US: 20 Jay Street, Suite 1010, Brooklyn, NY 11201
versobooks.com

Verso is the imprint of New Left Books

ISBN-13: 978-1-78873-822-4
ISBN-13: 978-1-78873-825-5 (US EBK)
ISBN-13: 978-1-78873-824-8 (UK EBK)

British Library Cataloguing in Publication Data
A catalogue record for this book is available from the British Library

Library of Congress Cataloging-in-Publication Data

Names: Jeffries, Stuart, author.
Title: Everything, all the time, everywhere : how we became post-modern /
  Stuart Jeffries.
Description: London ; New York : Verso Books, 2021. | Includes
  bibliographical references and index. | Summary: 'Where modernism was
  serious, absorbed in grand narratives and committed to social progress,
  its successor was a riot of colour and irreverence, toying with forms
  and styles, committed to none of them and to nothing. But beneath its
  glitzy surface, post-modernism hid a dirty secret: it was the fig leaf
  for a rapacious new kind of capitalism, the bridgehead of the
  'post-truth' era in Western values' – Provided by publisher.
Identifiers: LCCN 2021029491 (print) | LCCN 2021029492 (ebook) | ISBN
  9781788738224 | ISBN 9781788738255 (ebk)
Subjects: LCSH: Postmodernism.
Classification: LCC B831.2 .J44 2021 (print) | LCC B831.2 (ebook) | DDC
  149/.97–dc23
LC record available at https://lccn.loc.gov/2021029491
LC ebook record available at https://lccn.loc.gov/2021029492

Typeset in Sabon by Biblichor Ltd, Edinburgh
Printed and bound by CPI Group (UK) Ltd, Croydon CR0 4YY

Contents

Introduction:
Creative Destruction

I

In 1982, a puzzling message appeared in midtown Manhattan. 'Protect me from what I want', read huge LED lettering in Times Square. What was it selling? Why would anyone want to be protected from their own desires? Who would do the protecting? And who had made us desire what we should not? The person responsible for installing the sign, the artist Jenny Holzer, did not do answers.

She might have told you, though, that her sign was not advertising, it was art – just not the kind of art you normally see in galleries. Holzer is perhaps best known for the slogans she put on T-shirts and baseball caps and even condoms in New York in the late seventies and early eighties. She also art bombed the street at night, putting up posters with texts culled from Karl Marx, Susan Sontag and Bertolt Brecht, and others of her own such as 'The desire to reproduce is a death wish' and 'Romantic love was invented to manipulate women'. 'I would sneak around the morning after I'd pasted them up to see if anybody would stop', she recalled. 'That's the test of street art – to see if anybody stopped. People would cross out ones they didn't like and would start others. I liked that people would engage with them.'[1]

'The desperate things seem to require attention, the lovely things seem to elicit celebration', she told me in 2012. 'If I had to choose, I would go to the awful in the hope that doing something could yield a happier result.' Perhaps her hope was that, in taking art from gallery to street, she might indict a rampaging culture of consumerism and get her subversive message to new demographics.

The 'awful' that Jenny Holzer gravitates towards is to do with how, in our post-modern era, the existential human tragedy of desire followed by disappointment followed by desire followed by disappointment has been exploited as never before. Holzer, possibly, was highlighting how that cycle of desire and disappointment helps keep capitalism in business: we need to be protected from being corrupted by desire in general, and by shopping in particular.

Her sign became a striking emblem of the new, post-modern world in which we live. It is a world in which we know that we are ensnared in a system we feel scarcely able to change. Indeed, it is one in which we are oppressing ourselves with the very things we desire.

Holzer's piece invoked a different kind of 1984 from the one imagined in Orwell's novel. Big Brother needed electroshock, sleep deprivation, solitary confinement, drugs and hectoring propaganda broadcasts to keep power, while his Ministry of Plenty ensured that consumer goods were lacking to ensure subjects were in an artificial state of need. In our deindustrialised, neoliberal era, such biopolitics is obsolete, argues Korean-German philosopher Byung-Chul Han. What capitalism realised was that it didn't need to be tough, but seductive. Instead of saying no, it says yes: instead of denying us with commandments, discipline and shortages, it seems to allow us to buy what we want when we want, become what we want, and realise our dream of freedom.[2]

In this book I will argue that post-modernism originated under the star of neoliberalism, a global economic ideology whose heroes or devils, depending on your political persuasion, include Ronald Reagan, Margaret Thatcher, Deng Xiaoping and General Augusto Pinochet. It is an ideology that stands for liberating entrepreneurial acumen from the presumed dead hand of state intervention. Before neoliberalism got us in a chokehold, advanced industrial post-war states, especially in western Europe, had been committed to two things: the ladder and the safety net. The former gave the least fortunate the chance to rise; the latter caught them if they fell. Free education was part of the ladder, socialised medicine part of the safety net. Neoliberals such as Reagan and Thatcher kicked over the ladder and cut holes in the safety net. They shrunk the state to a humbler role. Its new task was to create a framework to defend and extend free trade, free markets and private property rights. Ameliorating poverty or creating equality of opportunity? The state could forget about such patronising nonsense.

Soon after neoliberalism was born, the world economy suffered economic recession. The 1973–74 recession and its successor in 1979–83 led to the collapse of the Fordist model of integrated industrial production. Instead, short-term contracts proliferated, work was outsourced from Walsall to Warsaw and still further east. The information age supplanted the manufacturing age, capital flowed more freely across the world, companies expanded globally. Your parents may have made worthwhile things for a living using now-obsolete skills, but you are more likely to work in a call centre for a loan-consolidation website.

In order that capitalism overcome recessionary crises, and indeed emerge stronger from them, neoliberalism required a populist, market-based culture of differentiated consumerism and individual libertarianism. 'As such it proved more than a little compatible with that cultural impulse called "post-modernism" which had long been waiting in the wings but could now emerge full-blown as a cultural and intellectual dominant', argued Marxist geographer David Harvey.[3]

But what is post-modernism? As the name suggests, it came after modernism. Post-modernism is a movement that disdained the modernist vision. Its enthusiasts saw it as a giddy, fun, libidinous carnival after the communal prison, a riot of colour and quotation that replaced modernism's acres of brutalising concrete. But post-modernism is more than cultural handmaiden to neoliberalism, as Harvey envisaged it. It is a paradox. It is at the same time both alibi for and indictment of the neoliberal order. Worse yet, its very indictments can serve as alibis.

Jenny Holzer's 'Protect Me from What I Want' is a case in point. She may have conceived of it as a radical subversion of consumerist mores, and maybe it was. But if, as she hoped, her art was 'doing something', it was not doing much to create a happier world, if by happier she means a more just one. Another of her street-art slogans from the 1980s captures this: 'Enjoy yourself because you can't change anything anyway.' No doubt that message was ironic, indicting the playful cynicism that some have found characteristic of post-modernism.

It could be decoded as saying that enjoyment and fatalism needed to be overcome in order to overthrow a demeaning economic system, and that such cynical fatalism in the face of overweening power was the problem. But, at the same time, it could be taken at face value, as recommending quietism of a rather clever and self-satisfied kind. Irony is necessarily subversive because it means the opposite of what it says; but the risk of post-modern irony is that it subverts not what it sets out to critique, but the critical agency of the message itself.

Just as sarcasm is the lowest form of wit, irony is the feeblest kind of indictment. And yet it has become the go-to rhetorical stance of the post-modernist. By maintaining a cool, affectless stance, irony colludes, unconsciously or otherwise, with what it overtly disdains. Many of Holzer's texts appear on consumer goods – baseball caps, T-shirts, skateboards, mugs. 'Have you ever worn one of your T-shirts?' I asked Holzer. 'No, that would be mortifying. Shoot me if you ever see me in one.' It's a revealing remark: as if she hoped to remain immune to the corrupting merchandise her ostensibly subversive art has been reduced to. Jenny Holzer is too cool to put her heart on her sleeve or her slogans on her chest.

Holzer is not a politically conscious artist bombing the street with politics, but something more typically post-modern: a semiotic terrorist blowing up language and subverting her own

4

authority as creator. Her fellow artist Dan Graham considered her street posters to be more than political: 'Unlike most "political" art, which a priori begins with a worked-out belief and then employs a methodology to prove it, Holzer's statements deconstruct *all* ideological (political) assumptions.'[4] She was producing what the Italian philosopher Umberto Eco called open texts, endlessly interpretable, shifting, unstable. French post-modern theorists such as Roland Barthes and Michel Foucault had recently argued for the sacrificial death of the author as guarantor of the meaning of a work. No longer, they gleefully argued, was the author of a work the one who decided for all time its immovable truth. 'We know now that a text is not a line of words releasing a single "theological" meaning (the "message" of the Author-God)', wrote Barthes, 'but a multidimensional space in which a variety of writings, none of them original, blend and clash.'[5]

For Foucault, the author needed to be murdered, since he was stopping the free flow of intellectual capital: 'He is a certain functional principle by which, in our culture, one limits, excludes, and chooses; in short, by which one impedes the free circulation, the free manipulation, the free composition, decomposition and recomposition of fiction.'[6]

Holzer's street slogans were, wittingly or otherwise, a product of these times: they served as celebrations of her own death as an authority figure, in favour of her work being erased, augmented and repurposed by a putative streetwise democracy of interpreters. Her slogans were akin to what Barthes wrote of literature: 'Literature . . . by refusing to assign a "secret", an ultimate meaning, to the text (and to the world as text) liberates what may be called an anti-theological activity, an activity that is truly revolutionary since to refuse to fix meaning in the end is to refuse God and his hypostases – reason, science, law.'[7]

At the same time as Barthes and Foucault were killing the author, their countryman Jacques Derrida sought to deconstruct what he called the 'metaphysics of presence': the notion that the meaning of a word has its origin in the structure of reality and makes the truth about that structure directly present to the mind. He posited that all kinds of disciplines – philosophy, science, history – were prone to this metaphysics. Each supposed that their claims about the world were made true by the world. Derrida, rather, insisted that we are caught in a linguistic system that does not relate to external reality. All conceptual systems, he argued, were falsifying and distorting, precisely because they seemed to make claims about the world; but really those claims could not be sustained since language was metaphor-ridden and its terms relative to other terms.

'Deconstruction is not an operation that supervenes from the outside, afterwards, one fine day', wrote Derrida. 'It is always at work within the work.'[8] Viewed thus, Jenny Holzer's work was taking itself apart as fast as she made it.

Holzer started out making street art and ended up working for luxury car brand BMW. Her slogans appeared on marketable T-shirts, hoodies, handbags. Holzer, in the playful way of post-modernism, also collaborated with capitalism. In 1990 she became the first woman artist to win the prestigious Golden Lion award at the Venice Biennale. Commissions began to pour in from banks, arts organisations and museums across the globe. Holzer worked obligingly within the system she ostensibly indicted. In 1999, she became the fifteenth artist to be commissioned for the BMW Art Car Project. She wrote 'Protect me from what I want' in metal foil and outlined the slogan with phosphorescent paint on a BMW that was due to race in that year's 24 Hours of Le Mans rally. She added more slogans to the car's side-pods: 'You are so complex, you don't respond to danger' and 'The unattainable is invariably attractive'. The car's rear wing read: 'Lack of charisma can be fatal' and 'Monomania is a prerequisite of success'. Holzer was perhaps deconstructing the boy racers' self-image even as they pulled on their helmets.

I say 'perhaps' because she was not clearly saying anything. What was clear, though, was how Holzer's art functioned as brand: her words were the brand even when it was not clear what they meant. And by associating their car with her clever oeuvre, BMW was itself burnishing its own image – even if what the slogans actually said might be taken to imply that those who drove BMWs were sociopathic narcissists.

Sadly, Holzer's car did not in the end race at Le Mans. Nonetheless, it looked like it had been defaced by a politically conscious graffiti artist indicting the commodified world she lived in. And yet it was also the work of the opposite, an artist who had been co-opted into the system she despised. What looked like subversion was at the same time submission. What looked like sticking it to the Man was also self-abasement before his motorised altar.

In the post-modern world, subversive art often risks such submission or co-optation into the system it seems to be submitting to critique. Not because of the willing collaboration of artists, but because of a leading feature of that world – appropriation. Everything is up for grabs, for sale at the right price, because there is nothing outside the market.

II

There is another narrative of what post-modernism means. It's one that doesn't involve seeing post-modernism as more or less cynical collapse into accommodation with a new mutant form of capitalism. Rather, it's the story of an idea as liberation from the constraints of the modern world that dehumanised us, reducing us to cogs in modernist machines. In this story, modernism has become oppressive; post-modernism is the revolution we need to restore our utopian hopes by means of a liberating free-for-all.

This is the story of post-modernism that David Byrne, one-time front man of New York indie band Talking Heads, told in the Victoria and Albert Museum's catalogue to its 2011 exhibition *Post-Modernism: Style and Subversion 1970–1990*. At its inception, Byrne suggested, post-modernism felt akin to a giddy, joyful liberation movement:

Like many others I felt [modernism] had both strayed from its idealistic origins and become codified, strict, puritanical and dogmatic . . . Besides, as lovely as it is, modern furniture is cruelly uncomfortable. If postmodernism meant anything is allowed, then I was all for it. Finally! The buildings often didn't get much more beautiful or the furniture more comfortable, but at least we weren't handed a rulebook.[9]

The great modernists of the early twentieth century were certainly idealistic. They called for creative destruction, for the detonation of frills, furbelows and floral fuss in favour of the functional. The pioneer of the International Movement of modernist architecture, Le Corbusier, argued that 'a house is a machine for living in', and believed the modern world had evolved beyond the need for decoration. Useful, well-designed things would fill the void, not just in architecture, but for furniture, furnishings and fixtures, too. He wrote in 1925: 'The almost hysterical onrush in recent years toward this quasi-orgy of decor is only the last spasm of a death already predictable.'[10] 'The evolution of culture marches with the elimination of ornament from useful objects', wrote another pioneer, Adolf Loos, in his *Ornament and Crime*.[11]

Where modernism was, to critics like Charles Jencks, functional, self-denying, austere, mechanical, utopian, led by a revolutionary cadre of technocrats and like-minded artists, and committed to progress, post-modernism, in contrast, was exuberant, fun, irresponsible, anti-hierarchical, and had lost faith in progress.

According to Jencks, in his 1977 book *The Language of Post-Modern Architecture*, the modern world died at 3.32 p.m. in St Louis, Missouri, on 15 July 1972 'or thereabouts'.[12] The dynamiting of the Pruitt-Igoe housing scheme was a noise that resonated around the world. Completed in 1954, the thirty-three eleven-storey buildings replaced entire slum neighbourhoods in inner-city St Louis, and were advertised as a paradise of 'bright new buildings with spacious grounds', indoor plumbing, electric lights, fresh plastered walls, and other 'conveniences expected in the 20th century'.[13]

Japanese-American architect Minoru Yamasaki, in common with the modernist architects who inspired him, believed that architecture could make people behave better. His design for Pruitt-Igoe followed the principles of the modern movement: cars and pedestrians were separated, open space was provided between the blocks, and flats were oriented to catch daylight. The austere blocks rising over the Missouri plains were designed to be machines for living in, part of a federally funded solution to rehouse poor folk from overcrowded slums. If there were to be crimes at Pruitt-Igoe, ornament was not to be one of them.

But, even from the start, the housing scheme was hardly paradise, but an expression of American racial segregation. The project was named after two soldiers: Captain Wendell O. Pruitt, an African-American fighter pilot in World War II, and William L. Igoe, a former US congressman of Irish ancestry. The Igoe apartments were intended for whites, the Pruitt for blacks. Yet, when it became clear that whites were unwilling to move into the development due to a racist unwillingness to live alongside African-Americans, it became all black.

Paradise soon became a dystopia. Federal money that had bankrolled the project did not cover maintenance costs. Rents were supposed to fund Pruitt-Igoe's upkeep, but they did not, not least because the residents were often poor: the median income of tenants was $2,718, the equivalent today of $25,000 (£19,000). Pruitt-Igoe became more of a slum than the ones its residents had escaped, notorious for violence, vandalism, chaos and squalor. It became an emblem of racially segregated America. 'Police must not sound sirens when approaching the Pruitt-Igoe homes', went one police directive. 'The residents come from the chain-gang and blood-hound country of the Deep South and are likely to react violently to sirens.'[14] Soon police stopped responding to calls from Pruitt-Igoe altogether.

What went wrong? Pruitt-Igoe 'would be here today if it had been maintained like it was when it opened up', one former resident told the makers of the 2011 film *The Pruitt-Igoe Myth: An Urban History*, 'but it went down and down and down and down'.[15] Down is right: less than twenty years after Pruitt-Igoe was completed, the first of its blocks were destroyed by controlled implosion. It was finally put out of its misery. 'Boom, boom, boom,' wrote Jencks, the arch-proselyte for post-modernism, triumphantly.[16]

Godfrey Reggio's 1982 film *Koyaanisqatsi* captured this destruction to the soundtrack of a doomy, minimalist piece by Philip Glass called 'Pruitt-Igoe'. In the Native American Hopi language, *Koyaanisqatsi* means 'unbalanced life'. That was the suggestion of the film: modernist architecture like Pruitt-Igoe was part of an off-kilter existence. Reggio showed this by means of slow-motion and time-lapse photography, speeding up traffic, slowing down demolitions. Reggio was dynamiting the modern world in his cinema. What we saw in *Koyaanisqatsi* was akin to the imposition of uniformity from above. Modernist architecture was, for its critics, totalitarianism in glass and steel, inhuman in scale, dismal to live in.

The blowing up of Pruitt-Igoe was a consummation devoutly to be wished by many American capitalists, too, who viewed public housing projects with suspicion. Such aspirations were un-American, smelling of socialism. And anything that smacked of socialism in an America obsessed with winning the Cold War between the capitalist West and the Soviet bloc was to be terminated with extreme prejudice.

What was terminated when Pruitt-Igoe fell was not simply a style of architecture. That was only the pretext for a more profound demolition: the commitment to the interventionist and regulatory powers of the state to improve the lot of society's most disadvantaged that had been orthodox in many advanced industrial nations since 1945. If post-modernism arose from Pruitt-Igoe's rubble, so did neoliberalism, the economic philosophy that sought to roll back the state and make the disadvantaged responsible for their well-being.

Both post-modernism and neoliberalism were couched in terms of liberation – the former from the tyranny of functional style, the latter from the state. And yet, the new neoliberal orthodoxy of minimal state and personal responsibility substituted one tyranny for another – namely the tyranny of the market. George Orwell foresaw this in his review of neoliberalism's bible, Friedrich Hayek's *The Road to Serfdom*: 'A return to "free" competition means for the great mass of people a tyranny probably worse, because more irresponsible, than that of the State.'[17]

Post-modernism's role in establishing this new tyranny was to extend that narrative of liberation into culture, to suggest that, instead of modernism's constraining rulebook, we were now in a free-for-all where anything goes. Behind the apparent free-for-all that David Byrne and others liked about post-modernism was a new system of control of the kind Byung-Chul Han describes, one that does not need torture chambers to keep its subjects compliant. Neoliberalism is at once more efficient than the totalitarian system of control that Orwell satirised in *Nineteen Eighty-Four* and more insidious, since it makes its subjects into ones who imagine themselves to be free while at the same time desiring their own domination.

The myth, then, is that modernist buildings like Pruitt-Igoe were oppressive and dehumanising. In truth, what was inhuman was not the architecture but the system that failed to maintain it. Residents interviewed for the documentary recalled their utter joy when they moved in, not only at the plumbing, heating and electricity, but also at the views and the 'warmth of community'. 'When I moved in, it was one of the most exciting days of my life', said one interviewee. People remembered 'a wonderful building with so many different smells of cooking' and 'so many kids to play with'.[18] To start with, at least, Yamasaki's modernism was not alienating. No one called it grim and inhuman, and when it was compared to a prison it was because of the management regime, not the design.

Post-modernism is often cast as a liberation from an oppressive predecessor. But that modernist predecessor was neither oppressive nor dehumanising. Pruitt-Igoe was allowed to become hellish for its tenants. The rot was allowed to set in because Pruitt-Igoe looked too much like an un-American, state-funded, socialistic experiment in communal living. The existence of Pruitt-Igoe was a symbolic blot on the neoliberal landscape. So when Pruitt-Igoe was blown up, the noise heard around the world signified not just the end of a style of architecture, but the end of the social-democratic consensus that had dominated the advanced industrial nations since World War II.

Today the ruins of Pruitt-Igoe are swathed in resurgent forest that critics have compared to the setting for horror film *The Blair Witch Project* – as if the very ground on which a modernist paradise once arose has become cursed. It became the prototype for the detonation of modernist public housing around the world.

In Britain, for example, where modernist public housing had been envisaged as a solution to post-war slum clearance, 'the great kerflumpf of a collapsing tower block became a form of civic festival, in which politicians would preside over bacchanals of cascading masonry'.[19] As state support for public projects dwindled during the seventies, so post-modernism supplied an alibi. In 1979, Margaret Thatcher was elected prime minister, and soon after embarked on a sell-off of Britain's council estates as part of her policy of reducing the public sector and giving the market free rein. The policy showed that the assault on state-funded property could not be solved with dynamite alone, but also required the expansion of the market into all corners of life.

This was the doctrine of the Viennese political economist Friedrich Hayek, a copy of whose *The Road to Serfdom* Thatcher famously brandished as she set out to explain her economic vision. This doctrine was, simply, one of minimal state intervention, negligible public ownership and a belief that private ownership of property was essential for civilisation. Socialism, by contrast, was slavery. Thatcher agreed: her dream of a nation of owner-occupiers was perhaps one of her most fully realised. Millions of Britain's better-off working class snapped up their own council houses at discounted prices under Conservative right-to-buy legislation. In 1981, two years into Thatcher's premiership, England and Wales had 10.2 million owner-occupiers. A mere decade later, their ranks had swollen to 13.4 million.

What arose in the place of these collapsing tower blocks and modernist estates? Just as Pruitt-Igoe went down, the World Trade Center in New York was going up. It was also designed by Minoru Yamasaki, but had very different occupants from those in his Missouri housing scheme. Indeed, the history of who worked in the Twin Towers exemplifies the rise of neo-liberalism. Their initial occupants were government bodies like the State of New York. As the state was rolled back during the seventies and eighties, Wall Street firms relocated there, including Morgan Stanley, the Aon Corporation and Salomon Brothers. Yamasaki's Twin Towers were destroyed with an even greater ruthlessness than the demolition of Pruitt-Igoe when, on 11 September 2001, two airliners were flown into them by terrorists, murdering thousands of the people inside.

One of the first architectural icons of post-modernism was John Portman's Westin Bonaventure Hotel in downtown Los Angeles. 'I am at a loss', the great critic of post-modernism, Fredric Jameson, wrote of this hotel, 'when it comes to conveying the thing itself.'[20] But he had a jolly good go: escalators and elevators were in dialectical relationship, the good Marxist noted, and effectively replaced the *flâneur*-haunted Parisian pedestrian arcades that modernists like Baudelaire and Benjamin had eulogised at the birth of the modern era; the cocktail bar rotated, making drinkers into passive consumers of the vista; the acres of glass were like 'reflector sunglasses which make it impossible for your interlocutor to see your own eyes and thereby achieve a certain aggressivity [*sic*] toward and power over the Other'. Not that Jameson was unimpressed: it was a kind of miracle. What he had already noted about post-modern literature and art was its depthlessness, its fixation on surface; he couldn't imagine depthless architecture as possible, but John Portman had realised it.

The whole complex of hotel, boutiques, restaurants and bars 'aspires to being a total space, a complete world, a miniature city', wrote Jameson. It was like a foretelling of the movie *The Truman Show*. Certainly, post-modern theorists had trouble leaving. 'Given the absolute symmetry of the four towers, it is absolutely impossible to get your bearings', wrote Jameson exasperatedly. He was not the only one to be baffled. In its first years, the hotel's many boutiques struggled because shoppers could not find them. Given that the Westin Bonaventure was designed by a post-modern architect who was also a millionaire developer, this was surprising. If post-modernism was the handmaiden of neoliberalism, keeping capitalism going, it did not always do a very good job.

III

What does this paradoxical term post-modernism mean? In *Philosophical Investigations*, Ludwig Wittgenstein considered games – tennis, ring-a-ring o' roses, chess, noughts and crosses, patience – and invited us to specify what is common to them all. 'Don't say: "There *must* be something in common, or they would not be called 'games'" – but *look and see* whether there is anything common to all', Wittgenstein wrote. 'And the upshot of these considerations is: we see a complicated network of similarities overlapping and criss-crossing: similarities in the large and in the small.'[21]

Wittgenstein was trying to get us to see that games do not have to have a single essence. Rather, he argued, each game stands in family resemblance to others. Just as some family resemblances – nose, eyes, gait, hair, temperament – overlap and criss-cross, without all resemblances being shared by all members, so all games need not share any one thing in common.

If post-modernism is, like games, a family-resemblance concept, then that may help us realise why so many disparate phenomena appear under its umbrella. Madonna may be a post-modern artist for revelling in such knowing paradoxes as being a queer icon while apparently straight, for being a feminist hero while dressing as if for the role of a soft-porn fantasy, and for multiplying her personae (virgin, saint, mother, femme fatale) often by retooling past icons such as Marilyn Monroe or Mae West. Salman Rushdie's *Midnight's Children* may be a post-modern novel for having an unreliable narrator and for its postcolonial liberation of polyglot and polyvalent India from the exoticising gaze typified by E. M. Forster's *A Passage to India*, effectively doing in fiction what Edward Said had done in his 1978 book *Orientalism* three years earlier. Stanley Kubrick's *2001: A Space Odyssey* may be a post-modern film for both its lack of affect and of linear narrative, and for its discombobulating suggestion that computers may feel more than humans. James Stirling's No. 1 Poultry may be Britain's leading post-modern building, its staircase quoting the Vatican's Renaissance Scala Regia, its clock quoting the fascist-era main post office in Naples, and the whole thing surmounted by a turret that looks like a submarine conning tower surfaced in the middle of London. But while these po-mo artefacts may share some resemblances, there need be nothing that all share in common.

But there's a problem. These post-modern phenomena seem to have no resemblance, family or otherwise, with another notion of what post-modernism is. The philosopher Daniel Dennett, for instance, thinks post-modernism is gibberish:

> Postmodernism, the school of 'thought' that proclaimed 'There are no truths, only interpretations', has largely played itself out in absurdity, but it has left behind a generation of academics in the humanities disabled by their distrust of the very idea of truth and their disrespect for evidence, settling for 'conversations' in which nobody is wrong and nothing can be confirmed, only asserted with whatever style you can muster.[22]

For Dennett, post-modernism has lost all relationship with what he values – truth, evidence and science.

There is a deeper reason for rejecting Wittgenstein's notion of family resemblance in our attempt to understand what post-modernism means, if indeed it means anything. Families descend from common ancestors. That is why we speak of the family tree. You may share brown eyes with your uncle, and madness may fortunately have skipped your generation – but you share your ancestry with everyone on that family tree. This tree metaphor was troubling for two of the leading post-modern thinkers I will be considering in this book: Gilles Deleuze and Félix Guattari. In their book *A Thousand Plateaus*, they suggested that the tree is an image of centralised power that we need to uproot.

In contrast, they proposed another network structure as a substitute for the tree: the rhizome. 'As a model for culture, the rhizome resists the organisational structure of the root-tree system which charts causality along chronological lines and looks for the original source of "things" and looks towards the pinnacle or conclusion of those "things".' A rhizome is characterised by 'ceaselessly established connections between semiotic chains, organisations of power, and circumstances relative to the arts, sciences, and social struggles'. Rather than presenting history and culture as narratives with beginnings, middles and ends, the rhizomatic approach presents history and culture as a map or wide array of attractions and influences with no specific origin: a rhizome 'has no beginning or end; it is always in the middle, between things, interbeing, intermezzo'.[23]

If post-modernism is rhizomatic rather than arboreal, then that might suggest things falling under its description – Madonna's or Salman Rushdie's respective oeuvres, the MI6 headquarters or the Westin Bonaventure Hotel, the limpid prose of the best post-modern critics or the gibberish spooling from the Post-Modern Generator – have no common ancestors; and that each can get on very well on its own without support from other examples of post-modern culture.[24]

There is a third possibility. Perhaps post-modernism cannot be explained by a Wittgensteinian family-resemblance concept, and neither is it genitally fixated in an arboreal manner, nor loved-up, anti-essentialist, anti-foundationalist and rhizomatic in character, but is instead a semiotic black hole, consuming everything but signifying nothing.

The critic Dick Hebdige supposed as much when he suggested that post-modernism was crazily polysemous. It might be intended to describe, he wrote, 'a process of cultural, political or existential fragmentation and/or crisis, or the "de-centring" of the subject, an "incredulity towards metanarratives", the replacement of unitary power axes by a plurality of power/discourse formations, the "implosion of meaning", the collapse of cultural hierarchies, the dread engendered by the threat of nuclear self-destruction'. If post-modernism could mean all that, and more besides, we are, Hebdige concluded, 'in the presence of a buzzword', and a semantically overloaded one at that.[25]

If so, that would be fitting, since one strand of post-modern thought that Hebdige identified is that it problematises signification, inhabiting the semantic black hole into which meaning has imploded. How post-modern thought might express its critique of signification from inside that black hole is an interesting question for students, though one they would have trouble communicating to the world outside.

In any event, the term post-modernism has a prehistory. Among the first uses of it was in 1939 by the historian Arnold J. Toynbee, who wrote: 'Our own Post-Modern Age has been inaugurated by the general war of 1914–1918.'[26] Precursors of post-modernism can also be found in 1964, with the start of US involvement in Vietnam (what Fredric Jameson calls the first post-modern war) and the publication of both Marshall McLuhan's *Understanding Media* and Susan Sontag's *Notes on Camp*. The former set the scene for humanity's post-modern switch into the screen-based information age. The latter set the tone for a sensibility that would become post-modern in the next decade. Sontag wrote in her essay: 'Camp is a woman walking around in a dress made of three million feathers', 'Camp sees everything in quotation marks' and 'The whole point of Camp is to dethrone the serious'.[27] She could have substituted 'post-modernism' for 'camp' in each of those sentences and captured the sensibility of post-modernism.

That said, post-modernism came out of the shadows in the early 1970s, just as neoliberalism was emerging as the new form of capitalism. The next ten chapters will dramatise the rise, fall and persistence of post-modernism, and how its cultural impulse did indeed change our lives. The book will not be a comprehensive history; rather, each chapter will focus on three striking moments from 1972 to today. Those moments might include, for example, the publication of a book, the first Gulf War, the release of a videogame or film or the first hip-hop single.

The juxtaposition of these narratives will show how neoliberalism and post-modernism shifted creativity from traditional arts and culture to new media industries that thrive online, and what its arrival meant for our economics and our souls. More broadly, I will be considering how the post-modern 'anything goes' philosophy took advantage of technological changes, and how the market-based culture of differentiated consumerism and individual libertarianism that post-modernism extolled was ultimately realised in Amazon, Facebook and Twitter.

One result of these changes is that we are today scarcely capable of conceiving politics as a communal activity, because we have become habituated to being consumers rather than citizens. Politicians treat us as consumers to whom they must deliver; we grumble about politics as consumers do about a disappointing product or service. Shock and buyer's remorse are the only fitting attitudes towards politics conceived as an extension of shopping. Without post-modernism, such attitudes might not exist.

Finally, I will ask whether post-modernism is over, as radical movements since 2008 might suggest, or if we remain trapped in its embrace. Perhaps post-modernism is not dead; perhaps, instead, we're all post-modernists now.

1

Shock Doctrines, 1972:

Nixon Shock | Martha Rosler | *Anti-Oedipus*

Only a few months before the Pruitt-Igoe complex was demolished, President Nixon took the United States off the gold. This move signalled the first of three shocking doctrines that revolutionised the world in the early 1970s. The first was economic, the second artistic, and the third philosophical. The first – what became known as the Nixon Shock – overthrew a seemingly stable system that had existed for millennia by which financial exchanges were backed by metal. The second, typified by the work of post-modern conceptual artist Martha Rosler, laid waste to the captivating idea that the artist captures reality without distortion or bias.

The third revolution catalysed French theory, in particular from an incendiary text by Gallic bad boys of philosophy Gilles Deleuze and Félix Guattari that overturned the idea that we are or have stable selves, inviting us instead into a giddy adventure of permanent instability wherein we did well to imagine ourselves as machines bent on producing and satisfying desire. For Deleuze and Guattari, freeing desire from the corsets of history would be revolutionary, though today we might demur: in the post-modern world untrammelled desire brought about not libidinal utopia, but Harvey Weinstein and shopping as the leading leisure-time activity. What seemed liberating was really oppressive. Together, all three of these shocks demonstrate how the rise of neoliberalism went hand in hand with that of post-modernism.

I

As so often when terrible things happen in history, the first of these revolutions was Britain's fault. In the summer of 1971, the UK demanded that the United States redeem $3 billion for gold. It was not a totally unreasonable request. For the previous 4,000 years humanity had consistently based its currency in metal, usually gold. Yet this changed after 1944. In July that year, the United Nations Monetary and Financial Conference was held in Bretton Woods, New Hampshire, with delegates from forty-four countries.

It was designed to produce an agreement to ensure exchange-rate stability, prevent competitive devaluations, and promote economic growth. It was nothing less than a new world order that might prevent any repeats of the 1930s international depression and, ideally, prevent war. The resulting agreement was designed by the chief international economist of the Treasury Department, and the man whose name became a byword for the post-war economic orthodoxy: John Maynard Keynes. Bretton Woods agreed not only the establishment of the International Monetary Fund and the World Bank, but more importantly a gold standard.

In order to convert currencies, countries settled their international balances in dollars, while US dollars were fully convertible to gold. The exchange rate applied at the time was $35 an ounce. Keeping the price of gold fixed and adjusting the supply of dollars was the responsibility of the United States. As David Harvey has noted, 'This system existed under the umbrella protection of US military power. Only the Soviet Union and the Cold War placed limits on its global reach.'[1]

But the system underpinned by American military might was destroyed by it. The high cost of the Vietnam War left the United States with its first twentieth-century balance-of-payments deficit, prompting investors, including Britain, to demand gold. In response, Nixon decided to decouple the dollar from the rigid gold valuation. In part, the president was attempting to pay for the longest and most expensive war the United States had ever fought. 'The debt crisis was a direct result of the need to pay for bombs, or to be more precise, the vast military infrastructure required to deliver them', wrote David Graeber.[2]

For the first years after World War II the Bretton Woods system worked. Assisted by the Marshall Plan, Japan and Europe were rebuilding from the war, and countries outside the United States wanted dollars to spend on American goods – cars, steel, machinery, movies, nylons, gum and, if they had any sense, Miles Davis albums. And because the United States owned over half the world's official gold reserves – 574 million ounces at the end of World War II – the system appeared secure. Leading industrialised countries such as the United States, Britain, France, West Germany and Japan enjoyed a long economic boom from 1945 to 1973.

This long boom defined the era of Fordism. In 1913, Henry Ford installed the first moving assembly line for the mass production of motor cars in Detroit, reducing the time it took to build a Model T Ford from twelve hours to two and a half. In doing so, he was applying the ideas of American engineer and pioneer of scientific management Frederick Taylor, set out in *Time Principles of Scientific Management* (1911). For Taylor, assembly lines sped up the production processes by reducing workers to cogs in a machine. *In extremis*, machines rendered them obsolete.

The Italian communist Antonio Gramsci wrote in his *Prison Notebooks* that Fordism was an attempt to resolve the dilemmas of capitalism. Ford trained his workers to specialise in one of the eighty-four discrete steps necessary in car production. This rationalisation of production into discrete parts raised output, which in turn cut the prices of the finished cars. That enabled workers to be paid relatively high wages, allowing them to buy the products they made, to become producers and consumers in one. Beyond such industrial core workers were the rest of the proletariat – the expendable unskilled workers and the unemployed. The proletarian solidarity between the two groups of workers that threatened capitalism was thereby undone.

Gramsci's analysis also foresaw the change in relationship between the worker and their work:

> It is certain that [Ford and Taylor] are not concerned with the 'humanity' or the 'spirituality' of the worker, which are immediately smashed. This 'humanity and spirituality' cannot be realised except in the world of production and work and in productive 'creation'. They exist most in the artisan, in the 'demiurge', when the worker's personality was reflected whole in the object created and when the link between art and labour was still very strong. But it is precisely against this 'humanism' that the new industrialism is fighting.[3]

Gramsci's sense – and it was shared by many on the left at the time – was that Fordism destroyed what was valuable for humans. He also supposed that Fordism needed the help of an obliging state to keep its wheels in motion. Such state intervention was conceived by Keynes to make capitalism less prone to such crises as the American Great Depression of the 1930s, which had been caused partly by a crisis of overproduction. To ensure such crises never occurred again, Keynesian economics suggested that, by lowering unemployment, raising wages and increasing demand for goods, the state could help realise economic growth and social stability.

Keynesianism had a global tenor too: to prevent another catastrophic war, its principles of demand management allied to social welfare reconstruction were seen as necessary government tools. For leftists, this was embedded capitalism, producing what anthropologist Jason Hickel calls a 'docile, productive middle-class workforce that would have the means to consume a mass-produced set of basic commodities'.[4]

Fordism and Keynesianism together delivered high growth rates throughout the industrialised West until the 1970s; the French called this post-war boom era *les trente glorieuses* – 'the thirty glorious years'. This was underpinned by gold, and in particular American, fiscal and monetary policy, exercised through the Bretton Woods system.

On Friday, 13 August 1971, Nixon arrived for a secret meeting with high-ranking White House and Treasury advisors at

Camp David. The British demand for $3 billion worth of gold was the last straw. Germany and Switzerland had already quit the system, and the French were seething. Economists and foreign politicians now appreciated the Bretton Woods system of US-backed exchange rates as one that shored up American power, as well as subsidising American living standards and multinationals. Economist Barry Eichengreen wrote: 'It costs only a few cents for the Bureau of Engraving and Printing to produce a $100 bill, but other countries had to pony up $100 of actual goods in order to obtain one.'[5]

At the time Britain's demand came through, the United States did not have enough gold to cover the volume of dollars circulating throughout the world. That anxiety eventually crept into the foreign-exchange market, making traders abroad fearful of an eventual dollar devaluation. As a result, they began selling US dollars in greater amounts and more frequently. After several runs on the dollar, Nixon sought a new economic course for the country.

But the unsustainability of Bretton Woods's linking of gold and money was not the only reason Nixon nixed the system. He was mainly concerned with domestic problems. Unemployment had just risen from 4 per cent to 6 per cent, and he needed something to boost jobs. His idea was that the Federal Reserve would be able to print money more easily since it had been decoupled from gold. True, that would have been inflationary, but Nixon proposed to outlaw inflation by imposing price and wage controls.

What the president and his aides decided that afternoon became known as the Nixon Shock. Once the Bretton Woods gold standard was abandoned, the relationship between money and value was severed.

On Sunday, 15 August, Nixon went on TV to announce that the United States had come off the gold standard. Earlier in 1971, Nixon had said: 'We're all Keynesians now!'; but one corollary of the Nixon Shock was to integrate international markets, thereby making national policies of Keynesian economic demand management ineffective. From its outset, the network age has been at odds with the age of the nation-state. What emerged was a globalised, hyperconnected world that favours the transnational flux of capital and labour, banking treaties and security pacts, drug cartels and terrorists.

The globalisation and deregulation of markets that followed the Nixon Shock helped nations such as the United States and Britain, which thrived in the Wild West of financial deregulation, and opened new markets for exports. But it also destroyed the social-democratic egalitarianism of advanced industrial nations, especially those in Europe, where there had long been widespread collective bargaining and welfare-state provision for society's least fortunate.

The arguments at Camp David were the economic equivalent to contemporary arguments in literature and philosophy departments. Those who sought the end of the gold standard envisaged an end to financial regulation. This was parallel to what Michel Foucault sought when he called for literature to be liberated from the constraint of authorial control in favour of the free composition, decomposition, recomposition and manipulation of texts. The Nixon Shock helped produce the world we live in – one of deregulation, free-floating signifiers and no less free-floating capital.

The Nixon Shock was also a disaster, even for capitalists. In his 1990 book, Paul Volcker wrote: 'The inflationary pressures that helped bring down the system did not abate for long; they got much worse as the controls came off and plagued the country for a decade or more.'[6] Worse, only three years after the Nixon Shock, oil-producing Arab nations administered another upset to the system when an embargo by OPEC – payback for US military aid to the Israelis during the Yom Kippur War – resulted in the quadrupling of oil prices.

This was a disaster for the American economy in general and Nixon's stewardship of it in particular. Inflation rose after the dollar was unpegged from the gold standard, the value of the currency plummeting and the price of gold skyrocketing (from $35 an ounce under the Bretton Woods gold standard to $600 in

1980). The stock market crashed, and the US economy went into a tailspin. Production slowed down, prices went up, and a new word was coined: stagflation – denoting a combination of inflation and stagnation.

That tailspin forced two salient moves. First, Nixon's diplomats scrambled to Saudi Arabia in the summer of 1974 to encourage the kingdom to finance America's widening deficit with its new-found petrodollar wealth. The world's key commodity, oil, was to be bought and sold in dollars, and so the United States would buy oil from Saudi Arabia and, in return, provide the kingdom with military aid and equipment. Saudi Arabia also pressured other members of OPEC to ensure that oil was paid for in dollars, while their oilfields would be protected by American arms. In return, Saudi Arabia and Kuwait effectively became US military protectorates.

Second, in 1974, US Treasury secretary William Simon managed to convince the Saudis and other oil-producing countries that America was the safest place to park their petrodollars. These dollars were therefore used to buy US Treasury bills, which effectively meant OPEC was buying American debt. As a consequence, the dollar remained the world's reserve currency – not because it was backed by gold, but because the world was buying American IOUs. The combined effect of low interest payments and inflation was, as David Graeber noted, the depreciation of the value of these IOUs to their holders, serving, as he put it, as a 'tribute' to the author of the new global economic system, the United States.

But while the United States didn't have to pay its debts, the rest of the world did. The neoliberal system that emerged from the Nixon Shock imposed tight monetary policies on those countries that held dollars as their reserve currency, especially when it came to how and when they had to repay their debts. The neoliberal system involved the International Monetary Fund and World Bank, institutions established under Keynes's imprimatur, chasing down debtor nations and imposing on them repayment regimes that hit the poor hardest, often working at the behest of the United States. When it came to debt, it was a question of who was to be the master, and who the slave.

The Nixon Shock hastened the ideological war Friedrich Hayek had hoped for in 1947. The stagflation that Nixon's policies helped produce led America, Britain, Chile and China, among others, to abandon their Keynesian commitments and roll back the state in order to combat unemployment and improve negligible rates of growth. These principles were evoked by Harvard philosopher Robert Nozick in his 1974 masterwork *Anarchy, State, and Utopia*, where he concluded 'that a minimal state, limited to the narrow functions of protection against force, theft, fraud, enforcement of contracts, and so on, is justified; that any more extensive state will violate persons' rights not to be forced to do certain things, and is unjustified; and that the minimal state is inspiring as well as right'.[7]

This individual right to act was also expressed in the development of personal credit. The first credit card, the American Express, came into operation thirteen years before the Nixon Shock, while others, including Visa and Mastercard, became increasingly popular during the 1970s. But while we could have what we wanted instantly, there were downsides: eye-watering interest payments only served to make the trade-off between desire and possession painful. In 2009, First Premier Bank issued a credit card featuring 79.9 per cent APR interest charges, targeted at making profits from the riskiest of borrowers (the so-called subprime credit card market). Although it was withdrawn two years later because of the number of defaults, the card typified how easily the most financially vulnerable could be seduced into choosing instant gratification, even though the certain result of that choice was, not pleasure, but debt peonage extending into the foreseeable future. Protect me from what I want, indeed.

According to David Harvey, the upper classes were in this moment reasserting their right to be masters after a forty-year post-war interregnum. During those decades, politics and economics had been configured together. Global finance was regulated and states cooperated internationally, while, domestically, advanced industrial nations intervened to ameliorate the worst effects of deprivation through public housing, welfare support and socialised medicine. In the struggle to reassert their mastery, the upper classes overturned Fordism as the prevailing economic order since World War II, and replaced it with a new one: post-Fordism.

The 'conceptual economy' is one way of describing what arose. David Graeber, in his 2013 article 'On the Phenomenon of Bullshit Jobs', put it more disobligingly. He noted that, in 1930, Keynes predicted that by the end of the century technology would have advanced sufficiently that in countries such as the UK and the United States we might be on fifteen-hour weeks:

> In technological terms, we are quite capable of this. And yet it didn't happen. Instead, technology has been marshalled, if anything, to figure out ways to make us all work more. Huge swaths of people, in Europe and North America in particular, spend their entire working lives performing tasks they believe to be unnecessary. The moral and spiritual damage that comes from this situation is profound. It is a scar across our collective soul. Yet virtually no one talks about it.[8]

Which jobs are bullshit? 'A world without teachers or dockworkers would soon be in trouble', wrote Graeber. 'But it's not entirely clear how humanity would suffer were all private equity CEOs, lobbyists, PR researchers, actuaries, telemarketers, bailiffs or legal consultants to similarly vanish.'[9] Understandably, Graeber didn't consider whether humanity would suffer if anthropologists disappeared, too.

In any case, one person's bullshit is another's desirable socioeconomic shift. Former Al Gore speechwriter Daniel H. Pink argued that the post-Fordist brain was different from the Fordist one: 'The future belongs to a very different kind of person with a very different kind of mind – creators and empathisers, pattern recognisers, and meaning makers. These people – artists, inventors, designers, storytellers, caregivers, consolers, big picture thinkers – will now reap society's richest rewards and share its greatest joys.'[10] Pink's idea was that not only had blue-collar manufacturing been outsourced from the formerly industrialised West to Asian countries, but so had logic-based white-collar work such as software development. What remained in the West was right-brain work. The heavy lifting would be outsourced, leaving the West to be creative.

But what was new about supply-side post-Fordism compared with its predecessor was that it required creatives to defibrillate our jaded sensibilities by acquiring products marginally, but, tellingly, different from the last model we bought. Creative genius here consists in evoking through a product a world of freedom and fulfilment that can be bought at the very moment one is on the proverbial wheel of Ixion, trapped by one's own desires. Fordism may have offered car buyers any colour so long as it was black; post-Fordism offers very nearly too many colours, including some that buyers had never heard of.

One unexpected corollary of this is what's become known in our post-Fordist, post-modern era as the paradox of choice. The standard line is that choice is good for us, that it confers on us freedom, personal responsibility, self-determination, autonomy and lots of other things that don't help when you're standing before a towering aisle of water bottles, paralysed and increasingly dehydrated, unable to choose. That wasn't how endless choice was supposed to work, wrote American psychologist Barry Schwartz in *The Paradox of Choice: Why More is Less*. 'If we're rational, [social scientists] tell us, added options can only make us better off as a society. This view is logically compelling, but empirically it isn't true.'[11]

We may be bored, sated, decadent and stuffed with food, drink, car ads and the bitter fruits of the cultural industry, but the most creative minds of the post-modern, post-Fordist era that Pink evoked are bent on keeping us buying so as to forestall crises of overproduction by tailoring demand to suit supply.

This shift from Fordism to post-Fordism in the developed nations can be exaggerated. Certainly, outsourcing became rife because of relatively low labour costs in the developing world; but manufacturing still exists in the old industrial heartlands. Take the birthplace of the industrial revolution, the United Kingdom. By 2018, its manufacturing sector made up roughly only 10 per cent of the economy and employed directly only 2.6 million people out of a population of 66 million. But that sector was key to the national economy: 44 per cent of total UK exports were manufactured goods.[12]

That said, the Fordist conveyer belt, turning out the same product hour after hour, is obsolete. Post-Fordism replaces the rigidities of that system of manufacture with what David Harvey calls flexible accumulation: 'It rests on flexibilities with respect to labour processes, labour markets, and patterns of consumption. It is characterised by the emergence of entirely new sectors of production, new ways of providing financial services, new markets, and, above all, greatly intensified rates of commercial, technological and organisational innovation.'[13]

Harvey divides the post-Fordist workforce into two groups – the core and the periphery. The steadily shrinking former group is made up of full-time skilled employees on permanent contracts, with pensions, benefits and other rights. But, under post-Fordism, even this favoured group were expected to be flexible (in terms of both hours and location of work); indeed, that was the trade-off for their permanent contracts and relatively high wages. Better that, though, than being a member of the periphery – the part-timers, those on fixed or short-term contracts, or no contracts at all, as well as exploited interns. As well as flexible accumulation, Harvey characterises the post-Fordist era as one of time–space compression.

> As space appears to shrink to a 'global village' of telecommunications and a 'spaceship earth' of economic and ecological interdependencies [the former was the notion of media theorist Marshall McLuhan, the latter of architect and systems

theorist Buckminster Fuller] and as time horizons shorten to the point where the present is all there is (the world of the schizophrenic) so we have to learn to cope with an over-whelming sense of compression of our spatial and temporal worlds.[14]

Harvey was writing in 1990, before the internet became the primary means of compressing time and space. But the internet intensified that compression, made us more schizophrenic in his sense – more capable of getting everything, everywhere all the time. This is what Frances Cairncross calls the death of distance. For her, at least initially, the internet was part of a welcome technological revolution in the wake of which 'transmitting information costs almost nothing and capitalism distributes resources more efficiently'.[15] For Harvey, though, this death of distance accelerated consumption and disposability. Which makes our world, quite possibly, work worse, or at least more degradingly.

Neologisms proliferate in the attempt to capture these changes. Post-Fordism is the time of the gig economy (in which labour markets are characterised by the prevalence of short-term contracts or freelance work, as opposed to permanent jobs; instead of a regular wage, workers get paid for the 'gigs' they do, such as a food delivery or car journey) and of zero-hours contracts (where the employer is not obliged to provide any minimum working hours, while the worker is not obliged to accept any work offered), but above all it is the era in which a new class has emerged: the precariat.

The precariat – combining 'precarious' and 'proletariat' – means those who suffer a precarious existence because they lack job security, but experience intermittent employment or under-employment. It has become such a fixture of our otherwise liquid neoliberal, post-modern times that, in 2011, the precariat figured in a new model of seven classes in the Great British Class Survey.[16] Below the Elite came the Established Middle Class, followed by the Technical Middle Class, New Affluent Workers,

Emergent Service Workers, Traditional Working Class and finally the Precariat.

The classes were divided according to the extent to which they possessed not only wealth or income, but various kinds of capital. Economic capital included income and the value of one's home and savings; cultural capital incorporates cultural interests and activities; social capital derives from the number and status of people you know.

Accordingly, the Great British Class Survey also asked participants whether they enjoyed any of twenty-seven cultural activities, including watching opera and going to the gym. The precariat is the most deprived class of all, with low levels of economic, cultural and social capital. The precariat doesn't have a box at the opera. 'People tend to think they belong to a particular class on the basis of their job and income', argued the survey's authors. 'These are aspects of economic capital. Sociologists think that your class is indicated by your cultural capital and social capital.' This redefinition of class in the neoliberal era is particularly significant for a book about post-modernism because it emphasises culture as a determinant of class. If neoliberalism was to succeed, it needed a cultural movement to support it: post-modernism was able to supply it.

This kind of class analysis is inimical to the ideology of neoliberalism that demands a minimal state as the precondition of individual freedom. At the end of *Anarchy, State, and Utopia*, Nozick insists that, in the neoliberal utopia, we will be inviolate individuals, free 'to choose our lives and to realise our ends and our conception of ourselves, insofar as we can, aided by the voluntary co-operation of other individuals possessing the same dignity. How *dare* any state or groups or individuals do more. Or less.'[17]

But one reason the state *should* dare to do more than Nozick allows is that we are better thought of not as inviolate individuals, but rather as violated individuals, thrown into a world with parents, traits and a level of wealth we did not choose, incapable of realising our ends or conception of ourselves – still less living lives of dignity – without assistance. All this is to say that, as neoliberalism was born, as Fordism was supplanted by post-Fordism, as post-modernism arose from the rubble of Pruitt-Igoe, as the Nixon Shock shook the world economy, another shock, less heralded but no less important, was administered to the system. It was a semantic shock, one revealing a vision of language more reminiscent of *Alice through the Looking Glass* than we hitherto supposed possible. It was typified by the Humpty Dumpties of neoliberalism, from Hayek to Nozick, who defined freedom as they saw fit, erasing any other way of conceiving it. 'The question is', said Humpty Dumpty, 'which is to be master – that's all.' But language was supposed to reflect the world as it is, to capture the truth of things, rather than codify and facilitate a struggle for mastery and power – wasn't it?

II

Into these multiple shocks, the American conceptual and performance artist Martha Rosler launched a work of art called *The Bowery in Two Inadequate Descriptive Systems*. It consisted of twenty-one black-and-white photographs and three blank panels that were paired with twenty-four panels of typewritten text. The photographs included decrepit storefronts, rubbish and a close-up of an empty bottle of Gallo White Port.

That bottle was significant. It eloquently conveyed the history of America's post-Prohibition booze industry. The Californian wine-maker's first commercial success was a lemon-flavoured wine called Thunderbird that, the obituarist for Julio Gallo reported, was the choice 'for oblivion of America's tramps'.[18] In the 1930s, Gallo employees were rumoured to spread empty bottles of Thunderbird around inner-city slums as a method of ensuring brand loyalty.

Rosler had returned to her native New York a few years earlier from the west coast, where she had studied at the University of California, San Diego – at the time a nerve centre for radical thought. Fredric Jameson and Herbert Marcuse were on the faculty, Angela Davis studied there, and Jean-Luc Godard visited to give lectures. In California, Rosler became part of a group of artists who were sceptical of the notion of photography as a form of visual truth. Documentary photography that simply reports or reveals, Rosler and her like-minded friends believed, merely affirms the status quo without criticising it. A different approach to photography was needed.

The Bowery was at the time a New York neighbourhood synonymous with bums and alcoholics. The street that Rosler photographed in the winter of 1974–75 was the place where the proto-precariat went when they fell off the wagon to live in hostels and low-rent lofts. Only a handful of artists hinted at the area's future gentrification. One of Rosler's shots prefigures this – an artist-in-residence sign denotes the presence of incoming creatives at the very moment the Bowery was bottoming out. Today the Bowery has been socially cleansed of those who went there to drink themselves to death.

One of the most astute critics of Rosler's work, Steve Edwards, thought that Rosler's images of the Bowery as a 'necropolis of old stuff', and, through their associations with an 'older mode of production', the goods on display, negated the 'hyperseductions of the late-capitalist commodity form'.[19] Her work thus echoes that of the critic Walter Benjamin. His great unfinished book about the birth of consumer capitalism in mid-nineteenth-century Paris, *The Arcades Project*, was a necropolist's montage of quotes, facts, playbills, the detritus of the past. He sought out the obsolete and discarded in order to give the lie to earlier hyperseductions of the late-capitalist commodity form. In doing so, he thought he could effect revolutionary change. Martha Rosler was doing something similar with *Inadequate Systems*, but with a post-modern twist: the hopes that Benjamin had expressed in the 1930s for photography and cinema to catalyse revolutionary change were not Martha Rosler's hopes. Her necropolis of old stuff had a different purpose.

A poignant absence haunts each of Rosler's shots: there are no humans. A discarded shoe figures in one image – as if a socially cleansing neutron bomb had vaporised the underclass. Rosler's contact sheets for the project, by contrast, teemed with people. One critic surmised: 'It's as if, after painstaking thought, she decided that one person shouldn't attempt to represent another person, or can't.'[20]

But why shouldn't one person attempt to represent another? Susan Sontag, in her 1977 essay 'The Image-World', gave one idea: 'To photograph people is to violate them, by seeing them as they never see themselves, by having knowledge of them that they can never have; it turns people into objects that can be symbolically possessed. Just as a camera is a sublimation of the gun, to photograph someone is a subliminal murder – a soft murder, appropriate to a sad, frightened time.'[21]

To take a photograph is to transform the subject into an image that can be reproduced endlessly. To make a movie is murder at the rate of twenty-four frames per second. In Billy Wilder's 1950 film *Sunset Boulevard*, silent movie icon Norma Desmond, played by Gloria Swanson, so identifies herself with her screen image that she loses her soul: she has no sense of her personal identity beyond her two-dimensional image on film. In this, Norma Desmond was modern. Under post-modernism, this gospel of photography gets its comeuppance. The ostensibly neutral gaze of the photographer or the viewer is challenged and revealed as imperial, colonising, raping and murdering its subjects, deciding even what counts as real and how it is to be represented. Best of all, the gaze is reversed, and its subject takes revenge.

Rosler's Bowery photographs were hardly revenge on the part of the bums whom she, out of ethical compunctions and political commitments, allowed to slip beyond her frame. She was thwarting rather than returning the gaze. Her project was to deconstruct the moves of a documentary photographer, to challenge the suggestion that photography was an accurate reflection of reality and to deflate its pretensions to objectivity.

But Rosler was doing something else, too. Photography has a long history of depicting human suffering and violence. The pioneer of documentary photography, the French photographer Eugene Atget (1857–1927), was described as investigating the streets of Paris as though they were crime scenes. Social-realist documentary photographers like Walker Evans and Dorothea Lange made images of the Great Depression that were hailed for the purportedly unflinching gaze they directed towards their deprived subjects. As post-modernism was born, the production of images generally, and the production of images of human violence and suffering in particular, rose exponentially, partly because of the growing popularity of photographic essays in glossy magazines. This was the context for Martha Rosler's Bowery project.

There was something perverse and obscene about glossy magazines unwittingly juxtaposing photographic essays of the most disgusting things happening in the world with titillating advertisements for the must-have fruits of neoliberal industrial production; and something perverse and obscene, too, about images of human suffering being consumed in middle-class living rooms. Rosler nailed this perversion in *House Beautiful: Bringing the War Home* (1967–72), a series of photomontages juxtaposing images from the war with domestic banality. In one image, 'Cleaning the Drapes', a woman vacuums her curtains, drawing them aside to reveal GIs holed up behind sandbags. In another, the First Lady, Pat Nixon, stands proudly in her regally appointed drawing room. But what is that image above the fireplace? A woman's corpse riddled with bullets. A third depicted an on-trend TV room with minimalist furniture and exposed brickwork, marred rather by the superimposed cut-out image of a Vietnamese girl missing part of her right leg. Its title: 'Tron (Amputee)'.

Eugene W. Smith's photograph of a Japanese mother cradling her severely deformed, naked daughter in a traditional Japanese bathroom appeared initially in a 1972 edition of *Life* magazine in a photo essay about the terrible consequences of Minimata disease (a form of mercury poisoning) in a Japanese fishing community.

Both Smith and fellow documentary photographer Don McCullin at the time argued strongly for the importance of their photographs in changing the world. 'I want to create a voice for the people in those pictures', said McCullin. 'I want the voice to seduce people into actually hanging on a bit longer when they look at them, so they go away not with an intimidating memory but with a conscious obligation.'[22] Eugene Smith said he contrived his image 'Tomoko Uemura in Her Bath' to raise the international profile of Minimata disease and the struggle of victims for compensation.

Rosler's friend and fellow member of the San Diego group of artists, Allan Sekula, wrote an essay called 'Documentary and Corporate Violence', in which he rounded on such explanations for documentary photography. He argued that 'the subjective aspect of liberal aesthetics is compassion rather than collective struggle. Pity, mediated by an appreciation of great art, supplants political understanding.' Sekula's concern was that documentary photography, as he put it, 'has contributed much to spectacle, to retinal excitation, to voyeurism, and only a little to the critical understanding of the social world'.[23] Images are narcotising, encouraging us to consume them in aesthetic delight rather than spurring us to take collective action to remedy social wrongs.

And there's clearly something in this. Take, for example, Koen Wessing's photograph of a dead child lying under a sheet in Nicaragua in 1979, during the Sandinista struggle. Roland Barthes wrote of it in *Camera Lucida*: 'a banal enough scene, unfortunately, but I noted certain interferences: the corpse's one bare foot, the sheet carried by the weeping mother (why this sheet?), a woman in the background, probably a friend, holding a handkerchief to her nose'.[24] This and other images of human suffering led Barthes to make his distinction between *studium* and *punctum* – *studium* meaning the cultural, linguistic and political interpretation of a photograph, perhaps in line with the photographer's intention, while the *punctum* was the personally touching detail that establishes a direct relationship with the object or person within it. The dead boy's foot and the question of the grieving mother holding that sheet were examples of the *punctum*, or, as Barthes put it, 'that accident that pricks me (but also bruises me, is poignant to me)'.[25]

However, without wishing to be disrespectful to Barthes, who cares about his bruises? Particularly when they were caused by exposure to images of real suffering. Susan Sontag wrote: 'To suffer is one thing; another thing is living with the photographed images of suffering, which does not necessarily strengthen conscience and the ability to be compassionate. It can also corrupt them. Once one has seen such images, one has started down the road of seeing more – and more. Images transfix. Images anaesthetise.'[26]

More than that, paradoxically, they anaesthetise by aestheticising: by making images beautiful, composing them to evoke art-historical allusions, by allowing the readier to consume them pleasurably, documentary photographs risk destroying their ostensible purpose, which is to present us with a slice of reality, the incontrovertible truth. 'The rhetorical strength of documentary is imagined to reside in the unequivocal character of the camera's evidence in an essential realism', wrote Sekula in his 1978 essay 'Dismantling Modernism, Reinventing Documentary'. 'The only "objective" truth that photographs offer is the assertion that somebody or something . . . was somewhere and took a picture. Everything else, *everything beyond the imprinting of a trace*, is up for grabs.'[27]

The camera never lies? Well, hardly, Sekula suggested; but, more importantly, the camera is not about telling the truth, either. Just as a courtroom, for Sekula, is a battleground of fictions each fighting to be named the truth, so the photographic image is always composed, edited or selected to serve a political agenda, especially when that agenda is erased by claims that it offers incontrovertible reality. How, then, can photography document reality? 'A truly critical social documentary will frame the crime, the trial, and the system of justice and its official myths. Artists working toward this end may or may not produce images that are theatrical and overtly contrived, they may or may not present texts that read like fiction. Social truth is something other than a matter of convincing style', wrote Sekula.

This is a Marxist argument: photographers have only interpreted the world in various ways; the point, however, is to change it. All these critical thoughts and more are explored in Martha Rosler's work. Her photographs are part of an inadequate descriptive system. Juxtaposed with another, the text cards accompanying each shot describe various states of drunkenness. One goes: 'the worse for liquor, top heavy, moon-eyed, owl-eyed, pie-eyed, shit-faced, snockered, shickered'. The result? As one critic put it, 'Each system undermines the other's self-consciously feeble attempts at portraying the social reality of skid row. Bouncing between a general lexicon of alcoholism and a visual vernacular borrowed from the likes of Depression-era social reformist documentarian Walker Evans, Rosler pokes fun at the mannerism that inevitably accompanies mediation.'[28]

But Rosler's was a more profound critique than this suggests, attacking not just documentary photography but any conceptual system. Words or images, Rosler feared, could never capture what they were supposed to. For her, truth collapsed from a transcendent absolute into a multiplicity of shifting truths that reflected power struggles. In this, Rosler's art had the same concerns as Barthes, Foucault and above all Derrida, for whom there was always a poverty of representation in any conceptual scheme. Like these French theorists, Rosler sought to tear off the mask of truth to reveal the power play beneath. Meaning wasn't a butterfly that could be pinned down, but a corrosive substance that no container could hold for long.

Martha Rosler's work is worth reflecting on as a challenge to those who see post-modernism as a giddy, irresponsible, consumerist free-for-all in cahoots with a neoliberal system that creates unparalleled inequality. While some fellow artists wallowed in the degrading exchange between commerce and art, Rosler critiqued the society she lived in and at the same time reflected critically on the power or otherwise of art to change that society. For the neo-Marxist thinkers of the Frankfurt School, steeped in the culture of mid-century modernism, the point of art was to exist as an Other that indicted, though could not change, society. In the post-modern age, that otherness of art was no longer possible. Artists, even radical, critical ones like Rosler, were enmeshed, often knowingly, in cultural, economic and language systems they could scarcely change: under post-modernism, there could be no avant-garde.

In the same year as she made her Bowery photography piece, Rosler produced a feminist parody video of cooking shows in her piece, 'The Semiotics of the Kitchen'. She took on the role of an apron-clad housewife and parodied the television cooking demonstrations of celebrity chef Julia Child in the 1960s. Standing in a kitchen, surrounded by refrigerator, table and stove, she moves through the alphabet from *A* to *Z*, assigning a letter to each of the various tools found in this domestic space. Wielding knives, a nutcracker and a rolling pin, she warms to her task, her gestures sharply punctuating the rage and frustration provoked by oppressive women's roles. Rosler said of this work: 'I was concerned with something like the notion of "language speaking the subject", and with the transformation of the woman herself into a sign in a system of signs that represent a system of food production, a system of harnessed subjectivity.'[29]

For two French theorists, writing as Rosler worried about such questions, it wasn't only women who could be reduced to cogs in a machine, be it semantic or literal. For Gilles Deleuze and Félix Guattari, everything was part of a machine.

III

Imagine, for a moment, that you are a lone male wasp flying through the Australian outback without a care in the world. Not long ago, you were an egg that had been laid by your mother in a beetle larva, but not before she had paralysed it with her sting, so that when you emerged from your egg you would have a ready supply of food. Suddenly, as you penetrate the summer breeze with the aid of your five-centimetre wingspan, you are attracted by a scent and set off in pursuit.

It is rare for a male wasp like you to scent a female wasp: flightless females spend most of their lives underground laying eggs in beetle larvae. So the fragrance piques your desire, and you speed towards her. You're not the only one on this irresistible trail of pheromones, though: competitors have joined the hunt. But then you see the source of the fragrance – a female thynnine wasp, swaying in the breeze, is advertising that she wants to mate. You race towards her, outstripping your rivals. You grasp her firmly and, soon afterwards, ejaculate.

But you've made a mistake. You haven't mated with a female wasp but with a flower. You've been hoodwinked, as so many thynnine wasps have before you, and so many more will in the future, into pollinating an orchid that smells and looks like a female wasp. Most orchids produce beautiful flowers to announce the presence of nectar; seduced into contact, the male wasps brush up against the pollen, which sticks to their bodies. But in Australia more than 250 orchid species have evolved in a different way: they seduce male insects, including wasps, with chemical copies of the female wasp's pheromones.

What's more, when you mated with the orchid, you may have been aided to pick up the pollen by the design of the flower's lip. If you were mating with a so-called hammer orchid, it would have flipped you upside down and smacked your body into the pollen. And then you would fly off into the summer breeze with pollen stuck to you, pollen that became detached by the next female orchid that seduced you.

The deception of the thynnine wasp captivated Gilles Deleuze and Félix Guattari. When they published *Anti-Oedipus* in 1972, they mused on insect behaviour and used it to explode the notion of identity. Just as Martha Rosler found documentary photography and language to be inadequate descriptive systems, so these two post-modern theorists found the usual binary oppositions – man versus nature, animal versus human, machine versus human, not to mention wasp versus orchid – to be hopeless. Man was nature, humans were animals, humans were machines, and wasps were indistinguishable from the reproductive systems of orchids. Identity was not fixed, but fluid.

Deleuze and Guattari's reflection on the thynnine wasp's sexual misadventures was the latest of French theory's playful attempts at destabilising speculation – one that would disturb the venerable project of dividing the world into discrete objects.

Plants would die out if they were not fertilised by insects foreign to themselves. And if one follows that thought, it leads one to realise that it scarcely makes sense to refer to insects and flowers embroiled in this great deception as independent entities. The thynnine wasp might be better thought of as part of the orchid's reproductive system. When it hooks up (sexually, and also quite literally) with the orchid, it is, in Deleuze and Guattari's terms, re-territorialised. This thought was not new. 'Does anyone say', asked Samuel Butler rhetorically a century before *Anti-Oedipus* was published,

> that the red clover has no reproductive system because the humble bee (and the humble bee only) must aid and abet it before it can reproduce? No one. The humble bee is a part of the reproductive system of the clover. Each one of ourselves has sprung from minute animalcules whose entity was entirely distinct from our own, and which acted after their kind with no thought or heed of what we might think about it. These little creatures are part of our own reproductive system; then why not we part of that of the machines?[30]

Deleuze and Guattari loved this passage from a section in Butler's satirical book *Erewhon*, called 'The Book of the Machines'. No wonder: it prefigures the shocking doctrines of *Anti-Oedipus* nowhere more so than when Butler considers what it is to be a machine. His thought was that there is no clear line between production and reproduction, nor between human and machine; nor was it helpful to think of the machine as a single entity. Butler wrote:

We are misled by considering any complicated machine as a single thing; in truth it is a city or society, each member of which was bred truly after its kind . . . The truth is that each part of every vapour-engine is bred by its own special breeders, whose function it is to breed that part, and that only, while the combination of the parts into a whole forms another department of the mechanical reproductive system, which is at present exceedingly complex and difficult to see in its entirety.

Anti-Oedipus updated this thought for post-modern, neoliberal times. Deleuze and Guattari's book – the first instalment of a pair entitled *Capitalism and Schizophrenia* – is shocking in part because it opens up possibilities of becoming something other than you are. Forget the values you were brought up with, overcome your biological make-up and environmental heritage, step beyond familial and societal structures, and affirm other possibilities.

Discard, in particular, the notion that you are some fixed self persisting through time. Consider instead that you change your identity incessantly. Just as a thynnine wasp becomes part of the machine of plant reproduction when it grips the relevant orchid, you too become part of whatever process – or, as Deleuze and Guattari phrased it, machine – you are plugged into. 'The self is only a threshold, a door, a becoming between two multiplicities', they wrote in *A Thousand Plateaus*, the 1980 sequel to *Anti-Oedipus*.

To be human was not to be a Cartesian subject in a theatre of the mind before which sense data presented themselves. It was to be part of a machine. Insofar as a ghost lingered in the machine, Deleuze and Guattari were bent on performing an exorcism.

Only four years after the *soixante-huitards* of Paris had chanted 'Sous les pavés la plage' ('Beneath the paving slabs, the beach'), Deleuze and Guattari were reviving the revolutionary spirit of May 1968 by tearing up the ground beneath our feet, if only figuratively: 'Courage consists, however, in agreeing to flee rather than live tranquilly and hypocritically in false refuges. Values, morals, homelands, religions, and these private certitudes that our vanity and our complacency bestow generously on us, have many deceptive sojourns as the world arranges for those who think they are standing straight and at ease, among stable things.'[31] The technical term for this revolution in thought was de-territorialisation. The courage we needed was to stop being sheep and become birds.

Territorialised humans are not dissimilar to sheep that have become so used to their field that they do not need walls to keep them in. Similarly, we can be given freedom because we are not expected to make use of it. We become de-territorialised when we leave the flock – when, like a bird, we 'flee rather than live tranquilly and hypocritically in false refuges'. The line of flight is another key term for Deleuze and Guattari. 'A flight is a sort of delirium', Deleuze told an interviewer:

> To be delirious is exactly to go off the rails (as in déconner – to say absurd things, etc.). There is something demoniacal in a line of flight. Demons are different from gods, because gods have fixed attributes, properties and functions, territories and codes: they have to do with rails, boundaries and surveys. What demons do is jump across intervals, and from one interval to another.[32]

For Deleuze and Guattari, the flight from stable identities and the reconceptualisation of humans as machines were parts of a subversive political project. *Anti-Oedipus*'s key thrust is to challenge our preconceptions of normality and madness. In this, *Anti-Oedipus* was of its time. The Scottish anti-psychiatrist R. D. Laing became celebrated in the late 1960s, and was admired by Deleuze and Guattari for his attacks on the madness of normality. 'What we call "normal" is a product of repression, denial, splitting, projection, introjection and other forms of destructive action on experience. It is radically estranged from the structure of being.' By contrast, Laing wrote, 'Madness need not be all breakdown. It may also be break-through.'[33]

43

Deleuze and Guattari added a political dimension to this topsy-turvy world where madness was sanity and sanity deadening conformity. Revolutionaries, they advised, 'should carry out their undertakings along the lines of the schizo process', because the schizophrenic 'has become caught up in a flux of desire that threatens the social order'.

They considered desire a productive or life force akin to Nietzsche's will to power, contrary to Freud and Lacan, who conceived it as a lack. For them, desiring production involved a pleasurable force of appropriation of what is outside oneself. Desire was ubiquitous. 'The truth is', Deleuze and Guattari explain, 'sexuality is everywhere: the way a bureaucrat fondles his records, a judge administers justice, a businessman causes money to circulate; the way the bourgeoisie fucks the proletariat; and so on . . . Flags, nations, armies, banks get a lot of people aroused.'[34]

Anti-Oedipus resonated for a new era whose radical spirit was bent on subverting hierarchies. But, just as the swinging sixties notion of the sexual revolution had concealed its opposite, namely the repressive desublimation Herbert Marcuse indicted in *One-Dimensional Man*, so *Anti-Oedipus*'s injunctions towards non-fascist living produced a cure worse than the disease; so, at least, argues psychoanalyst Rob Weatherill in *The Anti-Oedipus Complex: Lacan, Critical Theory and Postmodernism*.[35] Although preaching against the Oedipus complex, Deleuze and Guattari enmesh themselves deeper in it by gleefully slaying all forms of authority, tradition, morality and restraint, encouraging us to murder our patriarchal masters ecstatically, cheering our 'liberation' even as we remove the last bulwarks against the inhuman rapacity of the market, argues Weatherill. Instead of supporting, as Freud did, the basic matrix of marriage and family, they favour 'free-wheeling individualistic modes of pleasure'.

This critique of *Anti-Oedipus* is unfair, perhaps. After all, it is hardly a eulogy to individualism. In the introduction to *Anti-Oedipus*, Foucault wrote: 'Do not demand of politics that it restore the "rights" of the individual as philosophy has defined them. The individual is the product of power. What is needed is to "de-individualise" by means of multiplication and displacement, diverse combinations. The group must not be the organic bond uniting hierarchised individuals, but a constant generator of de-individualisation.'[36] The desire that Foucault, Deleuze and Guattari prized was a disappearing act in which one loses one's identity and merges into some collective – trippy crowds at a Grateful Dead gig, perhaps, or *enragés* at demonstrations in Paris or Tehran. Instead of resolving one's Oedipal complex on the couch, and sublimating one's incestuous desires into de-sexualised and thus socially acceptable activities, we should realise the revolutionary potential of desire. Libidinal flows were to be prized, hierarchies toppled, and the mad orgy of pleasure joined.

But is desire revolutionary? The Deleuze and Guattari thought so: 'It is explosive; there is no desiring-machine capable of being assembled without demolishing entire social sectors. Despite what some revolutionaries think about this, desire is revolutionary in its essence – desire, not left-wing holidays! – and no society can tolerate a position of real desire without its structures of exploitation, servitude, and hierarchy being compromised.'[37]

That jibe against 'left-wing holidays' makes it clear they thought proletarian struggle worth less than the ostensibly revolutionary potential of liberating desire. Deleuze and Guattari clearly cared little for collective norms as means of improving the workers' lot. In this, these post-modern French theorists were not so different from the neoliberals who would, before the decade was over, take power in the White House and 10 Downing Street. A society devoted to self-gratification is easier to control. Such, at least, had Marcuse argued eight years before *Anti-Oedipus* was published, in *One-Dimensional Man*. His notion of repressive desublimation was used to argue that the countercultural liberation of Eros is readily co-opted by conservative forces.

His point was that the unleashing of untrammelled desire seemed to end repression, but only resulted in another, more sophisticated system of exploitation. Under fascism we may have desired our own domination for sado-masochistic reasons; under late capitalism, we supposed that sexual freedoms and consumer choice would free us, while, Marcuse argued, in reality these freedoms were really new means for us to desire our own domination.

If the human world can be comprehended as a factory consisting of billions of desiring machines, as Deleuze and Guattari suggest, then those machines can readily be owned by capitalists and exploited for profit, like anything else that is produced. What's more, under neoliberalism the unrepressed transgressive flows of desire eulogised in *Anti-Oedipus* mirror the deregulated flows of capital unleashed as a result of the Nixon Shock. Deleuze and Guattari became, in effect, complicit with the system they ostensibly sought to destroy.

One corollary of Deleuze and Guattari's eulogies to the revolutionary potential of desire was what has been called the happiness fantasy – a deluded pursuit of power, sexual conquest and money that, as often as not, is a male masturbatory fantasy. Indeed, the history of happiness since the war can be traced from Reich's orgone accumulator through Marcuse's repressive desublimation and Deleuze and Guattari's desiring machines to Harvey Weinstein's sexual predation and Donald Trump. Deleuze and Guattari reckoned that desire would overturn the social order; more likely, its liberation, at least under neoliberal capitalism, has unleashed that order's most rapacious, exploitative tendencies.

And yet *Anti-Oedipus* did serve as a radical manifesto for the post-modern era, not least in its subversion of identity. Consider the thynnine wasp one last time. Instead of being trapped in the prison-house of being, it was engaged in a flight of becoming, its identity fluid, its passion spent as it fertilised the orchid. In the post-modern era, such becoming was part of a gleefully godless liberation theology for which Deleuze and Guattari had proselytised. Gender was fluid, identities exchangeable – perhaps even the biologically determinate constraints of sex could be overcome. Instead of being doomed to be, one could become multiple. Instead of remaining what one was born as, one could become what one wanted – multiple, provisional, fluid. Identities became masks one could pick up in the marketplace, wear, and discard at will. In this way, desire exploded identity.

2

Disappearing Acts, 1975:
The Passenger | Ziggy Stardust | Cindy Sherman

In Michelangelo Antonioni's 1975 film *The Passenger*, a burned-out political correspondent finds a dead body in a hotel room in the North African desert. The journalist, David Locke, played by Jack Nicholson, studies the body on the bed. The corpse looks a little like him. It could be his double. He rummages through the dead man's things and notices he shares not just David Robertson's appearance but his first name. He has an idea. He exchanges identities with the corpse. He swaps their passports, switches their clothes, tells the clerk that someone called David Locke is lying dead on the bed, rightly supposing that the two men look indistinguishable to him. Back in London, Locke's estranged wife is told her husband is dead. She and a colleague edit the footage her husband filmed in the desert, trying to find clues as to what happened.

What becomes clear through several flashbacks is that Locke is using the corpse to escape himself, to elude an identity that has become unbearable. And that is a very post-modern move. Post-modern artists including David Bowie and Cindy Sherman revelled in the liberation, creative and existential, of taking on new identities and performing characters in their works. Those alter egos became both lucrative brands that helped sell creative products and, sometimes, a means of subverting prevailing social norms.

In 1975 Harvard philosopher Robert Nozick published *Anarchy, State, and Utopia*. In it Nozick proposed a thought experiment. Imagine there is an experience machine that would give you any experience you desired: 'Superduper neurophysiologists could stimulate your brain so that you would think and feel you were writing a great novel, or making a friend, or reading an interesting book. All the time you would be floating in a tank, with electrodes attached to your brain.'[1]

Nozick's experience machine was to become the philosophical underpinning of many post-modern fictions, and arguably the basis for the videogame industry which, in 1975, had still not evolved beyond the on-screen tennis game, Atari's Pong. Kathryn Bigelow's 1995 film *Strange Days* was a sci-fi thriller whose story revolves around SQUID, an illegal electronic device that records memories and physical sensations directly from the wearer's cerebral cortex onto a MiniDisc-like playback device for others to experience. David Foster Wallace's 1997 novel *Infinite Jest* centres on a film of the same name that is so entertaining that, once watched, the viewer will desire nothing else but to watch the film over and over. Both William Gibson's 1984 novel *Neuromancer* and Neal Stephenson's 1992 novel *Snow Crash* develop virtual realities into which their protagonists disappear. In the Wachowski Brothers' 1999 film *The Matrix* (its title drawn from the virtual-reality network of Gibson's novel), artificial intelligence has wiped most of humanity from the earth, except for those it enslaves in a virtual-reality system as a farmed power source, and the relatively few remaining humans who are free of that system. Enslaved humans lie in pods, controlled by cybernetic implants connecting them to a simulated reality called the Matrix.

What Bowie and Sherman, among others, showed in 1975 is that we desire not to live in reality, but to create new possibilities for ourselves, to plug into other identities. Long before Second Life and other online means of presenting oneself behind virtual masks, these post-modern artists opened up the possibility that reality might be transcended.

I

On 3 July 1973, at London's Hammersmith Odeon, David Bowie told the crowd: 'Not only is this the last show of the tour, but it's the last show we'll ever do. Thank you.'[2] At the time Bowie was incarnating Ziggy Stardust, a space-age pop-star character whose androgynous allure made him a simulacrum of other real-life glam-rock stars, such as Marc Bolan. On his hit album of the previous year, *Ziggy Stardust and the Spiders from Mars*, Bowie had sung what in hindsight became the chronicle of a death foretold.

On that night in west London, Bowie killed Ziggy and broke up the band. But he didn't tell the bassist and drummer before making his on-stage announcement. Trevor Bolder is reputed to have mouthed to drummer Mick 'Woody' Woodmansey, 'He's fucking sacked us!' And then, fittingly, the band launched into their last number, 'Rock 'n' Roll Suicide', sacrificing Ziggy to the crowd, with whom Bowie symbolically merged as he sang the song's last line: 'Gimme your hands, 'cause you're wonderful.'

Bowie-as-Ziggy, argues fan-turned-philosopher Simon Critchley, captivated his fans because his persona refused the dominant norms of society – boy/girl, human/alien, gay/straight. In the anti-Oedipal terms of Deleuze and Guattari, Bowie de-territorialised himself in becoming the androgynous star-man, quitting the cul-de-sac of suburbia for the gender-bending, omnisexual fantasy realm of outer space.

At the end of 'Rock 'n' Roll Suicide', Bowie was reaching out to his target demographic, whom Critchley describes as 'millions of self-conscious mini-Hamlets, living out their loveless hells in scattered, sundry hamlets, towns'. Teenage Simon was just such a mini-Hamlet, dreaming of a life beyond his native Letchworth Garden City. Leafy Letchworth, like Bowie's Beckenham, might have seemed arboreal, rooted, stuck. That night in Hammersmith, Ziggy, as he sacrificed himself on stage, revealed himself as outlier, pointing the way – the Deleuzian line of flight for others to take from the spiritual lockdown of suburbia to the stars, propelled by the revolutionary force of desire-production. 'We heard those words', recalls Critchley, 'and were astonished at being forgiven. We just needed to reach out our hands. We did. We bought the album.'[3]

The spiritual rebirth from Ziggy's sacrificial death came with a price. But that's how it is: at the end of the post-modern show, the exit is always through the gift shop.

Ziggy's death was a necessary sacrifice. The mask had begun to stick, so Bowie cast it off. And after that sacrifice, he would be creatively born again many times. The Beckenham boy had already become existentially fraught spacemen Major Tom and Ziggy Stardust; he would go on to become the thin white duke, the man who fell to earth, Pierrot junkie, elephant man, goblin king. Ultimately, on his album *Blackstar*, released two days before his death in 2016, he left his fans an inscrutable testament that they could try, and most likely fail, to interpret.

Bowie was a virtuoso of becoming rather than being, and his long artistic career was a series of anti-Oedipal flights: he flitted from mask to mask the better to escape confrontation with what lies behind. ('I've never caught a glimpse', he sang on 'Changes', 'Of how the others must see the faker / I'm much too fast to take that test.')

His lyrics became parodies of meaninglessness, words in flight that were suggestive but never weighed down with anything as determinate as meaning. On the 1974 album *Diamond Dogs*, for instance, he employed the cut-up method developed by novelist William Burroughs and artist Brion Gysin. Like them, he took scissors to text, drew slips of paper at random to produce lyrics that were suggestive (or more or less random: the fact that they often rhymed suggests Bowie submitted to more order than he was letting on). Hence such lyrics as this verse from the album's title track:

> Meet his little hussy with his ghost-town approach
> Her face is sans feature, but she wears a Dali brooch

Sweetly reminiscent, something mother used to bake
Wrecked up and paralysed, Diamond Dogs are stabilised.

Meaning was a mask – something that could be picked up and discarded before it stuck. It was as though Bowie the author had committed suicide in a manner not foreseen by Barthes and Foucault, and left to his fans the burden of interpreting what it was, if indeed anything, he was on about. A poisoned chalice, given that it was conceived to be literally meaningless. And not only was meaning unstable: if you opened the gatefold sleeve to *Diamond Dogs*, the naked Bowie on the front was revealed to have a canine body, as if he was in the process of becoming a dog.

He was born David Robert Jones in Brixton, south London, in 1947, and formed his first band, The Konrads, in 1962, playing rock 'n' roll covers at youth clubs and weddings. He went on to front several other bands in the 1960s – including The Lower Third and The Riot Squad – and became a proselyte for identity fluidity. Indeed, Bowie's early years revealed him as a fashion outlier or proto–Gok Wan, persuading a series of unreconstructed white English blokes in the band to free their minds and wear make-up. In the back of the ambulance that served as The Lower Third's tour bus, Bowie argued they should emulate groovy mod bands in London with their sharp suits, amphetamine intensity and make-up. Bassist Graham Rivens 'turned round and said: "Fuck that" ', recalled guitarist Denis Taylor in a 2019 BBC documentary.[4]

Later, Bowie convinced Mick Ronson, Woody Woodmandsey and Trevor Bolder – who have, I would submit, the most hetero names in the glam rock pantheon – that they should not only stretch silver satinette over their beer guts, but conceal their stubble with foundation. Only then could they become the Spiders from Mars to his Ziggy Stardust. 'When they realised how many girls they could pull while looking otherworldly,' recalled Bowie off camera, 'they took to it like a duck to water.'

How did this suburban boy mutate into such a lubricious alligator, Major Tom, alien – not to mention squaddie amusingly buried up to his neck in sand by Japanese captors in the film *Merry Christmas, Mr Lawrence*? One theory, advanced by his cousin, Kristina Amadeus, was unrequited love. He was always trying to please his mum, Peggy. Childhood friend Geoff Mac-Cormack, writing to Bowie after her death, said he thought she had never approved of him. 'She never quite took to me either,' Bowie wrote back. Strikingly, he had a half-brother, Terry, who Bowie recalled as a rebel outsider and the catalyst for his escape from suburbia, introducing him to beat literature and rock 'n' roll (when he heard Little Richard's 'Tutti Frutti', Bowie would recall, it was like hearing God). Terry ended up hospitalised with schizophrenia until his suicide in 1985, while David made a career from slipping into and out of different personae.

Certainly Bowie wore many masks. By 1975, he had evolved from diamond dog to soul boy, sporting a new haircut and sound, plundering contemporary black American music for his album *Young Americans*. A year later, he recast himself as Thin White Duke for the album *Station to Station*, a character announced on the title track thus: 'The return of the thin white duke, throwing darts in lovers' eyes.'

The following year he pitched up in Berlin, where he produced what turned out to be a series of three albums – *Low*, *Heroes* and *Lodger* – in which he performed himself as world-weary Europhile. 'I've lived all over the world', he sang on 'Be My Wife', surely the most unconvincing marriage proposal in popular song, 'I've left every place.' The perils of taking Deleuze's line of flight were laid bare: perhaps the globetrotter was yearning for conjugal felicity and domesticity. Or perhaps not: Bowie was never more post-modern than in his ironic, unreliable narratives about the person we took to be 'David Bowie'.

By 1980, he was commenting ironically on his post-modern persona even as he developed another, the Pierrot junkie of 1980s 'Ashes to Ashes'. In that song, Bowie seemed to be inhabiting another future dystopia — at least in the video for the single — sinking in clown make-up into lime-green nuclear waste, a white-faced clown in Tarkovskian end-times:

> Ashes to ashes, funk to funky
> We know Major Tom's a junkie
> Strung out in heaven's high
> Hitting an all-time low.

Drugs indeed fuelled Bowie's mutations. He described himself as taking industrial qualities of cocaine during the 1970s, and ascribed the fascist salute he gave from an open-top car in character as Thin White Duke as a theatrical gesture devoid of political significance, and also symptomatic of his drug use. He wasn't flirting with fascism, as we were to suppose; he was playing a role. Even the hate speech of a Hitler salute was subordinate to spectacle.

Everything in Bowie's post-modern art was mutable, but most of all the artist himself. He was the personification of his friend and collaborator Iggy Pop's 1977 single 'The Passenger', taking a ride on others' texts, other identities. Critchley supposes that the title of the song may have been inspired by Antonioni's film. Iggy claimed in one interview he was the passenger, whom Bowie had driven around the United States because he did not have a driving licence. In that song, produced by Bowie and recorded at the Hansa studios in Berlin, the world is reimagined as nocturnal phantasmagoria created for consumption.

The most curious of David Bowie's personae, though, was humanoid alien Thomas Jerome Newton, whom Bowie played in Nicholas Roeg's 1976 film, *The Man Who Fell to Earth*. Not so much re-territorialised as territorialised, Newton has come to earth to seek a water supply after his home planet has dried up – but only after putting on a disguise to pass as human. Initially his mission is successful: he deploys his technological superiority to patent a series of inventions, and becomes immensely wealthy, using his money to pay for a spaceship that will transport water to save his home planet. In the meantime he lives with Mary-Lou, a rather simple hotel worker who, while not realising he is an extra-terrestrial, recognises he is not from these parts. He tells her he's English, which, hilariously, satisfies her suspicions.

She introduces him to two of her home planet's leading pleasures, TV and alcohol, and he becomes addicted to both, sitting before a wall of screens, drinking, stupefied and immobilised like the personification of Guy Debord's society of the spectacle, or the territorialised emblem of conformity from which Deleuze and Guattari sought to liberate us.

The most resonant scene comes when Newton reveals his true identity to Mary-Lou. He is not English, but something even more disturbing. He performs a striptease of the self, an alien dance of the seven veils, peeling off nipples and hair, removing his ears and contact lenses to reveal reptilian eyes beneath. Mary-Lou turns white with shock and wets herself in terror. Her desire to see a more true self beyond the performance, stripped bare of pretence, is satisfied, but only in a horrifying way.

Humankind, wrote T. S. Eliot, cannot bear very much reality. And reality, Newton's true self in *The Man Who Fell to Earth*, is literally alien.

The philosopher Charles Taylor argued that we live in an age of authenticity. The injunction to be authentic, he suggested, has replaced the injunction to submit oneself to God's will. This age of authenticity, in which we are individuals tasked with becoming ourselves, with finding our own way and doing our own things, is the Enlightenment's gift to us, or perhaps its curse. The idea that one had to use one's own reason and experience to find God, which arose with the Enlightenment and found expression in the philosophy of deism, instilled a sense of intellectual autonomy that led some to abandon God altogether.

What's this got to do with David Bowie? The one-time starman refused to be pinned down in one identity. Moreover, he was a reminder, in our age of authenticity, of the importance of inauthenticity. Simon Critchley wrote: 'Art's filthy lesson is inauthenticity all the way down, a series of repetitions and reenactments: fakes that strip away the illusion of reality in which we live and confront us with the reality of illusion.'⁵

Newton's disclosure of his authentic self is something David Bowie, the post-modern artist, the man who spent his careers flitting from mask to mask, never did in public. Indeed, as Newton he was hiding behind another mask even as – in the kind of multi-layered irony post-modernism is renowned for – he played a character revealing his true self: each day when Bowie became the alien for *The Man Who Fell to Earth*, he would spend eight hours in make-up.

What this amounts to is the realisation that micro-analysing Bowie's lyrics for hidden meanings misses the point of his art. In *Against Interpretation*, Susan Sontag called for an erotics rather than a hermeneutics of art. That idea was inspired by her friend, artist Paul Thek, who got sick of Sontag's clever theorising before artworks rather than doing what she should – namely, experiencing them and getting turned on by it. Bowie's post-modern music similarly opposes itself to interpretation.

As for Thomas Jerome Newton, he never did make it back to his home planet. Captured by a rival entrepreneur, he is held in a luxury apartment and subjected to tests, one of which involves X-rays, which cause his contact lenses to become permanently fixed to his eyes. The mask freezes to his face, isomorphising his identity. Unable even to die, Newton faces an eternity territorialised.

Not long before his own death, Bowie returned to the role, writing songs for a musical called *Lazarus* and a song of the same name for his final album, *Blackstar*. The song is enigmatic, but since the author is dead and he is no longer the authority, perhaps we can attempt an interpretation. Perhaps Bowie as Lazarus, consigned to endless posthumous interpretation, would have preferred to have been left in peace. In any case, he had offered his own, albeit ironic, interpretation littered through his songs. 'Ashes to Ashes', for instance, seems to express frustration for Bowie's de-territorialised, endlessly mutable personae, for the Sisyphean labour of endless strategising that a career of constructing new identities involves. He sang:

> I never done good things
> I never done bad things
> I never did anything out of the blue, woh-o-oh
> Want an axe to break the ice
> Wanna come down right now.

In this, we can imagine, he got to the point as a post-modern artist where he could perform his dissatisfaction at what being a post-modern artists entails: all masks and no authenticity, ubiquitous irony and forests of quotation marks. But with this twist: Bowie often added to his repertoire with the spiritually dissatisfied post-modern artist reflecting on the existential ramifications of a career spent as a chameleon.

That self-reflective role was often expressed in tragicomically self-destructive terms:

> I was going round and round the hotel garage
> Must have been touching close to 94
> Oh, but I'm always crashing in the same car
> I'm always crashing in the same car.

This was perhaps as much of a disappearing act as his other masks. Maybe Bowie was performing a post-modern persona – let's call him 'David Bowie' – who wanted an axe to break the division between his roles and the real self behind them. But, for David Bowie, there was no axe and no way down, nothing but masquerade. Prefiguring how the internet might work as a masked ball in cyberspace, the masks became the man, interposing themselves indefinitely between us and whatever was behind. If there was anything. Or maybe the real David Bowie was just good at protecting his privacy.

II

Cindy Sherman, like David Locke and David Bowie, spent much of the mid seventies disappearing. While Bowie was a chameleon and Locke a post-colonial subject casting off his past, Sherman was an artist who hid behind her roles, performing characters that resembled movie stars of earlier generations, women like Monica Vitti, Sophia Loren, Brigitte Bardot and Kim Novak. In *Complete Untitled Film Stills*, a series of sixty-nine black-and-white photographs, Sherman apparently sought to subvert cinematic stereotypes of women. 'I feel I'm anonymous in my work', she said. 'When I look at the pictures, I never see myself; they aren't self-portraits. Sometimes I disappear.'[6]

Or did she? Oscar Wilde argued the opposite: 'Man is least himself when he talks in his own person. Give him a mask, and he will tell you the truth.'

Sherman's early work captured the gaze of feminist critics who supposed that the truth Sherman was telling was about the objectification of women by men through visual imagery. There were altogether too many women reclining obligingly on tousled bed sheets to suppose otherwise. In 'Film Still #52', Sherman appeared curled up on a bed wearing a blonde wig and silken nightie, apparently lost in reverie, unguarded and undressed as if available for predatory consumption. Judith Williamson reckoned you could tell in each image which director – Hitchcock, Godard, a host of B-movie auteurs – Sherman was pastiching.[7]

Laura Mulvey astutely noted that Sherman's film stills depict women in Eisenhower's 1950s America, when the Cold War was fought not just with the threat of nuclear Armageddon, but with perhaps more potent weapons: desirable women's bodies.[8] The America of this era, Mulvey imagined, was the mythic birthplace of post-modernism, in which advertising, movies and packaging marketed glamour and America postured hubristically as a paradise on earth, as if paradise could be defined by its supply of consumer goods. True, desirable women's bodies have been consumable by the male gaze ever since Venus disported herself on a shell in Botticelli's *Birth of Venus* in 1480, and probably before. But the post-modern twist Mulvey saw in Sherman's work was that the women she performed were involved in a social masquerade. The constructed femininity of the movie stars that Sherman pastiched – with bullet bras, cinched waists and masks of make-up – were part of a culture industry bent on misdirection. Cold War terrors, from black-listing to mutually assured nuclear destruction, were hidden behind the smooth surfaces and sensuous curves, be they those of Marilyn Monroe or the latest Cadillac.

In 'Film Still #15' Sherman performed the role of a dancer sitting on a window sill in what we imagine to be a dance studio. She is wearing a tight, cleavage-revealing top, her long, elegant legs recalling those of Cyd Charisse or Shirley MacLaine and ending in period-specific ankle socks and heels. As if resting between takes for a dance sequence in *West Side Story* or *Singin' in the Rain*, she gazes demurely out the window, lost in thought – or, equally possibly, thinking about nothing.

Uncannily, the persona Sherman incarnates resembles Judy, a character played by Kim Novak in Hitchcock's 1958 masterpiece of male voyeurism *Vertigo*. In that film, James Stewart's ex-cop Scottie Ferguson becomes obsessed with a woman called Madeleine whom he is hired to follow through the streets of San Francisco by a worried husband. After Madeleine dies, Scottie transfers his obsession to Judy, a woman who looks rather like Madeleine (in fact both characters were played by Novak). And Scottie, like Cindy Sherman, though more fetishistically, devotes himself to making Judy into Madeleine, changing her hair, clothes and face until he can fall in love with Madeleine's doppelgänger.

Of course, there is a key difference between Scottie and Cindy: she doesn't transform other women to suit her erotic obsession – she transforms herself for her art. This was cinema's era of borderline misogynistic protagonists making over women until they matched their fantasies – from Scottie in *Vertigo* to Rex Harrison's Henry Higgins in *My Fair Lady*.

The scene set up in 'Untitled Film Still #15' recalls another Hitchcock film about voyeurism. In 1954's *Rear Window*, James Stewart plays photographer Jeff Jefferies (no relation), forced to recover from a disabling injury in his apartment – a kind of symbolic castration preventing him from going beyond the pleasures of the visual. The window he wheels himself up to in his wheelchair offers a view on the parade of overwhelmingly female life in neighbouring flats. Each window he looks into is framed like a movie screen, each woman inside it on the receiving end of his gaze.

He snoops on one woman, whom he dubs Miss Lonelyheart, as she makes a candlelit supper for a man who will never arrive, until she can sustain the illusion no longer and collapses in tears. In another window, he watches the ballet dancer he calls Miss Torso (soul sister to Sherman's dancer at rest) entertaining a bevy of men over drinks. But while Jefferies revels in this sexually charged voyeurism (complete with telephoto lens flexing as his gaze becomes more lubricious – a prosthesis you don't have to be a Freudian to decode), the nameless woman of Sherman's 'Untitled Film Still #15' is looking through the window, but what she's seeing and what she's thinking remain obscure. She is the ironic inversion of the male gaze; the female gaze in Hitchcock's cinema is programmatically irrelevant, as if Hitchcock were answering Freud's question 'What do women want?' with another question: 'Who cares?' All you need to know is that women are to be looked at and men take pleasure in looking at them.

Happily, there is a 'but' looming. Laura Mulvey saw Sherman's movie stills as a *trompe-l'oeil* in which the artist importuned the viewer into enjoying the voyeurisms on offer, inviting them to gaze at the erotic images of passive, available, consumable women in the manner of Jeff Jefferies consuming the images and dramas from his rear window – but then turned the tables. The viewer suffered a hideous realisation that these pastiches of erotic availability were performed by Cindy Sherman, and those performances destroyed the fourth wall necessary to the fetishistic fantasy, the implicit contract between available object (female) and pleasured gaze (male). Mulvey wrote: 'As is well known in the cinema, any moment of mar-velling at an illusion immediately destroys its credibility. The voyeurism turns around like a trap and the viewer ends up aware that Sherman-the-artist has set up a machine for making the gaze materialise uncomfortably, in alliance with Sherman-the-model.'[9]

This perceptual switch is called the oscillation effect. It's like the duck/rabbit illusion, which can be seen as duck or rabbit but never (or at least Wittgenstein supposed) both at the same time. But there is a difference between duck/rabbit and Sherman's many illusions. If you look at the duck/rabbit image, you can happily swing between two perceptions. You can see it as a duck and then see it as a rabbit, then duck, then rabbit. Not so with Sherman's *Untitled Film Stills*. Once you have seen through the illusion you cannot, or are at least very unlikely to be able to, beguile yourself by seeing the illusion again.

Cindy Sherman's art only swings one way. Never more so than in 'Untitled Film Still #6' in which the artist reclines on a bed in blonde bob and heavy make-up, thick gloss on slightly parted lips, peignoir opened to reveal mismatched bra and knickers, torso turned apparently obligingly, gazing off camera rather than troubling the voyeur by meeting their gaze, lost in some private, satisfyingly unknowable reverie. But something interferes with the consumption of this erotic image. The woman is reaching down for something with her right hand. What could it be? Phone, vibrator, gun, clutch bag? No, it was Sherman's remote shutter release, which thereby draws attention to the artifice.

Sherman was performing a dance of the two veils. The partial unveiling of her body by opening the peignoir seemed to offer sexual titillation, but revealing the shutter release told a differ-ent story: Sherman was the producer of the image, not – or not merely – object of consumption. This variant on the oscillation effect makes Sherman's art post-modern. 'The viewer looks, recognises a style, doubts, does a double take, then recognises that the style is a citation, and meanings shift and change their reference like shifting perceptions of perspective from an optical illusion', wrote Mulvey.[10]

In effect, Sherman was pouring cold water on predatory male genitals. Or, as the theorists put it, she problematised the fetishistic male gaze. In her essay 'Visual Pleasure and Narrative Cinema', Mulvey argued that mainstream cinema offers two types of visual pleasure: scopophilia, the voyeuristic delight in watching others when naked or engaged in sexual activity, which Freud insisted involved taking other persons as objects; and narcissism, the pleasure in identifying with a self-like image, an account developed in Lacan's theory of the mirror stage.

Because the 'pleasure in looking has been split between active/male and passive/female', scopophilia privileged the male gaze and made women in film things to be looked at. The function of woman in the patriarchal unconscious was to symbolise the castration threat by her absence of a penis, while, as Mulvey put it, 'in patriarchal culture [woman stands in] as signifier for the male other, bound by a symbolic order in which man can live out his phantasies and obsessions through linguistic command by imposing them on the silent image of woman still tied to her place as bearer of meaning, not maker of meaning'. Sherman subverted that symbolic order: she was maker of meaning, subverter of the patriarchal gaze.

Well, perhaps. But Cindy Sherman didn't care to be cast in that role:

I know I was not consciously aware of this thing, the 'male gaze.' It was the way I was shooting, the mimicry of the style of black-and-white grade-Z motion pictures that produced the self-consciousness of these characters, not my knowledge of feminist theory. I suppose, unconsciously, or semiconsciously at best, I was wrestling with some sort of turmoil of my own about understanding women.[11]

Perhaps one of the reasons Sherman's work feels so relevant to this day is that she's restrained herself from pigeonholing it. As the artist once said, 'There are so many levels of artifice. I liked that whole jumble of ambiguity.'

In this she was post-modern like the David Bowie of 'Changes' – she had, most likely, caught a glimpse of how the feminist theorist must see the faker, but was too quick to be consumed by that gaze. Naturally, this exasperated feminist writers who theorised elegantly about what Sherman was up to, to the point where Mulvey suggested that the artist's intentions have to be surrendered in favour of theory: 'It is necessary to fly in the face of her own expressly non-theoretical, even anti-theoretical stance.'[12]

Necessary, no doubt, to the theorist who seeks to flatter her self-image by seeing the artist's works as instantiations of her own theories. But necessary to Cindy Sherman? Not really. Indeed, just as Mulvey supposed Sherman suckered male voyeurs with her trompe l'oeil images, maybe Sherman importuned feminist theorists by inviting them to take her photographs as a reductive critique of voyeuristic patriarchal norms – and then turned around like a trap to show the feminist gaze that her photographed personae were not what they had been supposed to be by the theorists. 'The work is what it is and hopefully it's seen as feminist work, or feminist-advised work,' she commented. 'But I'm not going to go around espousing theoretical bullshit about feminist stuff.'[13]

In 1981, *Artforum* commissioned Sherman to make a series of photographs called *Centrefolds*. Each of the twelve images was in horizontal format and, at four feet by two feet, much larger than her previous work. The large colour-image format evoked the centrefolds of pornographic men's magazines. Sherman's centrefolds were erotic and contained fetishistic elements used in pornography to titillate the male gaze – wet shirts, matted hair, dishevelled nightgowns. They often also involved the performance of adolescent female characters in plaid kilts and gingham dresses, as if she was indicting the male desire for sex with underage girls. Sherman said she wanted a man opening up the magazine suddenly [to] look at it with an expectation of something lascivious and then feel like the violator that they would be looking at this woman who is perhaps a victim. I didn't think of them as victims at the time . . . Obviously I'm trying to make someone feel bad for having a certain expectation.[14]

In the end, *Artforum*'s editors decided not to publish the *Centrefolds* series, worrying that Sherman's subtle takedowns of the pornographic gaze would be misconstrued. Once more, what was striking was the reverie of her characters, each lost in thought, as if waiting, as Mulvey put it, 'in enforced passivity, for a letter or phone call'.

But these obligingly coy, demure, sexually passive, stirringly enigmatic characters in Sherman's voyeuristic masquerade, having played their role, were removed. As the 1980s unfolded, so did Sherman's women, as if they were losing their smooth, cosmeticised surfaces, their masks of femininity, to reveal the monstrous beneath. In 1984 she was commissioned by French *Vogue* to model clothes by Comme des Garçons and Issey Miyake. In doing so, she showcased the clothes while poking fun at the fashion industry. In 'Untitled #137', for instance, she wears a heavy, rust-coloured designer coat whose fabric folds around her slouching torso, her make-up is caked on, her hair bedraggled, and her oversized hands filthy. Even her expression subverts the conventional image of a fashion shoot, looking depressed rather than perky. In 1985 she was commissioned by *Vanity Fair* to make images illustrating fairy-tales. The result was a series of grotesques, as if Sherman was tearing off the mask of the enchantress.

In 1986, Cindy Sherman completed her disappearing act. In a series of photographs called *Disasters*, she removed herself from the photographic image and replaced the human figure with dismembered body parts strewn across toxic wastelands. In 'Untitled #167', fingers reached from the bug-infested dirt as if one of Sherman's glamorous women had been buried in a shallow grave but was now fighting to get out. Elsewhere, a dismembered nose lay in the dirt and – most uncannily of all – a discarded make-up mirror reflected to the viewer an inverted, hideous face.

In 'Untitled #173' flies feast on blood-stained tufts of hair seemingly torn from a woman's scalp. At the back of the image lies a woman, eyes open but devoid of life. It's as if the character of the adolescent girl from *Centrefolds*' 'Untitled #92', in her white shirt and tartan kilt, is making her final appearance. We're looking, for all the world, at a crime scene, at the dead end of the feminine masquerade, as if the girl has been raped, murdered, dismembered and, having been consumed and exhausted, her body parts thrown away.

In other images from this time Sherman depicts human figures composed of false breasts and buttocks. In 'Untitled', a woman's naked buttocks and prosthetic legs have been arranged as if on a forest floor. The torso is collapsing under foliage while the head is composed of a blonde wig and blushing face gazing off camera. It's not clear if this figure is dead, passively awaiting sex or resting after it. For Mulvey, such dismemberment compelled us to see the truth beneath the cosmeticised masks of Sherman's earlier female characters: 'In the last resort, nothing is left but disgust – the disgust of sexual detritus, decaying food, vomit, slime, menstrual blood, hair. These traces represent the end of the road, the secret stuff of bodily fluids that the cosmetic is designed to conceal.'[15]

All the make-up and outfits Sherman had meticulously applied to perform the feminine had been stripped away. For Mulvey, at least, Wilde was wrong: the masks didn't tell the truth. The truth was what ultimately broke through the masks: 'Sherman's ironic "unveiling" also "unveils" the use of the female body as a metaphor for division between surface allure and concealed decay, as though the stuff that has been projected for so long into a mythic space "behind" the mask of femininity had suddenly broken through the delicately painted veil.' Mulvey saw in the images of decaying food and vomit that appeared in

Sherman's photographs at the time the spectre of the anorexic girl who 'tragically acts out the fashion fetish of the female as an eviscerated, cosmetic and artificial construction designed to ward off the "otherness" hidden in the "interior".'[16]

But Mulvey's imposition of a truth beneath the surface of Sherman's art, though important and suggestive, is questionable. Bertrand Russell was confronted during a lecture on astronomy by a woman who claimed the world was held up by a giant turtle. 'What is the turtle standing on?' 'You're very clever, young man, very clever', said the woman. 'But it's turtles all the way down!' Post-modern art is like that: there is nothing but artifice, no truth that emerges at the end of its dance of the seven veils. Only interpretations that can be foisted, more or less brutally, on the work. This is partly because post-modern artists are alert to being consumed by the voyeur's gaze, especially that of a clever critic. If, like David Bowie and Cindy Sherman, they are any good, they are programmatically against having the meaning of their work frozen by another's interpretation.

In this, Sherman's photographs can be seen as precursors of the selfie, suggesting that being in public involves a process of becoming. We are always performing.[17] But the advent of the selfie is a game changer in this presentation of the self. Selfies, which involve uploading to social media photographs of oneself taken typically with a smartphone or webcam, make plain the ongoing process of identity construction.

In photographic or painted portraits and self-portraits, the photographer or painter is usually hidden. In most selfies, we see the subject's hand as she holds the camera up to capture her face. Not only is the fourth wall between spectator and subject made clear by the inclusion of the camera in the image, but something even more curious happens. The selfie is an externalised inward look, as if the human body were looking at itself; moreover, the selfie lets third persons on social media share that mirror view, that Narcissus gaze at our own image.

Nathan Jurgenson has argued that the selfie receives such opprobrium because it discloses the unbearable truth that we are always constructing our selves: 'The term selfie is widely used as shorthand for the exhibitionism, narcissism, and other enduring social worries aroused by technologies of visibility. But selfie taking is hardly aberrant; it is not rare or limited to some unusual subset of smartphone uses.'[18]

Selfies are not just scapegoats. They are also consumable images that worry us because they involve not just constructing our selves, but making those selves into things. If all that sounds rather glum, it's worth reflecting on the pleasures of self-performance. One reason selfie-taking has become so popular is because it allows all the fun of dressing up and wearing masks, with the frisson that comes from the implicit suggestion that one is disclosing one's true authentic self, even though that self is clearly a social construct.

The American sociologist Charles Horton Cooley came up with the term 'looking-glass self' in the nineteenth century; the selfie is the realisation and full disclosure of the truth about how we construct that self. It's a truth that sociologists may have known since Victorian times, but that we are having to deal with in the post-modern age – namely, the reification of the self. 'I am not what I think I am and I am not what you think I am; I am what I think you think I am', wrote Cooley.[19] The uncomfortable implication of this is that we come to know ourselves as selves precisely by taking on a third-person perspective on ourselves.

In this context, it's striking that Cindy Sherman, the proto-selfie artist, now thrives on social media. Her camera, though, is absent, as though she finds it unnecessary to draw attention to her fakery. We know she's not for real, and she knows we know it. From *Untitled Film Stills* onwards, her art has dealt with all the stuff that captivates and disgusts about social media in general: the narcissism, the perils and pleasures of self-exhibition, the cunningly filtered fantasies masquerading as the real thing. Her Instagram features Sherman performing different women in delirious costumes and make-up. Some images are the result of her playing about with Facetune, an app that allows her to reshape heads and eliminate wrinkles, or Perfect365, the make-up simulator she uses to give her subjects garish digital makeovers.

But online, as opposed to in her earlier photographs, the real Cindy Sherman appears. Possibly. There are holiday snaps of lighthouses, pictures of Mick and Keith bumping and grinding at a Rolling Stones gig, shots from the floor of a Dior show. Sherman's Instagram is incidentally fascinating because it reveals the woman of a thousand disguises letting her mask slip for once. Or does she? Maybe this virtuosa of self-disappearance is revealing nothing about herself, but rather presenting an unreliable simulation of a social media self-performance. That is one possibility. The other is that, in the post-modern selfie age as in the one that Oscar Wilde described, you disclose yourself as you attempt to hide, you appear at the very moment when you think you have successfully disappeared.

Consider Japanese artist Ayano Sudo. She is an ambassador for her country's leading wig manufacturer, Sugarcranz. That, in itself, is very post-modern: in the modern age countries had Japanese ambassadors; in the post-modern age wig companies have ambassadors too. And who's to say which is more important? Among her duties is taking one selfie a month in a different wig and posting it on her Instagram. 'Sometimes, when I wear a wig, I feel like I transform into a different person.' She believes this transformation gives her a kind of 'superpower'.

The superpower, if that's what it is, is the new identity that she creates. In another project, Ayano shot herself in the likeness of sixteen missing Japanese girls for her 2015 book *Gespenster*. She was inspired by missing persons posters in a Tokyo train station. Ayano searched for information about what the girls were wearing and how their hair was styled when they were last seen. 'When I posed [in] the clothes I had found . . . I fell under the illusion that I was one of the disappeared girls', she wrote in her artist's statement.

But, in impersonating these girls, Ayano was drawing on something that happened in Japan in the mid seventies, when

David Bowie was changing into the Thin White Duke, when Cindy Sherman was playing at Hitchcock heroines, and when Jack Nicholson was filling a dead man's shoes. At that time, Japan was revelling in what Ayano calls the golden age of shojo manga magazines. Shojo means girls between puberty and marriage, and manga means comics. And the girls depicted in those comics created an image that Japanese girls still imitate. 'Now girls today also take on that image', Ayano says. 'Big eyes and sparkling skin has always been and will continue to be the icon of a Japanese girl.'[20] This might seem tragic (in the way that Mulvey identified anorexia as tragic). Cindy Sherman deconstructed the mask of femininity, even reduced it to rubble, in her art, only to see it reassembled again and again as other women revelled in dressing up as what looked like, but were not, sexually available teenage girls. These masks of femininity were concerned not with servicing the predatory male gaze, but with something more interesting and post-modern – namely, fulfilling the fetishistic desires of women shaped in patriarchal society. Judith Williamson nailed this when she wrote about what she loved in Cindy Sherman's photographs. Williamson recalled standing before her wardrobe in the morning wondering what to wear today. Each outfit – smart suit, leather skirt, overalls, cotton dress – would send out different signals and determine how she would be seen that day. 'Often I have wished I could put them all on together or appear simultaneously in every possible outfit, just to say, "Fuck you, for thinking any one of these is *me*. But also, See I can be any of them." This seems to me exactly what Cindy Sherman achieves.'[21]

And this, to me, exactly captures what post-modern avatars like Bowie and Sherman bequeathed to the internet age. For self-presentation now delivers a fuck you to those dull-witted enough to mistake persona for person, or extrapolate truth from semblance. At the same time, it captures the desire to perform many identities rather than enduring the life sentence of having one mask congealing to one's face. Once only artists could do this. But we are all creatives now, all of us makers of masks. Art's dirty secret of inauthenticity has become ubiquitous and, as a result, stopped being a secret.

III

Which brings us back to Jack Nicholson in the desert. Depressed by his failing marriage and by a drab professional career, Locke discovers what he believes to be an existential way out: a suicide that isn't suicide – like David Bowie's killing off of Ziggy Stardust, but less rock 'n' roll.

There's more to Locke's depression than the foregoing might suggest. As a reporter, he is trying and failing to interview rebels in a postcolonial civil war in an African state (which may well be modelled on Chad). He can't find them; nor do they want to be found. Most strikingly, when Locke finds himself interviewing someone he supposes to be a witch doctor, he fails to realise that the man is in fact the rebel leader – the very interviewee he has been crossing the desert to interrogate. He asks if the witch doctor's ideology will be rendered obsolete by the arrival of Western ideas, to which the rebel leader-cum-shaman retorts: 'Your questions are much more revealing about yourself than my answers would be about me.' He then grabs the camera and turns it on Locke, who responds by turning it off.

This is a very freighted cinematic moment, seething with the post-modern interest in undermining hierarchies. And it also expresses in one elegant gesture of reversal something that postcolonial writers have found utterly exasperating. In her 1989 memoir of life in the newly created country of Pakistan, *Meatless Days*, Sara Suleri described being treated as an 'otherness machine', and being heartily sick of it.[22] The witch doctor is in a similar predicament, othered by Locke in the interview, made into something he is not – as if after the first rape of imperial occupation, comes the second: the postcolonial violation of being made into something else again by witless Westerners.

In his essay, 'Is the Post- in Postmodernism the Post- in Postcolonial?', Kwame Anthony Appiah worried that the manufacture of alterity has become the principal role for people of colour in former colonies.[23] In a later book, Appiah coined the term 'the Medusa syndrome' to describe such reductive gazes as the one David Locke tries to inflict on his interviewee.[24] Medusa's gaze turned everything to stone. Journalism does that a lot, but no more oppressively than in the kind of journalism David Locke does.

What the rebel leader does in turning the camera around is to subvert the Western gaze and make problematic the reporter's self-image, his pose as objective observer, ostensibly passively recording others' struggles but never taking sides, when in truth his questions already reveal which side he is on and that, worse, he utterly misconstrues his interviewee. In this, the scene dramatises Hegel's master–slave dialectic, wherein the slave knows more about the oppressor than the oppressor knows about the slave. And the oppressor knows little about the concrete struggles of the oppressed.

In 1975, such a scene was especially poignant. This was the year that America's disastrous colonial war against Vietnam ended – the year, too, that Portugal recognised the independence of two of its former colonies, Mozambique and Angola. Three years later, Palestinian intellectual Edward Said published *Orientalism*, which suggested that the West had created the cultural concept of 'the East'. This allowed Europeans to suppress the capacity of the peoples of the Middle East, of the Indian subcontinent, of Asia more generally and even of Africa, to express and represent themselves as discrete peoples and cultures, submitting them instead to a distorting gaze that helped justify imperial rule:

Arabs, for example, are thought of as camel-riding, terroristic, hook-nosed, venal lechers whose undeserved wealth is an affront to real civilization. Always there lurks the assumption that although the Western consumer belongs to a numerical

71

minority, he is entitled either to own or to expend (or both) the majority of the world resources. Why? Because he, unlike the Oriental, is a true human being.[25]

As for Chad, it had become independent from France in 1960 after forty years of colonial rule, and in 1975 was mired in a long-running civil war that, we can suppose, David Locke has been assigned to cover for the Western media. When the camera turns on Locke, then, it reveals something that the rebel leader has known all along: there is no one there. The reversed gaze turns Locke into airy nothing, rather than into stone. The former master in the master–slave dialectic, the civilised man among the ostensible barbarians, disappears. This conforms with what Locke's colleagues in London see later in the film, when they pay homage to their dead friend. One says Locke had 'a kind of detachment', a 'talent for observation. He was always looking, always noticing.' He had a 'fairness'. This went with his 'objectivity', with his 'control on life. He was always controlled.'

When Antonioni was interviewed about *The Passenger*, he claimed his film was against 'the myth of objectivity', and that in 'pretending to be objective, you annul yourself. What sense would life have then?' That self-annulling which is supposed to be the principle of objective journalism becomes a vice.

When Locke sees the opportunity to become Robertson and escape himself, he does so because the dead man was a globe-trotter, a freewheeling *flâneur* taking life as it came, devoid of commitment. What Locke dreams of, that is to say, is to float even more freely than he did before. And, having assumed that identity, he floats through Europe and Africa, hooking up with a nameless young architecture student (played by Maria Schneider), like him an ostensibly footloose Westerner. 'What are you running away from?' she asks him as they drive in a big American convertible through some dusty landscape. He tells her to look back. She does, sees the road receding behind her, and laughs. As Roger Ebert put it in his review, Locke 'is not running away, or toward. He is simply in motion. Many of the shots suggest people with time on their hands in empty cities.'[26] This is Antonioni's characterisation of the decadent post-modern Westerner – someone in mere motion and devoid of real commitments, disengaged and bored. Their enemy is little more than anomie.

But the freedom that Locke thinks he has found in becoming Robertson is illusory. It turns out that the man whose identity Locke has stolen is no free-floating *flâneur*, as he had hoped, but a gunrunner supplying rebels with the means to overturn their colonial masters. In the screenplay (by Antonioni, Mark Peploe and Peter Wollen), Robertson is described as having deserted from the British Army in Kenya to help Africans in their post-colonial political struggle. As one insightful critic put it, 'Robertson's a revolutionist, who is *engagé*, who participates, who acts, who is prepared to fight. Locke carries a Uher tape recorder, Robertson carries a Walther pistol.'[27]

Some early critics thought the film's title alluded to the woman in the passenger seat, but in fact the passenger is Locke – riding on someone else's identity, exploiting Africans for material, in a variation of what his ancestors did.

But what's particularly striking about *The Passenger* is that it involves turning the camera on Michelangelo Antonioni, too, in what could be decoded as a piece of Maoist self-criticism. His previous film had been a three-and-a-half-hour documentary about China made for Italian TV at the invitation of Mao Zedong's government. In *Chung Kuo* (1972), Antonioni favoured long sequences in which his camera simply watched groups of people engaged in various activities: tai chi exercises in a Beijing park, a caesarean procedure in which the woman receives acupuncture in lieu of an anaesthetic, a half-hour sequence of acrobats and jugglers performing feats of balance and dexterity. The results delighted some Western critics – the *New York Times*'s John J. O'Connor called it 'visually breathtaking' and characterised by 'a degree of sophistication that would appear to be beyond the capabilities or experience of most American television', noting too 'the degree of cool objectivity maintained by the director toward his subject'.[28]

But that cool objectivity was detested by the Chinese authorities, who had expected a propaganda film. As a result, *Chung Kuo* was banned there, and the director subjected to a campaign of denunciation. Wall posters in Beijing showed Antonioni's face covered with swastikas; he was branded a lackey of both Benito Mussolini and the Soviet leader Leonid Brezhnev. Back in his native Italy, the film was denounced by the Communist Party, and when it was screened at the 1973 Venice Film Festival, police held enormous crowds of protestors at bay.

Western intellectuals weighed in with their takes on the film. Umberto Eco wrote an essay describing the difficulty of being Marco Polo, the thirteenth-century Italian merchant and traveller to China, to whom Antonioni several times compares himself in the film.[29] Susan Sontag wrote that she understood why the Chinese authorities found the film condescending: he brought a Western eye to their revolution and traduced it in the process. He had taken their revolution and made it into something merely beautiful, thereby shattering the wholesome, revolutionary image of the people that the Chinese authorities hoped Antonioni might capture.

For instance, when he filmed Chinese tourists in Tiananmen Square taking photographs of their visit, the authorities believed their ritualised image-taking to express the reality of 'their deep revolutionary feelings'. But Antonioni, they claimed, shattered that reality, and disrupted that narrative. They issued a statement denouncing his project: 'But with bad intentions, Antonioni, instead of showing this reality, took only shots of people's clothing, movement, and expressions: here, someone's ruffled hair; there, people peering, their eyes dazzled by the sun.' The Western dismemberment of reality, the break-up of identity, was intolerable to the Chinese authorities. 'The Chinese', wrote Sontag in *The Image-World* in 1977, don't want very much or to be interesting. They do not want to see the world from an interesting angle, to discover new subjects. Photographs are supposed to display what has already been described . . . In China today, only two realities are acknowledged. We see reality as hopelessly and interestingly plural. In China what is defined as an issue for debate is one about which there are 'two lines', a right one and a wrong one.[30]

Whether this is a reflection of what was going on in Mao's China is at least contestable: Sontag was bringing her Western gaze to the matter just as much as Antonioni had. And yet, one implication of her analysis is that, in the post-modern world, reality, if there is such a thing, has become hopelessly plural, a matter of power and shifting perspectives.

The attacks by the Chinese authorities wounded Antonioni: 'I've been accused of being a fascist! Of having fought with the fascist troops!' he fumed in one interview. 'I want the Chinese to know this: during [World War II], as a member of the Resistance, I was condemned to death. I was on the other side! I must say these things, once and for all, because it can't go on that these people go around insulting me this way.'[31] What vexed Antonioni was what vexes the witch doctor in *The Passenger* – he's been traduced by the gaze of the other.

What wounded Antonioni, then, was the charge that the former resistance fighter had become a passenger, a tourist, a voyeur, floating through the world in the manner David Locke is dreaming of when he becomes David Robertson – at worst, out of touch with political reality. Signor Antonioni, indeed, could be seen as what the German poet and essayist Hans Magnus Enzensberger calls a 'tourist of the revolution'. Antonioni had left Italy to make *Blow-Up* (1966) in swinging London and *Zabriskie Point* (1970) in radical California, and now he had effectively made a travelogue in the People's Republic of China. Antonioni was reporting about what happened to other people, rather than being concretely involved in changing the world.

So when Antonioni came to make *The Passenger*, there was much that was self-critical in his portrayal of David Locke. Antonioni was now making a film about the existential crisis of the maker of a television documentary about a revolutionary country. Both Antonioni in *Chung Kuo* and David Locke in *The Passenger* hide behind the myth of neutrality, while at the same time bringing their own cultural presumptions to how they make their respective documentaries. Both are not just tourists of revolution, but something worse: manufacturers of alterity – a word that has become very popular in post-modern theory, since it designates making someone other; and being othered is a kind of violation.

The Passenger, then, is a post-modern film, since it subverts the hierarchical Western gaze, turning the camera around to excoriate the Western post-modern condition. Both Antonioni in China and Locke in Chad had detached themselves from the real world of struggle in favour of a free-floating existence, a lie-dream of disconnection that typifies the post-modern condition – one that decadently dreams of severing itself from the real world, of substituting surface for depth.

There are three key deaths in *The Passenger*. First, David Robertson dies in order to be replaced by David Locke. Second, the rebel leader is executed by a dictator's firing squad in painful detail. At the end, Locke is murdered off camera by the dictator's henchmen. He has escaped his own identity only to become caught up in another's, and gets wasted for another's deeds. The film makes Locke absent at his own death. And that is fitting, since he is dead already.

'Everyone can dream, and must have dreamed his whole life, of a perfect duplication or multiplication of his being, but such copies only have the power of dreams, and are destroyed when one attempts to force the dream into the real', wrote Jean Baudrillard in *Simulacra and Simulation*.[32] In realising his dream, David Locke must die.

3

No Future, 1979:

Sex Pistols | Margaret Thatcher | Jean-François Lyotard

A week before Christmas 1968, twenty-five Santas invaded the toy department of Selfridges store on London's Oxford Street. One of them was a young art student called Malcolm McLaren, a member of the situationist collective King Mob. 'Christmas: it was meant to be great but it's horrible. Let's smash the great deception', urged King Mob's manifesto. 'Let's light up Oxford Street and dance around the fire!' They didn't do any of those things. The Santas handed out toys to children until security staff and police chased them off.[1]

Ten years later, in 1979, this risible ex-Santa had become one of Britain's most notorious men. Like Oscar Wilde a century earlier, McLaren became a figure of nightmares for the British establishment: a corrupter of youth and inverter of values, unlikely to be invited to Buckingham Palace garden parties. Instead of handing out teddy bears to bewildered children, McLaren had found a better way of subverting straight society. He weaponised a bunch of roughneck white Londoners, called them the Sex Pistols, and encouraged them to administer the *coup de grâce* to the values and institutions that patriotic Britons clung on to as their empire sailed off towards the horizon and their economy sank into the Atlantic.

There is no future in England's dreaming, snarled the Pistols' frontman Johnny Rotten on their 1977 single 'God Save the Queen' – a sarcastic subversion of the national anthem released to coincide with Elizabeth II's silver jubilee. In what he called this 'fascist regime', the future had been terminated. In 1968, McLaren was teaching kids not to believe in Christmas; in 1977, through Rotten, he was teaching them not to believe in anything, least of all the festering dreams of their supposed betters.

There was not one but three punk movements in 1979. The first was created by Malcolm McLaren, fuelled by the wit and rage of Johnny Rotten and made possible by Britain's mid-1970s economic collapse. The second was the Conservative Party as revolutionised by its leader since 1975, Margaret Thatcher. In 1979, the Pistols had released an album called *Flogging a Dead Horse*; after her election in the same year, Thatcher spent the following decade flogging off council houses, public utilities and nationalised industries. She flogged the unions until their power was broken; abolished democratically elected local governments; gave young offenders 'short, sharp shocks'; unleashed police to carry out brutal attacks on striking miners, people of colour and poll-tax protestors; and sent a task force to the other end of the world to prove that Britain was not quite done – though after the smoke of war cleared over the Falkland Islands, what was left was more than 1,000 dead, while Thatcher herself remained master of a colony whose leading commodity was guano.

If there was anarchy in the UK, maybe our first punk prime minister was responsible for it. And yet, in May 1979, on the steps of 10 Downing Street, before she unleashed this decade-long flogging, Thatcher pretended, with unwitting post-modern irony, that her political project was one of healing rather than sadism. She quoted St Francis of Assisi: 'Where there is discord, may we bring harmony. Where there is error, may we bring truth. Where there is doubt, may we bring faith. And where there is despair, may we bring hope.' Taking her cue from King Mob, she brought none of what she promised.

The third punk, a French philosopher called Jean-François Lyotard, in 1979 published *The Postmodern Condition*. In it he argued against progress, against what he called grand narratives of history that he supposed beguiled humans but now needed to be exposed as delusions. While for the Sex Pistols there was no future in England's dreaming, for Lyotard there was no future in any dreams of progress or of history marching towards some goal, be that the Hegelian absolute or Marx's communist utopia.

And yet 1979 was a year in which the world descended into a number of crises that anticipated political theorist Samuel Huntington's 'clash of civilisations' thesis: the USSR invaded Afghanistan; Ayatollah Khomeini came to power in Iran; in Iraq, Saddam Hussein replaced Ahmed Hassan al-Bakr as president; China instituted its one-child-per-family policy, while embarking on a long march towards neoliberalism. Clearly, none of these powers had received Lyotard's memo: each in its particular way was committed to a grand narrative.

I

Punk was born, or so McLaren declared, in Selfridges' toy department. Pranks and punk were, for him, part of the same situationist subversion: a witty and yet savage demonstration that the world we see is not the real world, but the world we are conditioned to see. The Situationist International was a French invention, dreamed up in the aftermath of surrealism and codified in a 1967 book by Guy Debord called *The Society of the Spectacle*, which McLaren and his fellow Father Christmases took as gospel.

Debord argued that situationism should make individuals critically analyse their everyday lives, so as to free themselves from the economic treadmill of working at dismal jobs to pay off debts incurred by buying consumer goods and other pointless commodities of late capitalism and spending leisure time stupefied into passivity by other people – actors, footballers, rock stars – doing things in a great, pacifying spectacle. They would thereby become free to pursue their genuine desires, whatever they were. 'Young people everywhere have been allowed to choose between love and a garbage disposal unit', wrote poet and theorist Ivan Chtcheglov. 'Everywhere they have chosen the garbage disposal unit.'[2]

They were lost children deprived of the pleasure of play, and instead made to work at jobs that crushed their spirit. They had to remove the spectacles of conformism so as to see more clearly the system that made them passive consumers. Or, as Malcolm McLaren put it, situationist avant-gardists like him and other like-minded souls 'should be an insult to your useless generation'.[3] By which, presumably, he meant to indict not fellow situationist rebels, but their parents.

The tactic to awaken the slumbering masses was what was called *détournement* – the idea of recontextualising an event, work of art, piece of advertising, style of clothing, or the sacred precincts of a department store, ideally with wit, in order to shift their meaning radically. Hence, for instance, Johnny Rotten celebrating the Queen's silver jubilee by suggesting her subjects were dupes of 'a figurehead who is not what she seems'.

Three years after the Selfridges debacle, McLaren opened a boutique called Let It Rock at 430 Kings Road, in a part of London fittingly – given the sartorial and musical revolutions he would try to catalyse there – called the World's End. Above the shop was a clock that ran backwards and a quote from the French nihilist and surrealist Jacques Vaché: 'Modernity killed every night.'[4] It was perhaps the first post-modern shop, not least because it appropriated and repurposed old fashions for new times. His partner, art school drop-out and future doyenne of British couturiers Vivienne Westwood, had found the art world too snobbish to accommodate a working-class woman from Derbyshire, and instead sought to express herself through fashion.

The shop offered a style revolution to the hippie movement that, for McLaren and Westwood, had initially seemed countercultural, but had become a rancid orthodoxy, its music degenerating into pretentious concept albums and interminable guitar solos, its clothes into death by double denim. So, instead, they delved into fashion history and revived the style of the teddy boys and girls of the 1950s (itself a proto-post-modern reappropriation of Edwardian clothing from the beginning of the twentieth century), including the DA hairstyle (DA stood for 'duck's arse', and signified a pomaded hairstyle parted centrally down the back of the head). Against the perceived complacency of hippies, teddy boys and girls were, according to cultural historian Dick Hebdige in his 1977 book *Subculture: The Meaning of Style*, a reflection of the 'unexpected convergence of black and white, so aggressively, so unashamedly proclaimed, [that it] attracted the inevitable controversy which centred on the predictable themes of race, sex, rebellion, etc., and which rapidly developed into a moral panic'.[5]

McLaren loved developing moral panics, and would spend much of the rest of the decade, in the manner Debord recommended, devising situations that brought them about. Westwood became interested in appropriating and repurposing biker gear from the 1950s, and so started to make clothes in leather covered in zips and studs. To capitalise on its appeal to teens and twenty-somethings, the couple renamed their shop Too Fast to Live, Too Young to Die. In 1974, the shop was renamed SEX, and sold 'rubberwear for the office'.

McLaren set up the Sex Pistols in 1975 partly to promote the clothes that he and Vivienne Westwood were selling from their boutique. He hired the gobby, homeless and charismatic John Lydon, who used to hang out at the store, as singer, and renamed him Johnny Rotten. In 1976 the band had a mainstream hit with 'Anarchy in the UK'. A year later, another lost boy was recruited to this modern Fagin's gang when Rotten's Hackney Technical College mate, John Ritchie, joined. He was rebranded after John Lydon's pet hamster Syd (itself named after Pink Floyd's Syd Barrett) and the Velvet Underground's song 'Vicious'. As one probably apocryphal story has it, the hamster bit Ritchie, prompting him to say 'Syd's really vicious'.

Sid Vicious's music career was a post-modern triumph of surface over depth, of style over substance – and, in particular, of attitude over musicianship. When one of the band members, bassist Glenn Matlock, was fired, John Ritchie stepped into the breach. He had been a fan of the band, attending nearly every gig, and so effectively climbed from mosh pit to stage, changed his name to Sid Vicious, took off his top, strapped on the bass, curled his lip into a voguish sneer, and was good to go. It was immaterial, perhaps, that he couldn't play the bass; and that he struggled so badly with heroin withdrawal on stage that at one gig he carved 'I need a fix' into his chest with a razor blade – and immaterial, too, that his performing skills improved so little that he only played on one song on the band's album *Never Mind the Bollocks*.

His leading contribution to the band's song-writing was the manifold stupidities of the lyrics for 'Belsen Was a Gas'. He couldn't sing, he couldn't play, and he looked a fright. No matter: 'If Johnny Rotten is the voice of punk,' said McLaren, 'then Vicious is the attitude.'[6]

But what was the punk attitude? To shock the establishment at any cost. This involved not just sneering at sacred shibboleths such as the Queen, not just mocking values such as musician-ship, but a fetish for spitting. In fact, spitting has long been a shocking gesture. In Proust's *À la recherche du temps perdu*, Vinteuil's daughter spits on a photograph of her parents in an act of desecration aimed in part at arousing her lover. At gig after gig in the late 1970s, punk bands wiped audiences' expec-torated subversion of authority off their faces and guitars.

British punk appropriated Nazi chic to shock the older gener-ation, too. Vicious and Rotten both wore swastika shirts, while Siouxsie Sioux, once a part of the so-called Bromley Contingent of Sex Pistols fans, who later led the punk band Siouxsie and the Banshees, wore a swastika armband with S&M fetish gear, including fishnet stockings and a whip. Like the song 'Belsen Was a Gas', this seemed deeply offensive to many, and deeply stupid to others.

We should not take punk's flirtation with fascism very seri-ously. While their punk subculture appropriated Nazi iconography to shock the Britons who had fought in World War II, that shock was different from other contemporary subcul-tures, such as that of white-power skinheads, who embraced

Nazi or otherwise racist ideologies. The Pistols were, or so they claimed, being ironic in the song. 'The next one is meant as sarcasm, in case you get it wrong', said Johnny Rotten when, in February 1979, as his old friend Sid Vicious was living out his last days in New York, his new band Public Image Ltd performed 'Belsen Was a Gas' at King's Hall, Manchester.

At this moment in the narrative arc, the subculture seduces critics. 'And I'm hearing something I've never heard before', said the critic Greil Marcus of first experiencing the Sex Pistols:

> And I don't know what this is. I'm so moved by it, so trans-
> ported by it. I just wanted to hear more, and I'm afraid of what
> 'more' might be. That's a great feeling, you know, to be afraid
> to turn on the radio, afraid to walk into a record store. Because
> it's going to *do* something to you, and you don't know what
> that's going to be.[7]

After rebellion, Dick Hebdige hypothesised, comes accommodation. The lackeys of the hegemony (broadly, the media) discover the subculture, take it from the sidelines, project its distorted image into the mainstream, and thereby produce moral panic. This is what happened to the Sex Pistols in December 1976 when they, along with Siouxsie Sioux, appeared on Thames Television's *Today* programme with Bill Grundy. On the show, Siouxsie affected to flirt with Grundy, telling him, 'I've always wanted to meet you', to which he replied, 'Did you really? We'll meet afterwards, shall we?' It was a sleazy remark that prompted Pistols guitarist Steve Jones to call Grundy live on TV a 'dirty bastard', a 'dirty fucker' and a 'fucking rotter'.[8] This unprecedented swearing on early-evening TV kept tabloids in happy moral outrage for days, as did the punks' outfits. Despite record label EMI's decision to drop the band after the furore this TV appearance prompted, they were now a lucrative proposition. The band was signed up quickly by A&M, and then Virgin Records.

Hebdige supposed that the moment a subculture is brought into the mainstream represents its death knell. Worse, its protagonists are made laughable, satirised into absurdity by the media. Again, this is what happened to punk. 'Siouxsie is a punk shocker', went the *Daily Mirror* splash headline, simultaneously laughing at punk and feigning affront, the better to induce that sentiment in its readers – both astute moves to destroy its subversive power while allowing the continuation of business as usual.

And business did indeed carry on as usual after the Sex Pistols played their acrimonious final gig, at Winterland in San Francisco in January 1978. It was the final date of a US tour. At Randy's Rodeo in San Antonio, they had been pelted with hot dogs, beer cans and popcorn as they took the stage. 'You cowboys are all a bunch of fucking faggots!' Vicious yelled at the crowd, prompting a cowboy in the audience to attack him. Vicious hit him with his bass. The cowboy later denounced the Pistols on TV as 'sewer rats with guitars'. If this was the kind of situationist provocation McLaren sought, it is hard to see what its goal was.

In San Francisco, Johnny Rotten took the stage and shouted at the audience: 'Welcome to London!' By this point in the US tour, Vicious's descent into heroin addiction and unreliability was going beyond situationist prank and causing friction in the band. Rotten snarled his way through an encore of the Stooges' 'No Fun' as if commenting on his role as McLaren's mouthpiece and his old friend's sickness unto death. 'This is no fun, no fun / This is no fun at all, no fun', he sang, sounding like he meant every word. In his autobiography, *Rotten: No Irish, No Blacks, No Dogs*, Rotten wrote that he 'felt cheated, and I wasn't going on with it any longer. It was a ridiculous farce. The whole thing was a joke at that point.' As he left the stage, he shouted, 'Ever get the feeling you've been cheated?'

After this gig, Vicious set out on a more or less cynical solo career with Nancy Spungen as his manager – both of them heroin addicts with only months to live. As he edged towards death, Vicious released songs such as 'My Way', which made punk seem merely cynical, grotesque and thus devoid of subversive edge, just as Hebdige had theorised. When he died of a heroin overdose in New York City on 2 February 1979 while under suspicion of having stabbed Spungen to death, he was only twenty-one.

His posthumous career proved lucrative. 'Almost immediately, as soon as the news broke, T-shirts bearing the caption SID Lives or with screen printed headlines proclaiming his death were being churned out', wrote Hebdige in his essay 'Mistaken Identities: Why John Paul Ritchie Didn't Do It His Way'.[9] Four weeks after Vicious died, a mockumentary called 'The Great Rock 'n' Roll Swindle' was released. On 15 December 1979, a compilation of live material recorded during his brief solo career was released as *Sid Sings* – just in time to capitalise on Christmas.

After the Sex Pistols, Rotten became John Lydon again, ditching the moniker by means of which he had been beholden to the now hated McLaren. He formed Public Image Ltd, whose first single eviscerated McLaren and the manner in which Johnny Rotten's persona had been effectively collapsed from nihilist to fatuous style icon. If post-modernism was the time in which surface was depth, he was having none of it.

As for the two remaining and least interesting Pistols, McLaren took Steve Jones and Paul Cook to Brazil to record with Ronnie Biggs, the Great Train Robber who had fled Britain to evade jail. Lydon, as he became, despised this move, thinking it was an attempt to make a hero from a criminal who had attacked a train driver and then made off with what he called 'working-class money'.

A year after Sid Vicious's death in February 1980, the Sex Pistols – by now consisting only of McLaren and designer Jamie Reid, neither of whom played in the band – released an album of dregs from the band's catalogue under the title *Flogging a Dead Horse*. For the album sleeve, Reid produced a tacky illustration, using a photo of a model from the cheapest agency he could find, along with dull Letraset lettering, making the record look like a cheap easy-listening album, while the back cover featured a fake plastic dog turd on top of a gold disc of the band's debut album *Never Mind the Bollocks*.

Punk was dead, but its corpse was made to speak, while at the same time its image was posthumously being shat upon. The Pistols' management were overtly referencing the fact that they were trying to get as much money from the album's sales for as little effort as possible. And Richard Branson's label Virgin was knowingly making money from this cynical gesture.

What had started as *détournement*, an avant-garde subversion of the prevailing culture, ended in farce. Greil Marcus insisted nonetheless that punk had a utopian aspect, and had changed the world: 'Insisting on the bizarre and trashing standards of decency, punk shattered the mask of the dominant culture; by its very unnaturalness, punk made the host culture seem like a trick, the result of sadomasochistic economics.'[10]

But punk didn't shatter the mask of the dominant culture; that was simply Marcus's unreliable grand narrative. In the post-modern era, the dominant culture accommodates whatever is thrown at it. Indeed, McLaren's situationist pranks and the Sex Pistols' nihilism arguably heralded a new post-modern age, in which subcultures were destined either to destroy themselves or collapse into fatuous cynicism. There was, after all – or so argues Slavoj Žižek – something very dubious, even anti-revolutionary about the situationists' beloved *détournements*, of which the Sex Pistols were perhaps the gaudiest exemplar. By attacking and distancing itself from the sign-systems of capital, wrote Žižek, the subject creates a fantasy of transgression that covers up its actual complicity with capitalism.[11] Viewed thus, *Flogging a Dead Horse* was a post-modern admission of failure by Malcolm McLaren.

What the post-modern sensibility added to this symbolic murder of a subcultural form of resistance was merely a knowingness: everyone knew that the posthumously released material was a cynical move. The producers knew that the consumers of it were cynical; the consumers knew that the producers knew it was cynical – on and on, in a shameful spiral of degraded knowledge. And yet behind that cynicism, that pretence of affect-lessness that underpinned post-modernity, was the repressed sense that everyone was caught up in a system that they loathed but could not change.

In 2006, Selfridges, the department store that Malcolm McLaren and other situationist Santas had raided decades earlier, opened a festival called FuturePunk, which hosted films, lectures, live bands, fashion shows and workshops. McLaren died in 2010. In 2016, Joe Corré, founder of Agent Provocateur lingerie, joined his mother Vivienne Westwood in setting fire to £5 million worth of rare punk memorabilia. Punk, he reckoned, had become nothing more than a 'McDonald's brand . . . owned by the state, establishment and corporations'.[12]

II

The Sex Pistols were nonetheless more than applications of the Situationist Manifesto. Their rise was partly to do with Britain's calamitous economic performance in the mid 1970s, which also swept the Conservative Party under Margaret Thatcher into power in 1979. The Sex Pistols were not just a subcultural phenomenon, but a symptom of a broader malaise. In the terms of that other punk in this chapter, Jean-François Lyotard, the grand narrative that had sustained advanced industrial nations of western Europe and North America – namely, that of Keynesian demand management and state intervention to ensure full employment – was less convincing than ever.

The wheels had started to come off the British economy a few years earlier, under Edward Heath's Conservative admin-istration, when miners went on strike because their wages were not keeping pace with inflation, which had rocketed owing to OPEC's quadrupling of oil prices. The consequences of this industrial action were disastrous: Heath felt compelled to declare a state of emergency and mandate a three-day week in order to save electricity. In 1974, Heath decided to go to the polls to seek public backing against a capitulation to the miners' strike demands, asking the electorate: 'Who runs Britain?'

Heath's rhetoric backfired, and the Conservatives lost; but when the Labour Party took office under Harold Wilson, it found itself in deep financial trouble. This was partly because, in agreeing to meet the miners' demands, Britain now found itself struggling to foot the bill. This compounded the recessionary problems Britain was already experiencing. Consequently, unemployment soared, and the golden post-war age of economic boom and full employment was over. Disenchantment, especially among young people, with the government and with a time-honoured approach to the economy rose as fast as inflation and unemployment – or stagflation, as it was known.

The crisis led chancellor Denis Healey to turn to the International Monetary Fund for a multi-billion-pound loan – a desperate, even humiliating move, since, as patriotic Britons supposed, the UK was not a banana republic of the kind that usually went cap in hand to the IMF. The bank imposed an austerity regime on Britain that led to spiralling unemployment. In July 1973 there were 27,000 young people under eighteen out of work. In January 1977 the figure was 122,000 – an increase of 353 per cent.[13] By the time 'God Save the Queen' hit the charts, 6 per cent of working-age Britons were unemployed. This depressing backstory made the Sex Pistols' takedown of Britain's self-image all the more potent – and it also lent plausibility to the insistence of the new Conservative leader, Margaret Thatcher, that rolling back the state and cutting public expenditure was necessary to make Britain great, even if that insistence was itself part of a grand narrative of the kind at which Johnny Rotten and Jean-François Lyotard, in their different ways, would have thought ludicrous.

In the so-called 'Winter of Discontent' of 1978–79, unions took industrial action, with disastrous consequences: gravediggers refused to bury the dead, streets piled up with uncollected rubbish, medical care was rationed as hospital workers went on strike. Ad men Charles and Maurice Saatchi devised a slogan to capitalise on this disaster: 'Labour isn't working.' No matter that the image of a dole queue used on billboards to illustrate that claim was made up of twenty Hendon Young Conservatives – or that British dole queues under Thatcher's rule would become much, much longer.[14] The Conservatives went into the May 1979 general election in order, as they saw it, to put Britain back on track as a great international economic power.

After 1979, as Anne Perkins put it in her *Guardian* obituary of Margaret Thatcher, 'the ideals of collective effort, full employment and a managed economy – all tarnished by the recurring crises of the 1970s – were discredited in the popular imagination. They were replaced with the politics of me and mine, deregulation of the markets and privatisation of the state's assets that echoed growing individual prosperity.'[15]

Thatcher followed monetarist economist Milton Friedman, who argued that welfare practices created 'wards of the state' as opposed to 'self-reliant individuals'. In the name of this doctrine, she set about destroying the so-called Butskellite consensus (named after two politicians, Rab Butler and Hugh Gaitskell, the former Conservative and the latter Labour). Both leading parties had long been committed to Keynesian demand management, state ownership and extensive public services. This consensus had underpinned British politics since World War II, according to which Britons were to be offered the prospect of the so-called ladder and safety net – the ladder describing social mobility, the safety net referring to the provisions of the welfare state. Thatcher's brand of neoliberalism was from the outset a kind of sado-masochistic shriving whereby renewed virtue came from suffering. Britain's first woman prime minister became famous for killing off the nanny state.

Hers was a punk government – a rebellion against the smug, male consensus that had dominated British politics since World War II. In a sense, the eleven years of Thatcher's Britain constituted a piece of post-modern outsider art. The anti-establishment grocer's daughter from Grantham took on the men who had, she thought, made Britain mediocre: from Arthur Scargill, the

Marxist leader of the National Union of Mineworkers, to the so-called wets in her own cabinet – now forgotten men like Jim Prior, Francis Pym, Peter Walker, Ian Gilmour and Norman Antony Francis St John-Stevas (Baron St John of Fawsley). These were the mostly genteel, public-school-educated invertebrates raised in a venerable Trollopian culture in which compromise was favoured above conviction.

The only posh boy she kept in tow was Willie Whitelaw – because, as she said in a rare moment of humour, 'Every prime minister needs a Willie.' Whitelaw, who served as Thatcher's home secretary until 1983, once accused Labour's Harold Wilson of 'stirring up apathy' in the 1970 general election campaign. British politics was often like that until Thatcher came along: just as the Pistols had shocked Britain by swearing on TV while dressed as outlandish scruffs, so Margaret Thatcher shocked Britain out of its slumbers by transforming the landscape of British party politics. Her first order of business was to establish strict budgetary control, banishing the widespread idea that Britain was 'the sick man of Europe', as well as the Treasury motto that its business was overseeing the 'orderly decline of the British economy'.

Her economics advisor Alan Budd explained the policy after the fact, noting that 'the 1980s policies of squeezing inflation and public expenditure were a cover to bash the workers'.[16] High inflation, itself the product of public expenditure cuts, made unemployment rise sharply in the early years of her rule, creating an industrial reserve army that would chasten employed workers considering industrial action that might end up with their own addition to the dole queue. But the British electorate might well have thought itself misled. The electoral slogan 'Labour isn't working' was made to seem ridiculous by the fact that unemployment averaged 10 per cent between 1979 and 1985, compared with 3.3 per cent between 1955 and 1979 – the so-called golden years of Keynesian economics.

Union membership fell by more than 20 per cent between 1979 and 1988 as Thatcher introduced employment acts that undermined the disruptive power of organised labour, requiring secret pre-strike ballots and ending the closed shop.[17] She changed the rules of the game so that power shifted from labour to capital, enabling companies to close down inefficient plants and increase productivity – the latter itself a cause of higher unemployment during the 1980s. Thatcher's neoliberal economic revolution entailed that, by making workers more productive, fewer of them were needed to achieve the same levels of production. Hence redundancies. Hence too increased unemployment. And it worked: in 1979 German manufacturing productivity was nearly 20 per cent higher than Britain's; by 1989, it was just 5 per cent higher. Managers invested in new technology that would enable Britain to emerge as a world leader in the post-Thatcher digital revolution.[18]

In 1984 Thatcher provoked the miners into another strike and, after a bitter year of industrial action, broke the strongest union in Britain. It was a pivotal moment. In the 1950s, Labour politician Aneurin Bevan had evoked a self-reliant image of Britain surrounded by endless stocks of fish and built upon bottomless supplies of coal. The end of domestic coal mining contributed to the death of the vision of a self-reliant island Britain, replacing it with another: that of a country thriving in the globalised, post-modern free-for-all that neoliberalism had unleashed.

Coal wasn't the only nationalised industry Thatcher set about dismantling. She effectively destroyed the nationalised car manufacturer, British Leyland, thereby opening up Britain to become, as David Harvey has put it, 'an offshore platform for Japanese automobile companies seeking access to Europe'.[19] Much of the sell-off of public assets had this flavour of a fire-sale designed to attract foreign investors to snap up bargains.

Thatcher told the 1986 Conservative Party conference that the privatisation of public services was 'nothing less than a crusade to enfranchise the many in the economic life of the nation. We the Conservatives are returning power to the people.'[20] Irony was hardly an invention of the post-modern, neoliberal era, but in such utterances it reached a new level of brazenness: the enfranchisement and power of the people were dissipated as Thatcher's ministers sold off public assets.

Whereas, in 1945, Labour nationalised the commanding heights of the economy – rail, water, gas, electricity, coal, steel, public housing, airlines – for the common good, Thatcher sold them off. Only the National Health Service was ring-fenced: otherwise Britain's public assets were up for sale, often at bargain rates. The 1980 Housing Act, for instance, gave local-authority tenants the right to buy their homes at knockdown prices. Initially, council houses were sold off at a discount of between 33 per cent and 50 per cent of their market valuation, while flats were offered for up to 70 per cent of their market valuations. By 1987, more than a million council houses in the UK had been sold to their tenants. The policy proved popular, not only creating millions of property owners, but also eroding Labour's bedrock of working-class support. In the words of Thatcher's secretary of state for the environment, Michael Heseltine, 'Certainly no single piece of legislation has enabled the transfer of so much capital wealth from the state to the people.'[21]

Combined with cutbacks in local-authority expenditure, however, the sell-off meant that public housing, designed for the poorest and neediest of British society, whose numbers were rising fast during her years in power, would never be replaced. Successive prime ministers – Labour as well as Conservative – did nothing to reverse this policy; indeed, council housing, once the cherished centrepiece of Bevanite socialism, took only two decades to be dismantled.[22]

On Monday, 27 October 1986, the London Stock Exchange became a private limited company – an event that came to be known as the Big Bang. The privatisation of the LSE was a continuation of the remarkable sell-off of public assets credited with creating 1,500 millionaires. Before the Big Bang, City traders were divided between brokers and jobbers. The former, after liaising with clients, gave orders to the latter, who did the trading on the exchange floor. In what was called an 'open outcry' auction, bids and offers for stocks and shares were made using shouts and hand signals. Though the practice had originated in Amsterdam, in London the exchange of stocks and shares in this way had begun in 1773, in Jonathan's Coffee House, and been carried on for more than two centuries in various buildings. In one of them, Capel Court Stock Exchange, there were even staff called 'waiters', tasked with watering the floor of the exchange to keep down the dust – dust that the Big Bang, by making such practices obsolete, caused to gather copiously on the exchange floor. At the same time, the shift from traditional face-to-face share-dealing to computerised trading helped to cut costs.

By putting an end to fixed commissions, the Big Bang facilitated more competition; by ending the separation between dealers and advisors, it boosted mergers and takeovers; and by allowing in foreign owners, it caused London's financial markets to be opened up to international banks. Until then, the Bank of England had mandated that all of London's banks be within ten minutes' walking distance of the governor's office; that way, he could summon their elders to his office within half an hour. But the Securities and Investments Board (later the Financial Services Authority) now replaced the Bank's regulatory role.

On the day of the Big Bang, an advertisement in the *Financial Times* promised a new financial centre three miles to the east of the City, at Canary Wharf, rising on land where Henry VIII used to hunt, which would 'feel like Venice and work like New York'.[23] This was London's Docklands, the union of neoliberal deregulation with post-modern architecture. As the glass and steel of corporate offices and speculative apartments rose, Canary Wharf never for a moment felt like either Venice or New York. London became not just a centre of capital once again, but one of the most expensive cities in the world.

Thatcher's punk rebellion involved not the transfer of power to the people, but the shifting of income and wealth from poor to rich. In the first budget of her administration, Thatcher's chancellor of the exchequer, Geoffrey Howe, doubled VAT while slashing the top rate of income tax from 83 per cent to 60 per cent, and the standard rate from 33 per cent to 30 per cent (later in the decade, the standard rate fell to 25 per cent, and the top rate to 40 per cent). In the 1970s, Britain's Gini coefficient, measuring the gap between rich and poor, averaged 24.3, placing Britain near the bottom of the league table of economic inequality. By the mid nineties, it had jumped to 32.4, moving Britain well up the table; since then it has continued to rise.

'The secret to happiness', Margaret Thatcher once said, 'is to live within your income and pay your bills on time.'[24] If so, she was the prime minister of unhappiness. Household debt in the UK (including mortgages, student loans, personal loans and credit card balances) amounted to 56.9 per cent of GDP in the year after the Big Bang (1987), then peaked at 103.2 per cent in 2009, before stabilising around 90.5 per cent by 2019.

Bank of England analysts point out that households with the highest absolute levels of debt tend also to have the highest incomes and net wealth.[25] Those most troubled by debt, however, are those who have negligible or no income to live within, and no wealth to cushion their misfortune. Behind Gini coefficients and Thatcher's reassertion of the profit motive, after all, are food banks, soup kitchens and loan sharks. By 2017, one in eight people was classified as working poor; by 2019, 4 million children were living in poverty.

Much of Thatcher's punk revolution was a semantic one – a post-modern deconstruction of meaning in which the prime minister was akin to Humpty Dumpty in *Alice through the Looking Glass*, using words to mean just what she chose them to mean. Happiness became measurable by spreadsheets; society was meaningless. ('Who is society? There is no such thing!' she told *Woman's Own* in 1987. 'There are individual men and women and there are families.')[26] Freedom, opportunity and choice were reconfigured in narrowly economic terms that precluded selflessness, community-spiritedness and kindness.

After rebellion and money came the third part of the subcultural narrative arc predicted by Dick Hebdige: accommodation. The Thatcherite political project that had once seemed akin to avant-garde outsider art became the orthodoxy. 'Only an outsider could have given birth to an ideology as iconoclastic as Thatcherism, and Thatcher always regarded herself as a challenger of the status quo, a rebel leader against established power', wrote Anne Perkins. 'What mattered to her was less the breadth of her support than the depth of her convictions.'[27]

No British prime minister since Thatcher has dared to be such a conviction politician; rather, each has sought to preserve the gains her ideology supposedly brought to Britain, and has followed, more or less consciously, her neoliberal agenda. After her death in 2013, former Labour leader Tony Blair paid homage to her legacy: 'I always thought my job was to build on some of the things she had done rather than reverse them . . . Many of the things she said, even though they pained people like me on the left . . . had a certain creditability.'[28]

By the time the financial crash of 2008–09 unfolded, however, the Thatcherite model of boosting financial services and deregulation in order to unleash entrepreneurialism, yielding growth that might then increase tax revenues, had stalled. Maybe, critics suggested, more was needed than cuts to government spending in general and welfare payments in particular – perhaps more than privatisation and deregulation was required to spare the most vulnerable British people from the consequences of financial speculation. But when David Cameron's Conservative–Liberal coalition came to power in 2010, he carried on regardless, insisting, like his mentor before him, that there was no alternative to austerity – albeit austerity borne by the poor to pay for the bailed-out banks.

While Margaret Thatcher was revolutionising Britain by putting neoliberal ideas into practice, a French philosopher was seeking to deconstruct the narrative of progress that underpinned them.

III

Imagine, suggested Jean-François Lyotard in *The Postmodern Condition: A Report on Knowledge*, that a firm like IBM is authorised to occupy a belt in the earth's orbital field and launch satellites housing memory banks: 'Who will have access to them? Who will determine which channels or data are forbidden? Or will the State be one user among others? New legal issues will be raised, and with them the question: "who will know?" '[29]

Forty years after these words were written, in our age of techno-oligarchies like Google, Facebook and Twitter, each bigger and more powerful than many states, Lyotard's questions seem prescient in relation to current anxieties about what the commercialisation of knowledge will mean for us in the looming computer age.

In the year of Margaret Thatcher's election, though, Lyotard was writing at a time when neoliberal governments were bent on shrinking the state to a few minimal functions. Lyotard's sense was that the transformation in the nature of knowledge might compel states to reconsider their relations with large corporations. His concern was that the state could become so minimal that it would be reduced to the role of an impotent voyeur watching consenting adults buy and sell data.

During the 1970s, Lyotard contended, the state (at least in the advanced capitalist countries of Europe and North America) was being forcibly separated from the role it had enjoyed since World War II. 'The reopening of the world market, a return to vigorous economic competition, the breakdown of the hegemony of American capitalism, a probable opening of the Chinese market – these and many other factors are already, at the end of the 1970s, preparing states for a serious reappraisal of the role they have been accustomed to playing since 1930: that of guiding, or even directing, investments.'[30]

Margaret Thatcher undertook just such a reappraisal after taking power in 1979. But that changing role of the state was, thought Lyotard, further altered by the rise of computerisation and the mercantilisation of knowledge. Seven years after he wrote these words, Thatcher's government, in deregulating financial services and ending the era of face-to-face stock market transactions in favour of fast-moving, low-cost electronic ones, realised in practice what Lyotard had long suspected would happen.

The Postmodern Condition was the result of a commission Lyotard had accepted to write a report on the condition of knowledge for the Conseil des Universités of the government of Quebec, and his immediate worry was that universities were becoming corrupted by the unfettering of capitalism and the consequent reduction in the status of knowledge, from something whose pursuit was noble liberating to a mere commodity to be bought and sold.

There were two stories, he supposed – one French, the other German – that universities had historically offered to justify what goes on in lecture theatres, seminar rooms and laboratories. The French story was what he called a narrative of emancipation. Napoleon had reformed higher education to provide effective administrators, and thereby ensure the stability of the state; Lyotard argued that these reforms had an emancipatory role in spreading knowledge to the people.

The German narrative of legitimation was conceived less instrumentally. Prussian philosopher and government functionary Wilhelm von Humboldt was associated with the dictum 'Science for its own sake', and the university reforms he devised in 1790s Prussia were conceived in Hegelian terms: the subject of knowledge was not the people, but the speculative spirit. Universities, such as the one he founded in Berlin, must lay open the whole body of learning, and expound both the principles and the foundations of all knowledge. In his fragment *Theory of Human Education*, Humboldt argued that 'the ultimate task of our existence is to give the fullest possible content to the concept of humanity in our own person . . . through the impact of actions in our own lives'. This task 'can only be implemented through the links established between ourselves as individuals and the world around us'.[31] Humboldt's idea, Lyotard explained, was not that the university should serve the state, as Napoleon envisaged, but something more abstruse and yet cherishable. According to this narrative of speculation, there is 'a universal "history" of spirit, spirit is "life", and "life" is its own self-presentation and formulation in the ordered knowledge of all its forms contained in the empirical sciences'.[32]

Lyotard argued that these two grand narratives had been used to legitimise the idea of the university. But in the post-modern era such narratives of progress were no longer convincing. Under neoliberalism, when knowledge became like money, such stories were obsolete: the only legitimations were performance and efficiency.

'It is not hard to visualise learning circulating along the same lines as money', wrote Lyotard.[33] The pertinent distinction, he imagined, would then become not that between knowledge and ignorance, but that between payment knowledge and investment knowledge – the former concerned with survival, the latter with funds of knowledge dedicated to optimising the performance of a project. Education and learning were becoming, he feared, only instrumentally valuable, not intrinsically so. Humboldt's notion of pursuing science for its own sake was to become a casualty of post-modernism. 'Knowledge ceases to be an end in itself', wrote Lyotard.[34]

German philosopher Julian Nida-Rümelin argued that contemporary European education policy has understood education narrowly as preparation for the labour market.[35] It has breathed 'the spirit of McKinsey and not that of Humboldt'. Nida-Rümelin argued that we need to choose between Humboldt and McKinsey – the management consultancy firm renowned for improving companies' profitability, often by closing down offices and factories. Its efficiency ethos is global: its clients include 100 of the top 150 companies worldwide. It has consumed Mammon and God: among its clients have been the Bank of England and the Roman Catholic church in the United States.

The German government hired McKinsey after the fall of the Berlin Wall.

Lyotard went further in his shattering account of the debasement of knowledge and science. The rot had set in, he surmised, long before 1960s student radicals revolted against their professors. If the university Humboldt had devised was a rose – the flowering emblem of the Enlightenment's project of human intellectual mastery of the world – Lyotard showed that it had been sick from the beginning.

Lyotard supposed that the unfolding of the Enlightenment in tandem with the Industrial Revolution was not accidental. The latter supplied the former with technology. The laboratory needs money to perform its task since scientific instruments don't come cheap. As a result, Lyotard argued, knowledge becomes a commodity: science may posture as objective inquiry, but is really in the hands of those with the most cash: 'No money, no proof – and that means no verification of statements and no truth. The games of scientific language become the games of the rich, in which whoever is wealthiest has the best chance of being right. An equation between wealth, efficiency and truth is thus established.'[36]

Lyotard was calling into question the powers of reason – the very basis for the Enlightenment project of human mastery of the world through science. He argued that the procedures of science and the values of truth, seemingly so impartial and objective, are nothing of the kind. He also argued that there are two grand narratives that, in the past, have legitimised the pursuit of knowledge – namely, history as progressing towards social enlightenment and emancipation, and knowledge as progressing towards totalisation. In the post-modern era, these ideas no longer had any force: the corruption of the pursuit of knowledge by the spirit of McKinsey, as it were, meant that the only justification or legitimisation of the university, of science, or of the quest for knowledge, was to be found in efficient performance.

As neoliberal governments came to power in the years after the publication of Lyotard's book, the shortcomings of this approach to education in general, and to higher education in particular, became clear. Margaret Thatcher's governments slashed education budgets and held down the salaries of teachers and academics, provoking a brain drain, mostly to the United States. This hostility to public education was partly to a function of a commitment to reducing the role of the state; but it was also typical of the short-term focus of her approach to economic recovery – an approach shared by other neoliberals. Even though she was an Oxford-educated chemist, Thatcher cut research budgets for the sciences, for which she was rebuked by senior executives at pharmaceutical giants Glaxo and ICI.

'If there's one thing most economists can agree on, it's that in advanced countries economic progress depends on fostering scientific research and an educated workforce, two things Thatcherism failed to do,' wrote John Cassidy.[37] That's to say, even if knowledge has been reconfigured as having only use value, the short-term thinking and chronic underinvestment that neoliberalism encourages in relation to education can result in a neoliberal government creating circumstances for its policies to fail. If knowledge was to be considered as merely a means of material benefit, then Thatcher's governments, by favouring short-term gains over long-term results, spectacularly miscalculated even in their own terms.

Many years before he wrote *The Postmodern Condition*, Lyotard had been a member of the French group Socialisme ou Barbarie ('Socialism or Barbarism'). The Marxist beliefs he held in the 1950s and '60s, though, had long been discarded; he had come to see Marxism as yet another grand narrative, a Hegelian just-so story of human history, with the overturning of capitalism in favour of communist society substituting for the Hegelian goal of the self-revelation of the spirit. Such 'progress' had been made obsolete by the scientific, technological, political and cultural changes of the late twentieth century. The post-modern era was therefore characterised as 'incredulity towards meta-narratives': post-modernists no longer believed in progress or totalising stories about human goals. What remained was radical pluralism and the fragmentation of ideals.

This is the crucial matter. What Lyotard argued about the death of grand narratives applies beyond institutions of higher learning. Consider Nazism. In his notorious rector's address at the University of Freiburg on 27 May 1933, three months after Adolf Hitler's election as German chancellor, Martin Heidegger repurposed Humboldt's ideals, arguing that the questioning of being was the 'destiny' of the 'historico-spiritual people' – namely, the Germans. The university was essentially legitimised by serving the Nazi party, of which Heidegger was a member, whose 'historic mission' consisted in realising what Heidegger called 'the true world of the spirit', which is 'the most profound power of conservation to be found within its forces of earth and blood'.[38]

Such grand narratives have no force in post-modern times. They are supplanted by a world in which there is a shift from ends to means, reflecting the rise of technological innovation and what Lyotard calls the valorising of 'the individual enjoyment of goods and services'. And yet something remains of Lyotard's Marxism in *The Postmodern Condition* – most forcefully when he doubts scientific objectivity. Indeed, he applies Marxist analysis to knowledge itself, suggesting that items of knowledge are commodities just like apples or cars – that is to say, that they can be bought and sold for money. As a result, knowledge has not only a use value, but an exchange value: 'Knowledge is and will be produced in order to be sold, it is and will be consumed in order to be valorized in a new production: in both cases, the goal is exchange.' Later in the book, Lyotard added: 'Science becomes a force of production, in other words, a moment in the circulation of capital.'[39]

In the 1950s and '60s, Lyotard believed that, without socialism, there would be barbarism; in the 1970s, he believed that barbarism had triumphed. Beneath the objectivity of scientific inquiry, the apparently coolly rational pursuit of knowledge and the civilisation of university life, was the barbaric, neoliberal pursuit of money, and the power struggle to determine what was true and real using resources that only money can buy. Such was the post-modern condition, and so it remains.

While orthodox Marxism suggested that science could be legitimised according to the narrative of emancipation – that is to say, it could help the proletariat become fully human, and so no longer forced to sell themselves as commodities on the labour market – this was no longer available in the post-modern era. All that remained was what he called 'performativity – that is, the best possible input/output equation'. If science is a force of production, then, Lyotard breathtakingly suggested, among the things it produces are truth and reality: 'Scientists, technicians, and instruments are purchased not to find truth, but to augment power.'[40]

But surely, you might well object, truth and reality are not products, still less commodities: the latter is what science discovers with its instruments and then describes, thereby adding to human knowledge, while the former is a value of statements about that reality. But, in believing such statements, you are committed to the mirror theory of knowledge and art. According to that theory, the task of science is to capture the way reality is. Art and language, too, have the tasks of mirroring reality – hence realism in literature and painting; hence, too, the idea that language is structurally commensurate with the reality it represents.

But post-modern science, philosophy, art and literature, to put it mildly, do not perform such tasks. They are to truth and reality what Margaret Thatcher was to the British trade unions – or, if you prefer, what Sid Vicious was to bass playing.

Lyotard took a hammer to the mirror theory by suggesting that science is a productive force, and that there is no objectivity outside subjectivity, nor any coherent subjectivity either. He was not alone, in 1979, in philosophising with a hammer. The American philosopher Richard Rorty published in that year his book *Philosophy and the Mirror of Nature*,[41] a *succès de scandale* in philosophy and other university departments, arguing that we should stop imagining language as a mirror, but instead consider it a tool. Even more daringly, Rorty toppled truth from its pedestal. The truth or falsity of a statement was not to be determined, he argued, by whether it accurately described that world. This was the old correspondence theory of truth that, like the mirror theory of language, needed to be junked. Instead, for Rorty, describing a statement as 'true' was more like granting it an honorific status.

Both of these leading post-modern philosophers, Lyotard and Rorty, were in turn influenced by Ludwig Wittgenstein, the great Austrian Jewish philosopher whose first book was responsible for proposing an account of language as mirror, and whose later books are, among other things, extended meditations on why that first book was wrong. In *The Postmodern Condition*, Lyotard took Wittgenstein's insight about language games and used it to account for what he thought had happened to knowledge, science and human culture in the post-modern era. He tilted at the pretension of science to suppose that it and it alone produced knowledge.

Science, he argued, is composed of denotative utterances, such as 'Rain is wet', or, the one Lyotard himself significantly used, 'the university is sick'. He contrasted these with performative utterances, which may involve instructions, recommendations, requests or commands, such as 'Give me money', 'I promise to give you the money' or, in Lyotard's example, 'The university is open'. Following Wittgenstein, he argued that denotative utterances and prescriptive utterances are moves in language games, each having rules specifying the uses to which they can be put. But, just as the rules of chess and those of rugby are incommensurable, so are those of different language games. The rules of one cannot be used to judge whether the other game is being played properly.

Lyotard argued, then, that scientific knowledge includes only denotative statements, while other kinds of knowledge include several different kinds of statements. Science did not have a monopoly on what constituted knowledge. He cited other kinds of knowledge, including *savoir faire*, *savoir vivre*, *savoir écouter* and *savoir entendre* – respectively, 'to know how', 'to know how to live', 'to know how to listen' and 'to know how to understand'. 'Knowledge, then, is a question of competence that goes beyond the simple determination and application of the criterion of truth', he wrote, 'extending to the determination and application of the criterion of efficiency (technical qualification), of justice and/or happiness (ethical wisdom) of the beauty of sound or colour (auditory and visual sensibility).'[42]

Lyotard then distinguished scientific knowledge from narrative knowledge. Narrative knowledge is the kind of knowledge prevalent in 'primitive' societies, and is based on storytelling, sometimes in the form of ritual, music and dance. The narratives thus told are unquestionable, unlike the denotative utterances of science, which are in principle always questionable or falsifiable. For scientists, Lyotard maintained, narrative knowledge is no knowledge at all. The pragmatics of scientific knowledge do not allow narrative knowledge as legitimate, since it is not restricted to denotative statements.

Lyotard saw danger in the dominance of scientific knowledge, because of his view that reality cannot be captured within one genre of discourse or representation of events. Science will miss aspects of events that narrative knowledge will capture. In other words, Lyotard does not believe that science has any justification in claiming to be a more legitimate form of knowledge than narrative. To dismiss narrative knowledge in this way, he argued, is to use the rules of one language game to judge the competence of those playing another. That, for Lyotard, is as absurd as a rugby referee outlawing a knight's move in chess for being offside. Scientists might see the issue differently: for them, the oxymoron of narrative knowledge is like attempting to win a game of chess by means of the white pieces linking arms and shoving their way to the back row.

But, despite scientists' ostensible contempt for narrative knowledge, whenever they attempt to legitimise their work, ironically they do so by an appeal not to scientific criteria, but to narrative knowledge. Whenever you see a scientist on TV being interviewed after making a discovery, suggested Lyotard, they contextualise that discovery in terms of a grand narrative, an epic story of the progress of knowledge.

In the post-modern age Lyotard describes, though, no one believes grand narratives anymore, so their legitimising function is obsolete. Hegel speculated on the eventual totality and unity of all knowledge; Marx appointed science a role in the emancipation of humanity. Neither was any longer convincing. Nor was the epic narrative of heroic scientists capturing knowledge from the barbarian kingdom of ignorance.

So how is science legitimated in the post-modern era? Lyotard's answer was performativity. This is what Lyotard called the 'technological criterion' – the most efficient input/output ratio. Like everything else, knowledge has become primarily a saleable commodity, produced to be sold and consumed. What has been lost as a result is the aspiration to produce truth. The truth is expendable when knowledge is transposed into quanta of information.

In response to his fears of states being subverted by big data, and of humans being dominated by those corporations that control the dissemination of knowledge, Lyotard proposed that the public be given free access to computerised data banks. This would allow computerisation to contribute to the democratic dissemination of knowledge. But he had in mind a strange kind of knowledge that worked through what he called paralogy.

Paralogy is a method of reasoning that contradicts logical rules or formulas, on which Lyotard relied heavily – though critics have called him non-rational for doing so. By his invocation of paralogy, he hoped to overturn the notion of science as legitimised by performativity. Instead of science bending the knee to power, or to the forces of neoliberal profit-making, he hoped to reconfigure it as a human activity that involved the search for instabilities. In so doing, Lyotard drew from quantum mechanics, which showed the subatomic world to be nondeterministic, and from Kurt Gödel, who demonstrated that a complete and consistent set of axioms for all of mathematics is impossible.

Post-modern science, as conceived by Lyotard, was a child of these times, and concerned itself with 'such things as undecidables, the limits of precise control, conflicts characterised by incomplete information, "*fracta*," catastrophes, and pragmatic paradoxes'. It was thereby 'theorising its own evolution as discontinuous, catastrophic, non-rectifiable, and paradoxical. It is changing the meaning of the word *knowledge*, while expressing how such a change can take place. It is producing not the known, but the unknown.'[43]

What Lyotard wrote about science and knowledge had ramifying implications for politics. In the 1970s, philosophers worried about a democratic deficit affecting advanced capitalist countries. In 1973, Jürgen Habermas had written a book called *Legitimation Crisis*, in which he argued that, in countries such as the United States and the UK, where neoliberal regimes were then emerging, people often felt politically under-represented. The result has been variously called zombie democracy, façade democracy or even post-democracy.

Habermas coined the term 'civic privatism'. The idea was that electorates in democratic countries were generally willing to let the political classes get on with running the state because they were expected to be better off as a result. Effectively for the sake of material comfort, citizens willingly forwent their democratic duties. This strategy of civic privatism, in Habermas's Marxist jargon, 'admits bourgeois democracy only as a super-structure of capitalist class domination' – by which he meant that, instead of exercising their democratic rights and duties, citizens had been bought off with walk-in fridges and foreign holidays.[44]

The Frankfurt School, which Habermas headed in the early 1970s, had long worried that the proletariat had been bought off by consumer goods. In his *One-Dimensional Man*, Herbert Marcuse had supposed that those seeking to destroy capitalism would have to look elsewhere for revolutionary forces – among what he called subaltern groups, such as people of colour or women – because the workers had become too comfortable with the system that oppressed them.

The oppressed classes had become stakeholders in an economic system of which they should have been – according to the Marxist grand narrative – the gravediggers. Under post-war Keynesian capitalism, the state managed the economy more actively than ever before, manipulating the money supply or interest rates to stave off the worst systemic crises. It made welfare payments to unemployed workers, thereby mitigating the effects of business-cycle downturns by keeping those out of work functioning as consumers. In effect, the state was keeping capitalism from collapsing from the crises to which, Marxist theory predicted, it is inherently prone.

Meanwhile, Habermas argued, the ostensible role of the state in democratic polities – to serve as a reflection of the citizens' will – was quietly abandoned. Elections amounted only to a formal gesture towards democracy. The state, though, did not run smoothly, but was torn apart by conflicting demands:

> On the one hand, the state is supposed to act as a collective capitalist. On the other hand, competing individual capitalists cannot form or carry through a collective will as long as free-dom of investment is not eliminated. Thus arise the mutually contradictory imperatives of expanding the planning capacity of the state with the aim of a collective-capitalist planning and, yet, blocking precisely this expansion, which would threaten the continued existence of capitalism.[45]

The aim of the Enlightenment, Habermas supposed, had been thwarted, and the totality of life splintered into independent specialities, each left to the narrow competence of experts. What was needed was an overcoming of such splintering – a modernity or an enlightenment worth the name. Lyotard coun-tered that this was impossible. Post-modern societies were irredeemably fractured into mutually uncommunicative groups, each mired in its own language games, each committed to values that other groups did not share. In such circumstances, Habermas's dream of emancipating humanity through completing the project of modernity could not be realised.

Habermas yearned for a consensus inimical to the times, argued Lyotard, and his whole project depended upon the idea that there is a collective human subject that seeks its emancipation. On the contrary, insisted Lyotard, instability was not something that could be programmed out of such societies, least of all by rational discourse.

Lyotard thought Habermas's cause was good, but that the argument for it was poor because consensus has become an outmoded and suspect value. What was needed to hold society together was a notion of justice, Lyotard argued; this was not, he announced, a suspect value. Nevertheless, Lyotard had little to say about how post-modern justice might work.

Instead, at the very end of *The Postmodern Condition*, he once again took up the question of computerised knowledge. It could, he feared, become the 'dream' instrument for controlling and regulating the market system. 'In that case', he warned ominously, 'it would inevitably involve the use of terror.' But there was another possibility. Computerised knowledge might facilitate the free functioning of society as a set of heterogeneous elements rather than as an efficient system, removing the threat of terror. It hasn't worked out that way.

Who should own the great memory and data banks that he imagined IBM would install on satellites orbiting the earth? Not IBM, he argued: access should be freely granted to everybody. But he did not explain how this was to be achieved. And yet, for those of us today whose every keystroke supplies data for online techno-oligarchies, enabling their shareholders to become rich on our information, *The Postmodern Condition* seems entirely prescient.

4

Living for the City, 1981:
New York | London | Poundbury

In *Escape from New York*, ex–special forces soldier and convicted robber Snake Plissken (Kurt Russell) lands in a stealth glider on the roof of the World Trade Center. Then he descends to ground level on a mission to rescue the president from the tooled-up thugs who now run the city. American crime has risen by 400 per cent, and to deal with unprecedented numbers of convicted felons, Manhattan has been repurposed as a giant maximum-security prison surrounded by a fifty-foot wall, its bridges mined and the inmates doomed to life sentences. Feral gangs roam the island, and Manhattan's self-styled ruler is a warlord called the Duke of New York (played by Isaac Hayes), who cruises the streets in a flashy car that has – for reasons that have remained obscure to me for forty years – chandeliers for headlights. Yes, I know the chandeliers are expressions of conspicuous consumption, but think what the potholes would do to them.

In 1981, John Carpenter's film seemed a plausible depiction of New York in the near future. The metropolis had become known as Fear City – a place so overrun by gangs, rape, murder, serial killers, blackouts, looting, arson and muggings that abandoning it to criminals might have seemed like the best option. In 1961, there had been 483 murders in New York; in 1971, there were 1,466; and in 1981, this figure had climbed to 1,826.[1] The city's murder rate would continue to rise throughout the 1980s, fuelled in part by crime associated with crack cocaine.

But these figures conceal that it was the poorest of New Yorkers who suffered most. The Bronx, in particular – bisected by the Cross Bronx Expressway, which divided neighbourhoods, displacing residents and businesses as modernist city planners yielded to the demands of the car – was beset by thriving street gangs, while squatters took over abandoned tenements. The rise in crime had prompted middle-class white families to flee the city from the 1960s onwards, a flight that undermined New York City's tax base, rendering impossible the funding of public services – not least the police force. In 1975 New York declared bankruptcy, and mayor Abe Beame appealed to President Gerald Ford for a bailout. It never happened. The headline of the New York *Daily News* on 29 October 1975 read: 'Ford to City: Drop Dead. Vows He'll Veto Any Bail-Out.'[2]

Drop dead? This was a bracingly neoliberal response to a social problem. Bailouts were part of the social-democratic, interventionist past. The president's closest advisors, including Alan Greenspan and Donald Rumsfeld, urged Ford to make an example of a city living beyond its means, thus demonstrating the failure of big government. Ford was not a neoliberal, but was astute enough to recognise the drift of his party towards the anti-government, free-market ideology that would sweep Ronald Reagan into the White House in 1981. New Yorkers needed to realise that there was a new paradigm in town. It involved low taxes, minimal public services and a belief that the poorest were best served by creating circumstances fit for business.

The old paradigm it replaced was the set of policies launched by Democratic president Lyndon Johnson in 1964, known as the Great Society, which involved spending on education, medicine, poverty and transportation. Funded by means of the post-war boom, Johnson's utopian policy was aimed at eliminating poverty and racial injustice. New York was in step with Johnson's reforms, but now, with the post-war boom over, the city's very nearly social-democratic experiment was unsustainable – or so it was argued.

What did expire was a vision of how people might live together in a great city. New York mutated from modernist, social-democratic metropolis to a city amenable to Donald Trump, who in the 1980s leveraged his father's connections and the city's desperation into massive tax breaks, depriving New York of funds for education and other services as he developed properties for the rich. This Trump – the pre–White House property predator – figures as the personification of the new New York's values in Bret Easton Ellis's novel of 1980s Wall Street excess, *American Psycho*. It's a city where corpses lie on the street, the yuppie über-rich taunt the homeless, and brand-fixated conspicuous consumption is the highest form of human activity.

The 1980s was a time when the values of the prototypical post-modern city, Las Vegas, spread from the Nevada desert to the great metropolises of New York and London. It was also the decade when a prince created a post-modern fairyland in a corner of Dorset. Time was up for the modernist city.

I

At the start of *American Psycho*, a yuppie hero enters New York and notices some graffiti. 'ABANDON ALL HOPE YE WHO ENTER HERE is scrawled in blood red lettering on the side of the Chemical Bank near the corner of Eleventh and First.'[3] How very different this was to the neon-lit sign that greets drivers to Las Vegas: 'Welcome to Fabulous!' While New York was, apparently, dying, Las Vegas was rising from the desert, borne upwards by gambling receipts, mob money and a free and easy attitude to government regulation.

Las Vegas was founded as a city in 1905, but its business model was established in 1931, when the city legalised gambling and reduced residency requirements for divorce to six weeks. While New York was nicknamed Fear City, Vegas became known as Sin City. But there is a curious irony here. In Depression-era America, Vegas thrived while many other US cities struggled. One reason is that construction workers for the nearby Hoover Dam often lived in Las Vegas. The $165 million dam was built between 1931 and 1936, during the Great Depression, with funds from Public Works Administration – part of President Franklin D. Roosevelt's New Deal, a Keynesian social-democratic project to revive a country suffering mass unemployment. Without big government, Vegas might not have become the neoliberal, post-modern metropolis we know today.

Robert Venturi, the leading post-modern architectural theorist, loved the desert city. In 1972 he, his architect wife Denise Scott Brown and architect Steven Izenour wrote *Learning from Las Vegas*, arguing that the Vegas Strip was not a wasteland of kitsch but a cherishable urban landscape, a semiotic forest with layers of meanings.[4] The book was a jubilant retort to jeremiads that complained America was becoming ugly as it littered highways and cities with billboards and commercial signage.

Peter Blake's 1964 book *God's Own Junkyard: The Planned Deterioration of America's Landscape* concluded that there was a 'flood of ugliness engulfing America', typified by what a Long Island duck farmer had done in 1931. Martin Maurer asked Broadway set designers to design a building for selling poultry and eggs; local builders realised the vision by creating a big, hollow duck using wood frames, wire mesh and concrete. Its eyes, plucked from a Model T Ford, glowed red at night.

Meditating on the Big Duck led Venturi and his co-authors to make a distinction fundamental to post-modernism. For them, there were two kinds of buildings: ducks and decorated sheds. 'The duck is the special building that *is* a symbol', they wrote, while 'the decorated shed is the conventional shelter, that *applies* symbols.'[5] Duck architecture: littered or bejewelled America, depending on your tastes, from the hot dog stand at Coney Island styled as a hot dog, complete with inedible bun and eternally congealed ketchup, to the less jaunty Apple Store in Chicago designed by Foster + Partners to look like a giant

MacBook Pro. But in the co-authors' taxonomy, duck buildings didn't have to look like the things they symbolised. Consider, Venturi suggested, Boston City Hall, the rugged brutalist, modernist building that opened in 1968. It was a duck, just not the kind of duck he liked. 'It's all a big symbol, though it won't admit it', the architect said. 'How ridiculous – trying to make a *piazza publico*, like an Italian city-state! If they really wanted to make it so monumental, they should have built a plain loft building and put a sign up top saying, "I Am a Monument."'[6]

A better model in most situations, Venturi thought, was a conventional structure to which symbols were affixed. In 1992, when Venturi's firm designed the Children's Museum of Houston, he showed us what he meant. It was a plain box of a building, gaudily painted, with an entrance that looked like a toy Greek temple, a frieze below the pediment spelling out MUSEUM in big red letters.

Many of the world's greatest buildings, he thought, were both ducks and decorated sheds. The great Gothic cathedral of Chartres, for instance, was a duck, in that its floor plan takes the form of a Latin cross, while its façade is clamorous with attention-seeking signs. That said, Venturi was by temperament more of a decorated shed than a duck guy: he thought architects should be less concerned with space and structure and more with signs and symbols. Modernism was too concerned with heroic statement, too duck-like; it followed the venerable stricture of Walter Gropius in regarding ornament as a crime. But, for Venturi, those values were dead: post-modernism should learn from the ordinary, the kitsch, the ugly and the commercial, and try to tap into their vibrancy. Ornament wasn't so much a crime as a sign of life.

Accordingly, Venturi and Scott Brown hymned the architecture of the Vegas Strip, that ostensibly democratic conflagration of signs in the desert, that city bankrolled by means of human stupidity and cupidity. Venturi and Scott Brown looked on this post-modern Sodom and Gomorrah and saw it as a popular, commercial, fun retort to the patrician, mostly socialist and utterly funless architecture of modernism.

Venturi spent much of the 1960s tilting at modernist architecture, notably the International Style of Le Corbusier and Mies van der Rohe – the austere glass, steel and concrete block rising across American cities – while eulogising ostensibly obsolescent styles such as mannerism, rococo and decoratively flamboyant Edwardian architecture. Indeed, he and Scott Brown met while campaigning to save the University of Pennsylvania's Furness Library – an exuberant red sandstone, brick and terracotta building built in the nineteenth century, looking from the outside like a fortress struggling to become a cathedral, with an interior featuring a rotunda reading room and windows inscribed with Shakespearian quotations. It was as if Venetian Gothic had been airlifted to Pennsylvania, or as if post-modernism's joy in pastiche and appropriation, in exuberant bad taste and giddy decor, had a precursor.

Venturi adored such buildings, seeing them as spiritual antidotes to the modernist megastructures such as Pruitt-Igoe that were designed to liberate residents from the vicissitudes of market and money. The architectural past was conceived by Venturi, in post-modern fashion, as a resource to be plundered, a supermarket of styles, from which he returned with trolleys full of material to rebuff modernist aesthetics.

In *Learning from Las Vegas*, Venturi and his co-authors' distaste for modernism's aesthetic and political agendas became most apparent: 'Orthodox Modern architecture is progressive, if not revolutionary, utopian and puristic; it is dissatisfied with *existing* conditions.'[7] Modern architecture in that sense sought to revolutionise sensibilities, and even politics, by building imaginative spaces that effectively indicted existing conditions. The post-modern architecture that Venturi and Scott Brown favoured in their eulogy to Las Vegas sought to revolutionise nothing. 'Las Vegas's values are not questioned here', they wrote. 'The morality of commercial advertising, gambling interests and the competitive instinct is not at issue.' Venturi and Scott Brown loved Vegas's sprawl so much that, during the 1970s, they took classes of architecture students on tours of the Strip, and rented Howard Hughes's helicopter to fly over the city taking photographs that demonstrated how Vegas was a demotic takedown of modernism's elitism. Students called the course 'the Great Proletarian Cultural Locomotive', since Venturi affected to stand up to modernism's dictatorship of taste on behalf of the people. It might have been seen as the opposite; its fetish for vernacular Americana was a paean to ugliness that only the privileged could afford to indulge.

Venturi and his co-authors detested the planned monotony of modernism, favouring instead the plebeian, unplanned sprawl of Vegas. Its fetish object was Caesars Palace, which hotel owner Jay Sarno began building on the Strip in 1965. It had Roman arches and columns stuck on its façade, not to mention the tunic-clad cocktail waitresses inside, and spawned a host of imitations. It became the world's largest theme park, aimed at making visitors feel as though they were in Venice, Paris, Camelot or on a pirate's island – or, as Paul Goldberger put it in the *New Yorker* in 2010, 'given that these weird simulacra have become famous in their own right – that you are, quite simply, in Vegas'.[8]

In the same year as Venturi and his co-authors published their eulogy to Vegas, another book appeared that showed how timely this analysis was. In *For a Critique of the Political Economy of the Sign*,[9] the post-modern sociologist and philosopher Jean Baudrillard argued that traditional Marxist critiques based on Fordist production processes were increasingly obsolete. For Baudrillard, commodities were not only to be characterised in terms of their use-value and exchange value, as in Marx's theory of the commodity, but also in terms of their sign-value. Expressions of style, prestige and luxury become increasingly important if we are to understand the power of contemporary capitalism itself. Welcome to fabulous.

II

Four years before *Escape from New York* was released, America tuned in to ABC to watch the second game of the World Series from Yankee Stadium. The Yankees were down 2–0 in the bottom of the first inning when the aerial camera panned away from the game to capture a huge fire a few blocks away. An abandoned schoolhouse was ablaze. The scene came to define New York in the 1970s as hellishly out of control, not least because conventional wisdom at the time had it that many of the fires that destroyed the Bronx were caused by slumlords seeking to collect insurance money or tenants attempting to exploit housing law that prioritised fire victims for subsidies.

The South Bronx, in particular, became a symbol of America's dark side: a place ruined by heroin, gangs and citizens who, out of desperation or greed, were destroying where they lived. Viewed from a different perspective – that of hip-hop historian, say – it typified the abandonment of the poor, the needy and the communities of colour to brutal forces. 'America's dark side is comprised of those who don't fit neatly into official history – unneeded workers and uneducated youth whose contact with American government is usually limited to mean-spirited policing, their filthy, abandoned neighbourhoods covered up by graffiti', wrote Nelson George in *Hip Hop America*.[10] The flip side, he argued, was that the suburban revolution, 'the one supported by the government and celebrated by major industry (auto, oil, rubber, real estate), along with prejudice against blacks and Hispanics, had left large chunks of our big cities economic dead zones'.

Even before the Bronx burned, the borough had been ruinously bisected by the six-lane Cross Bronx Expressway, designed by city master-planner Robert Moses. Construction started in 1948 and ended only in 1972, by which time more than 60,000 residents had been forced to move, often being resettled in high-rise apartment blocks. The Bronx's local economy suffered as a result, with an estimated 600,000 jobs lost in manufacturing, and youth unemployment rising as high as 80 per cent.

'At first we couldn't believe it; it seemed to come from another world', recalled Marshall Berman in *All That Is Solid Melts into Air: The Experience of Modernity*. As a teenager, the Bronx-born Marxist professor saw the CBE cut through old neighbourhoods in what felt like wanton destruction of lifestyles and communities.

> First of all, hardly any of us owned cars: the neighbourhood itself, and the subways leading downtown, defined the flow of our lives . . . something like 60,000 working- and lower-middle-class people, mostly Jews, but with many Italians, Irish and Blacks thrown in would be thrown out of their homes. The Jews of the Bronx were nonplussed: could a fellow-Jew [i.e. Robert Moses] really want to do this to us?[11]

Apartment buildings that had been stable for thirty years emptied out as the Bronx became a vast construction site, Berman recalled, and black and Hispanic families, fleeing worse accommodation, moved in: 'I can remember standing on the construction site for the Cross Bronx Expressway, weeping for my neighbourhood.' Among the buildings that were destroyed were art deco houses on the Grand Concourse, which Berman described as 'our borough's closest thing to a Parisian boulevard'. 'As I saw one of the buildings being wrecked for the road, I felt a grief that, I can see now, is endemic to modern life.'[12]

Expanding modernity destroyed not just traditional and pre-modern architecture, Berman thought, but everything vital and beautiful in the modern world itself. Post-modernity often lived in or rose from the ruins that modernity had inflicted on itself: 'Thanks to Robert Moses, the modernity of the urban boulevard was being condemned as obsolete, and blown to pieces, by the modernity of the interstate highway.'[13]

While the Bronx spiralled into urban blight as a result of Moses's modernism, wealthier, whiter parts of New York City were spared that fate. In particular, when Moses settled on ripping up Manhattan's historic Washington Square so an expressway could be built through it, he was outmanoeuvred by a freelance journalist turned urban activist called Jane Jacobs. Her sense was that planners were ruining cities by imposing grid-like road structures, tidily zoned areas for business and residences, suburban sprawl for the anti-pioneers of white flight, and brutal public housing for people of colour. Her campaign to defend her beloved West Village from Moses's expressway achieved what the Bronx could not – successful resistance to the prevailing modernist ethos of what cities should be.

Jacobs liked cities that were plural, confusing, unpredictable. She favoured haphazard juxtaposition of everything – work and leisure, commercial and residential, black and white, rich and poor. Apart from anything else, having separate zones for homes, work and leisure led to traffic jams as everyone tried to get to the same place at the same time; such zoned planning also invited crime, since, if residential areas were empty during work hours, burglars were given free rein.

In her 1961 book *The Death and Life of Great American Cities*, written as city planners were genuflecting before architects like Le Corbusier and Mies van der Rohe, Jacobs extolled, without naming it, the post-modern jumble over the modernist grid.[14] Her biographer, Robert Kanigel, argued that Jacobs offered alternative ways to see: 'tottering old buildings could be sources of anarchic creativity . . . a factory near your house need not be unwholesome, but instead a nexus of economic and social renewal'.[15]

Jacobs's vision of urban renewal, rather than Robert Moses's, helps explain a key post-modern phenomenon: the gentrification of run-down urban areas. The revivals of New York's Lower East Side, Berlin's Mitte and London's Shoreditch have all involved artists moving into old buildings and revivifying depressed areas through their practices. Ultimately these outliers were too successful: in a post-modern irony, the run-down bits of cities into which artists moved became such lucrative real estate that they priced out artists and key workers. But this is a post-modern strategy for creating liveable cities – a contradiction of the principles that led Baron Haussman to bulldoze Paris or Robert Moses to bisect the Bronx in a tidy but misbegotten modernist project driven by the demands of the car.

Moses had earlier been responsible for transforming marsh and waste land on Long Island into the vast Jones Beach, which Berman described as the 'Rosebud of this Citizen Cohen'. He provided access to the beach and other Long Island state parks through two parkways.[16] But there was a problem Berman didn't consider: both parkways were crossed by a large number of low bridges. As a result buses could not run down them, and so state parks were out of the reach of poorer families who did not own cars. Moses's biographer Robert Caro also charged Moses with racism for making it difficult for black New Yorkers to get permits to the parks if they came by buses using other roads, and for assigning black lifeguards to distant, less developed beaches.[17]

For some, the Cross Bronx Expressway was a fast track to suburbia through what became known as white flight. Left behind were the Bronx's second-class citizens, mostly African-American or Hispanic, living often in slums. Robert Caro described the state of East Tremont, a section of the South Bronx, after the expressway had been completed that year. Streets were carpeted with broken glass; broken furniture, soaked mattresses and pieces of jagged steel filled the gutters.[18] And then the ruins of the Bronx were set alight.

The story of why the Bronx burned during the 1970s tells us a great deal about how cities work in the post-modern, neo-liberal, data-driven era in which we still live. It's a story that begins in 1971, when Mayor John Lindsay asked New York's fire chief, John O'Hagan, for savings to help close a budget deficit. To do so, O'Hagan brought in mathematicians and statisticians from the Santa Monica–based defence think tank, the RAND Corporation, to work with the mayor's office. RAND, started by the Pentagon after World War II, had a reputation for ingenuity, having all but invented game theory and systems analysis. It had also been at the forefront of the Cold War, producing war games strategies for the US military that led Soviet newspaper *Pravda* to dub it 'the academy of science and death and destruction'.

According to Joe Flood, the aim 'was nothing less than a new way of administering cities: use the mathematical brilliance of the computer modellers and systems analysts who had revolutionised military strategy to turn Gotham's corrupt, insular and unresponsive bureaucracy into a streamlined, non-partisan technocracy'.[19] RAND built computer models predicting when, where and how often fires would take hold in the city, and used that data to predict how quickly firefighters could respond to them. The aim was to show which areas received faster and slower responses, and thereby demonstrate which fire stations could be closed with least impact. But even that aim was dubious, since it relied on the only factor that could be easily quantified for determining which fire companies should be closed: response time. One RAND model Flood studied asserted that traffic had no effect on how quickly a fire engine travelled through New York City – which raised a laugh when he presented it to firefighters.

Fire captains were given stopwatches to time how long it took firefighters to reach a blaze. But often they lost or broke them, and submitted figures that showed them in the best light. RAND's number crunchers used simplified formulas to analyse flawed data. As a result, in 1972 RAND recommended the closure of thirteen fire companies, including some in the fire-prone South Bronx. They also recommended opening seven new ones, including units in suburban districts of Staten Island and the North Bronx. Flood asked RAND analysts how a model could recommend closing one of the busiest fire companies in the city: 'They'd cite a litany of equations and talk about how consistent the R-squares were, things like that. In effect, they were saying, "The Emperor is wearing clothes, because our calculations tell us he must be."'[20]

RAND was ostensibly presenting an objectively technocratic solution to help solve a political problem. In that sense it was akin to America's use of data in the Vietnam War, for which RAND was employed by the Pentagon. In Vietnam flawed data was used to determine military priorities, just as flawed data was used to determine public policy in New York. Both Defense Secretary Robert McNamara and the US military commander in Vietnam from 1964 to 1968, General William Westmoreland, were Harvard Business School graduates, familiar with and committed to the use of statistics in public policy. Both men favoured the collection of data on body counts and kill ratios to justify the war back home.

But, as in the Bronx, there was a problem with the data. In *The War Managers*, Douglas Kinnard quoted army generals who distrusted the data they were receiving. 'I had one Division commander whose reports I never believed or trusted', said one. 'The immensity of the false reporting is a blot on the honour of the Army.'[21] Long before the era of fake news, the data supplied to the media, and even to President Lyndon Johnson, was a simulacrum of transparency rather than the thing itself. And yet, as the war continued, Westmoreland increasingly came to rely on kill ratios to satisfy his thirst for data.

If post-modernism is about anything substantial, it is about countering these modernist myths of cool objectivity – or what Jean-François Lyotard called the language game of efficiency. Mayor Lindsay and fire chief O'Hagan sought to end Tammany Hall, the venerable administration of New York by Democratic patronage, and replace it with rational public administration. When Lindsay wanted to make cuts to the city budget in the early 1970s, he asked O'Hagan to come up with suggestions. It seemed to make sense to hire RAND analysts to work out where the axe should fall.

Ultimately, though, RAND's models fell prey to the very thing that technocracies are supposed to prevent: political manipulation. At the outset, the RAND studies didn't need to be manipulated – they provided what the politicians wanted to hear without prompting. As the cuts deepened, the models began recommending closures in wealthier, more politically active communities. But that was unacceptable to O'Hagan, who was well connected in the Democratic clubs of Brooklyn and Queens.

Retired fire chief Elmer Chapman, who ran the FDNY's Bureau of Planning and Operations Research, told Joe Flood that, instead of following the models, administrators scrolled down the lists of possible closures to a fire company or station in a poorer neighbourhood, and selected it for closure rather than the one recommended by the data: 'The people in those [poorer] neighbourhoods didn't have a very big voice.'[22]

As a result, poorer neighbourhoods burned. Over the next decade, a series of fires swept through New York, displacing more than 600,000 people, all thanks to the intentional withdrawal of fire protection from the city's poorest. Between 1970 and 1980, seven of the poorest areas in the Bronx known as census tracts lost more than 97 per cent of their buildings to fire and abandonment. What happened in the Bronx was echoed in Brooklyn's Brownsville, Bushwick and Bedford-Stuyvesant neighbourhoods, as well as Manhattan's Harlem and Lower East Side. 'The smell is one thing I remember', recalled retired Bronx firefighter Tom Henderson. 'That smell of burning – it was always there.'[23]

Post-modernity rose from the ruins into which modernity had collapsed. It was in this broken, burned-out Bronx that hip-hop emerged, creating art from junk, rubble, aerosol cans and old records. Chuck D, founding member of Public Enemy, recalled that hip-hop was born when impoverished residents of South Bronx 'started to look at old turntables and say "maybe we can actually make music out of the records that happen to be laying around" and they made something out of nothing'.

Not quite nothing. Initially, hip-hop musicians borrowed loop sections of funk, jazz and soul tracks and transformed them. For instance, the first hip-hop single, 'Rapper's Delight' by the Sugarhill Gang, would have amounted to nothing had it not repurposed the bass line from Chic's 'Good Times' and sampled Love De-Luxe with Hawkshaw's Discophonia's 'Here Comes That Sound'. Like punk, which, as Dick Hebdige put it, 'appropriated . . . commodities by placing them in a symbolic ensemble which served to erase or subvert their original straight meanings', hip-hop musicians took their raw material from anywhere and everywhere, subverting and sometimes honouring the music they quoted as a result.[24]

Orthodoxy holds that hip-hop was born on 11 August 1973, in the recreation room of a high-rise apartment building at 1520 Sedgwick Avenue in the Bronx. It was there that Clive Campbell, better known as DJ Kool Herc, held a back-to-school party for his sister Cindy. Admission was twenty-five cents for females, fifty cents for males, making the event affordable to low-income teenagers. Striking, too, was the fact that the music played was not disco, which was associated with expensive cover charges and wealthier, often white, club-goers. Instead, DJ Kool played eclectic, irresistibly danceable music, including James Brown's 'Sex Machine', Average White Band's 'Pick Up the Pieces' and Baby Hue's 'Listen to Me'. He had spent several months experimenting with two turntables, a mixer and two copies of the same twelve-inch vinyl records to develop a new technique involving, he said, 'playing the frantic grooves at the beginning or in the middle of the song'. At this point in a song, known as the break, vocals stop but the beat goes on. Herc marked the points on the record where the break began and ended with a crayon, so that he could easily replay the break by spinning the record and not touching the tone arm. He would play the break beat on one record, then throw it over to the other turntable and play the same part. Extending the break beat this way became popular, especially among b-boys and b-girls, the break dancers who loved this music because it gave them the opportunity to showcase their skills.

The Jamaican-born Herc brought his Caribbean heritage of sound systems to this Bronx jam. His sound system consisted of two turntables, guitar amplifier and huge speakers.

From the summer of 1973 onwards, DJ Kool Herc's parties in clubs, dance halls and even parks became weekend traditions for South Bronx kids. Herc was partnered by a master of ceremonies called Coke La Rock, who introduced the music in the manner of what Jamaican sound system pioneers called toasting. This appropriation of toasting by Bronx-based MCs became the basis of the beat poetry of rap. Coke's motivating slogans, like 'To the beat y'all!' and 'Rock on my mellow!', became hip-hop commandments, venerated by the faithful, quoted endlessly.

Yale anthropology and African-American studies professor John F. Szwed argues that rap's origins are rooted in a variety of African-American traditions, the chanted instructions of square dancing, bebop and even the speech patterns of great African-American orators such as Dr Martin Luther King Jr and Malcolm X, while the poetry of African-American poets such as Amiri Baraka, Gil Scott-Heron and Stanley Crouch served as a bridge to the creation of the MC and rap music. From the start, hip-hop artists were borrowing from the past and honouring those whose works they appropriated and quoted.[25]

Among those inspired by Herc and seeking to emulate him was a teenager called Lance Taylor, better known by the name he later gave himself, Afrika Bambaataa. If post-modern artists like David Bowie and Cindy Sherman playfully reinvented themselves in various guises, for this African-American artist from the Bronx, post-modern invention was as serious as a heart attack – a political statement and assertion of black pride.

Bambaataa had grown up in a family of Jamaican and Barbadian immigrants, developing a radical critique of white American society thanks to having a mother and uncle who sparred over black liberation movement politics. His home was an apartment in the Bronx River Houses, high-rise blocks constructed in 1951 to offer temporary housing to working-class families, among them the parents of many of hip-hop's founding fathers. He became a member of the Black Spades as a boy, rising to lead a division of what became the biggest gang in the city.

But after a trip to Africa, Bambaataa returned to the Bronx a different person, changing his name and turning his back on gang life.

Bambaataa was struck by the 1964 British film *Zulu*, which dramatised the Battle of Rorke's Drift, at which 150 British soldiers were outnumbered by 4,000 Zulu warriors led by King Cetshwayo kaMpande. But, while the film has long divided critics between those who see it as pro-imperialist and racist and others who took it as an indictment of war and British colonialism, what impressed Bambaataa were powerful images of black solidarity.

In 1974, Bambaataa founded the Zulu Nation, a collective of DJs, dancers and graffiti artists that, as Nelson George put it, 'fulfilled the fraternal role gangs play in urban culture while de-emphasising crime and violence'.[26] What he saw on screen in *Zulu* and among the African communities he visited, he tried to recreate with this collective. Inspired by Herc and by his mother's eclectic record collection, he started to DJ at the Bronx River Houses' Community Center, as well as at block parties and high schools in the Bronx. These parties often involved DJ battles. If Bambaataa sometimes had the edge in these throwdowns, it was partly because he had a wider playlist – he would sample from Caribbean soca, African music and even German electronica.

But he didn't have as much showmanship as another rival, Grandmaster Flash (a.k.a. Joseph Saddler), who spun records with his back to the turntables and used his feet as he developed two of hip-hop's key moves: 'punch phrasing', or clock theory, which meant playing a short burst from a song on one turntable while playing the same song on the other; and break spinning – alternately spinning both records backwards to repeat the same phrase over and over. Flash was thereby finessing the technique devised by Grand Wizzard Theodore (a.k.a. Theodore Livingston), who is reckoned to have invented scratching: moving a vinyl record back and forth on a turntable to produce percussive or rhythmic sounds. Theodore found that the 1972 Technics

SL-1200 turntable would continue to spin at the correct RPM even if the DJ wiggled the record back and forth with his fingers. Such manual manipulation was and remains key to hip-hop; but by the early 1980s computerised devices made sampling easier. The E-mu Emulator enabled artists to digitise, manipulate and play back music.

It didn't matter that doing this was, for some critics, artistic necrophilia. This was post-modern pastiche akin to post-modern architecture's quotations of past styles. Long before hip-hop, French anthropologist Claude Lévi-Strauss had called this way of working 'bricolage'. 'The bricoleur', he wrote in *The Savage Mind* in 1962, 'is adept at performing a large number of diverse tasks . . . and the rules of this game are always to make do with "whatever is at hand".'[27] Lévi-Strauss could not have foreseen that P.M. Dawn would sample Spandau Ballet's 'True' on 'Set Adrift on Memory Bliss', nor that Notorious B.I.G. would sample Diana Ross's 'I'm Coming Out' on 'Mo Money Mo Problems'; but he might well have seen each as confirmations of his thesis.

Hip-hop appropriation was part of a broader post-modern revolution that involved subverting myths of authorship, self, progress, origins, destinies and endings in favour of a new paradigm, described by French-Bulgarian theorist Julia Kristeva as intertextuality, whereby 'any text is the absorption and transformation of another'.[28]

All this may be true, but it would hardly have been an effective defence against, say, Gilbert O'Sullivan's legal action against rapper and DJ Biz Markie for not clearing the sample of the former's 1972 hit 'Alone Again (Naturally)' in the latter's 1991 song 'Alone Again'. O'Sullivan successfully compelled Warner Brothers to recall all pressings and stop selling the album on which the song appeared until the sample was removed. If post-modernism was going to subvert business norms, neoliberalism was going to thumb through its Rolodex and hire a lawyer to shut down post-modernism's free-for-all of creative quotation and appropriation.

The O'Sullivan–Biz Markie case sent a chill through the hip-hop community, preventing it from being as frenetically creative as Public Enemy had been at the outset. Instead, as George pointed out, hip-hop stars of the late eighties, when the music was becoming a global industry and MC Hammer, Coolio and Puff Daddy made millions in sales, paid their dues to the musicians they sampled and, as a result, transformed old R&B catalogues into gold mines.[29] Neoliberalism had found a way of monetising hip-hop. Indeed, hip-hop became even more profitable as it developed a back catalogue that could itself be plundered.

As hip-hop emerged in the Bronx, so did a new kind of visual art. In the 1970s, at East 180th Street Yard in the South Bronx, out-of-service subway trains became blank canvases, and the resulting works were sent on touring exhibitions all through the city. Initially, students of De Witt Clinton High School painted or sprayed what became known as 'tags' – the slang names of the artists – as part of vast painted subway-car artworks. One of the first was Clinton High student Lonny Wood, whose nom de plume, Phase 2, visited all points on the subway network.

Another street artist, the Puerto Rico–born, Lower East Side–raised Lee Quiñones, became famous for having painted as many as 125 entire cars by hand in the 1970s. They came with titles such as 'The Hell Express', 'Earth is Hell, Heaven is Life' and 'Stop the Bomb', and were so visually striking that other graffiti artists accorded Quiñones the ultimate honour – leaving them untouched by their own work. Post-modern art, at least for a moment, resisted being sucked into Manhattan's art world at a time when Wall Street money was eyeing artistic production as an investment opportunity.

Rampant inflation in the 1970s made the real interest rate negative, and so the usual monetary means of storing value became less attractive to investors. Instead, real estate, antiques and above all art became favoured investments. The result was a rapid expansion in the commercialisation and production of art, and spiralling inflation in the art market. Making work for galleries and collectors became what it had scarcely ever been before – a career, and, for some savvy post-modern artists, a means of getting very rich. For a while, graffiti art existed outside this commodification of cultural expression. Strikingly, Quiñones called the No. 5 subway line that runs through the Bronx the 'rolling MoMA'.[30]

Another street artist, the Brooklyn-born Jean-Michel Basquiat, started off as part of the duo SAMO (derived from 'same old shit'), daubing the doors and walls of the Lower East Side with enigmatic phrases. 'The paintings started coming right at the moment that the East Village transformed from a burned-out wasteland inhabited by heroin addicts to the epicentre of a startling art boom. There was a marketable glamour to being a down-and-out prodigy then', writes Olivia Laing, 'but it was an act for Basquiat, as much a way of satirising prejudice as the African chieftain outfits he'd later wear to the parties of wealthy white collectors.'[31]

His widow recalled a visit to MoMA during which he sprinkled water from a bottle, hexing the temple. 'This is another of the white man's plantations', he explained. But the outsider artist became part of the art world. In 1980, an abandoned massage parlour on 41st Street and 7th Avenue, in Times Square, played host to the Times Square Show in which Basquiat and Quiñones and fellow graffiti artist Fab 5 Freddy displayed their works alongside those of Kenny Scharf, Keith Haring, Kiki Smith and Jenny Holzer. The show brought Basquiat and Quiñones to the attention of the art world, resulting in exhibitions at major galleries around the world and wealthy collectors. Even as he was feted by the art world he had satirised, Basquiat's heroin addiction got worse. Andy Warhol worried in his diary about his friend's drug consumption after watching him nod out on the Factory floor, 'falling asleep as he tie[d] his shoes'.[32] He died of a heroin overdose in 1988 aged just twenty-seven.

Five years earlier, in 1983, one of Basquiat's friends had been killed by the police. Michael Stewart had been graffitiing the

14th Street subway station wall before he was beaten into a coma by three police officers. He died weeks later in hospital. Stewart's death, reportedly caused by an illegal nightstick chokehold on the artist's neck, became a cause célèbre for the African-American struggle against police violence, though six officers involved were acquitted of causing his death. 'It could have been me', Basquiat said at the time. In his painting *Defacement (The Death of Michael Stewart)*, two Mr Punch–like cops rain their nightsticks onto a silhouetted, faceless black figure in the middle of the canvas. Above, Basquiat has written in Spanish: '¿DEFACIMENTO?' Was it the subway wall or Michael Stewart who was defaced?

It was a tragically pertinent question for New York at the time. What was, for the likes of Basquiat and Quiñones, artistic expression was, for successive New York mayors, a symptom of lawlessness spreading throughout the city. Rather than seeing graffiti art as a sign of creativity, Ed Koch – mayor from 1978 to 1989 – regarded it as something that needed to be erased.

In 1982, Koch found the answer in an article in the *Atlantic Monthly* by two criminologists, George L. Kelling and James Q. Wilson. They argued that minor offences were evidence of a disregard for law that undermined neighbourhood pride and accountability, and that policing should have a zero-tolerance policy towards even minor infractions:

> If the first broken window in a building is not repaired, the people who like breaking windows will assume that no one cares about the building and more windows will be broken. Soon the building will have no windows. Fixing what is wrong with the city sends a message that the authorities are in control and that increases the power of authority to maintain order.[33]

Impressed by what became known as the 'broken windows theory', Koch spent millions scrubbing subways of spray-paint and trying to tackle the young artists who tagged the city's train yards, putting up fences around transit yards and guarding subway carriages with dogs. 'If I had my way, I wouldn't put in dogs, but wolves', Koch said.[34]

In any case, Koch was responding to the symptoms rather than the causes of crime in the city. One reason the mayor was so keen to implement Wilson and Kelling's broken-windows theory was that, unlike other sociological accounts, it didn't correlate rising crime with the level of poverty in an area; nor did it consider graffiti art as an expression of the otherwise powerless.

In *Fear City: New York's Fiscal Crisis and the Rise of Austerity Politics*, historian Kim Phillips-Fein argued that, instead of providing extensive public services, New York government at the time was mainly committed to making the city an attractive place for businesses, lowering taxes and relaxing regulations.[35]

It was less of a drain on the public purse to clean subway cars than to tackle the city's crumbling public transport infrastructure or growing social inequality; Koch's clean-up campaign was financially astute, if cosmetic. Koch's application of the theory proved popular, especially with those who daily had to strap-hang in a subway system in which chronic underinvestment had resulted in broken doors, cracked undercarriages and increasingly creaky tracks and signals. In 1980 Koch spent $5 million on cleaning all 6,424 trains on the network. It was a Sisyphean task: clean trains provided blank canvases that were soon re-sprayed and tagged anew. In hindsight, the policy seems like one of those barmy job-creation schemes that involved workers digging holes and filling them in again.[36]

The broken-windows policy was controversial. Urban theorist Mike Davis argued that its implementation was part of a bigger militarisation of public space – a classist and racist crusade against the poor predicated on misplaced fear.[37] Poor and needy New Yorkers, not to mention people of colour, were most likely to be arrested or held up by police more as a result of broken-windows policing, thus taking time away from more vital tasks.

The city was being sanitised in readiness for gentrification. It was being made safe for financiers and other suits, the kind of sociopathic Wall Street heroes satirised in a passage in Bret Easton Ellis's *American Psycho*:

> He places the Walkman in the case alongside a Panasonic wallet-size cordless portable folding Easa-phone (he used to own the NEC 9000 Porta portable) and pulls out today's newspaper. 'In one issue – in one issue – let's see here . . . strangled models, babies thrown from tenement rooftops, kids killed in the subway, a Communist rally, Mafia boss wiped out, Nazis' – he flips through the pages excitedly – 'baseball players with AIDS, more Mafia shit, gridlock, the homeless, various maniacs, faggots dropping like flies in the streets, surrogate mothers, the cancellation of a soap opera, kids who broke into a zoo and tortured and burned various animals alive, more Nazis . . . and the joke is, the punch line is, it's all in this city – nowhere else, just here, it sucks'.[38]

To the amoral beneficiaries of the post-modern era, the cancellation of a soap opera mattered as much or as little as murdered babies.

Its satire changed nothing. Thirty years after the novel was published, a musical version of *American Psycho* was launched; to capitalise on its release, fashion retailers offered the chance for their customers to get the Patrick Bateman look. 'Pinstripes are a must, as is condescension and an AmEx', wrote one fashion critic. 'Leave the humility at home.'[39]

Hip-hop, too, that most subversive of art forms, became a business opportunity. What Koch, the *New York Times* and angry commuters failed to realise was that graffiti was not so much vandalism as the birth of a New York art form that would take over the world and make some people very rich. In that sense, transgressive post-modernism and neoliberalism were made for each other – but neoliberalism just didn't realise it until much later.

In the end, graffiti art triumphed over the broken-windows policy. The art form became a global language – the go-to means of expression for alienated youth with spray cans. In 2015 graffiti art returned to New York subway cars. The MTA stuck laser-printed adhesive sheets to the sides of cars advertising *Street Art Throwdown*, a TV reality show. The MTA was capitalising on the art form it had sought to erase. Graffiti art was tolerable, at least in the city that created it, insofar as it could be monetised.

Nowadays, the hip-hop that Koch and his cleaners sought to whitewash is likewise part of New York's heritage industry. There are tours around the Bronx locales where hip-hop artists catalysed a cultural revolution. You too can visit the venues of rap battles, take selfies outside 1520 Sedgwick Avenue, and admire graffitied murals from back in the day. What happened in the Boogie Down – as the Bronx became known – once made history; now it is history. It's a risky thesis to suggest that great music and great art come from times of great oppression, that the creative spirit rises from rubble; but in this case and in this place, it did.

III

While New York was getting a makeover to function in the neoliberal world, a new approach to architecture was rising on the London skyline. The city took off its proverbial bowler hat, and yielded to architectural pastiche and the no-less-sexy allure of money. On 7 December 1981, the London Docklands Development Corporation was formed with the objective of regenerating London's former docks. The whole area was turned into an enterprise zone. Margaret Thatcher and her environment secretary Michael Heseltine granted the LDDC land, planning powers and a brief to think radically. The project was deliberately unplanned, low-tax and in theory low on 'big government', except for the not-so-small matter of massive public investment projects such as the Docklands Light Railway and the cleaning, dredging and decontamination of old industrial sites. Before long, Britain's first driverless trains whisked one through a vast construction site where a new capital of finance was to be built on top of what artist and enthusiastic avatar of post-modernism Pablo Bronstein called 'piles of burning rubbish and forgotten wastelands to the east of the city'.[40]

London embraced post-modernism only after having disdained the modernist architecture of the International Style. In 1963, for instance, Ludwig Mies van der Rohe, the last director of Bauhaus and the architect who was one of the models for Ayn Rand's Howard Roark, began work on a commission by developer Peter Palumbo to design a nineteen-storey office building and public square at the epicentre of the City of London. Part of the site was already occupied by a listed neo-Gothic Victorian building dating from 1870, which was used by crown jewellers Mappin and Webb.

Mies planned the building and Mansion House Square in minute detail, imagining it might be his last grand project. He designed bronze door-handles, specified the tree species for the square, and developed a heating system to keep the travertine steps dry. Shortly before his death in 1969, he was deciding the correct placement for the flagpole that would be situated at the heart of the new piazza, where he hoped there would be music festivals, concerts, exhibitions and flower markets – finally providing at the heart of London's financial district what it had long lacked: a public square free from traffic.

If Mies's bronze-clad, amber-glass tower had been built, it might have become as influential in London as his earlier Seagram Building in New York. But London never got either a Mies tower or Mansion House Square. In his 'carbuncle' speech at RIBA's 150th anniversary dinner in 1984, Prince Charles criticised Mies's tower and the Mansion House Square plans as follows: 'It would be a tragedy if the character and skyline of our capital city were to be further ruined and St Paul's dwarfed by yet another giant glass stump, better suited to downtown Chicago than the City of London.'[41]

In the same year, the architect Berthold Lubetkin – whose modernist jewels in London include the Finsbury Health Centre, Highgate's Highpoint apartment block and, best of all, London Zoo's penguin pool – told the public inquiry into Mies's plans: 'It is inconceivable that such a generous and unique gift to the City should be discarded in the name of a vague antiquarian pedantic prejudice.'[42] The Russian émigré was proved wrong. Existing buildings on the site that would have had to be redeveloped for Mies's design were listed, after conservationists successfully argued that they had historical merit.

It wasn't just antiquarian pedantry or royal architectural conservatism that did for Mies's plans. It was also fear of the people. Designer and author Jack Self detects behind the decision a neoliberal terror of the people. In the early years of Margaret Thatcher's eleven-year premiership, race riots, picket lines and political demonstrations against her economic reforms were common. Indeed, worse was to come in the form of the poll tax riots in Trafalgar Square. Self wrote: 'Large crowds – whether gathered out of civic pride or disobedience – were no longer desirable in the city. In effect, public space had become dangerous.'[43]

As the British state shrank according to neoliberal principles, public spaces disappeared. Squares and parks began to be superseded, as they had in Mike Davis's Los Angeles, by pseudo-public spaces – squares, parks and thoroughfares that appeared to be public but were actually owned and controlled by developers and their private backers, and policed by private security guards – as cash-strapped local authorities struggled to create or maintain such spaces themselves.[44]

Instead of Mies's modernist tower and public square, London got a post-modernist confection on the same site called No. 1 Poultry. Palumbo commissioned James Stirling, who had defended Mies's modernist design. Stirling's pink-and-yellow striped limestone building was completed in 1997. Prince Charles said that No. 1 Poultry looked 'rather like an old 1930s wireless'. It was voted fifth-worst building in London by *Time Out* readers in 2005, and described by one critic as 'a pink-striped stone galleon of an office building [thrusting] its jaunty prow into Bank junction like a slice of Battenberg cake gone astray, beckoning people inside to discover its great circular atrium lined with glossy blue tiles and pink and yellow window frames'.[45]

The criticism from princes and conservation groups got Stirling down so much that he contemplated emigration to the United States. He didn't entirely disagree with Prince Charles's crusade against insensitive modern building, but he abhorred the undemocratic manner in which he fought it. Stirling's plans were the subject of a long conservation battle. In 1988 the environment secretary, Nicholas Ridley, gave permission, seeing it as a potential masterpiece that was more important to the nation than the retention of the listed buildings – something that didn't seem to occur to the government when deciding against Mies's plans. But it was not until 1991 that the House of Lords finally gave consent for the redevelopment to proceed. Stirling never got to see his design realised: he died aged sixty-six in 1992 on the operating table.

No. 1 Poultry was seized on by American cultural theorist, landscape designer and architectural historian Charles Jencks as befitting London. Jencks described the city in which Stirling's office block rose as a heteropolis – a hundred-mile city made cosmopolitan by mass migration, and so rich in history that it offered a treasure house of architectural styles to be quoted and appropriated by any architect with a sensitivity to context. London was not, like Lutyens's New Delhi, Le Corbusier's Chandigarh or Niemeyer's Brasília, a city that could be built in one style – it was too old, too diverse and too contradictory for such tidy architectural solutions. Nor was it New York, a city that embraced modernist architecture.

London, Jencks argued, needed an architecture that was as multicultural and multi-centred as the city itself. Post-modern architecture, which Jencks called the new paradigm, suited a city whose financial districts were at least entering the turbo-charged, globalised world of unregulated finance with gusto. He saw the link between neoliberal commerce and London's many ethnic groups. 'As sure as exercise creates sweat,' wrote Jencks, 'multinationals create multiculturalism – not by intention but as a side effect of economic growth.'[46] It's a remark that makes better sense if we consider London's multicultural-ism as symptomatic, not just of the liberation of capital from the constraints of the Gold Standard in the early 1970s, which had unleashed globalisation, but also of Britain's earlier imperial project. The British East India Company, after all, was initially a multinational enterprise, and the immigrants from the Indian subcontinent who settled in London might well be seen as a corollary of the economic growth that Britain achieved through the plundering of their ancestors' homelands.

'Of course architecture does not change the facts of a compet-itive, multicultural society, but it can invent new strategies for dealing with pluralism', wrote Jencks. Londoners in the multi-cultural post-modern era were happy not to seek cultural integration, he thought, but to be 'ex-centrics' on the margins of a pluralist society. 'Taking advantage of heterogeneity is a matter of choice, desire, training and the style of life that celebrates difference.'[47]

Jencks took Stirling's No. 1 Poultry as just such a celebration, its mishmash of styles making it what he called a 'syncopated hybrid'. Outside, it has a glazed two-sided clock that quotes the fascist-era Palazzo delle Poste in Naples, and is surmounted by a turret that looks like a submarine conning tower, as if the building has surfaced through all the archaeological layers of London below. Inside, it has a ramped floor conveying an Ancient Egyptian mood, while its main staircase quotes the Vatican's Renaissance Scala Regia.

No. 1 Poultry today, though, is hardly as heterogeneous as the city it inhabits. It was designed as a speculative commercial building incorporating offices and retail units, and today is owned by a subsidiary of an asset-management firm. Its Conran-designed restaurant, the Coq d'Argent, has long been frequented overwhelmingly by stockbrokers, traders and bankers, and became notorious after the 2008 financial crash as the place where a succession of depressed City workers plunged eight storeys to their deaths.

Ninety years earlier, T. S. Eliot wrote *The Waste Land* while working in the foreign transactions department of Lloyds Bank in the Square Mile of the City of London, the venerable hub of British capital. He described it as Unreal City, a modern approximation of Dante's Hell, whose workers, each undone by death, walk through the brown fog of a winter dawn across London Bridge to their office desks.[48]

By the 1980s, the City Eliot hymned was no longer fit for purpose if London was to become a world capital of finance, and Britain to rise anew from its postcolonial welfare-state mediocrity – as Margaret Thatcher and her acolytes desired. Hence the development of Docklands.

What arose in Docklands was more hyperreal than unreal – a Disneyland in east London. Umberto Eco explained the difference between unreality and hyperreality in his essay 'Travels in Hyperreality' after visiting wax museums and Disneyland during a US tour: 'Disneyland is more hyperrealistic than the wax museum, precisely because the latter still tries to make us believe that what we are seeing reproduces reality absolutely, whereas Disneyland makes it clear that within its magic enclosure it is fantasy that is absolutely reproduced.' Disneyland involved misdirection, Eco noted: 'The Main Street façades are presented to us as toy houses and invite us to enter them, but the interior is always a disguised supermarket, where you buy obsessively, believing you are still playing.' What he called Disney's 'masterpieces of falsification' sold genuine merchandise: 'What is falsified is our will to buy, and in this sense Disneyland really is the quintessence of consumer ideology.'[49] Docklands, similarly, is a seeming carnival of fun, a metropolis of decorated sheds luridly garlanded in architectural quotations, inside which the business of capital accumulation carries on regardless.

'The postmodern reply to the modern consists of recognising that the past, since it cannot be destroyed, because its destruction leads to silence, must be revisited not innocently but with irony', wrote Eco.[50] And on Docklands' Isle of Dogs, a disused loop in the Thames where Henry VIII had once hunted, arose what Iain Sinclair called 'Anubis land, a reservation of jackals'. By Anubis land, Sinclair most likely meant the running dogs of speculative finance who filled the towers of glass and steel. Since the Docklands could not destroy its old associations with the East India Company and the rest of Britain's imperial project, it must revisit them with irony. Sinclair imagined this new capital of finance as Eliot had conceived the old one – as a near-death experience; he described the Isle of Dogs as 'Death's promontory. The whole glass raft is a mistake, glitter forms of anachronistic postmodernism (the swamp where *that* word crawled to die). Skin grafts peeling before completion. The seductive sky/water cemetery of Thatcherism, cloud-reflecting sepulchre towers.'[51]

But the Isle of Dogs wasn't where post-modernism went to die. It was where it went to roll over and wave its paws in the air at the feet of neoliberal capital. 'The liberation of PoMo is the liberation of capital; unrestrained, joyous and mad', wrote Pablo Bronstein. 'It was through postmodernism that architectural stories about business became romantic again.'[52] The romance of capital, if that was what it was, was rekindled in London in 1986 with the Big Bang. The resultant deregulation and computerisation of finance made the physical buildings of the Square Mile functionally useless, so great financial institutions began to move elsewhere in London – to Billingsgate and Victoria, but above all to Canary Wharf, at the epicentre of the old docklands. The dead zones of east London, from which Britain had launched its commercial and imperial navies to colonise nearly one-third of the world, were born again. Derelict industry was replaced by post-modern architecture, such as CZWG's 1986 waterfront housing complex, called Cascades, with its fantasy theme of nautical engineering that attracted yuppie financiers.

'The fizzy optimism of the Yuppie is celebrated in the jazz-age frivolity and ocean-liner detailing', noted Bronstein.[53]

The Big Bang meant that London had now outpaced its European competitors in deregulating its financial sector, and so became a magnet for international banks. Docklands rose from London's Luftwaffe-bombed, toxic eastern wastelands to accommodate incoming greed. Michael Lewis wrote in *Liar's Poker* of a modern gold rush: 'Never before have so many unskilled twenty-four-year-olds made so much money in so little time as we did this decade in New York and London.'[54]

The idea for an office complex in the Isle of Dogs came from two American bankers who sought funding for the project from Canadian property tycoon Paul Reichmann. They managed to lure business leaders to Canary Wharf, then an unfashionable wasteland in the east of London. 'I did not ask them if they would move to Canary Wharf', recalled Reichmann. 'The answer would have been no. My main question was: are you happy with your operating premises or do you see the need to do something dramatic?'[55]

The change was indeed dramatic. The era of red braces and greed-is-good was just beginning. Architects and artists were crucial in sustaining the era's optimistic mood. Over two nights in October 1988, for instance, the French musician Jean-Michel Jarre staged two concerts on a floating stage on the Royal Victoria Docks, with a vast *son et lumière* show using buildings as projection screens, deploying searchlights and 150,000 lbs of fireworks. Projections and music evoked the city's history, with one section about the industrial revolution, another about the swinging sixties, and a third about the computerised offices that were regenerating Docklands. Tricky matters like slavery, colonialism, plague and workers' uprisings were quietly omitted. Some 200,000 spectators saw the concerts, including Princess Diana, basking in the simulated spectacle of London's supposed progress.

Sinclair was right to call Docklands Anubis land. The dog-headed Ancient Egyptian god of mummification and the afterlife was a fitting spirit guide for the Isle of Dogs as it arose anew. Architects lured to east London bowed to Anubis with post-modern homages to Ancient Egypt. The Four Seasons Hotel, designed by Philippe Starck, is a case in point. 'It boasts', Bronstein wrote in his best estate-agent patter, 'a massive Luxor-style roof of green aluminium, protruding windows and a pair of multi-storey non-functional "doors" propped half open as if an excavation were in progress.'[56] It looks like a pharaoh's tomb in the Valley of the Kings midway through being plundered by astute Westerners – a fitting motif for a luxury hotel at the nerve-centre of deregulated neoliberal capitalism.

IV

One critic stood out against this post-modern architectural carnival. 'You have to give this much to the Luftwaffe', said Prince Charles at the Corporation of London Planning and Communication Committee's annual dinner at Mansion House in December 1987. 'When it knocked down our buildings, it didn't replace them with anything more offensive than rubble.' He was speaking against Richard Rogers's scheme to redevelop Paternoster Square, next to St Paul's Cathedral. 'Surely here, if anywhere,' added the prince, 'was the time and place to sacrifice some profit, if need be, for generosity of vision, for elegance, for dignity; for buildings which would raise our spirits and our faith in commercial enterprise.'[57] After that, Rogers's scheme was dropped.

Prince Charles didn't want to see his country 'disappear under a welter of ugliness'. In this, he postured as expressing the voice of the silent majority of Britons. At the time he gave this speech, his favourite architect, Léon Krier, was drawing up a masterplan for a village called Poundbury – a 400-acre site on the edge of the Dorset town of Dorchester. This was to be the prince's showpiece village, a retort to the ugliness of the built environment of the past century. It quickly became something much more interesting.

The first phase was built in the early 1990s. The results were mocked as Disney Feudal, and the village damned as a place where Prince Charles could play at being a planner, like Marie Antoinette with her toy hamlet in Versailles. Not so much 'Let them eat cake' as 'Let them eat the prince's own Duchy Original biscuits'. From flint-clad cottages and Scottish baronial villas to Palladian mansions and miniature pink gothic castles, Poundbury became a merry riot of porticoes and pilasters, sampling from the rich history of architectural pattern books with promiscuous glee, just as a hip-hop artist would do with a stack of old-funk twelve-inches. Prince Charles was blissfully ignorant of the fact, but Poundbury was impeccably post-modern.

Krier's plan was for 2,500 homes, two-thirds of which would be privately owned and the rest rented through housing associations. Cars would be confined to the rears of properties, shops and offices, so that street life would be overwhelmingly pedestrian. But Poundbury was not just backward-looking: cable TV was permitted, but satellite dishes were not, while condensing boilers, photo-voltaic tiles and ground-heat recovery systems were standard energy-saving devices. Beyond Poundbury, a Prince of Wales style of architecture emerged that was described by *Guardian* architecture critic Jonathan Glancey as 'promulgated by brogue-footed lickspits in search of, if not knighthoods and peerages, then a biscuit-tin architecture that was somehow meant to recall the glories of Georgian design'.[58]

By 2012, when Poundbury had finally received its town centre, in the form of Queen Mother Square, this conservative village had gone fully post-modern, quoting, appropriating and pastiching. A Greco-Roman Doric colonnade marches along one side of Waitrose, on one side of the piazza, facing the yellow façade of Strathmore House. Strathmore, a palatial pile that could have been airlifted in from St Petersburg, contains eight luxury apartments beneath its royal-crested pediment. Next door stands the white stone heft of the Duchess of Cornwall, Poundbury's first hotel, based on Palladio's Convento della Carità in Venice.

Krier was the intellectual father of New Urbanism, a movement that agitates for cities made up of close, walkable communities, in which places for living, working and leisure are built side by side and integrated with one another, rather than partitioned into separate areas. Indeed, Krier had a youthful model for this project. He was raised in Luxembourg, which he described as 'a small capital city of 70,000 souls' that was 'a miracle of traditional architecture . . . My father's tailoring workshop occupied the ground floor of the townhouse, and for my primary education I hopped across the street when hearing the school bells chime from our garden.'[59] He had been a youthful devotee of Le Corbusier's modernism, but a visit to the Radiant City in Marseilles cured him. He decried modernism's congestion of the skies with high-rise towers, arguing that their horizontal corollary was suburban sprawl. Both needed to be purged from the well-designed city.

These thoughts were developed in his book *The Architecture of Community*, where Krier argued that the best, most civilised cities observe a strict relationship between their economic and cultural wealth, on the one hand, while limiting their population, on the other. If they grew, cities should become 'polycentric', composed of relatively self-sufficient quarters. To convey what he meant, Krier compared Paris to Milton Keynes:

> The whole of Paris is a pre-industrial city which still works, because it is so adaptable, something the creations of the 20th century will never be. A city like Milton Keynes cannot survive an economic crisis, or any other kind of crisis, because it is planned as a mathematically determined social and economic project. If that model collapses, the city will collapse with it.[60]

This was perhaps a little unfair on Milton Keynes.

Krier also advised on the masterplan for Seaside, a planned town on the Florida panhandle, built according to principles of New Urbanism, with walkable streets, housing and shopping in close proximity, and accessible public spaces, just like the city of

Luxembourg, where he had grown up. Since development of the eighty-acre site began in 1981, Seaside has become a victim of its own success, with rocketing housing values and transportation problems. To enjoy the urban pedestrian experience, one journalist noted, visitors drive to the centre of town.[61] Krier's dream of a walkable city like the ones he knew in Europe has become a nightmare. The region's main traffic artery, Route 30A, is now simply a parking lot jammed with tourists.

One reason Seaside is overrun with tourists is because they are drawn there by the 1999 film *The Truman Show*, which director Peter Weir made in the town. The eponymous Truman Burbank is unaware that he is living inside a reality show about himself in a town populated by actors, including the woman he thinks is his wife. Seahaven is really a vast TV set delimited by a dome. Truman's world is a simulation of the real world; but when he ultimately realises his plight and tries to escape, Truman is told by the show's producer Christof (Ed Harris) over the PA that there is 'no more truth' in the real world, and that by staying in his artificial world he will have nothing to fear. Weir's only mistake was not to hire Jean Baudrillard or Umberto Eco to do the voiceover as Christof, since this thought echoes those philosophers' ideas about how, in our post-modern era, the simulation trumps the real.

Across the state of Florida from Seaside is another master-planned post-modern town. Celebration was designed for real-life Truman Burbanks fleeing the real world. It grew from an idea by Walt Disney, who, like Krier, worried about what suburban sprawl was doing to the souls of the people who lived there. Disney sought partly to create a space into which suburbanites could escape. Disneyland and its Florida counterpart, Disney World, were his first stabs at such spaces.

In 1966, he hoped to build Epcot (the Experimental Prototype Community of Tomorrow) on the forty-five square miles of land Disney had acquired in Florida. As in Seaside, the pedestrian, not the car, was at the heart of Epcot's philosophy. Transportation would be clean, and Epcot would have no slums and no unemployment. Some 20,000 inhabitants would live in a high-tech but old-fashioned city under a vast dome, travelling from skyscraper to skyscraper by monorail.

Epcot never got built, but in the late 1990s Disney CEO Michael Eisner decided that, instead of an experimental prototype community of tomorrow, the Corporation would build Celebration. Its principles were set out in the Disney Corporation's brochure for prospective residents:

> There was once a place where neighbours greeted neighbours in the quiet of summer twilight. Where children chased fireflies. And porch swings provided easy refuge from the care of the day. The movie house showed cartoons on Saturday. The grocery store delivered. And there was one teacher who always knew you had that 'special something'. Remember that place? Perhaps from your childhood. Or maybe just from stories . . . There is a place that takes you back to that time of innocence . . . That place is here again, in a new town called Celebration.[62]

Celebration was built on swampland at the edge of Disney World. The Disney Corporation's real-estate division hired post-modern architects Robert A. M. Stern and Jaquelin T. Robertson to draw up the plan for a high-density town with five or six dwellings per acre, rather than the standard suburban one or two. There were to be 2,500 houses in a limited range of styles and colours, all within walking distance of a shopping area. There were no front lawns, in order to encourage residents to use parks and piazzas, and thereby foster community interaction. When the first residents moved in in 1996, they were happy to sign guidelines prescribing how they should live.

What incoming residents were buying into was a new city that, in post-modern fashion, disinterred and animated a purportedly ideal American past and made it live, as a rebuke to a post-war world that had taken a wrong turn. One critic explained the thinking behind Celebration: 'It was necessary to go back in order to improve the future.'[63] Modernist architects like Minoru Yamasaki and modernist city planners like Robert Moses had ruined America with soulless apartment blocks and community-destroying expressways. The ills of the modern world – crime, poverty, incivility, government overreach – could be overcome only if a new way of living, an anti-modernist one, could arise according to the principles of Léon Krier's New Urbanism. Poundbury, Seaside, Celebration and other places like them were built according to those principles.

On Main Street in Disneyland, houses were full-size on the ground floor and two-thirds the scale on the floor above. Though nominally habitable, they were not inhabited. Rather, as Eco noted, the interiors were always disguised supermarkets. In Celebration, by contrast, the toy houses of Disneyland became dwellings for real people, where they could indulge in reality the fantasy of living in golden-age America, though with modern necessities such as high-speed broadband. Disneyland and Disney World were designed to offer respite from the real world. Now Celebration offered a complete opt-out for middle-class refugees engaging in 'white flight'.

Celebration was and remains devoid of crime, poverty, state regulation and people of colour. Professor of social and cultural analysis at New York University, Andrew Ross, who spent a year living in Celebration, reported that teachers could not afford rented apartments in town, while Disney employees, often Hispanic immigrants, earning the minimum wage of $5.95 an hour, could never hope to buy into Celebration. Brent Herrington, the Celebration Company's community manager, saw the lack of cheap housing as a plus:

> What happens is, in an affordable house that is couched as an entitlement, you don't have the same kind of personal commitment and pride in your accomplishment in this new home. If people come to a place just because their name popped up when that community had a vacancy, they are not going to have the same commitment to the town. That's the part I think the residents would probably have some squeamishness about.[64]

One resident told Andrew Ross he knew he was living in a white ghetto, adding: 'I would welcome more diversity as long as it doesn't drive the prices down.' For Ross, this underscored how, in this simulacrum of 1930s America, white-flight refugees could behave as though racism did not exist:

> Today, white people are often at their most white when they believe that consciousness of race is not natural . . . white-skin privilege abides and goes unexamined when it's no longer 'natural' to think about someone's racial background and is perceived to be racist to do so. As Malcolm X pointed out, 'racism is like a Cadillac. There's a new model every year.'[65]

Ross also detected a reason why so few residents of Celebration spoke out against the failings of the town. Celebration was perceived as a good investment opportunity, and people paid above the odds and put up with the vagaries of a town not yet fully built in the hope that their houses would rise in price. What kept them quiet was not so much community spirit as a desire to keep property values from plummeting.

Famous post-modern architects were hired to bejewel Celebration with public buildings. Philip Johnson built a town hall with fifty-two thin pillars crowded together beneath a pyramid-shaped roof – as if, one critic suggested, in this Disney-created world, he was spoofing a traditional town hall building by poking fun at the need for classical or neoclassical columns to lend it grandeur. César Pelli built a pastiche of an art deco cinema from the 1930s, complete with two spires that evoked a space-age future. Robert Venturi and Denise Scott Brown built the Bank of Celebration on a corner site to resemble a 1950s-era gas station or burger joint, with a three-sided façade designed to pastiche the House of Morgan at 23 Wall Street, near the US Stock Exchange building. In true Venturi style, it was a decorated shed, with colourful stripes wrapping around the white façades and the words THE BANK OF CELEBRATION written in unmissably huge letters.

The seemingly fun, joyful, irrepressibly upbeat post-modern architecture of Celebration veiled its neoliberal politics. The rollback of the state in this little corner of Florida was so decisive that there were no elected officials. One resident, a doctor, told Andrew Ross why he was happy to live under a Disney government rather than a democratically elected one: 'I'd rather live in a civil than a political society . . . What we have here is a deconstructing of government, a rollback of politicisation. In a civil society you feel a desire to fit into a community and satisfy your neighbours. In a political society, under the heavy hand of government, you expect your neighbours to satisfy you.'[66]

Ross worried about the future of a town based on corporate management: 'When a society allows public education to be dependent on lottery funds or the passing benevolence of toy manufacturers and soda producers, it has already walked away from its democratic obligations.'[67] When things started to go wrong at Celebration – jerry-built houses, planned state-of-the-art fibre-optic cables that never arrived – those who aired grievances received no answer from the Disney Corporation. In 2004, Disney sold Celebration to Lexin Capital, a private real estate investment company.

For all that, towns built according to principles of New Urbanism like Celebration have proved popular. After two critics of New Urbanism, Douglas Frantz and Catherine Collins, lived in the town for a while and published their book, *Celebration, USA: Living in Disney's Brave New Town*, in 1999, a review by a resident on amazon.com angrily retorted:

Written by left-leaning, snivelling reporters . . . They snipe about Disney not giving away part of their profit margin to accommodate low-income people, yet didn't rent out their 'granny flat' to an underprivileged person. As true liberals the authors see corporations as responsible for everyone's welfare . . . It would be nice at least once to hear them thank Disney. Thank you Disney for your vision. Thank you Disney for risking your capital. Thank you for fighting the political battles to make Celebration possible.[68]

Similarly, in Dorset, Prince Charles's village of Poundbury has proved popular, especially with older residents, perhaps seeking relief in retirement from a noisome, ugly world beyond.

As a result, the Duchy of Cornwall, an estate with the Prince of Wales as its head, has begun developing Baudrillardian simulacra of the prince's pet project on other land it owns in England. Hence, Nansledan, a town being built near the seaside resort of Newquay in Cornwall, complete with colourful terraced houses and 'edible streets', involving herbs and fruit trees planted next to houses. Another development on Duchy land outside Truro, also in Cornwall, was built with financial assistance from Waitrose supermarket. Critics have nicknamed the former Surfbury and the latter, because of the supermarket's support, Trolleybury, and accused both of turning back the clock in terms of design. But time travel has always been part of the post-modern architectural repertoire.

When Prince Charles made his famous speech in 1984 attacking the proposed extension of the National Gallery designed by Ahrends Burton Koralek, he said: 'What is proposed is like a monstrous carbuncle on the face of a much loved and elegant friend.'[69] ABK had won a competition to redevelop the bomb site next to the National Gallery in 1982, and had been given the green light to start work; but Charles turned it back to red. The year after his speech, a new, closed competition was launched, thanks largely to a £50 million donation from the Sainsbury family. The prince leaned in favour of a determinedly camp, post-modern design by Robert Venturi and Denise Scott Brown, which promptly won the competition and was built in 1991. Once more, the unelected royal was having a profound, and post-modern, influence on what Britain looked like.

It was a strange denouement. Venturi and Scott Brown were the architects who had argued two decades earlier that we had much to learn from Las Vegas, and called on architects to be more receptive to the tastes and values of 'common' people who liked the gimcrack pastiching of the Nevada city's Strip. Amazingly, the architects who eulogised Vegas were the people the conservative prince trusted to design an extension to the National Gallery – what he called 'a much loved and elegant friend'.

It's not clear whether the prince liked the results. Certainly he and Venturi clashed over a false Corinthian column that the latter wanted to add as a decorative element to his extension. 'A column as an architectural feature should act as a support', the prince, a trustee of the Gallery, told a board meeting in 1987. It was a remark that showed, at an intellectual level, that the prince did not understand Venturi's post-modern architectural theory – in particular his distinction between buildings that were ducks and those that were decorated sheds. The National Gallery extension Venturi designed was very much the latter, since its Corinthian column did not – and perhaps should not – support anything.

Venturi threatened to quit, and the column stayed. After the extension was completed, in 1991, Prince Charles wrote in the preface to a book about the new wing: 'The debate will now rage, I'm sure, about how good a building Mr Venturi has given us. I will leave that to others to decide – though I will say that I think the interiors are very promising.'[70] One way or another, we have all had to accommodate ourselves to post-modernism, even princes.

5

We Are Living in a Material World, 1983:

Sophie Calle | Apple Macintosh | Madonna

I

One summer's day in 1983, Sophie Calle found an address book on the Rue des Martyrs in Paris. Even though the owner's name and address were on the first page, the French artist decided not to return it immediately. Instead, she had an idea. She had been invited by the French newspaper *Libération* to produce a series of columns during the summer. This address book might give her a subject for those articles. She decided to make a portrait of the owner of the book, a certain Pierre D., by contacting his friends and building up a picture of him from their accounts.

What Calle plotted was appropriation art, dallying at the edge of legality and morality. Or, seen from another perspective, it was a new form of creativity, a post-modern one, that involves playfully subverting norms, particularly the idea that anyone has a right to privacy. In this, 'The Address Book', as Calle's project was called, prefigured what Apple, Facebook, Amazon and Google did to such success: amassing data on often unknowing or unwilling subjects.

At the time, Calle's project had a particular resonance as the Cold War accelerated, along with fears that the totalitarian society envisaged in George Orwell's novel *Nineteen Eighty-Four* might be realised. At the time, Big Brother was imagined as working from the Kremlin, not corporate offices in Cupertino, where Steve Jobs launched his Apple Mac computer in 1984 by proclaiming that his invention might free us from totalitarian overreach.

True, the Apple Mac may not have been the most important technological breakthrough of the time (1984 was the year British geneticist Alec Jeffreys developed genetic fingerprinting, allowing persons to be identified by means of their DNA, and also the year the NASA space shuttle Discovery embarked on its maiden voyage to deploy communications satellites in orbit); but its release catalysed a surveillance revolution beyond Orwell's imaginings. Sophie Calle's art project was a forerunner of that revolution.

She photocopied the address book, returned it to its owner, and set to work. 'Thus, I will get to know this man through his friends and acquaintances', she wrote in her first column for *Libération*. 'I will try to discover who he is without ever meeting him, and I will try to produce a portrait of him over an undetermined length of time that will depend on the willingness of his friends to talk about him – and on the turns taken by the events.'[1] Instead of a portrait painter sitting face to face with a subject and trying to depict her in terms flattering enough to fulfil the commission, Calle sought a new form of portraiture that broke the contract between subject and artist, and might be more truthful, if less direct.

But Sophie Calle is an unusual artist, one for whom stalking, seduction and self-disclosure are part of her creative repertoire. Born in Paris in 1953 to Monique, a critic, and Robert, an oncologist who was also a renowned art collector and director of a contemporary art gallery, she decided not to go to art school, but instead to study with the post-modern philosopher Jean Baudrillard. 'My father agreed he would pay me a sum of money if I got my diploma. But I didn't want to finish it. I told Baudrillard. He said, "Don't worry, I'll pass off some other student's exam papers as yours. You'll get your diploma."' The professor who famously argued that the first Gulf War did not take place ensured that Sophie Calle got a diploma for work she never did. 'I can tell this story now because Baudrillard is dead,' Calle told me in 2009.

What did her father think? 'I got my diploma,' she shrugged. 'How was not his concern.' After travelling to China, Mexico and the United States, she returned to Paris and decided to become an artist. Why, I asked her. 'To seduce my father.' Did you succeed? 'Oh yes. He collected pop art, and a lot of it consisted of photographs with accompanying text.' Just like your work? 'Just like mine,' she agreed. 'I came back to seduce him. I wanted to do something that made him happy for me.'[2]

She said that, bored and friendless back in Paris, she started following people in the street. 'Establishing rules and following them is restful. If you follow someone, you don't have to wonder where you're going to eat. They take you to their restaurant. The choice is made for you.'

One of her first art projects originated when a friend asked if she could sleep in Calle's bed. 'That made me think it would be fun to have someone in bed all the time.' So she asked friends and strangers to sleep in the bed for eight hours; one participant thought there was going to be an orgy. It sounds like a conceptual art project. 'It wasn't', retorted Calle when I put this to her. 'It only became so when the wife of a critic told him about it. He came along. He said, "Is this art?" and I said, "It could be."' She took photographs and wrote down everything everyone said. The result was 'The Sleepers' – text and photographs that could readily have hung on her father's walls.

One of the greater truths Calle's art discloses is how we change how we present ourselves according to our audience. 'We are all just actors trying to control and manage our public image', wrote Erving Goffman. 'We act based on how others might see us.'[3] We are, post-modernists realise, multiple.

The self-performance of the subject in 'The Address Book' became clear in some of the interviews Calle recorded with friends and acquaintances who agreed to meet her. Pierre D.'s Italian friend Enzo U. agreed to meet Calle while passing through Paris: 'He represented the burlesque and the romantic for me; he was the first of the new romantics. Then his image became more cultural. He started writing film criticism and scripts. His personality developed what could be called a "dirty side." ' By contrast, Sylvie B. told Calle: 'Physically, he's gorgeous. Thirtyish, white hair. A way of dressing with a certain proportion of intentional clownishness that he totally accepts.' Paul B. said: 'He is extremely intelligent. He is a real character. But he did not know how to "sell" himself. It is as a character that he failed.'[4]

To flesh out the portrait, Calle visited Pierre D.'s apartment building when he was out of town, but did not get into his flat. She rang people in the book to arrange meetings in person – only then would she tell them to whom the address book belonged. But when she rang Louis S. in Boulogne-sur-Mer, things did not go to plan. He yelled at her: 'I'll have no part in this! It's an outrage! Tell me his name! Tell me his name right now! I want to warn him!' Calle hung up.

'Why did that man refuse to understand me, to listen to me?' she wrote of Louis S. 'I can't take his refusal.'[5] It's as if Calle thought there was nothing wrong in plundering a stranger's personal data. But the France in which she worked on 'The Address Book' is not Palo Alto. And so her surprise at the outrage about her intrusion into Pierre D.'s private life is itself surprising. The French state has defended privacy more vigorously than many other countries. In 2008, a limitation to the right to privacy arose when a woman objected to the use of her image by the photographer François-Marie Banier in his book *Perdre la Tête*. An appeals court decreed that the right to control one's image must yield when a photograph contributes to the exchange of ideas and opinions, deemed 'indispensable' to a democratic society.[6] Was Calle's portrait of Pierre D. justified because she was creating a work of art?

When the subject of Calle's art project discovered these articles on his return from a trip filming wildlife in Norway, he was furious. Disclosing his identity as Pierre Baudry, he threatened to sue her and demanded, bizarrely, that *Libération* publish nude photos of her in a retaliatory invasion of privacy. In a sense, Calle had done to Baudry what male artists have done to women for centuries – namely, turned him into an object. So, insisting on her appearing nude in the same paper that had disclosed personal details about him looks like an attempt to revert to the old order whereby women are on the receiving end of the male gaze, ideally minus their clothes.

In her art, Calle often seems to be turning the tables on men, disempowering them against their will. She becomes the hunter, they the hunted. In 1980, for example, Calle followed a man she called Henri B. around Paris and tried to take his photograph. But she lost sight of him. That evening, she ran into him at a party, where he told her he was going to Venice. So she followed him there, phoned hundreds of hotels until she found out where he was staying, and then persuaded a woman who lived opposite to let her photograph his comings and goings from her window. The resulting book, *Suite Vénitienne*, included diary entries such as these:

> 9am: As I did yesterday, I settle down at Dr Z's window. I leave at 11am without having seen him.
>
> 11.20am: Piazza San Marco I have my picture taken in front of the church by a local photographer. In a blonde wig, my out-stretched hand full of seeds for the pigeons, strangers watching me pose, I'm ashamed. What if he saw me?[7]

Opposite these diary entries is the photograph of Calle in a ludicrous blonde wig to conceal her dark hair, as if she was playing the role of a stalker or spy badly on purpose: she looks like nothing so much as someone trying to hide their identity, and thus failing. Perhaps Henri B. did see Sophie Calle in Venice, or at least saw a very suspicious woman in an ill-fitting wig, hat and raincoat spying on him, but pretended not to notice.

That is, if Henri B. even existed; after all, all we know from the photographs is that Calle, or someone looking very like her though in a bad disguise, was in Venice. But maybe there was no Henri B. And perhaps all the situations she describes so meticulously and coolly are really figments of her imagination. At one point in the book, she shadows Henri B. as he walks around Venice with a woman. She writes: 'He points toward the canal as if to show something to the woman. I take a picture in the same direction.' Not of the couple, but of their view. And yet, from this absence, we are supposed to infer their presence.

In this, Calle was playing another role – that of the post-modern unreliable narrator, a character far from the omniscient author of realist fiction who controls the narrative and leads you to the singular truth of the book's revelation. For her, truth is multiple: it changes with the beholder's perspective.

During her thirteen-day Venetian stake-out, Calle behaved much like Stendhal's hero Fabrizio del Dongo. In *The Charterhouse of Parma*, Fabrizio is forever dressing himself up in ludicrous whiskers and other disguises, the better to glimpse his unattainable beloved Clélia Conti unobserved. 'I must not forget that I don't have any amorous feelings toward Henri B.', Calle wrote. 'The impatience with which I await his arrival, the fear of that encounter, these symptoms aren't really a part of me.'[8] Such symptoms, though, are typical of one in love, and it sounds from what Calle told herself as if, in the process of making art, she had alchemically created something that resembled love, merely by following rules.[9] 'I like being in control and I like losing control', Calle said. 'Following the rules of others is restful. A way not to have to think – to be trapped in a game and to follow it.' It is, as Schopenhauer put it, in such moments as these that we are 'set free from the miserable striving of the will; we keep the Sabbath of the penal servitude of willing; the wheel of Ixion stands still'.[10]

To live authentically is to experience what Sartre called the 'anguish of freedom',[11] the burden of responsibility to which the free person is shackled, forever having to choose who she wants to be and the life she wants to lead. Calle shrugs off this burden in her art along with the Sartrean insistence on what it is to be an authentic human, surrendering choices to others. Sartre died in 1980, and so did not experience her art; but had he done so he might well have seen it as an example of bad faith refusing the responsibility that freedom imposes on humans.

The French surrealists of the 1930s, notably André Breton, were excited by the notion of chance, and of will-less behaviours such as automatic writing or wandering the city without any aim: anything that subverted the tyranny of the will, the boring norms of freedom and responsibility. In the 1950s and '60s, the radical group of artists called the Situationist International embellished the Baudelairean notion of the *flâneur*, championing what the group's leading theorist Guy Debord called the *dérive*, which he defined as 'a mode of experimental behaviour linked to the conditions of urban society: a technique of rapid passage through varied ambiances'.[12] This technique, whereby the participants step outside their everyday relations for an unplanned walk through the city, was supposed by Debord to be a means of resistance to the false desires manufactured under capitalism.[13]

Through such psychogeographical *dérives*, we might encounter the spontaneous, the unexpected, the irrational – pop-up antidotes to what Debord called the society of the spectacle, wherein false desires are created and then fulfilled by passive victims of capitalism who have been duped into desiring what they are given. And what they are given is easy to produce, is profitable, and reduces humans to manipulable drones.

All these spectres stalk Calle, as she herself stalks male prey in *Suite Vénitienne* and 'The Address Book'. The traces of these avant-gardists' loathing for bourgeois values, and their strategies to escape the tedium and uniformity capitalism imposes on those who live under it, are echoed in her work. What Sartre took to be bad faith – namely, evading the responsibilities and anxieties of freedom – each of these precursors, and Calle herself, took to be ways of resisting. Yet there is no sense in her work that there is a more authentic way of being. Her art is critique rather than search for utopia beyond the dystopia of today. Sophie Calle's name, it's worth pointing out, means – as she often points out in interviews – street wisdom.

At its most political, Calle's art subverts male power and intrudes into others' privacy. It consists of a series of subversive games that challenge not only what art is, what counts as a portrait, how we present and hide ourselves from others, but also power structures, and not just male ones. Indeed, privacy itself might be thought of as akin to property – a commodity amassed and defended most assiduously by the powerful, whose loss provokes the biggest outcry from those who have most invested in the existing late-capitalist order. From this perspective, which I suspect is the perspective of Calle, Proudhon was right to say property is theft, but he should have added: privacy is theft, too.

In 1994 the novelist Paul Auster gave Calle a list of things to do in New York in order to make the city more cheerful. This project arose because Auster had created a character for his novel *Leviathan* inspired by Calle. She invited him to 'invent a fictive character which I would attempt to resemble'.[14] He invited her to roam the streets of New York armed with his instructions on how to behave. She must smile at and talk to strangers, help beggars and homeless people. Yet again, when Calle hit the streets to fulfil this contract, she had surrendered agency to another, or at least to the rules of Auster's game – even though, of course, her agency was demonstrated at the outset, since she had asked Auster to invent a role she could play. The results of her *dérive* included, she wrote, '125 smiles given for 72 received . . . 154 minutes of conversation'.[15] She filled a phone box with flowers and left a notepad for users to record their opinions. Some were abusive, some sweet. But, again, she was surrendering her will to another's rules.

Most striking for us is what she did in 1980, when she took part in an art project in the South Bronx, where she surrendered her will once more. Between 2 p.m. and 5 p.m. one day in 1980, she stopped passers-by to take her somewhere of their choice. This was a time when the Bronx was suffering from violence, destruction, fires and deprivation. The result, called 'The Bronx', is a collection of evocative photos and written accounts of her day in a neighbourhood falling apart.

One man took her to his ruined home, yet another showed her a sapling growing in the wasteland. Calle did not really explore the creativity that was exploding in the South Bronx at the time, so it was perhaps fitting that local artists imposed themselves on her art so as not to be culturally erased by this interloping Frenchwoman. On the night before the show opened at the Fashion Mode Gallery in the Bronx, someone broke in and tagged the works. Like Lee Quiñones spraying a subway car, they used her art as a blank canvas. Calle did not mind the erasure of her art. She left the tags as an intervention by 'an unexpected collaborator'. In this she was the proper descendant of the situationists, finding in chance an unexpected, serendipitously valuable experience.

It was no wonder, given the risks she exposed herself to in such *dérives*, that her friend and former teacher Jean Baudrillard worried whether Calle had a death wish in her art. Writing of *Suite Vénitienne*, Baudrillard wondered what she wanted from Henri B.: 'Did she secretly desire that he kill her or, finding the pursuit intolerable (especially since she wasn't consciously expecting anything, least of all a sexual adventure), that he throw himself upon her to do her violence?'

Calle thought she was turning the tables on men, perhaps, but the tables could be turned again. The murder Baudrillard had in mind was a symbolic one: 'It consists of following a person step by step, of erasing his traces along the way, and no one can live without traces. If you leave no traces, or someone takes it upon himself to wipe them out, you are as good as dead. That's what makes anyone turn around after a while when being followed.'

Baudrillard described Sophie Calle as 'the powerful blonde figure behind the scenes [who] leaves no traces as she follows him: she has lost herself in the other's traces. But she steals his traces. She photographs him . . . These are not souvenir snapshots of a presence, but rather shots of an absence, the

absence of the followed, that of the follower; that of their recip-
rocal absence.'[16] There is not one murder victim in 'The Address
Book', but two: Calle erases both her quarry and herself.

We can see now why Pierre Baudry's wish in demanding that
the artist appear nude in the newspaper was lame. He asserted
equivalence between having your privacy intruded upon and the
humiliation of appearing naked in the newspaper. In order to
restore his manhood after his humiliation by a woman in a
newspaper, he attempted to restore the heteronormative order
that she had overturned by her art project. His revenge, if that
is the right word, was both sexist and boring. He interpreted her
work of art, 'The Address Book', as humiliation of him, rather
than as art, or as an exploration of what portraiture might be in
our fragmented, post-modern age.

Baudry, no doubt, was trying to give Calle a sense of how it
felt to be publicly humiliated; but if he had known anything
about her, he would have realised that was fatuous. Calle used
to work as a stripper in Pigalle, Paris's red light district, and so
was professionally, so far as anyone can be, used to being on the
receiving end of the male gaze while naked. Indeed, she had
published a book called *The Striptease* featuring photos of her
unclothed at work juxtaposed with cards her parents had
received from friends when their daughter was born. 'They all
hoped Sophie will be a nice girl', she told me. Calle agreed to
Pierre's demand, and the nude picture appeared. 'He was trying
to be very aggressive. He disliked what I did', she told me.

Calle claimed she worked as a stripper because she needed the
money, but also as a self-imposed test. 'I asked myself, "Am I
refusing just because other feminists would oppose me?" And
I realised I feared being psychologically destroyed by the look of
others. But why did I think it OK to be a nude model for
artists?' Stripping made her feel powerful: 'To me they [her
clients] were pathetic, and I looked at them with a look of
contempt. I had made a style of this contempt and they were
paralysed.'[17] Once more, Sophie Calle was enjoying following
the rules of the game, overcoming her fear of psychological

destruction by the look of others (and, as it turned out, working on an art project that would bring her fame). If nakedness is the best disguise, then the naked stripper with her look of contempt is, of all the people in a Pigalle strip club, disclosing the least about herself. Her nudity is what she is not; unlike the lubricious punters, she's not there. Almost as if she were trying to feel nothing, or using art to escape – or, better, erase – herself. This is what makes Calle's art post-modern.

In 2007, Calle was dumped by email. Circumloquacious, pseudo-literary and self-serving, it ended: 'Take care of yourself.' And so she took care of herself. In 'Prenez soin de vous' ('Take care of yourself', 2007), she invited 107 women to analyse the email from their professional perspectives. A psychiatrist, a lexicographer, a crossword-setter, a psychologist, a lawyer and a Talmudic scholar were among the women who helped build what one critic called a towering babel of feminine scorn – though a very funny one – which showed Pierre Baudry how revenge was done: not through demanding the publication of naked pictures of the person who purportedly wronged you, but through merciless textual deconstruction.

Viewed thus, Sophie Calle is an organic intellectual, a revolutionary fighting not at the barricades but through art that challenges bourgeois norms and values that seem to be common sense. In stalking her male prey, she was attacking the very basis of the bourgeois French revolutionary heritage, showing that what seemed to be natural was really socially constructed and oppressive. If Pierre D. and Henri B. did not see matters that way when she intruded upon their privacy, that was because they were part of the problem. She was asserting something that the French tradition scarcely paid heed of: not the rights of man, but the right of woman to subvert the rights of man.

II

A few months after Sophie Calle stalked Pierre Baudry, Apple launched its first Macintosh personal computer. The launch heralded a new age in which technology – or so the faithful proclaimed – would free us from domination by overweening states. In that age, though, we would be pursued into places that Sophie Calle might have feared to tread. Our very psyches could be plundered for data. For critics, the age of Apple was one in which we desired our own domination by global cyber-oligarchies whose function was akin to the Christian religion.

Umberto Eco, not entirely joking, argued that Apple resembled the Catholic church and had a Jesuitical genius for developing user-friendly interfaces to keep the faithful abased before its altar. Meanwhile, its main rival Microsoft was Protestant:

> The Macintosh is counter-reformist and has been influenced by the 'ratio studiorum' of the Jesuits. It is cheerful, friendly, conciliatory, it tells the faithful how they must proceed step by step to reach – if not the Kingdom of Heaven – the moment in which their document is printed. It is catechistic: the essence of revelation is dealt with via simple formulae and sumptuous icons. Everyone has a right to salvation. DOS [Microsoft's operating system] is Protestant, or even Calvinistic. It allows free interpretation of scripture, demands difficult personal decisions, imposes a subtle hermeneutics upon the user, and takes for granted the idea that not all can reach salvation. To make the system work you need to interpret the program yourself: a long way from the baroque community of revellers, the user is closed within the loneliness of his own inner torment.[18]

Certainly, Jobs envisaged the Apple Mac, which was launched in 1984, as salvation, if by salvation one meant deliverance from woeful technology. It had been the result of a small research team he headed at Apple in the early 1980s to produce what he called 'the most insanely great computer', featuring a revelatory gizmo called a mouse, by means of which users could navigate an unprecedentedly graphics-rich interface more easily than with mere keyboard commands.[19]

The Apple Mac made its first public appearance during a commercial break in the 1984 Super Bowl, in an advertisement made by Ridley Scott, director of such nightmarish films as *Blade Runner* and *Alien*. Glum, grey workers (played by extras whom Scott, filming in the UK, had reportedly hired from Britain's skinhead community) sat in a vast grey hall listening to a portentous Big Brother declaiming from a huge screen:

> Today, we celebrate the first glorious anniversary of the Information Purification Directives. We have created, for the first time in all history, a garden of pure ideology – where each worker may bloom, secure from the pests purveying contradictory truths. Our Unification of Thoughts is more powerful a weapon than any fleet or army on earth. We are one people, with one will, one resolve, one cause. Our enemies shall talk themselves to death, and we will bury them with their own confusion. We *shall* prevail![20]

But, as Big Brother set out his philosophy, there was a disturbance in the hall. A young, blonde woman started to run towards the screen carrying a sledgehammer. You might think she looks like an escapee from a Leni Riefenstahl movie about the unstoppable athletic prowess of the *übermenschen*; but that would be to miss copywriter Steve Hayden's point. Unlike the glum drones she passed as she ran, this woman was in colour, with bright orange shorts and a white singlet bearing a line drawing of the Apple Mac on it. Four goons with nightsticks pursued our heroine, but they could not stop her hurling the sledgehammer into Big Brother's telescreen.

The successful candidate for the role, Anya Major, was a model and discus-throwing athlete. In the ad, her sledgehammer hits the target. Suddenly, the gloom is bathed in healing light.

'On January 24th', another voiceover announced, this time not from the sinister Big Brother, 'Apple Computer will introduce the Macintosh. And you'll see why 1984 won't be like [Orwell's] *Nineteen Eighty-Four*.' The screen faded to black as the voice-over ended, and the rainbow Apple logo appeared.

A few months after the ad was broadcast, George Orwell's estate sent a cease-and-desist letter to Apple and the Chiat/Day advertising agency, claiming that the commercial breached copyright. It had little effect. Indeed, the commercial has since been hailed as a masterpiece, winning many awards and in 1995 topping *Advertising Age*'s chart of the best commercials.

One of the reasons it won so many awards is that it tapped into contemporary American fears that computers could enslave the masses and invade their privacy. A Harris poll, taken the previous September, found that 68 per cent of Americans believed 'the use of computers had to be sharply restricted in the future in order to preserve privacy'.[21] At the time, the *New York Times* reported, the Internal Revenue Service had begun testing the use of computerised lifestyle information, such as the types of cars people owned, to track down errant taxpayers, while an FBI advisory committee recommended that the bureau computer system include data on people who, though not charged with wrongdoing, had associated with drug traffickers.[22]

In this context, Apple's Super Bowl advertisement effectively suggested that large computers, such as those manufactured by International Business Machines (IBM), then the dominant computer maker, were part of an Orwellian surveillance state, while personal computers manufactured by Apple were a revolution against such computerised Big Brothers. In a 1985 *Playboy* interview, Steve Jobs cast IBM as the great enemy of innovation, and framed the battle as nothing less than a battle of light versus dark in the race for the future. 'If, for some reason, we make some giant mistakes and IBM wins, my personal feeling is that we are going to enter sort of a computer Dark Ages for about 20 years', he said. 'Once IBM gains control of a market sector, they almost always stop innovation. They prevent innovation from happening.'[23]

Some experts were sceptical. 'The notion that a personal computer will set you free is appalling', Joseph Weizenbaum, computer science professor at Massachusetts Institute of Technology, told the *New York Times*. 'The ad seems to say the remedy to too much technology is more technology. It's like selling someone a pistol to defend himself in the event of nuclear war.'[24] What the Apple Mac represented, at least for its enthusiasts, was the potential for a democratic social revolution that would undermine state power and harness the power of the people. 'The Apple ad expresses a potential of small computers', one communications expert told the *New York Times*. 'This potential may not automatically flow from the company's product. But if enough people held a shared intent, grass-roots electronic bulletin boards (through which computer users share messages) might result in better balancing of political power.'[25]

Steve Jobs was an unlikely person to revolutionise the computer industry. He was a college dropout who visited India seeking spiritual enlightenment from Zen masters, and cited as his leading intellectual influence a venerable West Coast hippie. His parents, Joanne Carole Schieble and Syrian immigrant Abdulfattah Jandali, put Steve up for adoption not long after his birth in San Francisco in 1955. He was adopted by used-car salesman Paul Jobs and his wife Clara. Raised in Cupertino, California, Jobs met Steve Wozniak while at high school. Wozniak was a technical wizard with whom Jobs collaborated on making and selling what they marketed as 'blue boxes' – gizmos that users could use to piggy-back on phone lines in order to make free (and illegal) calls.[26]

After dropping out of college in 1972, Jobs worked as an engineer at videogames maker Atari, where he was relegated to night shifts because of his reportedly poor hygiene. After returning from India, where he had received guidance from a Zen Buddhist master, Jobs met up again with Wozniak, whom he urged to quit his job so that the pair could make computers. Apple Computers was born in Jobs's parents' garage in 1976. The pair named their first product, a version of Wozniak's circuit board, Apple I, and sold it for $666.66 – a sum that allegedly had no diabolical numerological significance (Wozniak just liked to repeat numbers). Apple II was a home computer featuring colour monitor and keyboard, both unusual at the time. In 1980, when Apple went public, the twenty-five-year-old Jobs made an estimated $217 million.

However, behind this story of Jobs's business acumen and corporate innovation was a countercultural figure called Stewart Brand. When Jobs gave a commencement address at Stanford University in 2005, he eulogised Brand for founding 'an amazing publication called the *Whole Earth Catalog*', which he called 'one of the bibles of my generation'. 'It was created by a fellow named Stewart Brand not far from here in Menlo Park, and he brought it to life with his poetic touch . . . It was sort of like Google in paperback form, 35 years before Google came along: it was idealistic, and overflowing with neat tools and great notions.'[27]

Brand came to public attention in the mid 1960s, with LSD-laced, proto-hippie gatherings in California. Along with *One Flew Over the Cuckoo's Nest* author Ken Kesey, he performed a multimedia presentation called 'America Needs Indians'. In 1968 he launched the *Whole Earth Catalog*, an encyclopaedia of items for people setting up communes: home weaving kits, potter's wheels, outdoor gear. But it was also essential reading for what became known as the counterculture, full of the ideas of Buckminster Fuller and Marshall McLuhan. In 1964 McLuhan wrote: 'Today we have extended our central nervous system itself in a global embrace, abolishing both space and time as far as our planet is concerned.'[28] The global embrace and the death of space and time that McLuhan envisaged would find their leading expression in the internet.

The *Whole Earth Catalog* was, for Brand, a combination of Diderot's *Encylopédie* and the LL Bean catalogue. The former was fuelled by the idea that knowledge had been kept from the people by aristocrats. But Brand's leading inspiration was Buckminster Fuller. 'Fuller said if all the politicians died this week it would be a nuisance, but if all the scientists and engineers in the world died it would be catastrophic. So where's the real juice here? . . . You can't change human nature, but you can change tools, you can change techniques.' And that way 'you can change civilisation'.[29]

On the cover of the first catalogue was a photograph of the whole earth, which Brand had lobbied NASA to release, and which became an iconic image for the environmental movement. The catalogue sold 2.5 million copies, and entranced tech people like Jobs. Brand was a post-modernist before the term was invented. He took influences from different parts of America – the art world, farmers, academic visionaries – and synthesised them into one ethos. He crowdsourced later editions of the *WEC*, asking readers to recommend other products to feature. And this open-source mentality governed what he did next. In 1972 he wrote a piece for *Rolling Stone* announcing the emergence of a new outlaw hacker culture. While in the 1960s computers had seemed like the ultimate establishment device – IBM and the government used them to subordinate people to punch-cards – in the 1970s, Brand imagined they could be used to launch a consciousness revolution.

Brand thought they were personal tools to build neural communities that would blow the minds of mainstream America. In his Stanford address, Steve Jobs told students how the *Whole Earth Catalog* had changed his worldview:

> It was the mid-1970s, and I was your age. On the back cover of their final issue was a photograph of an early morning country road, the kind you might find yourself hitchhiking on if you were so adventurous. Beneath it were the words: 'Stay Hungry. Stay Foolish.' It was their farewell message as they signed off. Stay Hungry. Stay Foolish. And I have always wished that for myself.[30]

There was more to Steve Jobs than hippie innovator, however. He loved to launch his new products wearing a black turtleneck and blue jeans, as if to say: 'I'm not a suit, and we don't make products for suits.' On one hand, Jobs was performing the role of countercultural icon; but, on the other, he turned the release of a new gadget into a quasi-religious event, with Apple acolytes lining up like pilgrims at Lourdes, each hoping to be cured not of some infirmity, but of a desire that could only be assuaged by shelling out for a 64GB iPod or an iPhone equipped with a voice-activated assistant.

Umberto Eco was right – Apple was Catholic. Indeed, that thought was picked up by Byung-Chul Han, who would later describe another of Jobs's inventions, the iPhone, as a modern rosary that is handheld confessional and effective surveillance apparatus in one. 'Both the rosary and the smartphone serve the purpose of self-monitoring and control', Han explained. 'Power operates more effectively when it delegates surveillance to discrete individuals.'[31]

In this sense, not only was Steve Jobs a brilliant innovator; he was also thoroughly post-modern. Jobs's post-modernism consisted in making us desire our own domination. He was selling conformity masquerading as personal liberation, and Apple was monetising what appeared countercultural.

A year after the successful launch of the Mac, though, Jobs was ousted from Apple. After Apple, he made computers for higher education and corporations. Among NeXT Computing's customers was scientist Tim Berners-Lee, who created the World Wide Web in the early 1990s. In 1986, Jobs also bought a small computer graphics division from filmmaker George Lucas's Lucasfilm Ltd, renaming the company Pixar. He sank $70 million of his fortune into it. In 1995, Pixar had a hit with *Toy Story*, the first feature-length computer-animated film, which was followed by other lucrative movies including *Up*, *Finding Nemo* and *Toy Story* sequels, prompting the Disney Corporation to buy Pixar.

Apple, which had foundered in Jobs's absence, bought NeXT Computing. As a result, Jobs became a billionaire and returned to Apple in triumph as special advisor. By 1997 he had mounted a successful boardroom coup and become chief executive. In that role he, along with British designer Jonathan Ive, was responsible for the creation of the iPod (launched in 2001) and the iPhone (2007) – two of the most successful personal technology products of the new millennium. The second coming of Steve Jobs (as one book was entitled) enabled the billionaire to present himself as a convention-bucking visionary whose genius could revitalise whatever industry he involved himself in – be it computers, films or mobile phones.[32]

This astute merger of cunning self-presentation and corporate branding reached its apogee with Apple's 'Think Different' ad campaign, which ran from 1997 to 2002 and responded implicitly to IBM's slogan 'Think'. The ad yoked together figures as disparate as Einstein and Gandhi to promote the idea of individual genius liberating humans from their shackles. Jobs, ran the implicit suggestion, was the latest in a historical line of liberators – though the ad-busters who scrawled over Apple's billboards thought otherwise. For them, Jobs wasn't a liberator, but a great dictator.

When he died in 2011, Jobs's legacy was ironically marked in Hong Kong. Demonstrators wearing Steve Jobs masks and dressed in black turtlenecks and jeans pretended to present new iPads outside an Apple store. In fact, they were protesting against conditions at Foxconn factories in China, where Apple products are made. Steve Jobs's legacy was not just cool products for countercultural hipsters, but anti-suicide netting beneath the windows of dormitories for exploited Foxconn workers.

Jobs's genius consisted not just in founding Apple and revolutionising personal technology, but in creating a liberation theology that, in the next few decades, converted many into believing computers and phones could deliver power to the people. That article of faith depended not just on hardware like Apple Macs, but on what came to be called the internet.

The internet was conceived not as a tool that could give power to the people, but as a means of ensuring the state could function in the event of nuclear war. The internet was developed in future decades not by buzz-cut grunts, however, but by hippie freaks more likely to spike the military's guns with flowers. People like Stewart Brand, who not only set up the *Whole Earth Catalog*, but in 1985 helped create the Whole Earth 'Lectronic Link (WELL), an early online platform by means of which computer enthusiasts in the Bay Area could meet and share ideas. WELL consisted of one computer in the Whole Earth office to which computers could connect by means of a dial-up modem, and have real-time conversations. Brand said: 'As it turned out psychedelic drugs, communes, and Buckminster Fuller domes were a dead end, but computers were an avenue to realms beyond our dreams.'[33]

The countercultural, egalitarian dreams of the likes of Stewart Brand and Tim Berners-Lee were shared by later proselytisers for how the internet and the World Wide Web could change the world for good. Wikipedia, the open-source online encyclo-paedia created by Jimmy Wales and Larry Sanger in 2001, was the bastard offspring of a failed collaborative effort to create a free online encyclopaedia called Nupedia, to which anyone could submit an article that would be reviewed in a seven-stage process by expert editors. That process proved cumbersome, so Nupedia's founders were introduced to a 'wiki' – a web page that could be edited by anyone with access to it. Any semi-literate jerk with an Apple personal computer could write the entry on, say, Heisenberg's uncertainty principle. The hope was that someone who knew a little more about the principle would read the first entry and, horrified, correct it. Another would fix spelling errors, and others still would add new material. Even efforts at sabotage would be corrected, so long as (and this was the important part) users cared enough.

Wikis and other web-based social tools encouraged extreme openness and decentralisation while discouraging the exercise of authority. But, instead of revivifying democracy and facilitat-ing greater equality, the web consolidated power in the hands of the few. In 2010, *Wired* magazine printed an all-orange cover with four black words that read: 'The Web Is Dead'. It argued that Berners-Lee's beautiful egalitarian vision had been supplanted by a commercialised online hell – or paradise (depending on your politics).

Apple spearheaded this transformation. Jobs in particular beguiled his customers with the purported countercultural cachet of his products. They seemed to promise an end to oppressive surveillance, while in fact not only making it more subtle and effective, but also making capitalists very rich. This, to put it mildly, is not what Steve Jobs's hippie mentors had had in mind. Neoliberalism sought to revive capitalism with a seductive, populist, market-based culture of differentiated consumerism and individual libertarianism. Steve Jobs made it happen.

Social critic Rebecca Solnit argued that Apple's Super Bowl ad of 1984 did not so much herald a new era of liberation as an age of unprecedented conformity and oppression:

> I want to yell at that liberatory young woman with her sledge-hammer: 'Don't do it!' Apple is not different. That industry is going to give rise to innumerable forms of triviality and misogyny, to the concentration of wealth and the dispersal of mental concentration. To suicidal, underpaid Chinese factory workers whose reality must be like that of the shuffling workers in the commercial. If you think a crowd of people staring at one screen is bad, wait until you have created a world in which billions of people stare at their own screens even while walking, driving, eating in the company of friends – all of them eternally elsewhere.[34]

III

On 14 September 1984, Madonna Louise Ciccone emerged from a seventeen-foot-tall wedding cake wearing a white wedding dress, a bustier, and belt buckle inscribed with the words Boy Toy, and began to sing her new single, 'Like a Virgin'. Like Sophie Calle, she was changing what it was to be a woman and subverting patriarchal norms in her art.

Conservatives had already called for the song to be banned. Its lyrics may have suggested to them an intolerably sexually promiscuous woman finding spiritual renewal in the fantasy of being a virgin. The meaning of the song provoked a welter of speculation. At the start of the 1992 film *Reservoir Dogs*, the colour-coded jewel thieves discuss the song in great detail at a diner before their disastrous heist. Mr Pink, played by Quentin Tarantino, offers his interpretation: 'Like a Virgin is all about a girl who digs a guy with a big dick. The whole song is a metaphor for big dicks.'[35]

When Madonna met Tarantino at a party for *Reservoir Dogs*, though, she demurred about Mr Pink's interpretation. 'So I asked her, "Am I right about the song?" because I *really* believed that was the subtext,' Tarantino recalled. 'She said, "No, it's about love, it's about a girl who's been messed over and she finally meets this one man who loves her." She signed my *Erotica* album, "To Quentin. It's not about dick, it's about love. Madonna."'[36]

That September, in 1985, the little known twenty-six-year-old singer had been booked to perform the song at MTV's first Video Music Awards, as a hip new counterweight to the ageing presenters Dan Ackroyd and Bette Midler. It was a pivotal pop-cultural moment: the multinational cable channel MTV, whose staple content was pop videos, had been launched three years earlier, and thereby made pop stars' mastery of television visuals as important as their music, if not more so. Emblematically, the first music video played on MTV was the Buggles's 'Video Killed the Radio Star'; Madonna capitalised on that murder. How she danced and what she wore were at least as important as what or how well she sang.

But at the MTV Awards that night in 1985, as she descended from the cake on stage, disaster struck. Madonna told Howard Stern in 2016: 'I had come down the wedding cake and my shoe fell off: I was like "Oh shit I can't dance in one shoe" . . . I proceeded to sing the song laying down on the ground. I was just making the best of the situation.' Madonna later protested that the performance was not planned, but a happy accident. 'What was I thinking? A million things were going through my head. It was scary and fun, and I didn't know what it meant for my future.'[37]

What it meant for Madonna's future was that she took hold of the world's consciousness. 'Since then', argues Georges-Claude Guilbert in *Madonna as Postmodern Myth*, 'she has never let go of it.'[38] By the beginning of the new millennium, she had sold about 140 million albums, performed in eighteen movies and three plays, made an erotic photo book called *Sex*, and become a fashion icon, music star and commodity so valuable that reporters who rooted through her rubbish bins sold the contents. Her music was studied at Harvard, Princeton and UCLA. After her mythic birth from a wedding cake, like a post-modern version of Botticelli's Venus emerging from a shell, she became ubiquitous – and, like Umberto Eco's notion of an open text, endlessly interpretable.

Madonna Louise Ciccone was born on 16 August 1958, the eldest daughter of six children, to Chrysler engineer Silvio Ciccone and Madonna Fortin, who died of breast cancer when her daughter was only five. Thereafter, her autocratic dad hired housekeepers to care for his children, one of whom became his second wife and, for Madonna, the wicked stepmother. According to biographer Lucy O'Brien, 'she channelled her feelings of loss into a restless search for love and recognition, expressing herself through dance'. 'The thing that stood out was how well she could dance', said one of her earliest boyfriends, Wyn Cooper. 'Everyone would get out of the way and watch her. She combined *The Temptations* with little syncopated routines . . . Her thing was a real mish-mash, but it worked.'

She attended the University of Michigan on a dance scholarship, but dropped out in 1987 to go to New York City. There she scraped a living as a dancer and an artist's model, before playing drums in ska/pop band The Breakfast Club. By 1980 she had branched out to form her own act with boyfriend Steve Bray, who would later produce several of her albums.

Madonna was a new kind of female pop star who, as Lucy O'Brien puts it, mixed 'punk attitude with cartoon sexuality'. 'My role models were people like Debbie Harry and Chrissie Hynde. Strong, independent women who wrote their own music and evolved on their own', Madonna said. 'They gave me courage.'[39] She also gained inspiration from becoming a regular at two clubs, the Mudd Club and the Danceteria, in the late 1970s and early 1980s. The former was a downtown riposte to the uptown chic of Studio 54. If Studio 54 on 54th Street had the glitz and glamour, the Mudd Club, at No. 77 White Street in TriBeCa, was more bohemian; it was one of the first clubs to double as an art gallery. Jim Jarmusch showed films there, while Jean-Michel Basquiat exhibited work and also took the stage as a DJ.

At the Danceteria, a four-floor club on 21st Street, Sade worked behind the bar, Keith Haring and the Beastie Boys were bus boys, and LL Cool J was the lift operator. It was there Madonna met Mark Kamins, a DJ and A&R man for Island Records. One night Kamins agreed to play a demo cassette of 'Everybody', her first single, which she had written with Bray. It showcased her treble voice against a spare disco bass and drum back beat, drawing on the music she would have danced to in downtown clubs.

Thanks to Kamins, Madonna was offered a $15,000 two-singles deal by Sire Records, which released her debut album in 1983. The third single from that album, 'Holiday', broke into pop charts around the world. 'Holiday' spoke the unthreatening international language of pop fatuity ('Just one day out of life / It would be, it would be so nice'), and Madonna's vocal performance highlighted her shortcomings compared with other singers of the time, but none of that mattered. What mattered was her upbeat performance and what Byung-Chul Han would doubtless call her 'libidinal-economic self production'. *Se produire*, Han noted, is a French expression meaning playing to the gallery. In the video for 'Holiday', Madonna skipped and strutted through the kind of dance moves that prepubescent girls would soon be copying in a million bedroom mirrors. Fans copied her bleach-streaked hair tied with lace, fingerless gloves and bra tops, fishnets with pumps, costume jewellery, and baggy, paint-spattered chinos.

For all the success of early singles, her breakthrough year was 1985. In that year, she not only appeared at the MTV Awards, but made her film debut in Susan Seidelman's *Desperately Seeking Susan*, appeared nude in *Playboy*, got married, and followed up 'Like a Virgin' with another hit single, 'Material Girl'. In *Desperately Seeking Susan* she played the eponymous Susan, a post-modern version of Rex Harrison's Henry Higgins in *My Fair Lady*. Henry Higgins transformed Audrey Hepburn's Cockney flower girl Eliza Doolittle into a lady. Madonna's Susan lured bored New Jersey housewife Roberta (Rosanna Arquette) from her staid suburban marriage to a hot-tub sales-man into an approximation of the glamorous Susan. In the process, like Jack Nicholson's David Locke in *The Passenger*, Roberta casts off her old identity. The film wants us to see this transformation as one woman's escape from boring bourgeois patriarchy norms; but it could equally be seen as her subjection to another controlling force. After Susan gives Roberta a style makeover, tying up newly tousled hair in a funky scarf, dangling rows of thrift-shop beads over her chest, and putting her in leather pants, along with white gloves that match Susan's own, Roberta looks not so much like her best self as like Madonna's mini-me. Henry Higgins might have been a misogynist, but at least he didn't make Eliza Dolittle dress like him.

Desperately Seeking Susan gave Madonna unprecedented exposure, cementing her cross-media brand. In July 1985, she got a different kind of exposure when nude pictures taken in the days when she was making ends meet as an artist's model appeared in *Playboy*.

In the celebrated video for 'Material Girl', Madonna wore a replica of Marilyn Monroe's shocking pink dress from the 1953 film *Gentlemen Prefer Blondes*, and echoed the drolly knowing and cynical sensibility of Marilyn's song from that movie,

'Diamonds Are a Girl's Best Friend'. Madonna was appropriating Marilyn's femme fatale persona, and updating her song's knowing materialism for a new era. Madonna sang: 'the boy with the cold hard cash is always Mister Right'. The boy toy of 'Like a Virgin', knowingly exploiting and yet refusing to be consumed by her sexual allure in a patriarchal world, now added what some construed as a eulogy to prostitution to her repertoire. Madonna didn't see it that way. 'Talk about the media hanging on to a phrase and misinterpreting the damn thing as well. I didn't write the song and the video was all about how the girl rejected diamonds and money. But God forbid that irony should be understood. So when I'm 90 I'll still be the Material Girl.'[40]

Madonna, the leading sex symbol of the post-modern era, is very different from Marilyn Monroe, the leading sex symbol of the modern era. And yet Madonna found Marilyn a soul mate. 'Marilyn was something not human in a way and I can relate to that. Her sexuality was something everyone was obsessed with, and that I can relate to.'

Both were stars in the sense defined by French philosopher Edgar Morin, namely 'beings that partake at once of the human and the divine, [who] are analogous in some respects to the heroes of mythologies or the gods of Olympus, generating a cult or a sort of religion'.[41] The star is always a sacrificial victim, exchanging privacy for fame, and allowing the public and the media to confuse her personae with her real identity.

The key difference between Marilyn and Madonna is that the latter knowingly appropriated the imagery of past stars like Marilyn, Jean Harlow and Marlene Dietrich in constructing her image. Hence Madonna's return to virginity: she was becoming shiny and new for her audience, piquing their desire even as she became untouchable to them. She seemed to be exploiting herself, but at the same time she was exploiting the gaze of her fans.

Like Sophie Calle, Madonna saw herself as a taboo-breaking feminist – no more so than when, after publishing the coffee-table book *Sex* in 1992, she was derided by some critics for promoting rape as entertainment and objectifying women. The 128-page book, written by Madonna under the pseudonym Mistress Dita, included photographs of the pop star naked wearing a rabbit's tail, kissing supermodel Naomi Campbell, shaving a naked man's pubic hair, romping with a dog in an image that purportedly suggested bestiality, and eating a pizza naked at a Miami restaurant while other diners primly averted their eyes. Zoë Heller saw this as the moment Madonna's post-modern crown slipped. It was 'the women who once saw Madonna as a witty feminist role model who have been most alarmist about her latest pornographic incarnation . . . Previously, they say, Madonna played with traditional images of feminine sexuality in a subversive, "empowering" way. But now, with sado-masochism and rape fantasies, she has gone too far.'[42]

Madonna's retort to her critics was that she was in control of the fantasies in her book. 'I put myself in these situations with men. Isn't that what feminism is about – equality for men and women? Aren't I in charge of my life?' The backlash against *Sex* led Madonna to pose too as a kind of sex therapist: 'I think the problem is that everybody's so uptight about it and have turned it into something bad when it isn't. If people could talk about it freely, we would have more people practicing safe sex, we wouldn't have people sexually abusing each other.'[43] *Sex* became the most successful coffee-table book of all time, selling 150 million copies worldwide – despite the Vatican calling on Catholics to boycott it (which may have unintentionally boosted sales).

When, in 2016, she won the Woman of the Year award at the Billboard Women in Music event, Madonna said: 'I stand before you as a doormat. Oh, I mean, as a female entertainer. Thank you for acknowledging my ability to continue my career for 34 years in the face of blatant sexism and misogyny and constant bullying and relentless abuse.'[44]

Madonna has become an open text, signifying incompatible things to different people. She has been hailed as a feminist icon and damned for using sex to sell product, praised by some for subverting patriarchal dominance but criticised by others for confirming it. She has become what beer is to Homer Simpson: a paradox. For Homer, beer is a symptom of and solution to our problems. Most of all, Madonna has astutely made and remade herself multiple times in post-modern fashion, not just as a pop star and film actor, but as a commodity. In a material world, it pays (and costs) to be a material girl.

6

The Great Acceptance, 1986:
Rabbit | Quentin Tarantino | Musée d'Orsay

I

Jeff Koons's *Rabbit* is larger than life – which is perhaps not surprising given the artist's genius for inflation. It is a forty-one-inch-tall stainless-steel casting of an inflatable bunny holding a functionally useless stainless-steel carrot. When *Rabbit* appeared for the first time at the Sonnabend Gallery in New York's East Village in the autumn of 1986, critics and curators were dazzled. 'You wanted to laugh, you were shocked, you were planted to the floor', recalled Kurt Varnedoe, chief curator of painting and sculpture at New York's Museum of Modern Art (MoMA).

> It has such an amazing physical presence. The swollen nature of it, the preternaturally round head and bulging seams of it, give it a kind of compressed and packed energy you feel instantly when you're in the presence of it. 'Uncanny' is the word that comes to mind. There were so many different things going on at once in the piece. It was hilarious, it was smart, and it was chilling.[1]

If, after the end of the human race, alien archaeologists unearth *Rabbit* from the toxic dumps and nuclear waste that our species has bequeathed to eternity, it is not impossible that it will be put in an intergalactic museum as the ur-fetish object of our planet's post-modern turn. Aliens could learn a lot about human society in the late twentieth century from *Rabbit*, since it is dense with semiotic signification. You can see Neil Armstrong's lunar helmet in it if you like, or the reflection of your kitchen sink. It also hangs heavy with allusions to high art and low culture: its leporine curves and shiny surface pastiche the austerely seductive forms of Constantin Brâncuşi's modernist sculptures while at the same time evoking the Playboy Bunny and Bugs Bunny – the latter's anatomically questionable grasp on a carrot clearly referenced by the artist.

But, while dense, it is also empty. It is post-modern in favouring style over substance and surface over depth, forcing high art and low culture into profane embrace. Indeed, its duplicitous stainless material reflects how it both means nothing and yet is open to suggesting anything that the viewer might wish. Its value is in the eye of the beholder, whose narcissistic desires *Rabbit* obligingly reflects: Koons's sculpture prefigures the age of the selfie, in which we only look in order to see ourselves. But it does something else, too. Wittgenstein, as we saw in Chapter 2, reflected on the drawing of a duck/rabbit – an image that, depending on perspective, can reveal in the eye of the beholder either a duck or a rabbit, but never both at once. Koons's *Rabbit* dramatises this oscillation effect. To look at it is to watch as it alternates from sublime to ridiculous, from rococo pastiche to cartoon bunny; sublime but ridiculous; sublime and then ridiculous.

Post-modernist art like Koons's *Rabbit* toppled old distinctions between high and low culture. In particular, it stood against modernism, if modernism can be taken as representing a utopian vision of human life and society and a belief in progress. Post-modernism junked such visions; or rather, given its fetish for appropriation and repurposing, it didn't put them in the trash, but instead recycled them. Post-modernism was concerned about the environment.

Rabbit is above all post-modern, incarnating the observation made by post-modern theorist Gilbert Adair that art need not be seen in order to be heard.[2] Millions of words have been written about this forty-one-inch metal bunny, a large proportion of them by people who have not seen it first-hand. And yet, paradoxically, *Rabbit* needs to be a physical object, not least because it would otherwise not fulfil its essential role: to be bought and sold, thus subjecting itself to the commercial norms of late capitalism. Of all artists, no one more than Jeff Koons, who once worked as a Wall Street commodities trader, has been so astute a businessman; nor has there been any artist more happy to collude with capitalism, even cannibalising his private life for material.

In 2007, a version of *Rabbit* joined other inflatables in the Macy's Thanksgiving Parade. This version eschewed the original *Rabbit*'s material duplicity by becoming a proper inflatable, and in that incarnation it was even bigger – fifty feet high and rising. *New York Times* critic Roberta Smith described the scene on Broadway: 'Floating overhead yesterday, it was a jubilant reminder of the way contemporary artists dip in and out of mainstream life, effortlessly working high, low and in between. That is where the latest, biggest "Rabbit" is suspended, and where it will stay. Owned by Macy's and slated to fly in future parades, it will not be turning up at auction any time soon.'[3]

Another version of Koons's *Rabbit* turned up at auction. In May 2019, *Rabbit* sold at Christie's for $80 million ($91 million including fees) to the art dealer and former banker Robert Mnuchin (father of Steven Mnuchin, the Trump administration's Treasury secretary and former Goldman Sachs partner), making Koons the world's wealthiest living artist, with a net worth estimated at $200 million.

After *Rabbit*'s birth in 1986, post-modern art divided into two warring factions. On the one side there were the Koonsians, who made fortunes for themselves through replicating his business model – namely, creating objects that loosened the purse strings of millionaire collectors. Post-modern culture, as Gilbert Adair argued, didn't involve looking at art so much as speculating about it, in both senses of the word; post-modern art and neoliberal capital were in cahoots. David Harvey argued that the growth of the art market and the commercialisation of cultural production since 1970 have a great deal to do with the search for means of storing value when money forms are deficient.[4] Thus, no doubt, the multiple iterations of Koons's inflatable but inflation-proof *Rabbit*.

In post-modern culture, the value of art isn't so much aesthetic as financial. The moment when this became true can be dated. On 18 October 1973, Robert Scull, a New York taxi-fleet impresario who was a passionate collector of abstract expressionist and pop art, sold off fifty works from his collection at Sotheby's. Jasper Johns's 1961 *Target*, for instance, was sold for $135,000, at that time a jaw-dropping price. In 1997, plastics mogul and art collector Stefan Edlis bought *Target* for $10 million. In 2018, Edlis appeared in Nathaniel Kahn's documentary *The Price of Everything* – a meditation on the role of art in a consumerist society – and claimed that the painting was worth $100 million. Kahn argued that, since the early 1970s, the art market has become a sophisticated stock market complete with trading, flipping and commodities futures.[5] 'The image is the commodity today', Fredric Jameson wrote, 'and that is why it is vain to expect a negation of the logic of commodity production from it; that is why, finally, all beauty is meretricious.'[6] His point was that, for artists, to produce beautiful commodities was to abandon the role the Frankfurt School had accorded to art: to indict an intolerable world. Jeff Koons, by contrast, encourages acceptance as the centrepiece of his artistic philosophy.

Jeff Koons was born on 21 January 1955 in York, Pennsylvania, to a mother who was a seamstress and a father who ran a furniture store. Koons likes to tell the story of how, aged nine, he would sign copies of old-master paintings that his father would place in the window of his shop in an attempt to attract visitors.

By 1986, after working on Wall Street, Koons was making a name for himself on the New York art scene as an appropriation artist, like his hip-hop contemporaries a few miles away in the Bronx. He repurposed vacuum cleaners and basketballs, putting the former in light-filled vitrines and the latter in glass cabinets suspended in water, as if to say: 'These humble objects are just as worthy of aesthetic appreciation as anything in a gallery or museum.'

In that respect, his art echoed that of Marcel Duchamp, who seventy years earlier had sought to install a urinal in an exhibition of the American Society of Independent Artists, signing it with the name R. Mutt and renaming it *Fountain* – though the society's board refused to exhibit the urinal. The poet Guillaume Apollinaire was among several avant-gardists who defended *Fountain* from its establishment critics: 'The viewpoint of the Society of Independent Artists is evidently absurd for it arises from the untenable point of view that art cannot ennoble an object.'[7]

Koons's basketballs and vacuum cleaners were similar attempts at aesthetic ennoblement. But there was a key difference between Duchamp's *Fountain* and Koons's ready-mades. The latter were the result of meticulous calibration by the artist. When he was working as a Wall Street futures trader in the early 1980s, Koons spent a lot of time on the phone. But instead of selling cotton futures he pumped scientists to find out how he could suspend a basketball in water without it sinking.

Eventually he tracked down Nobel Prize–winning physicist Richard Feynman, who explained it. The trick was to fill the ball with water and then layer the bottom two-thirds of the tank with salt water and the top third with fresh water. The suspension only lasts six months, though, after which collectors have to arrange for the basketballs to be reinstalled by specialists using Koons's helpful video and manual.

At the Sonnabend show in 1986, Koons exhibited a stainless-steel bouquet of flowers; and busts, also in stainless steel, of Louis XIV and Bob Hope. It was *Rabbit*, though, that made the biggest impression. 'In stainless steel, it provides a dazzling update on Brancusi's perfect forms, even as it turns the hare into a space-invader of unknown origin', wrote Roberta Smith.[8] It also made Jeff Koons rich and famous.

Art was not supposed to be like this. For the neo-Marxist modernists of the Frankfurt School, if art had a role in capitalist society, it was to become part of what the school's political philosopher Herbert Marcuse called 'the Great Refusal'. Such opposition, he wrote, is 'an elementary force which violates the rules of the game and, in doing so, reveals it as a rigged game'. The purpose of works of art, for Marcuse, was not to float above Macy's Thanksgiving Parade. Rather, it was to expose how late capitalism seduces us into desiring our own domination even as we queue at Toys 'R' Us: 'Now this essential gap between the arts and the order of the day, kept open in the artistic alienation, is progressively closed by the advancing technological society. And with its closing, the Great Refusal is in turn refused; the "other dimension" is absorbed into the prevailing state of affairs.'[9] Instead of indicting that which is, high art is repurposed to collude with it.

Marcuse, who died in 1976, did not live to see Jeff Koons collaborate with Louis Vuitton, but it would have clinched his point. In 2017, Koons produced a range of handbags emblazoned with old-master paintings – Leonardo's *Mona Lisa*, Van Gogh's *Wheat Field with Cypresses*, Rubens's *Tiger, Lion and the Leopard Hunt*, Titian's *Mars, Venus and Cupid*, Fragonard's *Girl with a Dog*, Manet's *Luncheon on the Grass*, Turner's *Ancient Rome*, Boucher's *Reclining Girl* and Poussin's *The Triumph of Pan*. Each bag displayed the name of the artist in large type. Instead of swanking down the boulevard with a bag that howled to passers-by it was a Fendi, Prada, Yves Saint Laurent, Gucci or even Louis Vuitton, the artists' names became the brands.

Nine-year-old Jeff had used old masters to help increase foot traffic to his dad's shop. Now, grown-up Koons was marrying art and shopping once again. One critic supposed that Koons's handbags might save art rather than bury it. 'High art needs all the friends it can get', wrote Jonathan Jones in the *Guardian*.[10] 'I can't think of a simpler way to put great art at the forefront of modern minds.' Prices were as much as $4,000, making these handbags, for most of us, not so much must-haves as can't-affords. But let's park our cynicism for a moment. If high culture comes out of the mausoleum, perhaps it can be born again to new demographics, and possibly to serve new purposes. 'True,' replied Marcuse, when he considered the repurposing of old art for new times, 'but coming to life as classics, they come to life as something other than themselves; they are deprived of their antagonistic force, of the estrangement which was the very dimension of their truth.'[11]

While I've been writing this, there has been a question nagging at the back of my mind. What is the difference between pop art and Jeff Koons's post-modernist art? After all, both involve breaking down hierarchies of value, and both use popular culture as raw material (Warhol's silkscreens of gun-toting Elvis and Koons's sculpture of Michael Jackson with his pet monkey are in this respect not dissimilar). But there seems to me a key difference between Warhol and Koons. In breaking down distinctions between high and low culture, arguably, Warhol and other pop artists functioned as an avant-garde performing what Luc Boltanski and Eve Chiapello, in *The New Spirit of Capitalism*, called 'artistic critique' of capitalism.[12] By the time Koons came to fame in 1986, by contrast, that critique had lost its subversive power – in fact, was no longer worth the name 'critique'. His art may not be so very different from pop art to look at; after all, in 1984 Warhol – long before Koons did his high-art handbags – had produced silkscreens that deployed details of great Renaissance art, placing Botticelli's *Venus* on a level with previous icons he had depicted, such as with Elizabeth Taylor, Marilyn Monroe and the Queen of England. But it is post-modern in the sense I have been trying to advance – namely, serving to appropriate and neutralise critique, and thereby serve as a cultural instrument of capitalism.

Koons does not make art of the Great Refusal, but of the Great Acceptance. 'The imperative of self acceptance is so important', he once told the curator Norman Rosenthal.

The motivation of art is the removal of any kind of guilt or shame, or anything that people have within their history that alienates them from just dealing with themselves. It's very important to try to remove these feelings if you want to function outside the self. If you can go inward you can eventually reach the bottom of the self and art is a great tool to enable that.[13]

Koons traced that vision of art back to his own feelings of inadequacy when he had visited the Baltimore Museum of Art as a child. He recalled that he had felt as though he had survived the experience, as though it had been an ordeal rather than a pleasure. 'I'm sure I felt a sense of inadequacy, a sense of "wait a minute, I don't know anything here."' Later, when he became an artist, he was bent on ensuring that his viewers did not feel that anxiety: 'I have always wanted to create art through which [the viewer] could realise that they were perfect . . . I wanted to keep in front of me that art is always about empowerment. It's about self-empowerment and your ability to empower other people.'[14]

One tactic for that empowerment is to disrupt the canon of art, to flatten distinctions between high and low, art and porn, even good and bad. Koons's aesthetic involves putting everything on the same level as everything else – classical sculpture and Disney ballerina, vacuum cleaner and martyred saint, basketball and infant Christ, Michael Jackson playing with his monkey Bubbles and an eighteenth-century girl getting pleasured by a dog's wandering tail. In one sense, this toppling of hierarchies, as if the Western canon were the oppressive statue of a dead tyrant that deserved demolition, is welcome.

But Koons's empowerment is a sham. To imagine yourself as perfect after all, which is Jeff Koons's cursed gift to his viewers, is to render yourself complacent, abandoning critique of the society you live in, or any sense that you might change it for the better. This is where post-modernism becomes a tool of domination, part of the culture industry that the Frankfurt School indicted. Jeff Koons encourages us not just to accept ourselves, but to accept a neoliberal order in which art becomes indistinguishable from narcissism, shopping and pornography.

'This is an art to deflect thought, and ultimately even viewing', wrote the *Observer* critic Laura Cumming, reviewing Koons's retrospective at Oxford's Ashmolean Museum in 2019. 'Look at it for too long and you sense its sterility. Koons's pitches for his work, which appear on wall texts throughout, are amiably generous and inclusive – but they never aim higher than platitude. And so it is with the objects themselves. Stare at their polished perfection and all you see is the shining fatuity of it all.'[15] The real worry with Koons's shining fatuity is that you look at it for too long and don't sense its sterility. You become inured to it.

II

The same thing happens if you look too long at the cinema of Quentin Tarantino, Jeff Koons's leading contender for the title of High Priest of Post-modernism. His too is an art that flatters his audience, bewitching them with intertextual references to other films and pop culture, thereby deflecting thought and encouraging acceptance of the self and the status quo. Or, as the critic bell hooks eloquently put it in an article entitled 'Cool Cynicism: Pulp Fiction':

> Tarantino has the real nihilism of the times down. He represents the ultimate in 'white cool': a hard-core cynical vision that would have everyone see racism, sexism, homophobia but behave as though none of that shit really matters, or if it does it means nothing cause none of it's gonna change, cause the real deal is that domination is here to stay – going nowhere and everybody is in on the act. Mind you, domination is always and only patri-archal – a dick thing.[16]

Another critic, James Wood, was no less scornful. When *Pulp Fiction* was released in 1994, he wrote: 'Only in this age could a writer as talented as Tarantino produce artworks so vacuous, so entirely stripped of any politics, metaphysics, or moral interest.'[17]

But Wood was wrong. Tarantino's vacuity is another way of doing politics, one fitting for post-modern times. And its moral interest consists precisely in its lack of interest in morals. It is of moral interest since, in appearing to be about nothing, it is as duplicitous as Koons's *Rabbit*. Just as *Rabbit* seemed to be light but was really heavy, Tarantino's cinema seems to be about nothing but is not as nihilistic as it purports to be. It is part of the Great Acceptance. As bell hooks argues: 'Tarantino's work lets us know it's a sick motherfucking world and we may as well get used to that fact, laugh at it and go on our way, cause ain't nothing changing – and that's Hollywood, the place where white supremacist capitalist patriarchy can keep reinventing itself no matter how many times the West is de-centered.'[18]

In 1986, Tarantino was a nobody working in a strip mall store called Video Archives near Manhattan Beach, California. This was the year he got the call to join the world capital of the white supremacist capitalist patriarchy's culture industry that so exasperated bell hooks – namely, Hollywood. It was at Video Archives, the legend around Tarantino has it, that he racked up a vast wealth of knowledge about cinema, rather than by attending film school. But the reverse is true: he was hired because he was a cinematic autodidact who already knew a lot about movies.

Born in Knoxville, Tennessee, in 1963, Tarantino moved to Los Angeles with his mother three years later, living in predominantly African-American neighbourhoods and educated in schools where he was one of the few white students. He assembled his first collection of films by taping late-night classic movies on TV. He spent much of his youth in picture houses serving African-American communities, immersing himself in blaxploitation cinema. He also steeped himself in other kinds of exploitation cinema – B-movies, spaghetti westerns, kung-fu flicks. All these genres would be appropriated by Tarantino in his later cinema.

Tarantino is post-modern, too, in taking his influences from high and low parts of the cinematic canon. His production company, emblematically, was called A Band Apart Films, in homage to his favourite of French *nouvelle vague* director Jean-Luc Godard's pictures, 1964's *Bande à Part*. Indeed, Tarantino once said that he had a eureka moment when he read Pauline Kael's review of that Godard film. Kael had written: 'It's as if a French poet took an ordinary banal American crime novel and told it to us in terms of the romance and beauty he read between the lines.' 'When I read that, I literally thought, "That's what I want to do",' said Tarantino, 'what I wanted to give to movies, I'd never heard anyone describe it so well before.'[19]

When Tarantino was interviewed by Bret Easton Ellis in 2015, post-modern novelist and post-modern movie director come together in their striking admiration for the critic. Easton Ellis wrote: 'Kael championed a kind of high-low trash-art aesthetic that was inclusive of both old-school foreign auteurs (Max Ophüls and Satyajit Ray) and new mavericks (Sam Peckinpah and Brian De Palma), while disdaining the polite, better-behaved American cinema of that era.'[20] Tarantino's cinema had a similar aesthetic: it has never been well-behaved, but rather clamorous in its high-low trash-art aesthetic. More importantly, it has often involved him pastiching the cinema in which he steeped himself while working at Video Archives, and studying acting at Allen Garfield's Actors Shelter, in Beverly Hills.

In 1986 Tarantino got his first work in Hollywood. He was hired, along with fellow video store employee Roger Avary, to work on an exercise video by muscled thespian Dolph Lundgren. He was also writing a screenplay for which he managed to get funding to film in the following year. *My Best Friend's Birthday* was written by and starred Tarantino and fellow trainee actors who he had been working with, while the rest of his video store colleagues served as crew and actors, and funded the film with $6,000. Much of that script would be recycled for *True Romance*, the 1993 movie he wrote for director Tony Scott.

Tarantino's first completed movie was *Reservoir Dogs* (1992), which provoked accusations that he was ripping off Ringo Lam's Hong Kong crime film *City on Fire* (1987). He admitted as much: 'I steal from every movie ever made . . . Great artists steal; they don't do homages.'[21] Post-modern appropriation was not something to be ashamed of – unless the lawyers advised otherwise. *Reservoir Dogs* is ostensibly a movie about a heist that goes wrong, but for Tarantino it had another resonance that may have made James Wood queasy. Near the denouement, he traps the remaining colour-coded putative diamond thieves in a room to settle their differences with guns, having bumped off all the potential heroes, so that there was no moral centre (a trope he also deployed in the 2015 western *The Hateful Eight*). He did so not because he is overtly amoral, but because, while plundering old cinematic genres for material, dialogue and structure, he refuses to do the thing that every Hollywood hack knows they are supposed to do – namely, ensure the hero triumphs in the final reel and, for bonus points, gets the girl before the closing credits. His films may have no moral centre, but they also refuse predictable Hollywood sentiment – which, if not progress, is something.

Tarantino's breakthrough film was the 1994 movie *Pulp Fiction*, which he co-wrote with Avary, and for which they won the Academy Award for Best Original Screenplay. The film starts with two murders. John Travolta and Samuel L. Jackson play two hitmen, Vincent and Jules, who enter a Los Angeles apartment to collect a briefcase for their gangster boss from a trio of terrified men. After Vincent checks the contents of the briefcase, Jules shoots one of the scared men and then declaims a passage from Ezekiel 25:17. Then he and Vincent shoot the second man.

These being post-modern times, a great deal of ink has been spilled in interpreting Tarantino's deployment of the Bible at this point. Is Jules righteous? Evil? Light in the valley of darkness? Or darkness itself? These questions seem pertinent because, at the end of the film, Samuel L. Jackson recites the same passage again, before renouncing his life of crime.

That ink has been wasted. The mistake for critics was to take Tarantino's deployment of the Bible seriously. We only have to look at Samuel L. Jackson's wig to realise that. It is far and away the most important character in the film, and makes meditating on *Pulp Fiction*'s ethical posture ludicrous. 'It's [Jules's] own signifying monkey', wrote bell hooks who, as an African-American woman, was rightly very suspicious of white director Quentin Tarantino ventriloquising a ridiculous black gangster – or, as she put it, 'our resident black male preacher-philosopher death-dealing mamified intellectual'. She added:

> No matter how serious Jules' rap, that hair always intervenes to let the audience know not to take him too seriously. Cause that hair is like a minstrel thing – telling the world that the black preacher-philosopher is ultimately just an intellectual arty white boy in drag, aping, imitating and mouthing intellectual rhetoric that he can't quite use to make sense of his own life.[22]

The wig is a helpful reminder not to take the film seriously. Quoting Ezekiel sounds cool, but it's folly to assume it means anything – still less to look for a hidden moral code. Cool, that must-have of post-modernism, is by definition devoid of morals.

In a second scene from the film, post-modernist theory's tendency to overthink and over-talk gets nicely, if unconsciously, skewered. Vincent, having shot up some heroin he bought from his drug dealer, escorts Mia, the wife of his gangster boss, while the latter is out of town. As he and Mia have dinner at Jack Rabbit Slim's, a 1950s-themed restaurant, the conversation peters out. 'Uncomfortable silences', says Mia. 'Why do we feel it's necessary to yak about bullshit in order to be comfortable?'[23]

Post-modernism, in *Pulp Fiction*, is all about the yak. Tarantino gluts our eyes and ears with audio and visual yak. The restaurant is an infernal theme park glutted visually with blaxploitation, *Shogun Assassin* and Roger Corman movie posters, and aurally with the soundtrack of music from a twenty-four-hour oldies radio station.

When Vince and Mia rise from their table to take part in the restaurant's twist competition, one of the pleasures for the viewer is to see John Travolta dance. Travolta reprises his celebrated Hollywood role in the 1978 homage to disco, *Saturday Night Fever*. It's a typical gambit, in Tarantino's movies in particular and post-modern culture in general: by referencing another movie or novel or painting that the audience is likely to be familiar with, the post-modern artist offers to us the pleasure of recognition – a self-contained system of quotations. This is what the critic Robert Kolker meant when he wrote that post-modernism 'consists of a flattened spatiality in which character and event are in a state of reminding us that they are pop culture figures and pleasure derives from its self-recognition'.[24] We are invited to be pleasurably lost in Tarantino's hyperreal simulation of a fifties diner, lost to his allusions to other movies and music, to the extent that we are able to anaesthetise ourselves to the venal things that happen in the film.

Pulp Fiction is not without moral interest, whatever James Wood has to say. The film has an ethical code – that of neo-liberalism. Human life may be expendable and women may be commodities to be looked after, but behind these self-evident truths of gangster ideology is the influence of globalised capitalism overrun by neoliberal ideals. *Pulp Fiction* constantly presents its characters in some state of consumption.

In between the conflicts, mishaps and freak coincidences that mark the film's different storylines, we repeatedly witness consumers who simply eat, watch movies, listen to music, take drugs and read *Modesty Blaise* in the toilet. And when not consuming, they are talking about consumption. On their way to slaughtering the three men in the flat, Vincent and Jules chat happily about the differences between Europe and America in terms of burger retail. Emblematically, Europe is busted down from the epicentre of civilisation to the continent where they do weird stuff to burgers.

No wonder this sort of dialogue affronted James Wood. The scene shows, if you like, the characters' amorality. How could

they discuss such trivia before a murder? One suggestion, identified by critic Alan Clarke, is that the effect of this scene is
to unmask the macho myth and make standard Hollywood
violence laughable. And, in general, *Pulp Fiction* might be seen
as a desirable subversion of terrible Hollywood mores: there is
no nudity and no violence directed against women, but there
are several examples of interracial friendship and cultural
diversity.

In this, some critics want *Pulp Fiction* to have its Royale with
Cheese and eat it. They want it to be a post-modern critique of
oppressive power structures even while confirming others.
Murder, the valuation of human life in terms of money, the
commodification of women – all figure in the film, and remain
largely unexamined. Tarantino is hardly proselytising for any of
these values, but his affectless post-modern stance, which allows
them to triumph in his film, suggests moral vacuity. In *Pulp
Fiction*, buying, consuming and owning have become dominat-
ing, self-justifying ideals, while the film's murders, racism and
homophobia go unchallenged. 'The film's cycle of racist and
homophobic jokes might threaten to break out into a quite nasty
view of the world', wrote Kolker, 'but this nastiness keeps being
laughed off – by the mock intensity of the action, the prowling,
confronting, perverse, confined, and airless nastiness of the
world Tarantino creates.'[25]

The airless nastiness of Tarantino's cinema is most evident in
the scene in which gangster boss Marsellus (Ving Rhames) is
raped by a pawn shop proprietor and his security guard, and
then saved by a boxer called Butch (Bruce Willis). For bell
hooks, there is more than the homophobic depiction of sexual
predation in this scene; there is racism, too. Marsellus, the
African-American gangster, is saved by a white man, and
'the film turns him into a welfare case – another needy victim
who must ultimately rely on the kindness of strangers to rescue
him from the rape-in-progress that is his symbolic castration,
his return to the jungle, to a lower rung in the food chain'. If any
African-American film maker had shot a scene as homophobic

as this, hooks suggests, there would have been protests from progressive critics.[26]

But ultimately what makes *Pulp Fiction* a post-modern film and amenable to neoliberalism is not what it does to its characters, but what it does to us. It empties violence of any critical social consequences, offering viewers only the immediacy of shock, humour, irony-without-insight and immersion in an airless world of pastiche and quotations. These are pleasures, no doubt, but degrading ones. We are made consumers first and critics of what we are seeing second – if at all. We lose our selves in the consumption of shocking violence and retro kitsch.

And then, having consumed, we transmit. One distinguishing feature of *Pulp Fiction* is that it circulates through online citation. In 'Say "*Pulp Fiction*" One More Goddamn Time: Quotation Culture and an Internet-Age Classic', Michael Z. Newman traces fans who share expressions of their fandom in YouTube videos and Tumblr postings of images and GIFs, repeat bits of dialogue, share images from the film – such as the shot of Jules and Vincent aiming their guns – and recreate scenes like the dance scene with Mia and Vincent.[27] Some have argued that post-modernism is essentially a pre-digital phenomenon. On the contrary, thanks to the internet, post-modernism can stupefy us more efficiently than before.

III

In the same year that Jeff Koons's *Rabbit* appeared and Quentin Tarantino broke into Hollywood, the Musée d'Orsay opened in Paris. The conversion of the Seine-side former railway station into one of the world's leading art galleries was a key moment for post-modernism. It was appropriation art, akin to Jeff Koons putting old-master paintings on handbags or hip-hop artists sampling other people's music.

The Musée d'Orsay was one of the eight monumental building projects that transformed the French capital from 1982 onwards. President François Mitterrand's *grands projets* included the Louvre Pyramid, the Institut du Monde Arabe, the Parc de la Villette, the Arab World Institute, the Opéra Bastille, the Grande Arche de La Défense, the Ministry of Finance and the Bibliothèque Nationale de France. This rash of buildings might be seen as the culmination of *les trentes glorieuses*, the three post-war decades after World War II, in which France, like many Western countries, thrived economically as a result of interventionist government policies, or what the French call *dirigisme*.

Indeed, these projects were an exercise in state-directed urban planning – perhaps not quite as radical as Haussmann's nineteenth-century bulldozing of Paris into a city of radiating boulevards, but, nonetheless, cumulatively producing a radical change in how the city looks and feels. They also typified something post-modern: France was becoming a post-industrial city of arts and culture. Its makeover by Mitterrand was an example of what the sociologist Daniel Bell called the post-industrial society, a term vague enough to encompass consumer society, media society, information society, electronic society and high-tech society.[28] With these contributions to the physiognomy of Paris, the city underwent a revolution as significant as those of 1789, 1848, 1871 and 1968. Of course, Paris has never been a cultural dustbowl; but Mitterrand's *grands projets*, by stressing the French capital's function as eternal capital of culture, were designed to revivify its brand.

Paris sought to join the post-modern carnival with the opening in 1979 of the Pompidou Centre, an arts complex that was post-modern not just in its stylistic pretensions, but in its conception as a place designed to keep visitors endlessly entertained. One of its architects, Renzo Piano, described it as 'not a building but a town where you find everything – lunch, great art, a library, great music'.[29]

It arose in the French capital's 4th arrondissement, according to *Le Figaro*, like Paris's answer to the Loch Ness monster. Given that there is no Loch Ness monster, that really underestimates the Pompidou Centre's impact on the city. It was brash, noisy, clamorous, ironic, playful and not a little infantile – utterly post-modern.

Like Le Corbusier's Unité d'Habitation or Portman's Westin Bonaventure Hotel, what became known as the Beaubourg (radical Parisians refused to use the name that honoured the conservative prime minister and president) was at odds with the city in which it was built, and threw down a challenge not only to the politesse of Parisian architecture, but also to designers of future museums. It wore its heart on its sleeve, and its guts on the outside – an exposed skeleton of brightly coloured tubes was initially colour-coded: green was plumbing, blue climate control, electrical wires were encased in yellow, and safety devices were red. For the Beaubourg competition, Piano, Richard Rogers and their colleagues imagined a big frame with pipes and structure on the outside, leaving the interior unencumbered and adaptable. Parts of the building could be clipped and unclipped in response to future needs. Its floors would move up and down. Huge electronic screens would interact with crowds in a piazza outside, and escalators in glass tubes would transport people towards the sky.

When, thirty years after it opened, the Beaubourg won the coveted Pritzker award, the jury argued that Piano and Rogers's art complex 'revolutionised museums, transforming what had once been elite monuments into popular places of social and cultural exchange, woven into the heart of the city'.[30]

The point was, as Richard Rogers put it, that 'culture should be fun'.[31] At the time, this was a radical idea. Before that, fun was something that intellectuals sneered at, and architects would not aspire to facilitate. 'Fun is a medicinal bath. The pleasure industry never fails to prescribe it', wrote Max Horkheimer and Theodor Adorno in *Dialectic of Enlightenment*, their jeremiad against the modern world in general and Hollywood in particular. 'It makes laughter the instrument of the fraud practised on happiness. Moments of happiness are without laughter; only operettas and films portray sex to the accompaniment of resounding laughter. In the false society laughter is a disease which has attacked happiness and is drawing it into its worthless totality.'[32] A worthless totality. That is, quite possibly, how Horkheimer and Adorno would have viewed Piano and Rogers's house of fun. What these two Frankfurt scholars had seen in their Californian exile was something called the culture industry, which used fun as an instrument to control the masses.

When the Musée d'Orsay opened in 1986, it was seen as a cultural mediator between the old masters of the Louvre and the contemporary art championed at the Pompidou Centre. 'We looked at the old station as a contemporary object, without history', wrote Gae Aulenti, the Italian architect hired to transform the station into a public art museum. 'We regarded the original architect, Victor Laloux, as a companion in the metamorphosis of the station into a museum.'[33] But that is a very strange approach, since Laloux's design for the station was steeped in architectural history. Laloux built a railway station that did not look like a railway station, but concealed its true function behind a beaux-arts façade that was already an anachronism when it opened in 1900. In Robert Venturi's taxonomy, it was a decorated shed, not a duck. From the beginning, it didn't look like a place for trains, but for paintings. The painter Édouard Detaille remarked at the time: 'The station is superb and has the air of a palace of art.'[34]

Eighty-six years later, after ornament-free modernism had risen and fallen, the Gare d'Orsay became a palace of art. But in the interim something had changed. Museums were not what they used to be. The French sociologist Pierre Bourdieu wrote in *Distinction: A Social Critique of the Judgment of Taste* that, for most visitors, trips to the museum had become dull.[35] Something needed to happen to make museums more exciting, and at the same time to court a new demographic of gallery-goers for whom, as Barbara Rose, the *Vogue* journalist who reviewed the Musée d'Orsay's opening, put it, 'museum visits are replacing country outings as a way to relax and revive'.[36] It also needed a really good gift shop, of which more later.

For art historian Patricia Mainardi, in her essay 'Post-modern History at the Musée d'Orsay', Gae Aulenti satisfied these conflicting demands by substituting spectacle for history. Post-modernism's central stylistic attributes, Mainardi wrote, were 'the appropriation of a historicising architectural vocabulary and the combination of mutually contradictory styles' to 'create a spectacle of historical refcrences while at the same time dissembling whatever historical meanings those references might possess'.[37]

Aulenti made the museum into a spectacle, deploying all the skills she had earlier acquired as a stage designer. She created a series of vistas and galleries so captivating to the eye as to make the art displayed in them expendable. Typical was the gallery for the nineteenth-century Barbizon school of painters, whose intimate, realist landscapes in gold frames hung paradoxically against black walls. Baroque and modern, ornate and functional, were juxtaposed in a historically contradictory way, according to post-modernism's law of the jumble that also governed the architectural makeover.

Visitors were encouraged to follow one-way processional routes through the gallery, to experience the spectacle as Aulenti and her French curators had devised it, with only a few short-cuts to abbreviate the visit (a tactic for visitor throughput later favoured by Ikea). In Paris, the city of the *flâneur* – that alienated modern temperamentally devoted to aimless wandering – this was heresy. At the same time, art that could be made to connive with Aulenti's deracinated spectacle was pushed into the foreground of the promenader's gaze.

Two sculptures typify this. Hippolyte Moulin's 1863 bronze statue *A Lucky Find at Pompeii* (*Une Trouvaille à Pompei*) stands on a large pedestal alongside Alexandre Falguière's 1864 bronze *Winner of the Cockfight* (*Le Vainqueur au Combat de Coqs*). Both are interesting sculptures – especially Moulin's, depicting a nude boy with a spade dancing for joy with one leg raised, because he has unearthed a Roman statuette whose pose he echoes (as if, critics have suggested, the statue depicts the excavator *imagining* himself in the original's pose). But the intrinsic interest of these two works of art is subordinated to their role in the spectacle: they flank the giant station clock which still overhangs the epic space beneath the vaulted ceiling, providing thousands of visitors with a ready-made view to photograph. In this way, the Musée became photogenic, adding to the post-modern curse of photographing art rather than looking at it.

The most popular exhibit at the newly opened Musée d'Orsay was Richard Peduzzi's multimedia installation of the Paris Opera House, which had been commissioned by Emperor Napoleon III in 1861 and completed by architect Charles Garnier in 1875. The installation included a beguiling cutaway model of the house, lighted vitrines depicting its leading productions and, best of all, a 1:100-scale model of the Opéra *quartier* under a glass floor over which visitors could walk, looking down, as Mainardi put it, 'like Superman'. 'The installation is something of a high-culture Disneyland,' she added, 'lacking any acknowledgment to the Haussmannisation of Paris.'[38]

It erased the political context that led Napoleon III to commission the opera house at the intersection of new Parisian boulevards. The emperor sought to bulldoze dangerous neighbourhoods and make the French capital militarily defensible, so as to thwart its revolutionary tendencies. Garnier's opera house was part of a process of increased state control and gentrification. That history was erased in Peduzzi's installation in favour of beguiling post-modern spectacle. In this, it was typical of the whole Musée d'Orsay.

The only problem was, as Mainardi put it, the 'resolutely inert' nature of the nineteenth-century impressionist, realist and post-impressionist art that was to be the big draw for the museum. But that very inertia gave the opportunity for post-modern revisionism. Modernism had polarised art into the anointed and the damned, erasing the latter from the museum. Post-modernism brought the damned back to prominence. The chief beneficiary of this revisionism was what French critics derisively call *l'art pompier* ('firefighter's art') – the academic paintings of historical or allegorical scenes that appealed to the values of the bourgeoisie. The term derives from the helmets worn at the time by French firefighters, similar to Ancient Greek Attic helmets; but it is also a pun on the French word for 'from Pompeii', *pompéien*, and the word for pompous, *pompeux*.

Moulin's *Une Trouvaille à Pompei*, is *art pompier* in at least one sense, but more typical are the works of William-Adolphe Bouguereau, Alfred Agache and Thomas Couture, whose often huge canvases depict historical scenes. Couture's 1847 painting *Romains de la décadence* (*Romans during Decadence*) was given pride of place in the museum, displayed alone on a prominent partition. Its position indicated that it was to be seen chiefly, Mainardi argued, 'not as a painting but as a part of the architectural decor'. Indeed, what got lost were the politics of Couture's allegory: the Jacobin, anticlerical and republican painter indicted the moral decadence of Louis Philippe's July Monarchy through his depiction of dissolute Romans; but that indictment was erased as the painting became subservient to Aulenti's spectacle.

L'art pompier experienced a critical revival after the Musée d'Orsay's opening, precisely because it was displayed as if it was at least as aesthetically significant as more-celebrated realist and impressionist paintings of the same period. Indeed, the Musée's overall scheme was reminiscent, Mainardi argued, of a famous Parisian cartoon depicting a cross-section of a typical Parisian apartment house: on the first floor the bourgeoisie live in opulence and splendour; further up, the ceilings become lower and the residents poorer, until on the top floor you find the bohemian artists. It was as if the revolutionary artists of the nineteenth century – Monet, Cézanne, Van Gogh – were marginalised in favour of the reactionary art that was rescued from obscurity, because its bombastic nature precisely fitted the design scheme.

The *New York Times* critic had some trenchant advice to visitors. 'Don't waste time downstairs in the impressive main hall. The Orsay museum's finest treasures, the collection of Impressionist paintings by Monet, Van Gogh, Renoir, Pissarro and others are all crowded into the last four rooms upstairs.'[39] One sculptor, Pol Burry, wrote an article reviewing the museum, called 'Cannibal architects', while the great anthropologist Claude Lévi-Strauss said that it gave him migraines. 'If a camel is a horse drawn by committee', concluded Mainardi, 'then the Orsay is a camel of a museum.'[40]

Aulenti was unrepentant. 'The press was very rude', she said shortly after the opening. 'But 20,000 people a day stand in line waiting to get in.'[41] Her post-modern makeover showed how to make museums popular again in an age of unprecedented competition to gratify our need for leisure-based consumption. Fredric Jameson described post-modernism as 'the consumption of sheer commodification as a process'.[42] The way the Musée d'Orsay organised its historical parade of artworks facilitated just such consumption, presenting the items in its great collection as variations of style, erasing the history of struggle that made those stylistic variations happen. The culture industry that Adorno and Horkheimer saw in Hollywood had invaded the temple of art – a place they and Marcuse saw as a sanctuary from and rebuke to the existing order. No wonder post-modernism became such an ugly term for left critics.

Let's not leave the Musée d'Orsay this way. Let's exit through the gift shop. Art in the post-modern era is inconceivable without some relation to shopping. In the Musée's gift shop you can buy reproductions of some of the paintings Jeff Koons printed on Louis Vuitton handbags – happily much cheaper than the originals. A Monet *Water Lily* scarf will cost you €39.90, for instance – a Van Gogh *Starry Night* fan €6, a Degas *Swaying Dancer* tote bag €11.95. You don't need to visit Paris, still less the Musée d'Orsay, to buy these must-haves. You could just shop online. That way, you needn't experience the museum's art, but you can still take part in the culture, still express yourself through shopping. That would be the post-modern thing to do.

7

Breaking Binaries, 1989:

'The End of History?' | Queer Theory | The Rushdie Fatwa

I

In 1989, the year the Berlin Wall fell and the Soviet bloc teetered on the brink of oblivion, a young American political scientist called Francis Fukuyama gave a talk at the University of Chicago called 'The End of History?' He suggested: 'What we may be witnessing is the end point of mankind's ideological evolution and the universalisation of western liberal democracy as the final form of human government.' Fukuyama argued that there could be no clashes over fundamental values, since 'all prior contradictions are resolved and all human needs satisfied'.[1]

For Fukuyama, the Cold War binary between Soviet communism and American capitalism had ended with the triumph of the latter. But that was hardly the end of history: a venerable conflict, between the West and the Islamic East, arose anew in its wake. At a geopolitical level, the West needed an enemy, be it Soviet communism or militant Wahhabism, to define its identity more clearly, to give itself an heroic mission, and to justify otherwise absurd levels of defence spending.

Strikingly, though, such binary thinking had been expressly rubbished by post-modern philosophers such as Derrida, Deleuze and Guattari in recent years. Western metaphysics, Derrida argued, created false binaries and, worse, privileged one term within each without justification – man over woman, say, or West over East.

Like history, though, binary thinking was not over. Rather, it took a new turn: a decadent, corrupt, gender-fluid, amoral and hideously post-modern West was confronted by Islamists. For the Islamists, among others, distinctions between sacred and profane, religious and secular, needed to be militantly upheld. What arose in the wake of the Cold War was conceived as a Manichean struggle between a godless post-modern West and the defenders of religious authority. One of those who suffered in this struggle was the post-modern novelist Salman Rushdie, who spent the following decade on the run from Islamists charged by Iran's Ayatollah Khoemeini with murdering the sacrilegious apostate. In this chapter I will explore how post-modernism, so long considered as a critique of modernism, by the end of the 1980s became itself the target of critique, from both left and right thinkers exasperated at its seeming political apostasy and its takedown of Western metaphysics.

At the time of his Chicago speech, Francis Fukuyama was moving from his job as Soviet foreign policy expert at the RAND Corporation in California to become deputy director of policy planning at the State Department in Washington. His analysis would have astounded Muslims in the Yorkshire city of Bradford, who the previous month had burned Salman Rushdie's novel *The Satanic Verses* as a blasphemous slur on their religion; or the students who in June 1989 protested in Tiananmen Square in Beijing calling for the communist Chinese state to allow greater freedom of speech and reduce censorship. But, most likely, neither group attended Fukuyama's talk. Nor did many women, or people persecuted because of their colour, sexuality, religion or gender, share Fukuyama's view that all contradictions were resolved and all human needs satisfied.

Despite the breathtaking complacency of Fukuyama's analysis, three years later, when his book *The End of History and the Last Man* was published, the question-mark had gone – as if to suggest he was now only more convinced he was right.[2] The doyen of the grand historical narrative, Georg Wilhelm Friedrich Hegel, had envisaged a future when a perfectly rational form of society and the state would become victorious. That moment,

Fukuyama claimed, had arrived: there could be no new stage beyond liberal democracy. Communism was dead; the grand narrative of history had concluded with a flourish, and the human race had achieved happy homeostasis.

All that remained was an eternity of what sounded very much like boredom. 'The end of history will be a very sad time', Fukuyama wrote. 'The struggle for recognition, the willingness to risk one's life for a purely abstract goal, the worldwide ideological struggle that called forth daring, courage, imagination and idealism will be replaced by economic calculation, the endless solving of technical problems, environmental concerns, and the satisfaction of sophisticated consumer demands.'[3] Perhaps the prospect of that boredom, Fukuyama mused, might restart history.

In his arrival at this view, Fukuyama's earlier brush with post-modern theory and deconstruction was important. As a graduate student, he had studied comparative literature at Yale with Paul de Man, before sitting in on classes with Roland Barthes and Jacques Derrida in Paris. 'I decided it was total bullshit', he told an interviewer.

> They were espousing a kind of Nietzschean relativism that said there is no truth, there is no argument that's superior to any other argument. Yet most of them were committed to a basically Marxist agenda. That seemed completely contradictory. If you really are a moral relativist, there is no reason why you shouldn't affirm National Socialism or the racial superiority of Europeans, because nothing is more true than anything else. I thought it was a bankrupt way of proceeding and decided to shift gears and go into political science.[4]

Perhaps Fukuyama had simply substituted one kind of bullshit for another. Certainly, his end-of-history thesis scandalised his teachers at Harvard so much that they came up with an alternative, more plausible account of geopolitics in the last decade of the twentieth century.

Fukuyama did his PhD at Harvard, studying with the political scientist Samuel Huntington. But it was the student who more powerfully influenced the teacher: reading Fukuyama prompted Huntington to posit that it wasn't history that had ended, but the age of ideology. Unlike Fukuyama, he recognised that the rise of East Asia and Islam was of central importance to the continuing grand narrative of history. Indeed, when he came, in 1993, to write an article for *Foreign Affairs* magazine titled 'The Clash of Civilizations?', Huntington implicitly diagnosed Fukuyama as suffering from the debilitating condition of hubristic occidental myopia. 'Every civilization sees itself as the centre of the world and writes its history as the central drama of human history', he wrote.[5]

Nor was boredom likely to be the world's biggest post–Cold War problem, Huntington supposed. Cultural and religious identities were going to be the primary sources of conflict in the wake of the Cold War. Nonetheless, by the time he expanded that hypothesis into his 1996 book, *The Clash of Civilizations*, the question-mark had gone, as if he, like Fukuyama before him, had become more convinced that he was right. Huntington wrote that the most dangerous clashes of the future were likely to arise from 'the interaction of Western arrogance, Islamic intolerance, and Sinic assertiveness'.[6]

By the time *The Clash of Civilizations* was published, not only had the Soviet bloc collapsed, but a Western coalition had unleashed Operation Desert Storm in Iraq to topple that country's leader, Saddam Hussein, apparently confirming Huntington's thesis that the world would revert to civilisational clashes between East and West after the distractions of fascism and communism.

Fukuyama's end-of-history thesis, despite having been criticised by his professor, represented an attempt, in the wake of the fall of the Soviet bloc, to sunder neoliberal triumphalism from its cultural wing: post-modernism. Post-modern philosophy had, in Fukuyama's opinion, undermined the ideology behind liberal democracy, leaving the Western world in a potentially weaker position. The cultural relativism he found in Paris and Yale offered no hope and nothing to sustain a necessary sense of community. It made Westerners believe in next to nothing, rendering us decadent, weak and pitiful. In this, he argued, we had truly become the last men envisaged by Nietzsche – anti-Napoleons who represent the decadent full-stop to the heroic adventure of Western civilisation.

If this was true, then, in the looming clash of civilisations, post-modernism made us unfit for purpose. The West's enemy wasn't just jihadists in suicide vests, but the pampered Westerners that post-modernism produced. 'Pampering,' wrote German philosopher Peter Sloterdijk in his book *In the World Interior of Capital*, 'the expectation of security without struggle, has infused almost every individual existence today, regardless of gender.'[7] If there was to be a clash of civilisations that the West could win, then it needed to junk such post-modern decadence with its mimsy culture of offence and its bastard offspring, moral relativism.

There is something worth salvaging from Fukuyama's end-of-history thesis beyond its dubious Western hubris. At the geopolitical level, he may have assumed that one binary had been broken – namely, the Cold War struggle between communism and capitalism – in favour of a monolithic polity. But in its wake he identified another kind of struggle, which he called the struggle for recognition, or what has become better known as identity politics. This was a struggle that he thought risked disastrously fragmenting and weakening societies. 'People felt unfulfilled', said Fukuyama:

> They felt they had these true selves that weren't being recog-nised. In the absence of a common cultural framework previously set by religion, people were at a loss. Psychology and psychiatry stepped into that breach. In the medical profession, treating mental health has a therapeutic mission, and it became legit-imate to say the objective of society ought to be improving people's sense of self-esteem.[8]

The therapeutic turn that Fukuyama noted of the 1960s had now expanded beyond the medical profession. 'This became part of the mission of universities, which made it difficult to set educational criteria as opposed to therapeutic criteria aimed at making students feel good about themselves. This is what led to many of the conflicts over multiculturalism.' He cited how Stanford's Black Student Union had argued in the late 1980s that the university's Western Civilization curriculum 'hurts people mentally and emotionally in ways that are not even recognised'. Fukuyama found such remarks exasperating:

> Instead of saying we want to read authors that are outside the canon because they're important educationally and historically and culturally, the way it's framed by that student leader is that the exclusion of those authors hurts people's self-esteem: 'Because my people are not equally represented, I feel less good about myself' . . . We think of ourselves as people with an inner self hidden inside that is denigrated, ignored, not listened to. A great deal of modern politics is about the demand of that inner self to be uncovered, publicly claimed, and recognised by the political system.

He suggested that many of these social-movement groups 'found a home on the left, triggering a reaction on the right. They say: What about us? Aren't we deserving of recognition? Haven't the elites ignored us, downplayed our struggles? That's the basis of today's populism.' Not all populism involved heterosexual, white, working-class men expressing their anger over being neglected while struggles for recognition by women, people of colour, the disabled, and gay and transgender people made significant strides in law and in society more generally. But quite a lot of it did.

One of Francis Fukuyama's insights persisted long after his end-of-history thesis had been consigned to history's junk heap. It was his notion that post-modernism was bullshit; or, if not bullshit, then an intellectual and political disgrace. By

1989, post-modernism, which had arisen as a critique of modernism, had itself become a subject of study. In 1989, the American Marxist critic Fredric Jameson published *Postmodernism: Or, the Cultural Logic of Late Capitalism*, which argued that, in the post-modern era, art had been colonised by commerce.

Jameson also wrote about 'the waning of affect' that he claimed characterised post-modern subjectivity. Artists don't cut off their ears these days, more's the pity. The great demiurges and prophets of modernism – Jameson cited the force of nature that was Picasso, the tragic Kafka, Proust in his cork-lined room, Frank Lloyd Wright in his cape and pork-pie hat – were not possible in the post-modern era. 'If the post-structuralist motif of the "death of the subject" means anything socially', wrote Jameson, 'it signals the end of the entrepreneurial and inner-directed individualism, with its "charisma" and its accompanying categorial panoply of quaint romantic values such as that of the "genius".'9 Modernism was an elite vision that couldn't survive in our putatively democratic age.

But there was something in post-modernism to be welcomed by leftists such as Fredric Jameson. It entailed a levelling process by means of which the great geniuses of modernism were cut down to size. As Perry Anderson wrote in *The Origins of Postmodernity*: 'Although not without its grim satisfactions, such plebeianization perforce denotes not greater popular enlightenment, but new forms of inebriation and delusion . . . Certainly, the phenomenon of cultural coarsening . . . is on global display.'10

Despite that coarsening, Anderson compared the transition from modernism to post-modernism with that from the Renaissance to the Reformation: 'The Renaissance had been essentially an elite affair, confined to privileged minorities even among the educated, whereas the Reformation was a mass upheaval that transformed the outlook of half the common people of Europe.' Perhaps post-modernism was a secular reformation after the elitist renaissance that was modernism. If so, Anderson mused, perhaps post-modernism might ultimately move us beyond inebriation and delusion. After all, the Reformation was, Anderson argued (following a line of thought developed by Italian Marxist Antonio Gramsci), a necessary prelude to the Enlightenment. The extraordinary sophistication of Renaissance culture needed to be 'coarsened and simplified if its break-out from the medieval world was to be transmitted as a rational impulse to those below. The reform of religion was that necessary adulteration, the passage of an intellectual advance through the ordeal of popularisation, to a broader and eventually stronger and freer social foundation.'[11] It was the Protestant churches that performed that popularisation.

'Are banks and corporations plausible candidates for the same historical role?' Anderson asked, only half seriously. He thought not. Post-modernism would not, despite popularisation, create a stronger and freer social foundation. Rather, it would mire us further in a society of the spectacle. That society, rather than rising up against its oppression, risked being stupefied. And yet spectacles – especially TV, cinema and sport – represented the very *raison d'être* of what the Frankfurt School had called the culture industry: namely, to make the masses desire their own domination.

Anderson seized on mass tourism as typifying the post-modern society of the spectacle 'in its awesome mixture of release and despoilment'. And yet this monument should be approached dialectically: the grand tour was once only for periwigged toffs; now it is for any roughneck with an Interrail card. On the other hand, the post-modern birth of mass tourism through encouragement of the masses to fly may well be hastening the death of the planet, not to mention banalising human experience by reducing nature, art and architecture to Instagrammable spectacles.

The point, then, is that Anderson's analogy – as he well recognised – breaks down: post-modernism has not created a stronger and freer social foundation, as did the Reformation. Rather, post-modernism has thrown humanity off course from its Enlightenment project, landing it in a place devoted to inebriation and base pleasures – a kind of Faliraki of the soul, where patrician professors, even neo-Marxist ones, would not be caught dead. Francis Fukuyama's neoconservative sense was that post-modernism needed to be overcome because it weakened the resolve of democratic liberalism. For leftists such as Anderson, that entirely missed the role of post-modernism in helping neo-liberalism thrive. The plebeianisation of culture, Anderson recognised, served neoliberalism by inducing consumerist political quietism and increasing opportunities for capital acc-umulation. If there was to be a socialist revolution in late-capitalist countries – and there probably wouldn't be – post-modernism should be the first against the wall.

For Jürgen Habermas, in one of the key jeremiads against post-modernism, the Enlightenment programme of modernity had foundered before its completion. In his 1980 lecture at Frankfurt titled 'Modernity: An Unfinished Project?', he claimed that project had two aspects. The first was that science, art and morality were divided into separate value spheres, each governed by its own norms – namely, truth, beauty and justice, respec-tively. The second aspect was the release of each of these value spheres into everyday life, enriching it and emancipating us.

But the latter had not happened: rather, these value spheres became esoteric specialisms, their meanings increasingly acces-sible only to experts – usually academics massaging each other's self-images with peer-reviewed gobbledegook. 'The distance between these expert cultures and the general public has increased', sighed Habermas. The optimistic dream of Enlightenment thinkers, he argued, was that the arts and sciences would 'not merely promote the control of the forces of nature, but also further the understanding of self and world, the progress of morality, justice in social institutions and even human happiness'.[12]

The Reformation (as Perry Anderson suggested) had prepared us for the enlightenment of the people, for the development of communicative rationality at an unprecedented level; but the Enlightenment itself had been perverted. Instead, systems of power and money imposed constraints on human action.

Habermas was embellishing the excoriating critique of the Enlightenment by his predecessors and mentors in the Frankfurt School, Adorno and Horkheimer, whose *Dialectic of Enlightenment* had argued that Enlightenment values themselves are not progressive, and that the potentially liberating process of the unfolding of human freedom, as Hegel and indeed Marx posited it, was a delusion. They were pessimists in arguing that we were enslaved within capitalism thanks to the culture industry, which creates a false consciousness about the world and makes us desire our own domination by the ruling class. Habermas demurred: for him there was no total system of delusion; rather, there was a project of modernity that could be restored to its proper path.

A year after his Frankfurt address, Habermas gave another talk in Munich, in which he expressed more doubt that the project could ever be completed. In a lecture called 'Modern and Postmodern Architecture', he reflected that one of modernism's great dreams had been that cities might be built in a rational way, liberating hitherto stymied human potentials.[13] Le Corbusier wrote that a house is a machine for living in. Cities, too, might be thought of as bigger machines. The corollary of such thoughts was that the way in which we live, both at home and in cities, could be rationally planned. But Habermas came to the conclusion that was a mistake. The crooked timber of humanity could not be so easily straightened; the city was beyond the grasp of mere human planning.

Perry Anderson accused Habermas of 'eudaimonism of the intelligence, defeatism of the will', suggesting that he had come to this bitter conclusion: 'There could be nothing but capitalism. The postmodern was a sentence on alternative illusions.'[14]

Two other left-wing critics saw post-modernism as arising in the wake of the left's historic defeat in its revolutionary struggles of the late 1960s. Alex Callinicos, in *Against Postmodernism: A Marxist Critique*, argued that post-modernism reflected the disappointment of the revolutionary generation of 1968 – especially those in France – and the incorporation of many of its members into the professional and managerial new middle class.[15] This was a theme developed most powerfully by French sociologists Luc Boltanski and Eve Chiapello, whose book *The New Spirit of Capitalism* argued that capitalism revivified itself from new blood sucked, ironically enough, from those who had tried to destroy it on the barricades in 1968.

For Callinicos, post-modernism wasn't an intellectual or cultural phenomenon so much as a symptom of political frustration. Terry Eagleton took up this theme in his 1996 book *The Illusions of Postmodernism*, arguing that its rise could not be wholly explained through the defeat that the political left had suffered in the late 1960s. Post-modernism, for Eagleton, had provoked a veritable revolution in thought about power, desire, identity and the body that any radical politics must take into account; but he balked at what he took as its 'cultural relativism and moral conventionalism, its scepticism, pragmatism, and localism, its distaste for ideas of solidarity and disciplined organization, its lack of any adequate theory of political agency'.[16]

The most frequent charge against post-modernism from both left and right is that of cultural relativism. In Eagleton's view, post-modern theorists have 'produced . . . an invigorating and a paralysing scepticism, and unseated the sovereignty of Western Man, in theory at least, by means of a full-blooded cultural relativism which is powerless to defend either Western or Eastern Woman against degrading social practices'.[17]

The problem here, it seems to me, is that Eagleton's critique of post-modernism has created a straw man. Richard Rorty captures this very well:

> 'Relativism' is the view that every belief on a certain topic, or perhaps about any topic, is as good as every other. No one holds this view. Except for the occasional cooperative freshman, one cannot find anybody who says that two incompatible opinions on an important topic are equally good. The philosophers who get called 'relativists' are those who say that the grounds for

choosing between such opinions are less algorithmic than had
been thought.[18]

There is no such person as a cultural relativist who accepts that
her values are no better than anyone else's.

And yet, for critics of post-modernism, its supposed relativism was its most damning defect. 'Seriously,' snarled the great
linguist Noam Chomsky, 'what are the principles of their theories, on what evidence are they based, what do they explain that
wasn't already obvious, etc.? These are fair requests for anyone
to make. If they can't be met, then I'd suggest recourse to Hume's
advice in similar circumstances: to the flames.'[19] Chomsky was
outraged at post-modernists' contention that there was no such
thing as truth and objectivity, only power and interests.
Chomsky's fury may have been misplaced. Book burning is no
way to settle an argument. A better tactic was ridicule. Consider,
suggested the post-modernism-despising philosopher Daniel
Dennett, in his 1998 paper 'Postmodernism and Truth', the
following story. A group of American researchers inadvertently
introduce a virus into a Third World country they are studying.
The virus raises infant mortality rates, leads to a decline in the
health and well-being of women and children, and strengthens
the hand of the ruling despot. These researchers surely have
something to answer for. Not at all, they reply. Their critics,
they contend, are trying to impose 'Western' standards in a
cultural environment that has no use for such standards.[20] But
here is the twist in Dennett's tale. These researchers were not
biologists, chemists or doctors, but

postmodernist science critics and other multiculturalists who
were arguing . . . that Western science was just one among many
equally valid narratives, not to be 'privileged' in its competition
with native traditions that other researchers – biologists, chemists, doctors, and others – were eager to supplant. The virus they
introduced was not a macromolecule but a meme (a replicating
idea): the idea that science was a 'colonial' imposition, not a

worthy substitute for the practices and beliefs that had carried the Third World country to its current condition.[21]

But science, argues Dennett, is not a colonial imposition; nor are all knowledge claims relative; nor is the pursuit of truth a dubious activity concealing power interests. And yet, he claims, post-modern thinkers suppose just such nonsense.

Dennett suggested three unquestionable truths: Life first emerged on this planet more than 3,000 million years ago. The Holocaust happened during World War II. Jack Ruby shot and killed Lee Harvey Oswald at 11:21 a.m., Dallas time, on 24 November 1963. 'These are truths about events that really happened. Their denials are falsehoods. No sane philosopher has ever thought otherwise, though in the heat of battle, they have sometimes made claims that could be so interpreted,' Dennett concluded.[22] Perhaps, but many philosophers – some of them even sane ones – have worried about who decides what counts as true. For them, truth is not innocent, but bound up with power.

In the post-modern era, Michel Foucault elaborated what that will to truth amounted to, suggesting that what counts as true shifts from one society to another.

> Each society has its regime of truth, its 'general politics' of truth: that is, the types of discourse which it accepts and makes function as true; the mechanisms and instances which enable one to distinguish true and false statements, the means by which each is sanctioned; the techniques and procedures accorded value in the acquisition of truth; the status of those who are charged with saying what counts as true.[23]

Clearly, there is something in this. Another regime of truth than ours might have accepted that the sun goes round the moon. The Catholic faithful have long accepted that God created man and woman, the latter as the former's helpmeet. British imperialists might well have taken it as axiomatic that they were intellectually superior to the people they subjugated. None of these propositions, asserted as true, are always and everywhere held to be so. For Foucault, facts are always products of what is sayable in a particular regime of truth. Not so for Dennett: for him, there are propositions whose truth is incontestable whatever regime of truth one lives under – such as the three given earlier. Only the insane or antisemites doubt that the Holocaust happened.

The battle over truth between post-modernists and their critics has been fought most strikingly over a passage in George Orwell's *Nineteen Eighty-Four*, in which the Party boss O'Brien makes Winston Smith believe that two plus two equals five is true by electrocuting him and threatening him with rats. Some have taken this scene as showing that Orwell defends common sense against those intellectuals who insist that there aren't any objective truths, only human interests and desires. In his 1989 classic of post-modern philosophy *Contingency, Irony and Solidarity*, Richard Rorty argued otherwise. The point of Orwell's story is not that it is true that two plus two equals four, but that the freedom to say it is what matters:

> The *only* point in making Winston believe that two and two equals five is to break him. Getting somebody to deny a belief for no reason is a first step toward making her incapable of having a self because she becomes incapable of weaving a coherent web of belief and desire. It makes her irrational, in a quite precise sense: She is unable to give a reason for her belief that fits together with her other beliefs. She becomes irrational not in the sense that she has lost contact with reality but in the sense that she can no longer rationalise – no longer justify herself to herself.[24]

It is this lack of coherence that matters in the story: if O'Brien can destroy Smith's rational sense by making him believe two plus two equals five, he has destroyed Smith. And this cruel destruction of another human being is the worst thing that anyone can do. As Rorty put it elsewhere in the book, 'liberals are the people who think that cruelty is the worst thing we do'. By contrast with such pressing concerns, philosophical navel gazing was unimportant: 'Somewhere we all know that philosophically sophisticated debate about . . . objective truth . . . is pretty harmless stuff.'[25]

Rorty was a post-modernist who wanted to deny the value of truth. For him, truth is not only dispensable; its pursuit by scientists and historians is a hopeless surrogate for humanity's earlier worship of God. Rorty agreed with Nietzsche that, now that God is dead, intellectuals replace him with metaphysical fictions like truth. Rorty argued that humans would be freer if we dispensed with such God surrogates. In this, post-modernist thought seems to be a liberation theology – freeing us from the tyranny of truth imposed on us by powerful elites. Post-modernism doesn't tell truth to power; rather, it tells power that truth is not what it seems to be.

But that post-modern denial of the value of truth scandalised critics. British philosopher Bernard Williams, in his book *Truth and Truthfulness*, argued that these values are essential in any human society, and that the twin virtues of truth – sincerity and accuracy – should be prized.[26] In a 2002 Oxford talk, to clinch this point, Williams considered the scene in Orwell's *Nineteen Eighty-Four*: 'Why is it better to believe with Mrs Harrison [a woman he has invented for the evening] that Africa is a continent that has the equator running through it than with O'Brien that 2+2=5? It can't be because Mrs Harrison is nice and O'Brien has tortured you with rats. It's because Mrs Harrison's belief is linked with the truth.'[27] The truth, that is to say, is not just about power and interests. It deals in objective facts.

And indeed that seemed to have mattered very much to Orwell. He certainly thought of what it was to be a liberal in a different way from Rorty. 'There is some hope . . . that the liberal habit of mind, which thinks of truth as something outside yourself, something to be discovered, and not as something you can make up as you go along, will survive.'[28] In another essay,

Orwell wrote of the disorientating horrors of fascist propaganda, which left him 'feeling that the very concept of objective
truth is fading out of the world'. He added, 'Nazi theory indeed
specifically denies that such a thing as "the truth" exists . . . This
prospect frightens me much more than bombs.'[29]

Orwell's suggestion in *Nineteen Eighty-Four* is that the claim
that there are hard facts that can be doubted by philosophers in
theory is a luxury the rest of us cannot afford in practice.[30] Only
the force of doublethink might lead us to suppose that what is
true in one epistemic domain is not also true in another.

Post-modern scepticism about truth, for the likes of Rorty,
Foucault, Jacques Derrida and others – including historians
like Paige Dubois, who contended that truth is historically
bound up with Greek slavery, and so its pursuit does nobody
any good – was supposed to liberate us, to free us from our
metaphysical illusions and enslavement under regimes wherein
only certain authorities get to say what is true and what is false.
But, while post-modernists have undeniably striven to take
down Western metaphysics in general and its respect for truth
in particular, it's not clear that this leaves us at a philosophical
swingers' party where facts and values can be swapped with
grubby disregard for standards of intellectual decency like the
guests' car keys. As Rorty argued, there is no such person as a
cultural relativist who accepts that her values are no better than
anyone else's. Viewed thus, the parable that Daniel Dennett
devised above conflates two phenomena: the cultural relativist
(who can't exist) and the absurd figure of the guilt-ridden Westerner (who can and does exist) striving not to repeat the sins of
their fathers by imposing imperial values on historically
oppressed persons in developing countries – even at the expense
of oppressing them further.

Post-modernism is both less silly than Dennett's tale suggests
and capable of being more subversive than Eagleton and other
left critics allow. It subverts our convictions with the same
disturbing force that Judith Butler's gender theory overturns our
notions of sexual identity. Rorty puts it well:

All human beings carry about a set of words which they employ to justify their actions, their beliefs, and their lives. These are the words in which we formulate praise of our friends and contempt for our enemies, our long-term projects, our deepest self-doubts and our highest hopes . . . I shall call these words a person's 'final vocabulary' . . . Those words are as far as [their user] can go with language; beyond them is only helpless passivity or a resort to force.[31]

Against such convictions, Rorty proposed something typically post-modern: irony. The ironist, for Rorty, is someone who doubts that there is one final vocabulary, as much as she doubts there is such a thing as absolute truth or a reality independent of us. He defines this ironist thus:

(1) She has radical and continuing doubts about the final vocabulary she currently uses, because she has been impressed by other vocabularies, vocabularies taken as final by people or books she has encountered; (2) she realizes that argument phrased in her present vocabulary can neither underwrite nor dissolve these doubts; (3) insofar as she philosophizes about her situation, she does not think that her vocabulary is closer to reality than others, that it is in touch with a power not herself.[32]

But this makes the post-modernist sound like a cosy figure devoid of real commitments and happy to float in a bottomless ocean of irony. Even a Marxist critic of post-modernism like Terry Eagleton recognised there was more to it than that. Post-modern politics also involves 'the appearance on the theoretical centre stage of millions who have been dumped and discarded, as often by traditional leftists as by the system itself'.[33]

Traditional Marxism had little to say about the plight of women, people of colour or LGBTQ people. Even the so-called New Left, spearheaded in the 1960s by Herbert Marcuse, seemed a dubious phenomenon. In 1964, it was Marcuse who, in

One-Dimensional Man, said that now the proletariat had become too comfortable with material goods to fulfil its manifest destiny of overthrowing capitalism. The revolution would have to be fought by a new army composed of what he called subaltern groups: women, civil rights activists, students. At least some of those groups, though, did not care to be recruited to the cause by an old white Marxist man.

II

Among the sceptical was feminist thinker Kate Millett, celebrated for her 1970 book *Sexual Politics*. When, in 1975, Marcuse and Millett shared a platform at the University of California, San Diego, sponsored by the university's women's centre, Millett said of Marcuse: 'One gets the impression, and I'm sure it is unintended, of political opportunism. The time is right, the women's movement is getting along nicely . . . let's utilise this in the eternal struggle, the great holy war, to bring about the fall of capitalism. Women are used to being used.'[34]

Instead of being co-opted into someone else's idea of a revolution, the hitherto dumped and discarded created their own. And one of the leading revolutionaries in this was Judith Butler, whose book *Gender Trouble: Feminism and the Subversion of Identity* was published in 1990. Butler queried the notion of stable sexual identities, and in so doing challenged the heteronormative orthodoxy. In this, she took her cue from what the French feminist philosopher Simone de Beauvoir had written in *The Second Sex* in 1949, namely: 'One is not born, but rather becomes, a woman.'[35]

This claim created space for Butler to think that, while one might be born anatomically female, it does not follow that one identifies with or displays a female gender. 'If there is something right in Beauvoir's claim that one is not born, but rather becomes a woman, it follows that woman itself is a term in process, a becoming, a constructing that cannot rightfully be said to originate or to end.'[36] For Butler, gender is not innate:

just because you are born with a penis or a vagina does not mean you identify as a man or a woman, respectively. Instead, one performs one's gender according to social norms. This possibility opens the way to thinking that one's sex may not decide one's gender – indeed, that some people will identify with a gender different from their sex. Some people may not identify with either of the traditional genders, but consider themselves gender fluid, or between, or neither.

More revolutionary yet, Butler doubted even that the distinction between sex and gender was between biological fact and cultural construction. For her, the apparent existence of sex prior to discourse and cultural imposition is only an effect of the functioning of gender.

> We are assigned a sex, treated in various ways that communicate expectations for living as one gender or another, and we are formed within institutions that reproduce our lives through gender norms. So, we are always 'constructed' in ways that we do not choose. And yet we all seek to craft a life in a social world where conventions are changing, and where we struggle to find ourselves within existing and evolving conventions. This suggests that sex and gender are 'constructed' in a way that is neither fully *determined* nor fully *chosen* but rather caught up in the recurrent tension between determinism and freedom.[37]

The problem here is the word 'assign', with its connotations of a high-handed, arbitrary bureaucratic decision. But if the claim is that a baby is treated as a boy or girl by his or her parents after being born on the basis of which sex the parents think the baby to be, that seems uncontroversial: indeed, experiments have shown that, when parents see a baby crying, they will identify it as indicating fear if they think it is a girl but as anger if they think it is a boy. But this doesn't seem to be the distinction Butler is making when she talks about assigning sex. She seems to want to argue that babies have no tendencies or abilities prior to their experience of gendered society.

This thought still outrages many scientists and doctors, for whom sex is a biological fact, and whether one is born male or female is a matter of biology – namely the presence or absence of a Y chromosome in the human embryo. Genes on the Y chromosome cause changes that produce the male testes in the typical male foetus; without that stimulus from the Y chromosome, the gonad turns into an ovary. QED.

Well, not quite. There are, for instance, cases of androgen insensitivity syndrome, as a result of which someone may be born with male or female external genitalia, or something in between. But females with AIS are not fertile, because they have testes rather than ovaries. In such cases who decides what sex a person is? Moreover, what is the point of doing so? Butler noted that 'intersexed people have become increasingly critical of the fact that medical authorities have often mis-categorised them and subjected them to cruel forms of "correction"'.[38]

What does 'correction' mean? 'In many places surgeons have often tried to "tidy up" the genitalia of babies born with nonstandard sexual bodies, soon after birth', writes Kwame Anthony Appiah. 'So they've sought to bring everybody into a binary system, in which everyone is more or less clearly male or female. Not everyone agrees that this is a good idea.'[39] This sort of surgical 'tidying up' was objectionable to Judith Butler – though, to her satisfaction, it at least clinched the point that sex can be culturally decided: 'Even if the sexes appear to be unproblematically binary in their morphology and constitution (which will become a question), there is no reason to assume that genders ought to remain as two. The presumption of a binary gender system implicitly retains the belief in a mimetic relation of gender to sex whereby gender mirrors sex or is otherwise restricted by it.'[40]

For Butler, we need not only to overcome a binary gender system, but also to realise that gender is scripted, rehearsed and performed. Post-modern artists like Cindy Sherman, David Bowie and Madonna had already playfully demonstrated this through their works. Butler has also championed drag, since it destabilises the heteronormative binary. In *Bodies That Matter*, she wrote: 'Drag is subversive to the extent that it reflects on the imitative structure by which hegemonic gender is itself produced and disputes heterosexuality's claim on naturalness.'[41] True, this quote never appeared on billboards for Danny La Rue or RuPaul's shows, but doubtless it was implicit. Queer identities, for Butler, should be celebrated because they disrupt our ideas of gender and challenge the traditional structures of society.

For critics, though, this challenge is feeble. In a devastating critique of her intellectual contribution, philosopher Martha Nussbaum wrote that Butler's

> best known idea, her conception of politics as a parodic performance, is born out of the sense of a (strictly limited) freedom that comes from the recognition that one's ideas of gender have been shaped by forces that are social rather than biological. We are doomed to the repetition of the power structures into which we are born, but we can at least make fun of them; and some ways of making fun are subversive assaults on the original norms.[42]

For Nussbaum, Judith Butler's quietist politics were a tragic betrayal of the struggles of feminism. Butler did nothing to improve women's economic opportunities, working conditions or education; nor did she fight for pregnancy benefits for female workers or campaign against sex trafficking of women and girls, argued Nussbaum.

And yet the trouble Butler stirred up with her book stimulated the rise of what has come to be called queer theory, or gender theory – and it has had real-world effects beyond academia. The rights of trans people in the military, gay marriage, and other movements in favour of gender equality and sexual freedom have gained a lot of ground since *Gender Trouble* appeared.

What Butler subverted was the traditional taxonomy in which there were only men and women. Men and women knew which gender they were because they were born with bodies that helpfully informed them of the fact. If you had a penis, you were a man; if you had a vagina, you were a woman; and the task of humanity was to bring the former into close interaction with the latter for the sake of the species. There were only heterosexual, cisgendered men and women, and everything was very simple.[43] Trans people did not exist – or, if they did, there was something terribly wrong with them, and they needed to be brought into line with the existing order.

Such traditional views have hardly disappeared in the thirty years since *Gender Trouble* appeared. 'God created man and woman; God created the world like this and we are doing the exact opposite', said Pope Francis in 2016. 'We are experiencing a moment of the annihilation of man as the image of God.'[44] Gender theory as advanced by the likes of Judith Butler had contested the natural, hierarchical distinction between male and female upon which family values and social life are based, and the leader of the Catholic church thought the impact of this challenge was disastrous. In an encyclical *Laudato Si*, the Pope criticised gender theory's disruption of stable male and female identities: 'Thinking that we enjoy absolute power over our own bodies turns, often subtly, into thinking that we enjoy absolute power over creation.'[45] Once this Pandora's Box of gender theory had been opened, he feared, all kinds of monstrosities would emerge. He even connected gender theory with the exploitation of human beings and of the natural world; both came from a lack of appreciation of humankind's God-given dignity. Nonsense, retorted Butler:

> Ultimately, the struggle for gender equality and sexual freedom seeks to alleviate suffering and to recognise the diverse embodied and cultural lives that we live. Teaching gender is not indoctrination: it does not tell a person how to live; it opens up the possibility for young people to find their own way in a world that often confronts them with narrow and cruel social norms. To affirm gender diversity is therefore not destructive: it affirms

human complexity and creates a space for people to find their own way within this complexity.

The world of gender diversity and sexual complexity is not going away. It will only demand greater recognition for all those who seek to live out their gender or sexuality without stigma or the threat of violence. Those who fall outside the norm deserve to live in this world without fear, to love and to exist, and to seek to create a world more equitable and free of violence.[46]

In the same year as *Gender Trouble* appeared, Eve Kosofsky Sedgwick published *Epistemology of the Closet*. Both books appropriated the abusive term for gay people 'queer' and used it to subvert binary oppositions – man–woman, gay–straight – and argue that genders are fluid and fictional rather than fixed. In this, they were elaborating on Michel Foucault's argument that bodies are given meaning by discourse and by social structures of knowledge and power. This argument is profoundly post-modern: it is one that blurs another binary, that between facts and values.

For queer theorists like Butler and Sedgwick, the idea that sex is a biological fact, or that women have cervices, is itself the product of the values of the prevailing discourse. Sedgwick held it to be axiomatic that people are different from each other: 'It is astonishing how few respectable conceptual tools we have for dealing with this self-evident fact.' All we have, she argued, is a 'tiny number of inconceivably coarse axes of categorisation . . . [namely] gender, race, nationality, class [and] sexual orientation'. Such crude categories were hopeless in comprehending the diversity of humans:

> The sister or brother, the best friend, the classmate, the parent, the child, the lover, the ex- . . . not to mention the strange relations of our work, play, and activism, prove that even people who share all or most of our own positioning along these crude axes may still be different enough from us, and from each other, to seem like all but different species.[47]

Since *Gender Trouble* and *Epistemology of the Closet*, the mainstream has certainly been destabilised, if only somewhat and only in some polities. Take the United Kingdom in 1992. At that time, Section 28 of the Local Government Act stated that a local authority 'shall not promote homosexuality' or 'promote the teaching in any maintained school of the acceptability of homosexuality as a pretended family relationship', and gay marriage was illegal. The former law was repealed in 2003, and the Marriage (Same Sex Couples) Act passed in 2013. Of course, it would be hard to show that queer studies as pioneered by Butler and Sedgwick changed the public mood on these questions, and very easy to show that homophobia and transphobia thrive today. And yet it would be trite to suggest that queer theory has not improved some people's lives. Consider, for instance, how Kwame Anthony Appiah tips his hat to feminist theorists: 'Without the reshaping of gender that has increasingly liberated us all from old patriarchal assumptions, I could not have lived my life as a gay man married to another man, making a life, in public and private ways, together.'[48]

That is to be cherished. But it is also worth noting that queer theory has also been rubbished for its politically inert academic preening by tough-minded feminists, nowhere better than in Andrea Dworkin's 1990 novel *Mercy*. There Judith Butler, so keen to argue for the subversive role of parody, gets mercilessly parodied. Dworkin has the thinly veiled Butler tell her academic faithful:

> The notion that bad things happen is both propagandistic and inadequate . . . To understand a woman's life requires that we affirm the hidden or obscure dimensions of pleasure, often in pain, and choice, often under duress. One must develop an eye for secret signs – the clothes that are more than clothes or decoration in the contemporary dialogue, for instance, or the rebellion hidden behind apparent conformity. There is no victim. There is perhaps an insufficiency of signs, an obdurate appearance of conformity that simply masks the deeper level on which choice occurs.[49]

For Butler's critics, this satire was justified, since her work is preaching to a choir of academic faithful while refusing to engage in the real struggles to improve the lives of women. While Dworkin and her colleague Catharine MacKinnon were fighting for changes to laws against sexual harassment, Judith Butler was part of a new feminism that refused direct engagement with power. Martha Nussbaum described Butlerian quietism thus:

> We are all, more or less, prisoners of the structures of power that have defined our identity as women; we can never change those structures in a large-scale way, and we can never escape from them. All that we can hope to do is to find spaces within the structures of power in which to parody them, to poke fun at them, to transgress them in speech. And so symbolic verbal politics, in addition to being offered as a type of real politics, is held to be the only politics that is really possible.[50]

Nussbaum blamed post-modernism for this new feminism – and in particular the post-modern French theory that infuses Butler's writings. Foucault in particular has infected his faithful with the fatalistic idea that we are prisoners of an all-enveloping structure of power, and that real-life reform movements usually end up serving power in new and insidious ways. So it was better not to bother with them. 'There is despair at the heart of the cheerful Butlerian enterprise', wrote Nussbaum:

> The big hope, the hope for a world of real justice, where laws and institutions protect the equality and the dignity of all citizens, has been banished, even perhaps mocked as sexually tedious. Judith Butler's hip quietism is a comprehensible response to the difficulty of realising justice in America. But it is a bad response. It collaborates with evil. Feminism demands more and women deserve better.[51]

That charge – of collaborating with evil – is a strong one to make. But Nussbaum's point here shows why post-modernism, from which queer theory and new feminism derive, has attracted a bad name. It postures as subversive and ends up either co-opted into supporting the system it affects to subvert or relegated to the margins, burnishing its hip academic credentials but otherwise changing nothing very much. In architecture, post-modernism erects beguiling façades before temples of neoliberal capital. In terms of women's fight for equality, it does something similar, dressing itself in drag and beguiling itself at the results, while the struggle against patriarchal power is challenged, if at all, by other means. Catharine MacKinnon put it this way: 'Post-modernism is an academic theory, originating in academia with an academic elite, not in the world of women and men, where feminist theory is rooted.' MacKinnon argued that until sex inequality was tackled legally, women would continue to be raped, murdered and served up as masturbation fantasies for men.[52] The post-modern queer theory pioneered by Judith Butler has never been part of that struggle.

III

On Valentine's Day 1989, Iran's Ayatollah Khomeini declared a fatwa against Salman Rushdie. 'I inform all zealous Muslims of the world that the author of the book entitled *The Satanic Verses* – which has been printed and published in opposition to Islam, the Prophet and the Qu'ran – and all those involved in its publication who were aware of its contents are sentenced to death. I call on all zealous Muslims to execute them quickly wherever they may be found, so that no one else will dare to insult the Muslim sanctities.'[53]

Soon afterwards, the Indian-born British novelist joined the elite Level One Club, which gives members 24/7 police protection. Rushdie became, after the Queen and prime minister, its third member. He went into hiding, and for thirteen years played and was compelled to play the role of someone else. His protection officers suggested he choose another name, to increase his security when he turned up at a new home (though being flanked by four armed men in bulletproof Jaguars usually did the trick). It was probably better not to make it an Indian name, counselled his minder, Stan. And so Salman Rushdie became Joseph Anton – what he called 'an invisible man in a whiteface mask'. Joseph was Conrad's first name, Anton was Chekhov's.[54]

What had prompted the fatwa was Rushdie's 1988 novel *The Satanic Verses*. The satanic verses of Rushdie's novel were those Muhammad believed were dictated to him by the archangel Gabriel. They said that the pagan goddesses worshipped in Mecca 'are exalted females whose intercession is to be desired' – a contradiction of the nascent monotheism of Islamic orthodoxy.[55] Only later did Muhammad repudiate these verses, argues Rushdie, saying he was deceived by the devil, who had disguised himself as the archangel.

As a history undergraduate at Cambridge twenty years before he published *The Satanic Verses*, Rushdie had written about this historical Muhammad, wondering why, 1,400 years ago, the prophet had temporarily accepted the first false revelation as true. One possible answer, Rushdie argued, following certain Western scholars of Islam, was that Muhammad was a political figure who, briefly, realised that his shaky Meccan power base could be made more secure if the monotheistic religion he had founded could make accommodations with followers of then-popular pagan deities. But this makes the founder of Islam look more like canny politician than divine vessel – a seeming slur against Islam at the moment of its birth.

Between Cambridge and fatwa, Rushdie spent ten years writing advertising copy. The man nicknamed 'Salmon Fishcake' by colleagues was responsible for slogans such as 'Incredibubble' (for Aero chocolate) and 'Naughty. But nice' (for the UK Milk Marketing Board's cream cakes), and for the *Daily Mirror*'s 'Take a look in the Mirror. You'll like what you see.' But during his mad-man years, Rushdie was also working on his first novel, *Grimus* (1975), about a young Indian man who gains immortality after drinking a magical potion. With the £800 he earned from his debut novel, Rushdie quit advertising to go backpacking around India. The trip catalysed his imagination. He realised he could write something that would 'presumptuously and self-defeatingly' try to capture India's polymorphous spirit in a single book.[56]

The result was *Midnight's Children*, the 1981 Booker Prize–winning novel whose hero, Saleem Sinai, was born at the very moment India became independent from Britain, at midnight on 15 August 1947 (Rushdie himself was born in Bombay – now Mumbai – on 19 June in that same year). Perhaps the novel was not the birth of postcolonial literature, but it typified the sub-version of the colonial gaze. While travelling, Rushdie realised that the cool prose that 'Indian writers such as R. K. Narayan, Anita Desai and others' had appropriated from the English nov-elist E. M. Forster, author of *A Passage to India*, was not adequate to the task of capturing the country:

> Don't get me wrong – I love Forster. In fact I knew him at King's [College, Cambridge] when I was there. He served me tea and I recognised him as someone brave enough to have been anti-imperialist in *A Passage to India*. But the Forsterian way of writing coolly and classically did not match the India I saw.
>
> It wasn't cool, it was hot. It's a country where, even if you're in a rural area, you're never alone. I wanted to write the literary equivalent of a crowd. So it was a trick, a deliberate attempt to have too much incident so that you feel pushed this way and that, as if you're in a crowd.[57]

Rushdie told the *New York Times* that his third novel, *Shame* (1983), was 'a sort of modern fairy tale', which the author says nobody need take seriously and which, since it is set in 'not quite Pakistan', need not provoke the authorities to ban the book or have it burned.[58] Nevertheless, it was an indictment of a country that had abjured polymorphousness and turned unitary. Pakistan freed itself from the colonial yoke only to mutate into a dictator-ship, with informers ready to betray to the authorities those who spoke out of turn. Rushdie may have claimed that this was fiction – magical rather than conventional realism – but the real rulers of Pakistan thought otherwise: *Shame* was banned in Pakistan by President Zia.

Some critics have taken these two subcontinental novels as demonstrating that, far from being a postcolonial novelist, Rushdie is in league with dominant European power structures, rather than seeking to challenge them. For them, he is a rootless, privileged cosmopolitan educated at Mumbai's elite private Cathedral School and Cambridge University – a life scarcely comprehensible to those who live in the countries he celebrates or indicts. For them, his is a Eurocentric vision that reduces India to exotic other and Pakistan to Third World dictatorship. For his part, Rushdie sees his multiple roots and multiple displacements as helping him to view contemporary history through satirical, magical-realist fiction more powerfully. 'I am an emigrant from one country (India) and a newcomer in two (England, where I live, and Pakistan, to which my family moved against my will)', he said once.[59]

The ban and criticism he faced for *Shame* hardly chastened Rushdie. After its publication, he began thinking again about the historical Muhammad, whom he had studied at Cambridge twenty years earlier. When the result of these meditations, *The Satanic Verses*, was published in 1989, it provoked outrage. Many thought Rushdie was attacking their religion and mocking its prophet. Syed Shahabuddin, an Indian MP, wrote in the *Times of India* that the novel was 'suggestively derogatory'. Rushdie, Shahabuddin claimed, had depicted the prophet's wives as prostitutes working in a brothel called the Curtain – a translation of *al-hijab*, the Arabic word for veil. Not true: in the novel, Muhammad's wives don't work in a brothel, but the prostitutes take the names of the prophet's wives – which is doubtless offensive to the faithful. Shahabuddin, like most of those condemning the book, had not read it. 'I do not need to wade through a filthy drain to know what filth is', said Shahabuddin.[60]

Otherwise, though, the Rushdie affair resembled the clash of civilisations Samuel Huntington had feared arising in the aftermath of the Cold War. On the one side, the pre-modern Islamic faithful believing in the absolute truth of the word of God given to the prophet and written in their holy book; instead of reading *The Satanic Verses*, they burned it from Bradford to Islamabad, and hunted down its author and his hirelings. On the other, a sophisticated post-modern novelist who had embraced the godless West and sneered at the Muslim sancti- ties. And indeed, Rushdie told me he is 'a profoundly irreligious man' and 'of the Hitchens camp' (his late friend Christopher Hitchens wrote the incendiary bestseller *God Is Not Great*).[61] In his memoir of the fatwa, *Joseph Anton*, Rushdie argued the case in favour of blasphemy: 'The writers of the French enlighten- ment had deliberately used blasphemy as a weapon, refusing to accept the power of the Church to set limiting points on thought.'[62]

This clash-of-civilisations narrative gained support from Rushdie's literary friends who wrote about Islam. Fellow novel- ist Martin Amis, writing after 9/11, argued: 'All over again, the West confronts an irrationalist, agonistic theocratic/ideocratic system which is essentially and unappeasably opposed to its existence.' Amis described moderate Islam as 'supine and inau- dible' in the face of what he called 'Islamism'. Amis was also quoted in a newspaper interview as saying that he felt an 'urge' to favour 'discriminatory stuff' against Muslims living in Britain 'until it hurts the whole community and they start getting tough with their children'.[63]

In fact, the story is not so simple. Rushdie conceived *The Satanic Verses* not as a slur against religion but, in more post- modern fashion, as a critique of religions' claims to absolute truth. '*The Satanic Verses* isn't – or is not only – about Islam', he told me:

> It deals with the origin story of religion, closely following Islam. It's about the nature of revelation, about the seeing of visions. There are close parallels between Joan of Arc and St John the Divine's revelations and Muhammad's descriptions of seeing

the Angel Gabriel. It seems to me that's a subjective reality, not an objective one. If you'd been standing with Muhammad, would you have seen this big angel? Probably not, but at the same time Muhammad was not making up what he saw. For him it's not a fiction. That's interesting to write about.[64]

But that very word 'interesting' is revealing: what the post-modern, secular novelist – friends with taunters of religion such as Christopher Hitchens – found 'interesting', or a fit subject for satirical magical-realist fiction, was precisely what the faithful took as sacred, which was profaned by Rushdie's book.

Equally, Rushdie situated the prophet Muhammad as an historical figure engaged in a power struggle, rather than one tasked simply with communicating the sacred word of God. Behind the supposed absolute truth of angelic revelation was the pursuit of power and interests, rather in the manner of what Nietzsche and Foucault posited. Rushdie's questioning of the nature of revelation and the historical basis of putatively sacred texts, though, hardly pertains only to Islam. Open your Bible at I Corinthians 14, for instance, and read the wisdom of St Paul: 'Let your women keep silence in the churches: for it is not permitted unto them to speak. And if they will learn any thing, let them ask their husbands at home: for it is a shame for women to speak in the church.'

For Dominican New Testament scholar Jerome Murphy O'Connor, this is a 'post-Pauline insertion' – that is, words put into St Paul's mouth by those hoping to give their misogyny the spurious imprimatur of biblical authority, pickling it in sacred aspic and thereby upholding the patriarchy until the Four Horsemen saddle up.[65] De-sanctifying religious texts by setting them in their historical context in this way is apt to make the more literally minded faithful sharpen their ancestral swords to take down the apostates.

The clash-of-civilisations narrative, pitting pre-modern faithful Muslims against post-modern secular faithlessness, is dubious for another reason. The Rushdie affair may have seemed to play out between mad mullahs and book-burning barbarians, on the one hand, and the smug, decadent, nihilistic literati in Armani, on the other – but that's an oversimplification. When the writer and journalist Kenan Malik visited Bradford to find out about opposition to Rushdie's novel, he ran across an old mate. Hassan had been a member of the Trotskyist Socialist Workers Party. He enjoyed Southern Comfort, smoking weed, supporting Arsenal and listening to bands like The Specials and The Clash. Along with Malik, he had been arrested for chucking bricks at the racist National Front. True, he had attended mosque as a child but, as Malik put it later, 'the only God he worshipped was Liam Brady, Arsenal's magical midfielder. But now here he was in Bradford, an errand boy to the mullahs, inspired by book-burners, willing to shed blood for a thousand-year-old fable that he had never believed in.'[66]

Malik took his friend's metamorphosis from left-wing wide boy to Islamist militant to be emblematic of a different clash of civilisations from the one Samuel Huntington envisaged. The clash was not just between civilisations, but within Western societies. Contemporary Islamic radicalism, far from being an expression of ancient theological beliefs, is really a reaction to new political and social changes: the loss of a sense of belonging in a fragmented society, the blurring of traditional moral lines, the increasing disenchantment with politics and politicians, the growing erosion of the distinction between our private and public lives. Radical Islamists have responded to these changes by seeking succour in the Qu'ran, and taking its strictures literally.

But there is another factor behind radical Islam's rise in the West that needs stressing – racism. As Salman Rushdie himself put it: 'Four hundred years of conquest and looting, four centuries of being told that you are superior to the fuzzy-wuzzies and wogs, leave their stain.'[67]

In Hanif Kureishi's 1994 short story 'My Son the Fanatic', Ali tells his Pakistani-born father Parvez that he is going to give up his studies because 'Western education cultivates an anti-religious attitude'.[68] Radical Islam offers a seeming escape from the free-for-all of Western society in the post-modern era. In a world where everything else is shifting and fragmenting, where life presents itself as a fatuous Sisyphean task of production and consumption, Islam offers stability.

In *You Must Change Your Life*, Peter Sloterdijk writes that the impulse to join a radical Islamist group, or even to become a jihadist terrorist, is part of a post-secular drive towards self-training and self-discipline.[69] In a disenchanted world of production and consumption, he argues, some of us look to re-enchant our dreary selves through religious observance or spiritual exercises that might allow us to become more than mere *homo economicus*.

Christianity, Islam, Scientology, the Olympic movement and, possibly, the rise in home baking have more or less transcendent pretensions; but their real importance and seductive power is their response to the injunction 'You must change your life'. Each gives you a role in changing yourself from mere drone into a sovereign agent through a process of self-mastery. Whether such makeovers take place in mosques or Pilates studios is of only local interest. Each is a post-modern solution to a post-modern problem. Radical Islam, then, might best be understood as a negative form of Westernisation. It is a religious experience of a new kind – one born in reaction to the post-modern world in which its faithful live.

The West, Rushdie argued in *Joseph Anton*, is partly responsible for the rise of Islamic fundamentalism not just in the West but in countries such as Iran. When I interviewed him, he explained that the West was involved in the coup in 1953 that brought down Iran's democratically elected prime minister, Mohammad Mosaddegh, in favour of strengthening the monarchical rule of the shah, Mohammad Reza Pahlavi. The coup, orchestrated by the United States and the United Kingdom, was an attempt to thwart the nationalisation of Iranian oil refineries and the possibility of a communist takeover. In 1979, the shah was overthrown during Iran's Islamic Revolution, led by Ayatollah Khomeini – the very man who later issued the fatwa against Rushdie.

Another aspect of the West's responsibility for Islamic fundamentalism's rise was its support for the House of Saud, Rushdie claimed:

> The decision to place the House of Saud on the Throne that Sits Over the Oil might well look like the greatest foreign policy error of the Western powers, because the Sauds had used their unlimited oil wealth to build schools (madrassas) to propagate the extremist, puritanical ideology of their beloved (and previously marginal) Muhammad ibn 'Abd al-Wahhab, and as a result Wahhabism had grown from its tiny cult origins to overrun the Arab world. Its rise gave confidence and energy to other Islamic extremists.[70]

Rushdie survived the fatwa. He played the role of Joseph Anton until 27 March 2002, when the police Jaguars finally drove out of his life for the last time. During that time his first wife, Clarissa, died of cancer, his second and third marriages broke up, his fourth became shaky, his Japanese editor was murdered, his Norwegian publisher shot, and his Italian translator stabbed, while hundreds died in riots protesting against his novel, and his books were burned. Meanwhile, writers he admired, including John Berger and John le Carré – both writing in the *Guardian* – attacked him for not withdrawing the novel.

His chief regret, though, was that during this time he was lured to play another role, that of what he calls 'a dentist's zombie'. On Christmas Eve 1990, at the behest of six Muslim scholars whom he had agreed to meet at Paddington Green police station, he signed a paper saying he had intended no offence to Islam, and that he re-embraced the religion. The man who brokered this meeting, Harley Street dentist Hesham el-Essawy, sought to return Rushdie to the faith into which he had been born in Bombay in 1947.

Soon after that meeting, Rushdie wrote an article called 'Why I am a Muslim' for *The Times*. 'I am certainly not a good Muslim', he wrote then. 'But I am able now to say that I am Muslim; in fact it is a source of happiness to say that I am now inside, and a part of, the community whose values have always been closest to my heart.' It was as if, in Richard Rorty's terms, he had stopped being a post-modern ironist and instead become a believer in the final vocabulary that was the word of God expressed in the Qu'ran.

'I was physically sick after that', he recalled. 'I felt I had lost my mind. Reading through my journals of that time, I see it was the blackest period. I became the dentist's zombie, thinking he was giving me [spiritual] Novocain. But everybody who loved me told me I was insane.' He remembers his sister, Sameen, ringing him from across London after she heard of her brother's abject and futile attempt at appeasement. 'She said: "I don't fucking believe it. Have you lost your mind?" The problem was I had acted alone, without consulting my supportive friends and family.'[71]

He resolved that he would never succumb to such approaches again. Instead he repudiated his supposed faith, setting himself self-consciously in the tradition of writers such as Osip Mandelstam and Federico García Lorca, who had stood up to tyrants. And he condemned the very cultural relativism that Daniel Dennett took to be characteristic of post-modernism, arguing for the superior virtue of freedom of speech over what he called the culture of offence. 'The refrain is: "Oh dear, Muslims might be angry and we must respect them." Not true. When people do the cowardly thing, it's not about respect, it's about fear.'[72]

Free speech must trump the offence claimed by those on the receiving end of expressed opinions, he argued:

I may despise you personally for what you believe, but I should be able to say it. Everybody needs to get thicker skins. There is this culture of offence, as though offending someone is the worst thing anyone can do. Again, there is an assumption that our first duty is to be respectful. But what would a respectful cartoon look like? Really boring! You wouldn't publish it. The nature of the form is irreverence and disrespect.[73]

Rushdie said this to me in 2012. Three years later, two brothers, Cherif and Said Koauchi, entered the offices of French satirical magazine *Charlie Hebdo* in Paris, killing twelve people and injuring eleven others. The magazine had published cartoons depicting and satirising the prophet Muhammad. It was significant that the attack happened in France and was carried out by Muslims born in Paris to Algerian immigrant parents. France champions two things that produce resentment among alienated Islamic youth: firstly, its government-defined policy of *laïcité*, and secondly its almost religious reverence for its intellectual life and freedom of expression.

The tradition of *laïcité* stems from a revolutionary tradition that insisted on the creation of a secular public space, where individuals renounced part of what French feminist philosopher Hélène Cixous called their 'personal particularity', while the right to religious expression was guaranteed only in their private lives. What this came down to was that, if you were a Muslim woman who wore a headscarf, then, to be properly French, you had to check in that item of clothing as the price of admission to French public spaces such as schools. You had to deny part of what you were in order to be integrated. In the post-modern age of authenticity, the era of identity politics, a policy aimed at integration in practice produced alienation.

Meanwhile, France's hallowed intellectuals, argues Shlomo Sand, 'have inherited both the role of the court jester, able to say whatever was in their minds without being punished, and of the priest, serving as intermediary between the believer and divine truth'.[74] The murder of *Charlie Hebdo*'s court jesters was mourned by 4 million demonstrators in Paris, and by millions around the world who declared their solidarity by wearing 'Je suis Charlie' badges. The cultural relativism that Eagleton thought characterised post-modernism had been replaced, if only temporarily, by secularism's negative of religious worship, complete with martyrs, parades of the faithful, expressions of piety and disdain for apostates.

As for Salman Rushdie, he lived on to play a court jester himself. In 2017 he appeared in the US comedy *Curb Your Enthusiasm*. He played himself meeting the star of the show, Larry David (the writer/director played an on-screen Baudrillardian simulation of himself), to discuss David's plans to make a musical about the Rushdie affair called *Fatwa!* (their exclamation mark).[75] For daring to make such a musical, and for promoting it on a talk show at which he does a mocking impersonation of an ayatollah, David himself attracts a fatwa, and thereafter appears in public wearing a wig to disguise himself from potential assassins. David, understandably, seeks advice from Rushdie on how to survive this existential setback to his lifestyle.

Don't worry, Rushdie counsels David over tea. There are upsides to being on the ayatollah's Most Wanted List. 'It can be scary, it can be bewildering, etcetera, but there are things that you gain.' You can, he suggested, shirk social commitments you'd rather miss on the grounds of your current threat level. And then there was the fatwa sex. 'There are a lot of women that are attracted to you in this condition. You are a dangerous man.' In the next episode, we see rehearsals for *Fatwa!*, including an intentionally terrible duet between Rushdie (played by Lin-Manuel Miranda) and Ayatollah Khomeini (F. Murray Abraham), the former in hiding in London, the latter in Tehran. Their duet goes as follows:

RUSHDIE: What am I gonna do? His death sentence is the worst friggin' book review.
KHOMEINI: Talkin' trash about the scripture, not a pretty picture.
RUSHDIE: All I wanted was to win the Booker Prize, guys / Not have him slit my throat and gouge out my eyes, my, my.
KHOMEINI: I can't allow this desecration / This irritation, indignation – Not while I lead this nation.

By this time, David has abased himself before a panel of muftis who convince the ayatollah to renounce the fatwa. At the end of the episode, Larry leaves the rehearsal theatre only to be spotted by an Iranian man on the street who does not know the fatwa has been revoked and begins chasing him as the credits roll.

In this way, comedy writer and actor Larry David created a simulation of the clash of civilisations, turning a real-life injunction to murder into entertainment; submitted religion to bottomless irony; and gave a fatwa survivor the chance to joke about the upside of the experience. If there is anything more post-modern than that, I'd like to see it.

8

Deserts of the Real, 1992:
Gulf War | Vegas Revisited | Silicon Valley

I

Jean Baudrillard was drawn to deserts. In 1981, in *Simulacra and Simulation*, he wrote of the desert of the real. His thought was that there are three orders of simulation. The first order consists of imitation that refers to an original work, like a painting or a manuscript. This reproduction, or counterfeit, represents the original, which preceded it. The second order of simulacrum is mass production. There is no original work for the items to represent, and the reproductions are all of equal importance. The third order of simulacrum is that of the 'hyperreal', and need not bear any resemblance to anything in the real world:

> Today abstraction is no longer that of the map, the double, the mirror, or the concept. Simulation is no longer that of a territory, a referential being or a substance. It is the generation by models of a real without origin or reality: a hyperreal. The territory no longer precedes the map, nor does it survive it. It is nevertheless the map that precedes the territory – *precession of simulacra* – that engenders the territory . . . It is the real, and not the map, whose vestiges persist here and there in the deserts that are no longer those of the Empire, but ours. *The desert of the real itself.*[1]

In 1991 Baudrillard wrote about a different kind of desert, one in which the United States and its allies were, at least ostensibly, fighting against Saddam Hussein's Iraq. His polemic consisted of three parts. 'The Gulf War Will Not Take Place' was published on 4 January, during the American military and rhetorical build-up; 'The Gulf War Is Not Taking Place' was published on 6 February, during the military action; and 'The Gulf War Did Not Take Place' appeared after it had concluded, on 29 March. The three articles appeared in both the French newspaper *Libération* and, across the Channel, in the *Guardian*. What he wrote became notorious – for critics not just of Baudrillard or of French thinkers, but of intellectual bankruptcy and philosophical obtuseness in general, it came to be taken as symptomatic of post-modern theory itself. 'Baudrillard is undoubtedly the one who has gone furthest toward renouncing enlightenment reason and all its works', wrote the philosopher and literary critic Christopher Norris.[2]

For Baudrillard, bringing Vegas rules to his rhetoric was a crazy but necessary literary strategy. He wrote: 'To demonstrate the impossibility of war just at the moment when it must take place, when the signs of its occurrence are accumulating, is a stupid gamble. But it would have been even more stupid not to seize the opportunity.'[3] He was also accused of immorality, since, his critics thought, to write of the unreality of war ignored real suffering. Without truth and reality, a critique of the war could not even begin.

The truth that needed to be told about the Allied campaigns in Kuwait and Iraq, Christopher Norris argued in his 1992 book *Uncritical Theory: Postmodernism, Intellectuals and the Gulf War*, was that they were fought in order to keep the oil flowing to the United States and western Europe. When Saddam Hussein's army invaded Kuwait, this flow had been interrupted, and the continued security of oil exports from the Gulf imperilled.[4] Saddam, for his part, imagined that, since he had been brought to power and sustained by the United States, his invasion of Kuwait would not be punished. But he was wrong: the United States feared he had become dangerously unstable and so needed to be thrown out of Kuwait – and, if the Iraqi people could manage it, removed from power. Norris also wrote that the Allies' real atrocities of attacking civilian infrastructure and bombing the retreating Iraqi army amounted to mass murder. And yet, these horrors were airbrushed from media coverage, which instead was beguiled by the technological fantasies of smart bombs and other ostensibly precise military techniques.

None of these judgements could be elicited from Baudrillard's aloof and deluded philosophical claim that we were living in a hyperreal world devoid of truth and objectivity. Norris, at the outset of his book, quoted Theodor Adorno:

> The confounding of truth and lies, making it almost impossible to maintain a distinction, and a labor of Sisyphus to hold on to the simplest piece of knowledge, marks the victory in the field of logical organization that lies crushed on that of battle. Lies have long legs, they are ahead of their time. The conversion of all questions of truth into questions of power not only suppresses truth as with earlier despotic orders, but has attacked the very heart of the distinction between true and false, which the hirelings of logic were in any case diligently working to abolish.

Adorno seemed to be predicting our post-truth world. But he is not so readily made a warrior for truth against the spineless forces of post-modernity as Norris seems to suggest by citing him. Adorno elsewhere wrote that the conversion of truth into power is 'a process that truth itself cannot escape if it is not to be annihilated by power'.[5] Here Adorno was not endorsing a return to the real, but rather melancholically describing how it cannot be rescued from questions of power.[6] For Adorno, there was a real war going on between truth and power, and truth was on the losing side long before Baudrillard wrote his fateful essays on the Gulf War.

In any case, it is unfair to frame Baudrillard as in effect a quietist in the face of real bombs, real murdered women and children; nor should he be cast as an uncritical theorist pitted against critical theorists like Adorno. Baudrillard's response to his critics, in his 2004 book *The Intelligence of Evil*, was laconic: 'If you speak of the virtuality of war, then you are in league with it and have no regard for the hundreds of thousands of dead . . . It is not we, the messengers of the simulacrum, who have plunged things into this discredit, it is the system itself that has fomented this uncertainty that affects everything today.'[7]

Baudrillard noted that both the Pentagon and the Iraqis ran computer simulations of their strategies before putting them into practice. These simulacra called into being actual events according to their models, just as Baudrillard had argued that the map precedes the territory it ostensibly depicts. The war that unfolded on Western TV screens was an atrocity masquerading as a war. It was one where, as in a videogame, Allied forces with overwhelming airpower dropped bombs from great heights and Western troops suffered few casualties, while Iraqi deaths were left out of the triumphalist narrative.

Baudrillard cited three scenes to clinch this point. In one, CNN journalists wore gas masks, even though they were in a studio in Jerusalem. In another, drugged and beaten prisoners appeared on Iraqi TV repenting for their supposed crimes. In a third, a seabird covered in oil pointed its blind eye towards the Gulf sky: 'It is a masquerade of information: branded faces delivered over to the prostitution of the image, the image of an unintelligible distress. No images of the field of battle, but images of masks, of blind or defeated faces, images of falsification. It is not war taking place over there but the disfiguration of the world.'[8]

Baudrillard wrote that the rhetoric of the Allies was that this would be a clean war with precision bombs that would hit their targets with minimal risk to pilots or to the civilians below. Baudrillard thought this was nonsense. This soap-bubble dream of a clean war was, he thought, like Walt Disney's Epcot theme park, gated communities and the terrifying fiction of *The Truman Show*, symptomatic of a Western delusion that technology and design could keep untoward elements (viruses, blood, Arabs) at bay.

Ever since an Italian lieutenant threw a grenade from his plane on 1 November 1911, the dream of exterminating enemies from the air with minimal risk to the aircrew has been a focus of military innovation. Read sympathetically in its context, Baudrillard's insistence on the unreality of a war visited on Iraqis from mostly airborne Western forces seems less crazy. What's more, since the Gulf War, the Western fantasy of a clean war has been further fuelled by technological change: the policy of unmanned drones controlled from Nevada bombing Afghan villages had its roots in the colonial policy of exterminating 'savages' from the air. But, as Sven Lindqvist argued in *A History of Bombing*, drones are cheap.[9] Perhaps in the future Nevada will be bombed by drones controlled from Afghan villages.

In between writing of the desert of the real and the virtual Gulf War, Baudrillard went on a road trip to America and found himself in another desert. He originally went to California to explore the idea that it was 'the testing ground of simulation', that the American state was pioneering what would soon spread back to Baudrillard's native Europe in a form of reverse colonialism. But he was blindsided by the desert landscapes he encountered in the American West.

The purpose of *America*, which was published in 1986, was to do what Alexis de Tocqueville, D. H. Lawrence and Jean-Paul Sartre had already done – namely, travel around the United States and report back. De Tocqueville's *Democracy in America* (1835–40) was written from the conviction that France was moving rapidly towards complete social equality, and that democratic America, rather than Britain's constitutional monarchy, provided the model for that. Baudrillard's book was spurred by a similar conviction: he thought Europe was going to become American, for better or worse.

From the start, he supposed America to be culturally null – a desert that was nothing like Europe. It was almost as if he had created a computer simulation of America before heading there and, once on US soil, used that simulation to prove what he saw:

'Here in the US, culture is not that delicious panacea which we Europeans consume in a sacramental mental space and which has its own special columns in the newspapers – and in people's minds. Culture is space, speed, cinema, technology. This culture is authentic, if anything can be said to be authentic.'[10]

He wrote of Americans as 'naive', but, as Geoff Dyer argued in his introduction to *America*, it was Baudrillard who was naive, 'given that since the Second World War at least, Americans have occupied the highest ground in every area of cultural endeavour'.[11] The days when Europe could look down its nose at America, and America could envy the cultural sophistication of Europe, were long over. And yet Baudrillard carried on regardless in a book that amounts to a series of wonderfully irresponsible rhetorical flourishes that, if you're in the mood, are poetically insightful, but, if not, may seem to typify the tendency in French theory to assert implacably, without argument or apology, high-stepping nonsense. 'America is neither dream nor reality', wrote Baudrillard. 'It is a hyperreality. It is a hyper-reality because it is a Utopia which has behaved from the very beginning as though it were already achieved.'[12]

This sort of stuff, understandably, drove some critics nuts. Some suggested he had crossed the Atlantic to find not America, but himself. Even Baudrillard's editor, Mark Poster, reckoned his client had gone too far.

> Baudrillard's writing is open to several criticisms. He fails to define key terms . . . His writing style is hyperbolic and declarative, often lacking sustained, systematic analysis when it is appropriate. He totalises his insights, refusing to qualify or delimit his claims. He writes about particular experiences, television images, as if nothing else in society mattered, extrapolating a bleak view of the world from that limited case. He ignores contradictory evidence.[13]

All this is true, but there is method in Baudrillard's drive-by philosophising. One could certainly read *America* as a symptom of what he was criticising. His book was as detached from reality as its subject. It was itself an expression of the third order of simulacrum, which need not bear any resemblance to anything in the real world. Americans might reasonably retort that his book had no resemblance to the real world either, and so nothing in it applied to them.

Other philosophers had found post-modern hyperreality in America, but had not discovered it to be as omnipresent as Baudrillard had. Fellow hyperreality tourist Umberto Eco, for instance, reported on his pilgrimage in search of the 'absolute fake', by which he meant imitations that don't merely reproduce reality but improve on it. In the Italian professor's book, *Travels in Hyperreality*, he reported finding in a wax museum a copy of the Venus de Milo that had been 'restored' – with arms. But it was at the two 'absolutely fake cities' of Disneyland and Disney World, with their imitation castles and animatronic robots, that Eco found what he was looking for.

After visiting these fakes, he found reality disappointing. On a trip down the real Mississippi, Eco wrote balefully that the river failed to reveal its alligators, whereas on an artificial river in Disneyland, the animatronic imitations of animals had performed obligingly for him. 'You risk feeling homesick for Disneyland,' he concluded, 'where the wild animals don't have to be coaxed. Disneyland tells us that technology can give us more reality than nature can.'[14] Indeed, this is one aspect of the post-modern condition: reality can be improved upon by technology. And today we see examples of that post-modern condition everywhere. The sand on Tenerife is imported from the Sahara. Dubai has built the World Islands – an artificial archipelago in the shape of a world map. And our experiences online often make real life pallid and uninteresting by comparison.

More significantly, Eco saw in Disneyland a connection between post-modernism and neoliberal consumerism: 'An allegory of the consumer society, a place of absolute iconism, Disneyland is also a place of total passivity. Its visitors must agree to behave like robots.'[15] If post-modern hyperreality had a function, it was to make us passive consumers.

Baudrillard disagreed with Eco's analysis. Disneyland wasn't hyperreal. Rather, the whole of the United States was. He argued that Disneyland was an alibi for a perfect crime: the murder of reality. In his 1983 essay 'Simulations', he wrote that Disneyland presents itself as an imaginary space to conceal the fact that it is 'all of "real" America that is Disneyland (just as prisons are there to conceal the fact that it is the social in its entirety, its banal omnipresence, which is carceral)'.[16]

The same illusion was fostered, Baudrillard argued, by the Watergate scandal – the 1972 break-in to the Democratic National Committee headquarters in Washington and subsequent attempted cover-up by President Richard Nixon's administration. Baudrillard's sense was that, though Nixon's cover-up had been disclosed, the very exposure of that cover-up produced an illusion – namely, that law and morality exist on a real level and that the American political system is not corrupt.

This sense that America is a society of simulations is, argued Douglas Kellner, symptomatic of Baudrillard's cybernetic imaginary, which regards contemporary society as providing an elaborate system of deterrence against collapse or revolutionary change.[17] This deterrence is not just made manifest in weapons systems or policing, but in the educational system, in the democratic system, and in what Americans do for fun. Disneyland and Disney World foster the illusion that they are amusement parks that simulate the real world; rather, they conceal the truth that the distinction between reality and the imaginary no longer exists. The real has been trumped and replaced by the hyperreal. And nowhere is more hyperreal than Las Vegas, the city in the Nevada desert that Baudrillard visited during his road trip.

II

In the terrible 1992 Hollywood film *Honeymoon in Vegas*, Nicholas Cage and Sarah Jessica Parker play a couple who arrive in town to get married. They check into Bally's Casino Resort, and are observed in the lobby by a wealthy professional gambler called Tommy, played by James Caan. He notices that Betsy (Parker) looks like his dead wife, and so proposes to Jack (Cage) a poker game which is crooked, with the sole aim of fleecing Jack, and thereby compelling him to agree to Tommy's indecent proposal – namely, that he spend the weekend with Jack's fiancée. During the game, Jack is dealt a straight flush and, thinking he can't lose, borrows $65,000, only to lose to Tommy's better hand. Tommy, however, promises to erase the debt – if he can spend the weekend with Betsy – who, understandably, is more than disappointed at the prospect, telling him: 'You brought me to Las Vegas and you turned me into a whore, Jack!'

The ludicrous premise typifies the post-modern Vegas. Here, a man can realise his fantasy of replacing his dead wife with a living copy, in much the same way as the old Eiffel Tower is replaced by its Vegas simulacrum, even if the living copy is prostituted as a result. At one point, Betsy hesitates over getting married to Tommy, so he offers her $1 million if she will hurry through the ceremony at a Vegas chapel. The mad idea that everything, even human beings and love, can be bought and sold is a notion that is fetishistically disavowed in the final reel. In the last moments of the film, Jack, having heroically parachuted into Vegas with a skydiving team of Elvis impersonators, for reasons that need not detain us, hurries to the chapel. There, still wearing his Elvis suit and flanked by his new friends, he marries Betsy. True love, we are supposed to believe, triumphs over Mammon and the other false values of Vegas, and by extension those of the neoliberal West.

The diabolical genius of Andrew Bergman's comedy is to make us swallow this nonsense and buy its Hollywood ending.

It does so by evoking all the things Vegas stands for – gambling, corruption, the monetisation of love, the replacement of the desert of the real with its upgrade, the dizzying parade of simulacra. Then it symbolically loads the responsibility for all these onto one bad man, making Tommy the gambler into a scapegoat. This leaves the film's hero and heroine uncorrupted – perhaps even born again to what are supposed to be marvellous American values: marriage, fidelity and dressing up for special occasions. We must forget, as part of the indecent proposal that Bergman urges on us, that Jack did indeed prostitute his fiancée, and that Betsy did trade in her fiancé for a more lucrative model. We must forget how Vegas values, the values of post-modernism and neoliberalism, permeate the film's everyday American protagonists, and by extension also us.

Betsy and Jack stand for the impure values they disavow when taking their vows. Just as the architecture of Vegas is a postmodern façade behind which the real business of making money goes on, so the marriage of Jack and Betsy was misdirection to convince us that values neoliberalism consumed long ago still exist in our hearts.

The neon sign that Jean Baudrillard passed by as he drove into Vegas read: 'Welcome to Fabulous'. It's an ingenious pun: Vegas is sold to us as both extraordinary and at the same time mythical, as though it has no basis in reality. The American desert expressed a Puritan psychology that he took to be essential to the nation's identity: 'America always gives me a feeling of real asceticism. Culture, politics – and sexuality too – are seen exclusively in terms of the desert, which here assumes the status of a primal scene. Everything disappears before that desert vision.'[18] This blank canvas recapitulates the distance that Americans maintain from each other, socially and politically. In this desert, Baudrillard supposed, was the American desire for the disappearance of humanity: 'If humanity's language, technology, and buildings are an extension of its constructive faculties, the desert alone is an extension of its capacity for absence, the ideal schema of humanity's disappearance.'[19]

The desert did not end when Baudrillard's car arrived in American cities. He wrote of Los Angeles as a mobile desert. After French cities, it scarcely made sense to him. Nothing converges on a single point. So it also becomes impossible to hold a demonstration – that acid test for a Parisian of a proper urban space: 'Where could you assemble?' Baron Haussmann bulldozed radical Paris into radial routes to stop the mob revolting; Los Angeles showed a better way of thwarting them. Revolt was sublimated into endless driving, which Baudrillard called a 'total collective act, staged by the entire population, twenty-four hours a day'. Americans have updated Jack Kerouac's beatnik notion that the road is the destination: whereas the French, argued Baudrillard, drive aggressively, the Americans have created a road network in their own image, 'a milieu into which you insert yourself gently, which you switch over to as you might switch over to a TV channel'.

While Robert Venturi found that Vegas incarnated what he loved – compromise, distortion, ambiguity, richness, vitality and creative disorder – Baudrillard instead found stultifying order. Vegas, like gambling, 'has a strict limit and stops abruptly; its boundaries are exact, its passion knows no confusion'. In this, Vegas was not just a forest of simulacra with half-size Eiffel Towers and faux Caesars Palaces. Vegas, he wrote, is 'a privileged immemorial space, where things lose their shadow, where money loses its value and where the extreme rarity of traces of what signals to us there leads men to seek the instantaneity of wealth'.[20] In other words, it was the post-modern city par excellence.

In Martin Scorsese's 1995 film *Casino*, the desert beyond the Vegas city limits has yet another significance. 'At night', recalls Robert de Niro's casino manager Sam 'Ace' Rothstein, 'you couldn't see the desert that surrounds Las Vegas. But it's in the desert where lots of the town's problems are solved.'[21] And it was his mafia enforcer Nicky Santoro, played by Joe Pesci, who solved those problems, by burying bodies where the neon of the Strip didn't shine.

The thing to learn from Las Vegas was not its model of unplanned and therefore democratic architecture, as Robert Venturi suggested, but the opposite. Vegas architecture, like Potemkin villages or the glass and steel of London Docklands, exists to hide what's going on inside. Because what is going on inside is the separation of gamblers from their hard-earned cash, and its diversion into the pockets of mobsters and junk-bond speculators.

The truth about Las Vegas is that it supplies a front to facilitate business; and not just business, but unregulated and often lawless business. The Tangiers casino works on a principle that mixes Jeremy Bentham's panopticon, Orwell's Big Brother and Bitcoin's blockchain. The casino system is based on a lack of trust. As Rothstein puts it:

> The dealers are watching the players. The box men are watching the dealers. The floor men are watching the box men. The pit bosses are watching the floor men. The shift bosses are watching the pit bosses. The casino manager is watching the shift bosses. I'm watching the casino manager. And the eye in the sky is watching us all. We're the only winners. The players don't stand a chance.[22]

The casino system, that is to say, is based on a lack of trust – the same distrust that led Bitcoin inventor Satoshi Nakamoto to develop a distributed ledger of transactions called the blockchain, replacing the uncertain trust of humans in each other with cryptographic proof.

Vegas, that's to say – from Caesars Palace to the basest slot machine – is a grand illusion, a post-modern fantasy built to separate players from their cash and funnel cash to the mob.

In the 1970s, it was the International Brotherhood of Teamsters, the union led by Jimmy Hoffa, that directed loans from its pension fund to bankroll casino projects, including the Desert Inn, Caesars Palace and the Stardust – the last of which provided the inspiration for Scorsese's picture.

By the 1980s, though, it wasn't the mob and organised labour financing the big corporations that ran the Vegas machine, but more reliable suppliers. 'Today, it works like Disneyland,' laments Rothstein in voiceover near the end of *Casino*. 'While the kids play cardboard pirates, mommy and daddy drop the house payments and junior's college money on the poker slots.' Now Vegas's post-modern money doesn't do the dance of the seven veils from count room to suitcase to mob, but races through cyberspace at the speed of light with a few keystrokes. The hyperreal imagined by Eco and Baudrillard in the 1980s has gone into cyberspace. Money, like war, has gone virtual. And in the virtual worlds of cyberspace, the real is more desert than ever.

III

On 3 December 1992, Neil Papworth, a twenty-two-year-old software programmer, sent the first text message. 'Merry Christmas', it read. To be fair, when Alexander Graham Bell made the first telephone call on 10 March 1876, to his assistant Thomas Watson, his message was just as unmemorable: 'Mr Watson – come here – I want to see you.' Mr Watson did not reply. Nor was the recipient of Papworth's text, Vodafone executive Richard Jarvis, who read it on his Orbitel 901 cell phone – a phone that weighed more than four and a half pounds – able to return the greeting.

'I had no idea just how popular texting would become, and that this would give rise to emojis and messaging apps used by millions', said Papworth.[23] At first, text messages had a 160-character limit. Early adopters got round this by inventing 'txt spk', such as LOL ('laughing out loud') and emoticons – symbols made from keyboard characters to show emotions. These would later inspire the creation of the first emojis (characters symbolising emotions and objects). Later, SMS would be joined by MMS (multimedia messaging service), whereby users could send and receive pictures, videos and audio clips. Texting developed beyond Neil Papworth's wildest imaginings.

What was revolutionary about text messaging is something that the sociologist Zygmunt Bauman describes in his 2003 book *Liquid Love*:

> One message flashes on screen in pursuit of another . . . You *stay connected* – even though you are constantly on the move, and though the invisible senders and recipients of calls and messages move as well, all following their own trajectories . . . Cocooned in a web of calls and messages you are invulnerable . . . Into that network you can always run for shelter when the crowd that surrounds you becomes too madding for your taste.[24]

Indeed, texting is emblematic of a new spirit of capitalism identified by sociologists Luc Boltanski and Eve Chiapello.[25] They call it connexionist, or network, capitalism, and it is thoroughly in step with post-modernism and neoliberalism. The metaphor of a network used to have associations with crime and subversion, but now it is a term used to capture a new spirit of capitalism. Capitalism now has a friendly face: its icons are Ben and Jerry, Bill Gates and Steve Jobs, entrepreneurs who have freed themselves from the trappings of authority. They are informal and seemingly friendly network-extenders, devoid of the trappings of authority and centralised control, mobilising staff to work better and harder by encouraging them to share in their boss's quasi-religious philosophies. Just as these entrepreneurs grew up in and were influenced by sixties counterculture, so the new spirit of capitalism draws on libertarian and romantic currents of the late 1960s.

In this context, texting is useful for a new society in which our traditional bonds are loosening their choke-holds. The purportedly fixed and durable ties of family, class, religion, marriage, and perhaps even love, aren't as reliable or desirable as they once were. For Zygmunt Bauman, the network extender – or, as he calls her, the liquid modern – has no kinship ties and constantly has to use her skill, wits and dedication to create provisional bonds that are loose enough to prevent suffocation, but tight enough to give a needed sense of security now that the traditional sources of solace are less reliable than ever. We must keep on the move, reinventing ourselves if we are to triumph over our fears of becoming obsolete at work, friendless, unloved. Bauman's later book, *Liquid Life*, was prefaced by a quotation from Emerson's *On Prudence*: 'In skating over thin ice, our safety is in our speed.' The network, once again, is crucial: our safety is in the speed of our internet connection.

We're torn, as Freud recognised, between freedom and security; but our task under network capitalism is to create a liveable balance between the two. Those who tilt the balance too far towards freedom are often to be found by Bauman rushing for home, desperate to be loved, eager to re-establish communities. But that's not to say that the liquid moderns want their old suffocating security back. We want the impossible: to have our cake and eat it, to be free and secure.

For Bauman, the medium isn't the message. The technologies we use hardly determine who we are. Nor are the messages that people send each other significant in themselves; rather, the message is the circulation of messages. The sense of belonging or security that the liquid modern creates consists in being cocooned in a web of messages. That way, we hope, the vexing problem of freedom versus security will disappear.

Texting enables users to set personal parameters on freedom and security. This, apart from anything else, explains why texting superseded phone calls. By 2014, texting had become more common for Americans under fifty than phone calls. In 2016, more than three-quarters of all adults in the UK owned smartphones, but 25 per cent didn't – or so they claimed – use them to make calls. Since then, the popularity of text-based communication tools such as WhatsApp and Instagram has meant that direct messaging has exploded.

People currently in their twenties and thirties, in particular, have developed a reputation for being allergic to phone calls. The *Guardian* columnist Daisy Buchanan explains why fellow millennials in particular are unlikely to make phone calls, still less answer them. 'We've grown up with so many methods of communication available to us, and we've gravitated towards the least intrusive ones because we know how it feels to be digitally prodded on a range of different channels.' Smart phones are valuable because they give users not just the freedom *to do* things, but the freedom *from* things. Only a mug is going to answer a call from a withheld number. 'I assume that whenever anyone does try to reach me on the telephone,' writes Buchanan, 'it's because of a serious emergency and I need to be reached urgently, possibly for a telling off. So I fling the phone from my hand, as if it's a live snake.'[26] Texting, be it via SMS or direct messaging apps, offers a way of optimising the balance between personal freedom and security from importunate callers, while at the same time ensuring that you are never outside the network.

Derrida was thus on to something when he wrote 'Il n'y a pas dehors du texte' – though not for the reason he supposed. The fear of silence and the exclusion it implies makes us anxious that our ingeniously assembled security will fall apart. Indeed, the fear of exclusion that Bauman identified as the reason we spend too much time texting has since become central to the success of Silicon Valley.

While some have argued that post-modernism is a pre-digital phenomenon, many of the phenomena of post-modernism – especially the notions of simulacra, fakery, irrationality, scorn for truth and doubt about reality – have reached their apogees thanks to another desert that captivated Baudrillard – namely, Silicon Valley. This is not the desert of Death Valley, or the Iraqi desert, but what Baudrillard calls a 'desert zone, given over to ions and electrons, a supra-human place, the product of human decision-making'.[27] For Baudrillard, Silicon Valley, like the university of Santa Cruz, was populated by what he called 'refugees from the orgy – the orgy of sex, political violence, the Vietnam War, the Woodstock Crusade, and the ethnic and anti-capitalist struggles too, together with the passion for money, the passion for success, hard technologies etc., in short, the whole orgy of modernity'.[27]

After the orgy of modernity, the former countercultural veterans of that libidinal conflict in Silicon Valley proposed a de-eroticised post-modernity: 'Reduced pace of work, decentralisation, air-conditioning, soft technologies, Paradise.' But Baudrillard can't resist a diabolical twist: 'But a very slight modification, a change of just a few degrees, would suffice to make it seem like hell.'[28]

Baudrillard also called these Silicon Valley refugees neo-gnostics, as if – following their predecessors who supposed this material world to be the creation of an evil blind demiurge – to turn from the desert of the real and make the garden of cyber-space flourish was not just possible, but right. Certainly, as Silicon Valley developed its unreal worlds, the money followed. In the 1990s, the internet was commercialised as never before, and from 1995 onwards dotcom start-ups fuelled a surge on the stock market. Like Vegas gamblers suckered by the distracting glamour and glitz, venture capitalists invested in any company with a '.com' after its name. Nobody wanted to miss their chance to cash in on the growing use of the internet and online applications. Capital poured into start-ups, which in turn raced to get big fast, even if they had little in the way of a proprietary product. The result was that, between 1995 and 2000, the technology-dominated Nasdaq index rose from under 1,000 to over 5,000. By the end of 2001, most dotcom stocks had gone bust. Even the share prices of blue-chip technology stocks like Cisco, Intel and Oracle lost more than 80 per cent of their value. Several leading high-tech companies, such as Dell and Cisco, placed huge sell orders on their stocks, sparking panic-selling among investors. Within weeks, the stock market lost 10 per cent of its value. Investors had lost confidence in technology.

But that was not the end of Silicon Valley. Foreign investors, particularly ones based in China, Saudi Arabia and Japan, pumped huge sums into start-ups. The first decade of the new millennium, moreover, would see the creation of many of the most profitable Silicon Valley businesses, most relying on business models that kept their users inside social networks, while their personal data was plundered and monetised. LinkedIn was founded in 2002, Facebook in 2004, Twitter in 2006, WhatsApp in 2009 and Instagram in 2010. The strategies of these companies were all predicated on what made texting popular: instant communication, addiction, being part of a network, and enabling us to set the parameters of mixophobia and mixophilia to suit us.

True, some of social media companies' business models left many critics baffled. Of LinkedIn, a start-up that Microsoft bought for $26 billion in 2016, *Esquire* magazine's Ken Kurson wrote: 'It provides people you don't like enough to take a telephone call from or even answer an e-mail from a way to get in touch with you when they're at their most boring and desperate – i.e., when they need a job.'[30] And yet LinkedIn grew, partly by selling information about its half a billion users. Other social media companies have done the same; indeed, one might say that they have lured us in with the desire to be part of the network. Trapped alive in the web, we are fresh meat for big data.

Social media companies are more than vast asset-stripping machines that feed off our anxieties, though they are that. They also offer performance spaces. Slavoj Žižek wrote that online we are able to create a 'space of false disidentification', by which he means that we can put on a mask to reveal who we want to be if not who we truly are.[31] Online, we can assume fake identities that we would never admit to or condone in the real world.

Žižek, though, spotted a lie in this purported revelation of our true selves online: 'The much-celebrated playing with multiple, shifting personae (freely constructed identities) tends to obfuscate (and thus falsely liberate us from) the constraints of social space in which our existence is caught.'[32] Facebook friends may well not be real ones; losing yourself in your World of Warfare avatars' lifestyle issues wastes valuable time you could spend changing your real world. But for the neo-gnostics of

Silicon Valley and their followers, the real is a desert. The hyperreal is where the action is – where one can become something one could not be otherwise.

The great dream of many post-modern artists was to pick up and discard identities at will. David Bowie and Cindy Sherman were the advance guard. But Žižek's worry is that the supposed liberation such performances offer us, in allowing us to escape ourselves and realise our fantasies, is a false freedom. For Boltanski and Chiapello, the values of expressive creativity, fluid identities, autonomy and self-development were touted by the counterculture of the 1960s against bureaucratic discipline, bourgeois hypocrisy and consumer conformity. Over time, however, these values were co-opted into becoming new values by means of which capitalism could reinvent itself to survive.

In reinventing itself – by creating a new spirit of capitalism – what seemed liberating, and indeed had its roots in the consciousness-raising movements of the 1960s, had become constraining and exploitative. Not only were our personal details sold to third parties by social media companies to make money out of us, not only was face-to-face communication forgone in favour of the Sisyphean labour of updating your Facebook timeline, but all human relationships have become reconfigured according to the norms of shopping. Lovers have become disposable commodities, Facebook friends junked when they don't deliver customer satisfaction, personal conflict avoided in favour of anonymous reviews more toxic than one would give to a malfunctioning vacuum cleaner. Bauman argued that social skills decline as we treat 'other humans as objects of consumption and judge them after the pattern of consumer objects by the volume of pleasure they offer . . . At best the others are companions in the essentially solitary activity of consumption.'[33] What gets lost in the process, he concluded, is human solidarity.

What is also lost is our ability to tell fake from real. There are fake Twitter feeds, phony Facebook accounts, staged internet suicides, sock puppets and twitterjackers – not to mention

Wikipedia pages undetectably mined with lies. This explains, perhaps, some of my favourite satirical fake Twitter feeds, such as 'Dick Cheney': 'Won a baboon on eBay. Condition as-is, but I'm going to use the little guy for parts anyway. Never know when the ticker might blow a valve.' Or 'Osama Bin Laden': 'Door-tag from UPS Ground says hazardous materials can't be delivered – curse the infidels! Off to UPS depot.' Or *Transformers* director 'Michael Bay': 'No, I don't know who "Fellini" is and quite frankly I don't give a shit.'[34]

Today's digital technology offers us even more chances than Disneyland ever could to revel in hyperreal fakery. Eco was unwittingly prescient when, in 1975, he wrote, 'the frantic desire for the Almost Real arises only as a neurotic reaction to the vacuum of memories; the Absolute Fake is offspring of the unhappy awareness of a present without depth'.[35]

9

That's Entertainment, 1997:

I Love Dick | Netflix | *Grand Theft Auto*

I

One night in the early 1990s, an experimental filmmaker fell in love with a post-modern intellectual called Dick. Chris Kraus had followed her husband, Sylvère Lotringer, also a post-modern intellectual, to California, where he was on sabbatical. Over dinner at Dick's house, Kraus later related, 'The two men discuss recent trends in postmodern critical theory while Chris, who is no intellectual, notices Dick making continual eye contact with her.'[1] The following morning, Chris told Sylvère that her flirtation with Dick the previous night felt like a 'conceptual fuck'.

Instead of feeling betrayed, Sylvère joined in his wife's obsession, and the two began writing letters to Dick. Both were turned on by the letters they wrote, prompting them to have sex together for the first time in years. Sylvère signed himself off as Charles Bovary, thereby casting himself as cuckolded husband to Emma, the heroine of Flaubert's novel *Madame Bovary*, and Dick as her adulterous lover Léon Dupuis.

And then Chris had an idea: why not make this whole obsession into an art project, mixing performance and film? Sophie Calle made a woman's obsessive pursuit of a man into art. Maybe Kraus could take it a step further by making hunter, hunted and conceptually cuckolded husband into co-creators and co-performers in a post-modern artwork blurring fiction and reality. She and Sylvère wrote to Dick on 10 December 1994:

'We've had an idea for a collaborative piece, inspired by and hopefully involving you. It's kind of like Calle Art . . . I guess the piece is all about obsession, although we wouldn't think of using images that belong to you without your agreeing to it. What do you think? Are you game?'[2]

One of the things that makes this letter so funny is the mismatch between Chris and Sylvère's glee and the probable reaction of its recipient. The pair were proposing that Dick participate in a high-concept post-modern stalking-cum-art project involving, as the letter goes on to suggest, pasting the correspondence on his car and house and around his garden. Who among us would want that?

And yet, a post-modern intellectual whose academic career involved problematising bourgeois notions of privacy ought to have responded positively to Chris and Sylvère's indecent proposal. Sylvère realised as much when he wrote to Dick: 'It seems to be a step towards the kind of confrontational performing art that you're encouraging.'[3] One post-modernist critic was throwing down the gauntlet to another.

Dick didn't pick up the gauntlet, and so Chris Kraus went on to write her memoir-cum-novel *I Love Dick*, including in it all the correspondence cited above. After the book was published in 1997, it became clear that, unlike *Madame Bovary*, *I Love Dick* was based on the author's life. 'It all happened,' Kraus told a book reading. 'There would be no book if it hadn't happened.'[4] Journalists were scrambled by editors to unlock this presumed *roman à clef*. Dick was soon revealed to be English cultural critic Dick Hebdige, theorist of subcultures and Sid Vicious. At the time the book was published, Hebdige was dean of the California Institute of the Arts. Kraus acknowledged that Dick was based on Hebdige, and that their brief relationship fell along the lines described in the novel. Not only was Hebdige unhappy at his portrayal, telling one reporter 'the book was like a bad review of my presence in the world'; he was upset at the invasion of his privacy.[5] Hebdige sent her a cease-and-desist letter in 1996 when he learned that Kraus was planning to publish the book.

But Kraus didn't cease or desist. Instead, she invited him to become a collaborator, just as the fictional Kraus in the book had. 'I said, "Why don't you write an introduction, and people will think we cooked up the whole joke together,"' she told the *New Yorker*. Hebdige declined: he didn't want to be in Calle Art. It's a shame, in a way, that Dick declined, but as a result he got to play an inversion of fiction's role – that of the wronged woman, stoic in her silence. When asked by the *New Yorker* for an interview about his relationship with Kraus and Lotringer, Hebdige replied: 'I really have no comment to offer either on them or the book.'[6]

Kraus was attempting something distinctively post-modern with *I Love Dick*, blurring the lines between fiction and memoir, and thereby subverting what she called the hetero-male novel. She wrote to Dick:

> Because most 'serious' fiction, still, involves the fullest possible expression of a single person's subjectivity, it's considered crass and amateurish not to 'fictionalise' the supporting cast of characters, changing names and insignificant features of their identities. The 'serious' contemporary hetero-male novel is a thinly veiled Story of Me, as voraciously consumptive as all of patriarchy. While the hero/anti-hero explicitly is the author, everybody else is reduced to 'characters'.[7]

Kraus argued in *I Love Dick* that even her inspiration, Sophie Calle, had been reduced to a cipher in a man's Story of Me. In Paul Auster's 1992 novel *Leviathan*, Kraus detected a thinly veiled version of Calle in the character of Maria, an artist whose art seems uncannily similar to 'The Address Book' and *Suite Vénitienne* – except Maria has been obligingly reduced to, as Kraus puts it, 'a waif-like character relieved of complications like ambition or career. When some try to pierce this false conceit by naming names because our 'I's are changing as we meet other 'I's we're called bitches, libelers, pornographers and amateurs.'[8] An insightful passage, since Kraus effectively anticipated her hostile reviews. When the book came out, it largely disappeared beneath the weight of huge realist novels mostly by men, including Philip Roth's *American Pastoral* and Don DeLillo's *Underworld*. Some male critics felt affronted on Hebdige's behalf. Kraus's book was, *Artforum*'s writer complained, 'not so much written as secreted'.[9] *I Love Dick* was just confessional with literary pretensions, some critics argued. 'The word confession is so odd', Kraus retorted in an interview with *Dazed*:

> As if any discussion of female experience, because it is so inherently shameful, would have to be a confession rather than a description. I was surprised that people took the book that way. It came out at the end of 1997, and by that point there had been the whole East Village transgressive art thing. People biting the heads off rats in a performance, or spattering HIV tainted blood at the audience. And this was a book about having an affair? Has no one left a husband before?[10]

A good question – especially in 1997, when the death of a princess who left a husband destined to become king was making headlines around the world. On 31 August, Princess Diana died in a car crash while she and her lover Dodi al-Fayed were being driven through Paris by a drunk chauffeur trying to elude paparazzi on motorbikes. Her end had the aura of myth: Diana the huntress had been hunted to death by media running dogs. In life, though, Diana was a virtuosa of the secular confessional, like Chris Kraus finding liberation in seizing control, wresting narrative and sexual power from the male author-God, be it a prince called Charles or a professor called Dick. In so doing, they became outliers for the spirit of self-revelation and self-disclosure that would in a few years make social media such as Facebook, Instagram and Twitter not just spaces for self-performance and self-disclosure, but massively successful businesses.

The profanation of the confessional was taken a step further by Chris Kraus, in that she was knowingly engaged in wresting narrative and sexual power from the male author-God. While Diana sought to be the queen of people's hearts, Kraus wanted to be the queen of her own story. And yet they were soul sisters. In a 1997 interview, Kraus defended the kind of public confessional Diana had made her own, without citing the princess by name: 'I think the sheer fact of women talking, being paradoxical, inexplicable, flip, self-destructive, but above all public is the most revolutionary thing in the world.'[11]

Diana's life and death were emblematic of the post-modern condition for another reason. She reinvented herself following her marriage in 1981 to Prince Charles in order to escape the identity that had been foisted on her. 'He'd found the virgin, the sacrificial lamb, and in a way he was obsessed with me', she said of her husband.[12] While Madonna was playing at being shiny and new, subverting the male fantasy in 'Like a Virgin', Diana was invited to play that role for her husband – though with the crucial difference that it was a role devoid of irony. Her wedding to Charles was the beginning not of a marriage but of an unsustainable and misogynistic fantasy, an infantilising prison from which she did well to escape.

Even though the 1981 wedding of Charles and Diana was watched by a global audience of 750 million viewers, she later described it as 'the worst day of my life'.[13] The royal family, Diana related, treated her with indifference. Her husband was in love with another woman, Camilla Parker Bowles, and he conducted an affair with her during his marriage to Diana.

Diana emerged from Charles's shadow to become a mythic character in a post-modern fairy-tale who needed no prince to redeem her. She would do that herself. In this she was an exemplar of a world that her in-laws did not comprehend. Royals, by definition, are not self-made. Unlike the Firm, she used TV as a confessional tool. In 1995, she was interviewed by Martin Bashir for the BBC, and disclosed to 15 million viewers that she had had an affair with her riding instructor, James Hewitt; she also spoke about her depression and bulimia, her children, the media and the future of the monarchy. In this, she was representative of the West's age of authenticity – an individualistic era in which people are encouraged to perform themselves in public rather than nurse wounds in private.

She was the heroine of a book yet to be written. In 2003, six years after her death, Zygmunt Bauman published his book *Liquid Love: On the Frailty of Human Bonds*.[14] We 'liquid moderns', who have been disappointed in love and find ourselves suffocated by traditional ties, cannot commit to relationships and have few kinship ties, Bauman suggested. If the royal family symbolised stolidity and solidity, Diana personified the liquid modern: a woman who reinvented herself and escaped the fusty destiny that seemed to be her lot. Her struggle with chilly in-laws and an aloof husband resonated for many viewers.

'I think every strong woman in history has had to walk down a similar path, and I think it's the strength that causes the confusion and the fear', she told Bashir. 'Why is she strong? Where does she get it from? Where is she taking it? Where is she going to use it? Why do the public still support her?' asked Bashir.[15] Good questions, but another question arose. Why was she talking about herself in the third person? It was almost as if she was putting on a mask to play the role of the authentic self. Or rather that, since she was a post-modern princess, the mask was her authentic self.

Certainly, she could no longer open supermarkets, read speeches written by others, or stand by her adulterous man. She knew that her access to her emotions and her confessional integrity resonated with many people. 'I'd like to be a queen of people's hearts, in people's hearts, but I don't see myself being Queen of this country', she said. 'I don't think many people will want me to be Queen.'[16]

'We are now living in a spiritual super-nova, a kind of galloping pluralism on the spiritual plane', wrote Charles Taylor in his book *A Secular Age*.[17] But that post-modern spirituality needs no god; Diana consulted many different gurus and healers, but her faith was in her self. In this she was representative of those who gathered outside Westminster Abbey and Kensington

Palace to mourn her death. Her life resonated with their struggles, with their projects of self-becoming, of disclosing what had been immemorially repressed. For Hilary Mantel, the princess we consumed was not her authentic self, but rather the projection of our desires: 'The princess we invented to fill a vacancy had little to do with any actual person.'[18] Even if Diana was a princess for our times, she was also a sacrificial being of our celebrity age, one who existed only as what we made of her. She was open text, endlessly interpretable and readily used and abused, not just by a media that quickly realised on which side its royal bread was buttered, but by admirers who had only seen her on telly. Her control of her own narrative was more apparent than real.

Her fame was unthinkable without her prettiness. Before selfies and Instagram filters, she concerned herself profoundly with how her surfaces would be consumed worldwide. 'Her dealings with the press and photographers were not innocent', noted Mantel. 'The images had to be carefully curated.'[19] If Diana was a feminist icon, she wasn't one to challenge the idea that to be a woman is to be looked at.

As for Chris Kraus, soon after *I Love Dick* appeared, she and Sylvère appeared on a radio show. They read aloud from their letters to Dick. Neither qualified the letters as fiction: they were piercing the false conceit of literature that protected the privacy of the author. Indeed, it was almost as if neither recognised that there was a line to cross. 'Nothing seemed unusual about it', Kraus said. 'I mean, who cares? The things that people consider private, they're so common. My past is really so trite, it could be the past of the whole creative class of a certain era. There's a great Gilles Deleuze quote on this subject: "Life is not personal." '[20]

And yet, Kraus was also playing a common post-modern game, framing reality to pass it off as fiction. In this sense, *I Love Dick* is a Baudrillardian simulacrum, wherein reality, once the ultimate guarantor of truth, is reduced to a pale imitation of art. 'When I started writing the book, I had a strong sense of things taking place in a frame. The space in performance is always framed . . . It makes it more possible to see it.'[21]

What made Kraus's book challenging was not just its reclamation of female subjectivity and sexuality, but its still-shocking sense that truth and fiction were not opposites, but locked in a lubricious lambada. 'What makes something fiction isn't whether it's true or not – it's whether it's bracketed in time, how it's treated and edited, and whether it's construed as a work of fiction', she wrote.[22] In the book, Kraus sent a letter to Dick citing Søren Kierkegaard's concept of the 'Third Remove' – that 'art involves reaching through some distance'. The distance is decided through framing and context, not through protecting somebody's privacy. In such a context, privacy was expendable at best – at worst a bourgeois patriarchal norm configured to keep women dumb.

At the end of the book, Kraus lets hitherto dumb Dick speak. Dick writes a letter addressed to Sylvère. In it, he argues that too much damage has been done to restore the friendship. 'That said . . . I still enjoy your company and conversation when we meet and believe, as you do, that Kris [sic] has talent as a writer. I can only reiterate what I have said before . . . that I do not share your conviction that my right to privacy has to be sacrificed for the sake of that talent.'[23]

Bad enough to spell her name wrong; but worse was to come. She too gets a letter from Dick. In a cab she opens the envelope excitedly, but it turns out to be a photocopy of Dick's letter to Sylvère. Thus, the patriarchy attempts to reassert itself by erasing the woman. Women may write more letters than they post; men post more letters than they write. After reading the letter to Sylvère, Kraus reels a little at this attempt at erasure, and then carries on. 'She gasped and breathed under the weight of it and got out of the cab and showed her film.' He didn't kill her, nor could he: he had become a character in her book, subsumed into the real Chris Kraus's desires.

If Chris Kraus never cited Princess Diana as spiritual soulmate, Dick Hebdige did. 'Dick outed himself in a *New York* magazine gossip piece by giving a quote about how reprehensible the book was', recalled Kraus. 'And yes, he compared himself to Princess Diana, as if the book was trading on his "celebrity." '[24] But there was more to his complaint than that: Hebdige compared Kraus's intrusion into his private life to the tabloid stalking of Diana. Dream on, professor. Rather, Hebdige better resembles Prince Charles than Princess Diana – the man reduced to a bit-part in a mere woman's story.

II

'One of the things that makes the people on TV fit to stand the mega-gaze is that they are, by human standards, really pretty', wrote the novelist David Foster Wallace in his 1997 essay on post-modern fiction and television, 'E Unibus Pluram':

> Because of the way human beings relate to narrative, we tend to identify with those characters we find appealing. We try to see ourselves in them . . . The same ID-relation, however, also means that we try to see them in ourselves. When everybody we seek to identify with for six hours a day is pretty, it naturally becomes more important to us to be pretty, to be viewed as pretty.

This has deleterious consequences. 'The boom in diet aids, health and fitness clubs, neighbourhood tanning parlours, cosmetic surgery, anorexia, bulimia, steroid use among boys, girls throwing acid at each other because one girl's hair looks more like Farrah Fawcett's than another's . . . are these supposed to be unrelated to each other? To the apotheosis of prettiness in a televisual culture?' asked Wallace, rhetorically.[25]

If he was right about this, how poignant that Princess Diana – who remade herself not just existentially and spiritually but physically, through bulimia and fitness regimens, becoming consumably pretty and thus able to withstand TV's mega-gaze – encouraged viewers to undergo similar makeovers. But the tyranny of pretty does not just compel us to change; it changes television, too, forcing it to foreground increasingly pretty people. Good-looking people kept us watching, which kept TV's ratings up, which kept shareholders happy:

> But it's less great for us civilians, who tend to own mirrors, and who also tend not to be anywhere near as pretty as the images we try to identify with. Not only does this cause some angst personally, but the angst increases because, nationally, everybody else is absorbing six-hour doses and identifying with pretty people and valuing prettiness more, too.[26]

The year before this essay, Wallace published a sprawling 1,058-page post-modern novel, *Infinite Jest*.[27] The title refers to an elusive film that terrorists are trying to get their hands on, because to watch it is to be debilitated, even killed by enjoyment. Perhaps these terrorists – a bunch of testy wheelchair-using Quebecois separatists called Les Assassins des Fauteuils Rollents – will be able to entertain Americans to death, destroying the evil empire with the very cultural weaponry it deployed on its own citizens and exported around the world.

'Entertainment's chief job is to make you so riveted by it that you can't tear your eyes away, so the advertisers can advertise', said Wallace in a 1996 interview to promote the novel. 'And the tension of the book [*Infinite Jest*] is to try and make it at once extremely entertaining and also sort of warped – and to sort of shake the reader awake about some of the things that are sinister in entertainment.'[28]

In reality, disappointingly, there are no Quebecois terrorists plotting the overthrow of America by weaponising its own culture industry. And yet the idea that Americans were amusing themselves to death through television was not new. In 1985, the critic and media ecology professor Neil Postman suggested that it was not George Orwell's *Nineteen Eighty-Four* that best predicted our current dystopia, but Aldous Huxley's *Brave New World* : 'In Huxley's vision, no Big Brother is required to deprive people of their autonomy, maturity and history. As he saw it, people will come to love their oppression, to adore the technologies that undo their capacities to think.'[29]

Postman contrasted the written word with television. The former encourages linear thinking and delayed response, the latter short circuits thinking and, while content arrives and disappears in seconds, the constant flickering parade of moving images makes it difficult for the viewer to turn away or off. For Postman, McLuhan was right: the medium was the message. TV made us passive and unthinking consumers of trivia. News programmes had to become entertaining spectacles; shows overtly aimed at educating children such as Sesame Street undermined education because TV viewing is essentially passive, while learning is necessarily active and, ideally, demanding.

Postman's jeremiad underpins much of Wallace's thinking on TV. But other critics of the medium have seen television not as inherently evil, but as a missed opportunity. TV could have become a tool to increase freedom and democracy, a bulwark against the dominant market-driven society. The cultural theorist Raymond Williams, for instance, wrote: 'We could have inexpensive, locally based yet internationally extended television systems, making possible communication and information-sharing on a scale that not long ago would have seemed utopian. These are the contemporary tools of the long revolution towards an educated and participatory democracy, and of the recovery of effective communication in complex urban and industrial societies.'[30]

That term 'long revolution' was Williams's hopeful idea that, alongside the industrial revolution, there had been a gradual extension of popular and democratic control over society. That long revolution is not done, and is always menaced by the dictates of market-driven society. Indeed, Williams went on to imagine what TV might become if it didn't help serve the long revolution. It is very much like the dystopias imaged by Postman and Wallace.

Certainly, that counterrevolution seemed plausible in America. In the early 1970s, when Raymond Williams left Cambridge to teach at Stanford, he was bemused by the television he saw in the States, not least by how advertising spots interrupted TV programmes. In California he began his book *Television: Technology and Cultural Form*, in which he developed the notion of flow. Flow is 'the defining characteristic of broadcasting, simultaneously as a technology and as a cultural form . . . It is evident that what is now called "an evening's viewing" is in some ways planned, by providers and then by viewers, *as a whole*; that it is in any event planned in discernible sequences which in this sense override particular program units.'[31]

Flow was a compelling metaphor for how broadcast TV worked at the time Williams was writing. But, two years after Williams's book on television was published, JVC launched the first VCR system. Flow became obsolete when we learned how to programme our VCRs. They enabled us to time shift programmes – to record programmes onto videotape to be watched at a viewer-chosen rather than scheduler-determined time, thereby subverting broadcast TV's schedulers. By 1997, VHS tapes were being replaced by DVD technology, which enabled viewers to flip through chapters rather than laboriously fast-forward through hours of tape. In turn, DVDs were supplanted by digital means of time shifting. We were no longer couch potatoes; we were active curators of our own entertainment.

In *Infinite Jest*, Wallace imagined two new television technologies – neither of them as liberations from the flow of broadcast TV, but as superior means of controlling couch-prone viewers. He also imagined broadcast TV being replaced by Interlace TelEntertainment, a company from which cartridges could be bought or rented on demand and played on home cinema systems. The 'on demand' invited customers to suppose that they were controlling the supply and curating their entertainment.

Interlace TelEntertainment, in its essentials, was Netflix, the home-entertainment streaming service that was launched in

1997, the year of *I Love Dick* and of Diana's death, and now consumes about 15 per cent of the world's internet bandwidth. Started by two Silicon Valley entrepreneurs, Marc Randolph and Reed Hastings, Netflix at first enabled its users to order DVDs from its website that would arrive days later in the post. When users had finished with them, they returned the DVDs in the envelopes provided. At the time, Netflix was valuable to those who had no video rental stores nearby, or couldn't be bothered to leave their homes.

But the revolution Netflix effected on home entertainment began a few years later, when it hired Ted Sarandos and embraced what became known as predictive analytics. Sarandos had been working at a video store in a Phoenix strip mall, not dissimilar to the one where Quentin Tarantino developed his encyclo-paedic knowledge of cinema. What Sarandos did next, though, would make video stores obsolete. Sarandos recognised that viewers were addicts, and that his role was to supply what they wanted. Viewers have long been battling schedulers bent on stopping them seeing what they want, when they want, he argued: 'Before time shifting, they would use VCRs to collect episodes and view them whenever they wanted. And, more importantly, in whatever doses they wanted. Then DVD box sets and later DVRs made that self-dosing even more sophisticated.'[32]

But 'self-dosing' makes it sound as though viewers were in control. In the same year as Sarandos was hired, Netflix intro-duced a personalised movie recommendation system, which used viewer ratings to predict choices for all Netflix subscribers. In 2007, it introduced a streaming service called 'Watch Now', allowing subscribers to watch TV shows and films on their personal computers. Ultimately, DVDs would become expend-able: Netflix's streaming model spread around the world not through snail mail, but through fibre-optic cables. 'People have always been frustrated when they can't get to see what they want', Sarandos told me. 'Today you can't stop spreading the joy for long. That's where I come in.'

Spreading the joy – a resonant phrase. In the post-modern age, helped by technology, we dream of achieving 24/7 joy. But behind the joy are the algorithms. In 2012, for instance, when Sarandos commissioned a political drama for Netflix TV called *House of Cards*, starring Kevin Spacey and Robin Wright, predictive analytics helped justify his decision. 'It was generated by algorithm', Sarandos told me. 'I didn't use data to make the show, but I used data to determine the potential audience to a level of accuracy very few people can do.'

Netflix's use of predictive analytics has changed since its inception. Initially, Netflix worked on the same sort of principle as Sarandos used when he worked in a video shop. He was a human gatekeeper, designing his store's content according to the tastes of his customer. This 'if you liked that, then you'll like this' facility has become commonplace in the new millennium, tailoring cultural supply to your tastes. And yet, customised culture such as that devised at Netflix risks creating what inter-net activist Eli Pariser in 2010 called 'filter bubbles': each of us isolated intellectually in our own informational spheres.[33]

Customised culture has become much more sophisticated. Today, at least 800 Netflix engineers work behind the scenes at their Silicon Valley HQ to try to predict what you might want to watch next. Tom Vanderbilt, author of *You May Also Like: Taste in an Age of Endless Choice*, discovered that when Netflix was a DVD-by-mail company, customised recommendations were based on the ratings of users for particular content; but the ratings of viewers, and the predictions based on those ratings, were insufficiently accurate when Netflix went digital.

The problem for Netflix engineers is to monitor behaviour less explicit than viewer ratings. In the old days of DVD rental, you added a movie to your queue because you wanted to watch it a few days later; there was a cost in your decision, and a delayed reward. 'With instant streaming, you start playing something, you don't like it, you just switch. Users don't really perceive the benefit of giving explicit feedback, so they invest less effort', says Netflix engineering director Xavier Amatriain.

As a result, to model tastes, more sophisticated algorithms are needed – algorithms that make Netflix sound more Orwellian than Huxleyan: 'We know what you played, searched for, or rated, as well as the time, date, and device', said Amatriain:

> We even track user interactions such as browsing or scrolling behaviour. Most of our algorithms are based on the assumption that similar viewing patterns represent similar user tastes. We can use the behaviour of similar users to infer your preferences . . . We have been working for some time on introducing context into recommendations. We have data that suggests there is different viewing behaviour depending on the day of the week, the time of day, the device, and sometimes even the location. But implementing contextual recommendations has practical challenges that we are currently working on.

This observational data is more accurate than self-reported ratings: 'A lot of people tell us they often watch foreign movies or documentaries. But in practice, that doesn't happen very much.'[34]

By this means, Netflix was delivering in reality what Wallace had imagined in fiction. He imagined the Interlace as an enormous gatekeeper deciding what you would watch while seeming to offer viewers choice. He supposed the internet would evolve similarly. Because the information supply is in principle infinite, we demand some kind of digital gatekeeper to protect us from being overwhelmed. Wallace told an interviewer: 'If you go back to Hobbes, and why we ended up begging, why do people in a state of nature end up begging for a ruler who has the power of life and death over them? We absolutely have to give our power away. The Internet is going to be exactly the same way . . . We're going to beg for it. We are literally gonna pay for it.'[35] What dies as a result is the utopian idea that the internet or digital culture in general is democratic.

What we're literally paying for is what Ted Sarandos calls the joy, the pleasurable experience of not deferring our pleasures. In that sense, Raymond Williams's notion of flow – a term coined for an age before post-modernism – is not obsolete. What Netflix's notorious binge culture results in is flow by another means, more efficient and more insidious – insidious in that we seem to be getting what we want all the time, and we suppose we have liberated ourselves from the gatekeeper of TV (schedulers), only to be ruled by another, much more sophisticated group of gatekeepers, whose task is to keep us watching while at the same time suggesting that viewers are being liberated by being given more choice.

Wallace wrote about television at a pivotal moment. In 1997, broadcast TV was not yet supplanted by streaming services, nor were the internet or social media the great sucking maws of time and attention they have since become. But at least he was not snootily deriding the medium from the outside. He called himself a TV addict, watching television pretty much indiscriminately as 'an easy way to fill in the emptiness'. As a recovering drug addict, he knew something about addiction and how dealers profit from grooming users. In 'E Unibus Pluram', he analysed how TV ensnared its viewers and emptied their pockets. Most TV criticism, he argued, indicted the medium for lacking any meaningful connection with the world outside it.

There was a generation gap between TV viewers. Those who started watching television before about 1970 watched it very differently from those who came to it later. You could call the former TV viewers modern and the latter post-modern. Those who started watching TV in the 1960s were trained to look where TV pointed, Wallace argued – 'usually at versions of "real life" made prettier, sweeter, livelier by succumbing to some product or temptation.' But no longer: 'Today's mega-Audience is way better trained, and TV has discarded what is not needed. A dog, if you point at something, will look only at your finger.'[36] Post-modern viewers, in this sense, were like dogs.

Around 1970, TV became self-reflexive; it did not need real life to justify its existence. Something similar happened to literature. Realistic fiction was ostensibly about what it portrayed;

post-modern meta-fiction turned from the world and withdrew into itself, drawing attention to the conditions of its construction in ironic and absurdist ways, often by playfully engaging with mass culture and the society of the spectacle. This change in literature, and its poisonous consequences for how we live, troubled Wallace when he wrote 'E Unibus Pluram'. He cited Don DeLillo's 1985 novel *White Noise*, in which there's a fabulously absurd passage involving a pop-culture scholar called Murray and his friend Jack. On their way to visit a tourist attraction, they drive past signs directing them to the most photographed barn in America, walk up a cow path past a kiosk selling postcards of the barn, and finally join tourists taking photographs of the barn. 'Can you feel it, Jack?' Murray asks. 'An accumulation of nameless energies . . . Being here is a kind of spiritual surrender . . . We've agreed to be part of a collective perception. This literally colours our vision. A religious experience in a way . . . They are taking pictures of taking pictures.'[37]

What fascinated Wallace about this passage was not so much the parodic regress – the tourists watching the barn, Murray watching the tourists, Jack watching Murray, us watching Jack watching Murray watching the tourists watching the barn – but Murray's assumption of the role of scientific critic at a remove from the culture of gawping. Wallace's sense was that we're all gawpers now, lens-dangling barn-watchers as much as pop-cultural theorists. The most absurd aspect of this parodic regress is the person who thinks he can stand outside it, observing with ironic detachment.

This applies not just to barns, but to how TV has changed to cultivate a knowing audience of ironists. In the cultural shift from modernism to post-modernism, TV has led the way. Wallace recalled that the first TV ads evoked the communities it was desirable to belong to. To sell Pepsi to a sad, lonely, pathetic TV viewer (called, for the sake of Wallace's argument, Joe Briefcase), a commercial would depict a bunch of beautiful people having fun with the branded cola drink. The implication was that, by buying it, Joe Briefcase could become a member of that group – the 'Pepsi Generation', if you will.

This sort of misdirection at the heart of advertising was analysed by Judith Williamson in her book *Decoding Advertisements*. She argued that, in advertising, real objects are taken out of physical reality and absorbed into a closed system of symbols.[38] The slogan for Kraft Superfine, for instance, was 'Is your mum a Superfine Mum?' There was a clever pun at work here: the capitalised S of Superfine goes beyond suggesting that your mother is superfine (in other words, a woman of taste and beauty), and asks whether she is a member of the Superfine clan – an implied cabal of Kraft margarine users. Better, it implies that only Superfine mums can be superfine.

For Williamson, the advertisement works by going a step further than the Pepsi Generation ad cited by Wallace. For her, advertisements paradoxically work by inviting us to create ourselves 'in accordance with the way that they have already created us'.[39] We do not buy Kraft Superfine margarine because we want to become superfine or Superfine; rather, we are already both superfine and Superfine – or, thanks to the advertisement, suppose ourselves to be so – which is why we buy the product. Advertising thus decoded is ideological, in that it misdirects us, diverting us from our real desires and real identities, and obscures the real structure of society.

Advertisements invite us to join confected social groups defined through consumed products. For Marxists, this programmatically obscures what is really important – namely, what people produce rather than what they consume. Social classes are ideologically erased by advertising, usurped by aspirant groups to which we are supposed to yearn to belong. Advertising deludes us about what we desire and leaves us, quite possibly, with margarine on our faces.

The ideology of freedom and choice is part of the misdirection industry: we suppose that we are freely choosing to buy particular brands of margarine, just as we suppose that Netflix offers us the freedom to choose. But, as the Frankfurt

School thinkers Max Horkheimer and Theodor Adorno wrote in *Dialectic of Enlightenment*, we have only 'the freedom to choose what was always the same'.[40] Advertising, and later the internet and social media and Netflix, are high-tech prophylactics against contamination by ideas that might challenge your worldview.

But something happened to TV ads in the 1980s that reflected both individualistic neoliberal values and the rise of ostensibly cool post-modern knowingness. We became ironic consumers of advertising, knowing that we were being manipulated, and yet manipulated all the same. How do you make somebody buy something when they are savvy about traditional sales techniques? Through the disarming deployment of irony, argued David Foster Wallace. A 1985 TV ad for Pepsi clinched this point. A van pulls up at a beach, and the pop jockey opens a can of soda right next to the van's PA system, filling the sunny afternoon with effervescent, thirst-quenching possibility. The heads of the sunbathing *jeunesse d'orée* turn as one. Moments later, the pretty things are flash-mobbing the van as the camera pulls back and the slogan fills the screen: 'Pepsi – the choice of a New Generation.'[41] The image undid the slogan: there is no choice for these beach narcissists; they respond to the amplified can-opening like Pavlovian dogs at a soda orgy. But the ad invites complicity between Joe Briefcase and the advertisement's copywriters. Their ad makes fun of the product, of the people who buy it, and of advertising itself. Joe Briefcase is invited to sneer at the suckers in the ad who have been duped thus into buying what Wallace called 'sugary crud'. And yet, at the same time, the ad thereby encourages all those lonely Joe Briefcases to buy the very product the ad has effectively derided. And it worked. The ad campaign boosted Pepsi sales through three successive quarters and won awards.

Through such content, TV becomes the most knowingly ironic of media. Irony on TV often works by juxtaposing images that contradict speech. It took a TV addict like Wallace rather than a snooty outsider (think Theodor Adorno, Neil Postman or Murray,

Don DeLillo's pop-culture scholar) to appreciate how irony is used to keep TV viewers buying goods they overtly despise.

It's striking that Wallace imagines Joe Briefcase as alone, and that through consuming Pepsi he might become part of a group. Joe Briefcase is a symbol of the decline of America in the post-modern era. In *Bowling Alone: The Collapse and Revival of American Community*, Harvard political scientist Robert D. Putnam found that Americans were much less likely to bowl in teams and leagues than in the past, but instead bowled – whether by choice or sad circumstance – on their own.[42] He took this to be symptomatic of the atomisation of society.

In the late 1970s, for instance, the average American entertained friends at home about fourteen times a year; by the late 1990s, it was more like eight. But while earlier advertisements – the Superfine Kraft margarine cited by Judith Williamson or the soft-drink ads that David Foster Wallace saw as a child – invited viewers to join imagined elite communities of margarine or sugary crud, such appeals are today less likely to be made; or, if they are made, less likely to be effective. We are too knowing in the post-modern age to believe that the Pepsi Generation is a community that we want to join; we are too self-consciously ironical to submit to such crude techniques. The trick of the ad is to keep us buying Pepsi even while we are critically aware of the techniques used to make us buy the product.

Such knowing irony became characteristic of the post-modern sensibility, and it worried Wallace. TV had become a bad influence, not just because people watch it for six hours a day and become addicted, but because it makes TV viewers become ironists in real life. By contrast, in the 1960s, perhaps, TV irony was a good thing – a rebel yell against cultural norms. We might watch a cowboy series and realise that its message of manliness, lone-gunman individualism and patriarchal stolidity was an apologia for a society in which those virtues were in decline. Joe Briefcase and other powerless white-collar workers decoded cowboy TV series such as *Gunsmoke* and *Bonanza* as ironic commentaries on their own passivity and effeminacy as they sat inert for six hours, symbolically castrated by a night's viewing of tooled-up horse-riding stetson-wearers. TV became a hypo-critical apologist for a lost set of values in the sixties, sure – but its viewers could see through that hypocrisy.

TV irony changed in post-modern times. Irony, which exploits the difference between what is said and what is meant, and between how things appear and how they really are, used to be a reliable trope for exposing hypocrisy. Post-modern irony is not liberating, but rather imprisoning. Wallace quoted the poet and philosopher Lewis Hyde: 'Irony has only emergency use. Carried over time, it is the voice of the trapped who have come to enjoy their cage.'[43]

Irony, in becoming ubiquitous, becomes tyrannising. There is no position from which to rebel when irony becomes institution-alised. TV, Wallace thought, teaches us to crave that feeling of canny superiority – a desire similar to drug addiction. That craving encourages us to laugh at other people's put-downs of each other on screen, and to protect ourselves by any means at our disposal from the most frightening prospect imaginable in post-modern culture: to leave oneself open to others' ridicule by betraying expressions of value, emotion or vulnerability. Sincerity becomes expendable, and boredom the knowing, default position – prophylactic against revealing oneself as the sucker who believes the crap flung at him.

Watching TV becomes research on how to fit in with affect-less crowds without inviting derision. It offers 'lessons in the blank, bored, too-wise expression Joe [Briefcase] must learn how to wear for tomorrow's excruciating ride on the brightly lit subway, where crowds of blank, bored-looking people have little to look at but each other'.[44] Just as the tyranny of pretty people on TV made viewers more concerned about their own relative ugliness, so it has also made us become chronically ironic, distant, knowing, heartless and lonely. Such is the post-modern predicament.

Wallace could only foresee the affectless, knowing, cool, ironic nature of post-modern subjectivity becoming more prevalent and intense due to the evolution of technology. In the new millennium that Wallace only experienced for a few years (he committed suicide in 2008), Joe Briefcase would spend hours not just in front of a TV screen but on the internet – whether via his laptop or smartphone. And yet, Wallace pretty much predicted how we could be entertained to death. 'And it's gonna get easier and easier, and more and more convenient, and more and more pleasurable, to be alone with images on a screen, given to us by people who do not love us but want our money. Which is all right. In low doses, right? But if that's the basic main staple of your diet, you're gonna die. In a meaningful way, you're going to die.'[45]

III

But before you die, you will kill. You will shoot strangers in the face, steal their cars, invade their countries, blow up their homes, preside over mass suicides. You may feel a rush of adrenaline, you may feel bored, you may feel nothing at all – but never will you feel that you have done anything wrong. Not really. Videogames realise the fantasy of action without consequences, lawlessness without breaking laws.

When *Grand Theft Auto* was launched in 1997, what was to become the fastest-selling cultural product in history was ingeniously marketed as morally scandalous. The game gave players a satellite view of Liberty City, a simulacrum of New York streets, and their task was to drive around the grid of streets, pulling over to receive missions from payphones. You might be commissioned to destroy a car or rob a bank, and as you raced through the streets you might mow down cops or civilians, who would make satisfying squelching noises as they were crushed by your tyres. Bonus points were given for exterminating dancing lines of orange-robed Hare Krishnas. 'It was just so much more fun doing all the crazy wrong stuff', said Dave Jones, one of the founders of DMA Design, which created *Grand Theft Auto*. 'There was no way we could get as much fun from being the good guys. Eventually, we just dropped the two-sided approach and fully embraced the dark side.'[46]

Max Clifford, the notorious publicist renowned for representing troubled celebrities, creating the *Sun* headline 'Freddie Starr Ate My Hamster' and ultimately for being jailed for child sex offences, was hired to head the PR campaign for *Grand Theft Auto*. Just as Malcolm McLaren had marketed the Sex Pistols two decades earlier by scandalising tabloids into pleasurable outrage with tales of the band's foul-mouthed antinomian tirades on live TV, so Clifford capitalised on DMA's embrace of the dark side, drip-feeding the media with stories about the game's outrageousness. 'It was scary and impressive how he laid out his plan to manipulate the media and the politicians', Jones said. 'It culminated in a two-hour feature on breakfast TV debating the game.'[47]

Many of those condemning *Grand Theft Auto*, Jones reckoned, had not seen the game, still less played it. The British Police Federation called the game 'sick, deluded and beneath contempt', while US Senator Hillary Clinton delivered a speech, saying: 'The disturbing material in *Grand Theft Auto* and other games like it is stealing the innocence of our children.' She called for a federal inquiry.[48] You couldn't buy such publicity, and Max Clifford didn't: he got it for free, and *Grand Theft Auto* became a huge hit.

At the time, *Grand Theft Auto* was the most convincing digital simulation of New York, but designed by a bunch of Scottish computer programmers based in Dundee and Edinburgh. The future creators of *Grand Theft Auto*, including Jones, Russell Kaur, Steven Hammond and Mike Dailly, met at Kingsway Amateur Computer Club in Dundee in the early 1980s. There, and later at Dundee Institute of Technology, they devised games on and for the Amiga 100, Sinclair Spectrum and Commodore 64 computers, and established a firm called DMA Design. Jones devised the first game that became commercially successful in a bedroom of his parents' house.

Menace, as it was called, was a single-player game that tasked its player with piloting a spaceship equipped with lasers and cannons to destroy the defence systems erected against them on the planet Draconia, and eliminate its population of evil creatures. As players ascended through six levels, debris from earlier explosions would mutate into tokens that could be traded in for high-grade weaponry or shields for the spacecraft. And that weaponry was ultimately used not just to kill the evil creatures, but to battle the diabolical guardian of Draconia. When released in 1988, *Menace* told 20,000 copies.

In 1991, DMA had its first big hit with *Lemmings*. Twenty million copies of the original game and its sequels and reboots were sold – including *Christmas Lemmings*. But the game's goal remained the same: players had to guide a percentage of suicidal green-haired, blue-robed lemmings from the entrance to the exit by clearing or creating a safe passage through a virtual landscape. The game was more sophisticated than Menace, not least in having more levels – and, crucially, allowing more than one player. Failed missions were marked by piles of squished lemmings who had fallen to their violent deaths because you or your fellow player could not be trusted to guide them to safety. But no Senate committee investigated the desensitising effect of witnessing such mass suicide on teenagers' brains. Nobody ever wrote a hand-wringing op-ed about how real-life lemmings might suffer after their depiction in a video game.

Grand Theft Auto was a different matter. DMA's greatest success, which at the time of writing has become a series of eleven standalone games and four expansion packs, provoked many complaints and accusations that it had caused murder and promoted misogyny in the real world. Each player took the role of a rookie gangster at the bottom of the city's organised crime structure. By carjacking, murder, pimping and various forms of torture, each player would impress mob bosses, and thereby climb through the ranks,

When *Grand Theft Auto III* was released, in 2001, one technical breakthrough was to shift the player's perspective from an aerial view to first-person. More than ever, driving these streets felt like being immersed in reality.

'Life is a video game. Everybody's got to die sometime', Devin Moore, an Alabama teenager, told police in 2003. Moore, reportedly influenced by playing *Grand Theft Auto*, was arrested on suspicion of stealing a car. At the police station, he grabbed an officer's .45 calibre pistol, shot two officers and a dispatcher dead, and escaped in a police cruiser, before being recaptured.[49]

The following year, Rockstar North (of which DMA Design was by this time a subsidiary) released *Grand Theft Auto: San Andreas*, set among drug and prostitution gangs in a simulated 1990s Los Angeles. Its arrival was initially welcomed by critics, not least because it was singular in having a black protagonist. But Rockstar made a terrible misjudgement with the game. Rockstar president Sam Houser called on his creatives to feature porn scenes in the game depicting fellatio, dildo sex and whipping. They obligingly did so, only for Rockstar to realise just before publication that the sexual content would cause retail chains to refuse to sell the game. So the offending parts were suppressed: they would never appear when you played the game – or so Rockstar hoped – but nonetheless remained on the discs' data.

A modder (a slang term for a hacker who modifies mass-manufactured software) discovered the deleted pornographic scenes in the data, and released a software patch to the internet that enabled other players to unlock them. The patch became known as the 'hot coffee' modification, because in the deleted scenes the protagonist's girlfriend invites him into her house for a euphemistic coffee. After the Entertainment Software Rating Board investigated *Grand Theft Auto: San Andreas* and changed its rating to adult-only, production was suspended and copies withdrawn from shelves by many retailers, at huge cost.

The makers continued to dwell on the dark side. *Grand Theft Auto IV*, published in 2008, was criticised for allowing drunk driving in the game. *Grand Theft Auto V*, published in 2013, was condemned for enabling, even encouraging, players to have sex with and then kill prostitutes. Cassie Rodenberg, a school-teacher in the South Bronx, wrote in the *Guardian*: 'This is all possible, even encouraged by tips on YouTube and chatrooms, in *Grand Theft Auto V*. In fact, your character's health (aka life points) goes up when you have sex with a prostitute.'[50]

Rodenberg worried about the real-life consequences of the game for her students. 'How perverse that *Grand Theft Auto* took place in ghettos suffering high crime, poverty and gang violence', she reflected. 'Many Bronx students, mostly males, many of whom live in shelters or subsist in the foster care system, play GTA V and laugh.' Sam Houser, for his part, doubted the real-life consequences of playing videogames. He recalled New York cops telling him that they didn't mind players killing cops in *GTA*. 'There's a lot of people out there trying to kill cops, and we'd rather they did it in your game than on the street.'[51]

Grand Theft Auto V sold 11.21 million copies during its first twenty-four hours on sale in 2013. By 2019, *GTA* had become the fourth-largest video game franchise ever – after *Tetris*, Nintendo's *Super Mario* and *Pokémon* – amassing an estimated gross revenue of $9 billion. Rockstar has published no figures for all the virtual prostitutes, police officers, pedestrians or Hare Krishna devotees slain between 1997 and today, but you would think the body count also runs into billions.

Since 1997, *Grand Theft Auto* has become part of a global industry that dwarfs cinema box-office and recorded-music receipts. The global games market was estimated to generate $152.1 billion from 2.5 billion gamers around the world in 2020. By comparison, the global box-office industry was worth $41.7 billion, while global music revenues reached $19.1 billion in 2018.

This revolution in the entertainment industry happened quickly. In 1972, the world's first videogame, *Pong*, was released by Atari, and consisted of a two-dimensional graphical representation of a tennis-like game. Players used rectangular paddles to hit a ball back and forth on a black-and-white screen. As the world plunged into recession in 1974, Atari engineer Harold Lee proposed a home version of *Pong* that would connect to a television: *Home Pong*. Sears Roebuck financed the production of 150,000 units. It became the hottest-selling Christmas present of that year. From these humble beginnings began a domestic revolution in entertainment.

One reason for the success of this new form of entertainment from 1972 onwards is that videogames offer what cinemas and recorded music do not. We can reinvent ourselves, cast off our disappointing real identities for avatars in videogames and online personalities very different from our own. Your first life may be disappointing, but your second life need not be. Videogames, and later the online world, let us be born again.

In 2003, San Francisco–based firm Linden Labs launched an online virtual world called *Second Life* that, a decade later, had a million users. *Second Life* was inspired by Neal Stephenson's 1992 novel *Snow Crash*, in which he described an online environment called the Metaverse where users interacted using the real world as a metaphor. 'It is by engaging its users in the act of creation that *Second Life* provides opportunities that are not necessarily available in real life', argued Douglas E. Jones. In *Second Life*, users construct personae that are either normative or fantastical. Women avatars usually have bigger breasts, while male avatars are often implausibly buff. The fantasists include a great number of fairies, Jedi warriors and Tolkien characters, but also a group called 'furries' – avatars created by people who yearn to role-play as cuddly squirrels or rabbits in a safe environment. In *Second Life* you could change gender, be more talkative, or less, or you can have sex of the kind you wouldn't dare experience in real life.[52]

And yet videogames, predicated on pleasurable fantasy role-playing, and on disconnecting from the real world, often replicate virtually the structure and demands of real work. Videogames are another kind of post-modern misdirection. We hunt for tokens to add to our life expectancy, battle aliens to shorten theirs, often within discrete task-based levels that replicate in cyberspace Taylorist and Fordist assembly-line production processes.

Videogames blur the line between reality and fantasy, but not in the way we might expect. What we do at leisure echoes, often clumsily, what we do at work. Mark Twain wrote in *Tom Sawyer*: 'Work consists of whatever a body is obliged to do. Play consists of whatever a body is not obliged to do.'[53] Not so, countered Adorno and Horkheimer in *Dialectic of Enlightenment*, contending that the obligations of labour continued after working hours were done:

> Amusement under late capitalism is the prolongation of work. It is sought after as an escape from the mechanised work process, and to recruit strength in order to be able to cope with it again. But at the same time mechanisation has such power over a man's leisure and happiness, and so profoundly determines the manufacture of amusement goods, that his experiences are inevitably after-images of the work process itself.[54]

In *Grand Theft Auto IV*, players have to complete missions if they are to rise through the gang hierarchy. Even maintaining friendships in the game, noted videogames critic Steven Poole, involves work – players must perform the chore of taking a friend to a bar or lap-dancing club in order to assure his 'loyalty'. Perhaps, Poole mused, performing this kind of task is a solace in the post-modern, flexible labour market. More irksome yet, in *GTA IV* you manage your interactions through a virtual mobile phone which, given the shortcomings of videogames consoles, was hard to operate. 'We thus arrive at the absurd position where it is supposed to be fun to use a complex piece of technology to emulate badly the experience of using a less complex piece of technology.'[55]

Certainly, playing games always requires that one follow rules; otherwise one is not playing the game, but doing something incomprehensible. And yet, we've all wanted to break out of the iron cage of rules while playing videogames. You don't get points for shooting your comrades rather than the enemy in *Call of Duty*, but it remains a temptation. When playing *Race Driver:*

Grid, Poole decided to crash his car into barriers and then park it in the middle of the track so that other players crashed into him.[56] While playing *The Sims*, my wife built a swimming pool, put her Sim in the water, then removed the steps so he drowned.

But what's striking is how little one can achieve by trying to break out of videogames' iron cages. In 'I Fought the Law: Transgressive Play and the Implied Player', Espen Aarseth wrote: 'These marginal events and occurrences, these wondrous acts of transgression, are absolutely vital because they give us hope, true or false; they remind us that it is possible to regain control, however briefly, to dominate that which dominates us so completely.'[57] Perhaps. But Poole found that, after his car was totalled, there was nothing to do but reload and try again. You might be able to be a drop-out in real life, but not in videogames.

What's more, many videogames express free-market ideology. In *The Sims*, for instance, you build your home by shopping for items that you pay for through work. You have a better house and a better career through work. More money makes your Sim happier.

The pleasures of playing videogames are not always associated with replicating capitalist work patterns, nor with instilling capitalist values. *Grand Theft Auto*, in its amorality and hyperreality, is the best exemplar of a post-modern entertainment in offering a fantasy of lawlessness. One of the great pleasures of *GTA* is that you get to break laws without consequence; moreover, you earn points by breaking laws. Paradoxically, our lawless impulses are contained within a rule-bound structure. In *GTA*, the points you earn for law-breaking are only accrued within the context provided by the rules of the game. You can kill innocent strangers, but you can't go on strike against your bosses. Some actions just don't make sense in this game.

Just as the NYPD might be happy that *Grand Theft Auto* players killed cops online rather than in real life, so capitalism benefits from oppositional energies being harmlessly diverted online. We could have overthrown the system; instead, we deluded ourselves with fantasies of law-breaking. We might have put our energies into creating a better real world; instead, we used them to murder virtual prostitutes.

10

All That Is Solid Melts into Air, 2001:

9/11 | iPods | Debt

I

'You've got to hand it to them on some level,' said Damien Hirst, 'because they've achieved something which nobody would have ever have thought possible.' The British artist was talking about the 11 September 2001 attacks on New York's Twin Towers and the Pentagon in Washington, DC, in which 2,977 people died, nineteen hijackers committed murder-suicide, and more than 6,000 others were injured:

> The thing about 9/11 is that it's kind of an artwork in its own right. It was wicked, but it was devised in this way for this kind of impact. It was devised visually. So on one level they kind of need congratulating, which a lot of people shy away from, which is a very dangerous thing. I think our visual language has been changed by what happened on September 11: an aeroplane becomes a weapon – and if they fly close to buildings people start panicking. Our visual language is constantly changing in this way and I think as an artist you're constantly on the lookout for things like that.[1]

Other artists were similarly awe-struck by 9/11, envious of the terrorists for shaking the world. Only a few days after the Twin Towers were destroyed, the composer Karlheinz Stockhausen held a press conference in Hamburg in which he called the attack on the World Trade Center 'the greatest work of art that is possible in the whole cosmos'. Extending the analogy, he spoke of human minds achieving 'something in one act' that 'we couldn't even dream of in music'.[2] The Spanish artist Santiago Sierra said: 'The problem now is that it's hard to be an artist and make the west sit up and take notice because of September 11.'[3]

All three felt overshadowed by the visual flair of what Bin Laden's terrorists had achieved by means of mass murder on 9/11. Robert Hughes described modern art as offering the shock of the new. Now art could not shock, because reality trumped art. Stephen King once told me that, after 9/11, he was approached by TV executives hoping to adapt his 1987 novel *The Running Man* as a topical satire of reality TV. 'And I'm like "Sure, but you've got to film the ending." The ending is a guy hijacks a jet and flies it into a skyscraper killing everybody. The guy does it because he perceives everybody in the skyscrapers as agents of the great Satan. The execs lost interest pretty quickly.'[4] The visual power of 9/11 was such that it could not be copied.

Several theorists argued that 9/11 ended post-modernism. Crashing two planes into the Twin Towers returned the world to the real after its decadent dalliance with post-modernism and hyperreality. To argue this way was appealing, because it suggested that post-modernism had a birth date and a death date, both of them associated with the detonation of buildings by Minoru Yamasaki. In 1971, his Pruitt-Igoe complex was blown up; in 2001, his Twin Towers were destroyed. Bin Laden had shocked us back to reality.

'That morning', wrote the novelist Hari Kunzru of 9/11, 'it became clear that "hostility to grand narratives", as Jean-François Lyotard defined it, was a minority pursuit, an intellectual Rubik's cube for a tiny western metropolitan elite. It seemed most of the world still had some use for God, truth and the law, terms which they were using without inverted commas.'[5] Others, such as *Vanity Fair* editor Graydon Carter, proclaimed that the attacks signalled 'the end of the age of irony'.[6]

But reports of the death of post-modernism were exaggerated; the age of irony, ironically, survived the crushing literalism of

9/11. The world after 9/11 was different from the one before it, but not in the way these critics of post-modernism imagined. Kunzru's suggestion that 9/11 made it clear that post-modernism was a minority pursuit is fanciful. It was apparent long before 9/11 that very few humans had the knowingly ironic qualities necessary for the post-modern sensibility; that grand narratives persisted in the minds of many of the world's citizens; that most of the world believed literally in varying degrees and varieties of nonsense, such as God, truth, law, American exceptionalism, and divine revelation through sacred texts, irrespective of Derridean deconstruction or Lyotard's analysis of the post-modern condition.

Even among tiny Western metropolitan elites, some continued to believe in grand narratives. Samuel Huntington's 'clash of civilisations' thesis was predicated on the notion that grand narratives motivated both sides in the global civilisational conflict that arose in the wake of the Cold War. Post-modernism had long functioned not as the end of grand narratives, but as a critique of their plausibility. They were believed, yes; they motivated some of the most grisly human actions, true; but they were also greeted by what Lyotard called 'incredulity' – roughly: how could clever humans believe such nonsense?

Post-modernism isn't to be swept into the dustbin of history so readily. The idea that a new seriousness arose from Ground Zero, of a renewed respect for the old values of truth and God that had been trashed by post-modernism, doesn't bear scrutiny. The age of irony curdled after 9/11 into something yet more degrading: our post-truth world.

Artists may have been confounded by 9/11, but another kind of creative virtuoso managed to do something with it. In 2015, Donald Trump, then the Republicans' presidential nominee, told a rally in Alabama: 'I watched when the World Trade Center came tumbling down. And I watched in Jersey City, New Jersey, where thousands and thousands of people were cheering as that building was coming down. Thousands of people were cheering', Trump said.[7] Days later he repeated the assertion in an interview on ABC's *This Week*, as host George Stephanopoulos explained to him that police had refuted any such rumours at the time. 'It did happen. I saw it', countered Trump. 'It was on television. I saw it. There were people that were cheering on the other side of New Jersey, where you have large Arab populations. They were cheering as the World Trade Center came down', he said.[8]

Trump later cited an 18 September 2001 *Washington Post* story that said 'law enforcement authorities detained and questioned a number of people who were allegedly seen celebrating the attacks'. But one of the story's authors, the *New York Times*'s Serge Kovaleski, retorted that the article did not stand up Trump's account. Kovaleski said he had tried to find out whether any Muslims had celebrated the attack, and reported that he had been unable to prove that point.[9] Abdul Mubarak-Rowe, spokesperson for the New Jersey chapter of the Council on American-Islamic Relations, called Trump's version of events 'a bald-faced lie', and 'bigoted, racist rhetoric'.[10]

It was more than that. It was the fault of post-modernism. Post-modern theory counselled that the signifier had floated free of the signified. The former, which after all was the vessel of meaning, was a dubious, incorrigible character, prone to the chronic disease of logorrhoea. The pleasure to be had in such free-floating polysemous creativity became less appealing when the lacuna between signified and signifier became a petri dish for fake news. It was, argued Matthew d'Ancona in *Post Truth: The New War on Truth and How to Fight Back*, post-modernists' fault for arguing that there were no such things as truth and objectivity, only power and interests.[11]

In 2017, White House press secretary Sean Spicer told the media that, contrary to photographic evidence, the crowd at Trump's inauguration was the largest ever. The following day, Kellyanne Conway, then senior counsellor to the president, appeared on NBC's *Meet the Press*, where host Chuck Todd told her that Spicer's claim was a falsehood. 'Don't be so overly dramatic about it, Chuck', she replied. 'Sean Spicer, our press secretary, gave alternative facts to that.'[12]

As for irony, it too survived 9/11 – not least as a tool for understanding American foreign policy. George W. Bush articulated the goals of the 'war on terrorism' in a speech of 20 September 2001, in which he said it would 'not end until every terrorist group of global reach has been found, stopped and defeated'.[13] In that same speech, he called the war 'a task that does not end'. Irony, the tool for enabling us to appreciate the opposition between what is said and what is meant, helped show Bush's speech was nonsense: there could be no war against terror, because terrorism was not a force but a tactic. Nor, in truth, was Bush announcing a war against all terrorism: there was no sense that he had in his crosshairs, for instance, the Irish Republican Army or Euskadi Ta Askatasuna, the Basque separatist group.

Moreover, the first salvos in the war on terror involved the invasion of Iraq in 2003, despite the fact that the country had no links to 9/11, or – despite Bush and Tony Blair's claims to the contrary – any weapons of mass destruction. It was a conflict steeped in tragic ironies. The war on terror was launched in Iraq not to free the world from terrorism (an impossible goal), but so as to create a smokescreen for the maintenance of Iraqi oil production, so that oil prices could be kept down. There was an ironic distance between stated war aims and real objectives. In 2003, British politician Dame Shirley Williams warned that 'the British government, with its American partner, must stop to think whether it is sowing the kind of resentment which is the seedbed of future terrorism'.[14] She was prescient: from war-ravaged Iraq arose Islamic State, which in 2014 overran northern Iraq and eastern Syria with the aim of establishing a caliphate. The war against terror, ironically, produced terror.

Kunzru argued that – 'crucially' – post-modernism was a pre-digital phenomenon. To back this up, he consulted Google's Ngram Viewer to look at the incidence of the word 'post-modernism' in books since 1975. The use of the term peaked around 1997 and then declined, overtaken in around 2000 by the term 'internet'.[15] I think this is mistaken. For a start, post-modernists were not an avant-garde; rather, insofar as they could be lumped together, they were the murderers of the avant-garde. As Fredric Jameson noted in *Postmodernism: Or, the Cultural Logic of Late Capitalism*, high modernism stood for a conception of unique style, along with the accompanying collective ideals of an artistic or political vanguard or avant-garde. Post-modernists had no such collective ideals, and no such unique style. Post-modernism, particularly in architecture, favoured multiple styles taken from the supermarket of history, and it doubted the model whereby an elite's ideas ultimately permeated the whole of culture, thereby powering human progress.

Moreover, the rise of the internet did not spell the death of post-modernism. Even if it had, that could not be demonstrated by the rise and fall of usages of the two terms in books. The internet is a symptom of post-modernism. If, as Kunzru realised, the internet is the realisation of a post-modernist dream, then that hardly means we are no longer post-modern. It is a very strange argument to suggest that, if something becomes real, it no longer exists. If anything, we are more post-modern now than before the digital age. The waning of affect that Jameson took to be characteristic of our souls under post-modernism thrives more than ever in the decades since 9/11. Joe Briefcase – the post-modern figure whom David Foster Wallace imagined alone yet connected, entranced yet immobilised before screens of various kinds – remains emblematic of how we live. The medium is the message, whether it is TV, the internet or the iPhone.

'The "content" of a medium', wrote Marshall McLuhan in 1964, 'is like the juicy piece of meat carried by the burglar to distract the watchdog of the mind.'[16] Society's values, norms and ways of doing things change because of technology and how we are encouraged to use it. The dream of infinite choice and endless entertainment that these technologies seem to offer us also has its nightmarish flip-side: the tyranny of control. The difference between the modern age and the post-modern one is that we know what the steak is for, but we carry on drooling over it while we are ransacked – while our privacy is eliminated, our pockets picked, and our time exploited with a sophistication that would have astounded McLuhan.

In response to 9/11, the philosopher Slavoj Žižek wrote *Welcome to the Desert of the Real*. In it, he argued that global capitalism and fundamentalism are two parts of the same whole, and that paradigms such as Fukuyama's 'end of history' and Huntington's 'clash of civilisations' restrict the range of apparent conflicts to cultural, ethnic and religious ones, masking anything more fundamental, such as economic conflict. His suggestion was that 9/11 and its aftermath had obscured reality rather than bringing us back to it. Global capitalism was itself a variety of fundamentalism, and America was complicit in the rise of Muslim fundamentalism, argued Žižek. Neoliberalism emerged more strongly after 9/11, since it harnessed the war on terror to suppress dissent, and used the tragedy to legitimise torture, rendition flights, and the horrors of Abu Ghraib and Guantánamo Bay.

To make sense of his argument, Žižek applied Baudrillard's ideas to the World Trade Center attacks via the 1999 science-fiction film *The Matrix*.[17] In *The Republic*, Plato imagined ordinary humans as prisoners tied firmly to their seats and compelled to watch the shadowy performance of what they falsely suppose to be reality on the walls of the cave. When some individuals escape the cave, they find that their 'reality' has merely been a shadow of the true reality. And that true reality is the Earth illuminated by the rays of the Sun, the supreme Good. In *The Matrix*, by contrast, those who awaken from the virtual reality generated by the eponymous mega-computer find the true reality to be nightmarish. The enlightened realise that each of us is effectively just a foetus-like organism immersed in amniotic fluid. Each of us is hooked up to cables that drain us of our life energy to power the Matrix itself.

For Žižek, the metaphor of the Matrix could be seen as representing how neoliberal capitalism colonises culture and subjectivity. For him, the Matrix is the Lacanian Big Other: 'This utter passivity is the foreclosed fantasy that sustains our conscious experience as active, self-positing subjects – it is the ultimate perverse fantasy: the notion that, in our innermost being, we are instruments of the Other's (Matrix's) *jouissance*.' The very reality we live in, the atemporal utopia staged by the Matrix, is produced so that we can be effectively reduced to the passive state of living batteries providing it with energy.

When the hero, played by Keanu Reeves, awakens into 'real reality', he finds himself in the burned-out ruins of Chicago after a global war. 'Was it not something of a similar order that took place in New York on September 11? Its citizens were introduced to "the desert of the real" – for us, corrupted by Hollywood, the landscape and the shots of the collapsing towers could not but be reminiscent of the most breathtaking scenes in big catastrophe productions.'[18] The simulation preceded the real. The towers being hit by planes and then tumbling into rubble were not so amazing because we couldn't believe it was happening, but because we'd seen it before in movies.

II

In the same year as 9/11, Apple released the iPod. The iPod was born and digital culture had its ur-fetish object. Digital technology accelerated, enabling individuals to manipulate every aspect of the media environment. In the digital world, you the consumer could do what cultural producers had always done: you could be your own DJ, photographer and filmmaker. Better, you could do what the Man said you shouldn't: sample, pastiche, cut-and-paste others' work, riff on the results, and pass it off as your own. But, if you follow Žižek, what the iPod does is give the illusion of creative activity, while in reality we are made into instruments, keeping the system we should overthrow on life support.

The iPod was the idea of Steve Jobs, the Silicon Valley revolutionary who pioneered home computing. But it was realised by Jonathan Ive, senior vice president of industrial design at Apple, who designed the iMac and iBook laptops. Ive's genius consisted partly of appropriating minimalist design for the digital age. He was hugely influenced by the great German industrial designer Dieter Rams, who at Braun designed a host of classic gadgets, from radios to juicers, and later was responsible for minimalist shelving design at Vitsœ. 'No part appeared to be either hidden or celebrated, just perfectly considered and completely appropriate in the hierarchy of the product's details and features', said Ive of Rams's designs. 'At a glance, you knew exactly what it was and exactly how to use it.'[19]

One of Dieter Rams's most celebrated design features was a click wheel for a Braun radio. This was echoed in the iPod's click wheel, which relies on an ingenious technology called capacitive sensing. Under the iPod's plastic click wheel is a grid of metal conductors that is supplied with electricity. If you bring your finger near to the click wheel cover, the current wants to flow to your finger, but is stopped by the plastic click wheel cover. As a result, a charge builds up between two conductors – the grid and your finger – which is known as capacitance. As your finger moves around the wheel, the charge build-up moves around the wheel with it. The faster you move your finger around the wheel, the more compacted the stream of signals it sends out, which results in the microprocessor increasing or decreasing the volume. Ive was drawn to Dieter Rams's design work because he 'remains utterly alone in producing a body of work so consistently beautiful, so right and so accessible'.[20] Rams's slogan 'Less, but better' was applied by Ive to the digital age, when he created in the iPod an object of fetishistic beauty – one whose function followed its form so perfectly that an instruction manual was scarcely necessary.

The hardware was ingenious enough, but what was most revolutionary about the iPod was the software. By means of the iPod you could download thousands of tunes and carry them in your pocket. It suddenly made previous personal stereos, such as Sony's Walkman and Discman, seem ludicrously cumbersome. The first MP3 player, the MPMan, released in 1998, held only thirty-two megabytes of memory. As one megabyte played about one minute of music, the MPMan held eight or nine songs. The iPod had a five-gigabyte hard drive, enabling users to carry about 1,200 song files; later versions multiplied memory storage.

This fetish object, like the later iPhone, soon acquired worshippers. In *iPod, Therefore I Am*, Dylan Jones described it as 'a cigarette pack for those addicted to music instead of tobacco'.[21] It was at once a lifestyle accessory that one could embellish with customised plastic skins, supported by in-car and at-home docks, and an existential statement of who you were, showing you to be a hipster with your finger on the pulse, both figuratively and literally.

It was a post-modern piece of kit, too, enabling the user to democratise music and flatten distinctions. The shuffle mechanism randomised the history of music, juxtaposing Wu Tang Klan with Mozart. That makes the iPod sound more serendipitous than it was. You were still in the prison of your own tastes (whatever you uploaded to your iPod was chosen by you), but the randomised juxtapositions made new connections and distinctions possible.

Technology is often like this. It changes us by making the hitherto unimaginable become first desirable, then ubiquitous. 'A light bulb', Marshall McLuhan wrote, 'creates an environment by its mere presence.'[22] Thanks to light bulbs, we can colonise the dark. Similarly, TVs, newspapers and the internet (McLuhan died in 1980, so he missed the rise of that technological innovation) extend our prosthetic reach; but their content may blind us to how technology has changed us. McLuhan had a relatively benign vision of technological innovation. It was our tool. The subtitle of *Understanding Media* was 'The Extensions of Man', and his vision was of technological innovations as human prostheses.

Friedrich Kittler, the German media theorist, was of a more dystopian temper. 'The development of the internet has more to do with human beings becoming a reflection of their technologies', he once argued. 'After all, it is we who adapt to the machine. The machine does not adapt to us.' Against McLuhan, he argued that 'media are not pseudopods for extending the human body. They follow the logic of escalation that leaves us and written history behind it.'[23] Copernicus showed the universe did not revolve around the earth. Darwin showed we descended from apes, and did not control our evolution. Freud said we were at the mercy of unconscious impulses. Now Kittler was suggesting we weren't masters of our technological domain, but rather its pawns.

His phrase – the logic of escalation – is telling. Like many post-modern thinkers about the media in continental Europe, including Paul Virilio and Jean Baudrillard, Kittler had a dystopian vision of technology that was influenced by early experiences during World War II. One of his first memories was seeing Dresden ablaze from a distance, bombed in February 1945 by the Allies. He also recalled being frequently taken by his mother to a Baltic island to visit the site where Hitler's V2 rockets had been developed.

Virilio, the French theorist, also had a childhood marked by war. He recalls living in occupied Nantes as it was bombed by France's allies. He once wrote: 'History progresses at the speed of its weapons systems', adding: 'The physical world ceases to be the battlefield and instead the battle becomes one of ideologies and economics and speed.' By this he meant battles would be won by the fastest: 'The class struggle is replaced by the struggle of the technological bodies of the armies according to their dynamic efficiency.'[24] Virilio's best-known statement, 'the invention of the ship was also the invention of the shipwreck', expresses in a nutshell his career-long scepticism for those Panglossians who argue that technology is entirely about progress.[25]

But as Silicon Valley boomed in the 1990s, investors in what became known as the dotcom bubble didn't read Kittler or

Virilio. Instead they read breathless encomia to digital technology. Rich Karlgaard, publisher of the money magazine *Forbes*,
for instance, wrote in 1999: 'The pace can go on. The physics of
the Information Age is a sure bet. [Silicon] chips are headed
towards infinite speed at zero cost . . . The radical new software
and e-commerce business models that will follow in their wake
can only be guessed at. But their arrival is . . . locked in.'[26] Such
believers in the transformative power of the New Economy, as
the digitised breakthroughs created mostly in Silicon Valley
became known, believed that it would not only make investors
rich but revolutionise society and business, and supersede
democracy as it was currently practised.

Thomas Frank, author of *One Market under God*, argued
that the period of the late 1990s, when the commercialisation of
the internet skyrocketed, was underpinned by a quasi-religious
phenomenon – an ideology that hinged on millennial ideas as
dubious as Francis Fukuyama's end-of-history thesis of a few
years earlier.[27] While Fukuyama had suggested that history had
ended with the triumph of liberal democracy, New Economy
proselytisers suggested that the problems of capitalism had
been solved by digital technology and that, as Frank claimed,
'therefore government regulation, taxes, labor unions, etc. were
no longer needed. As it happened, these theories were mostly
invented and trumpeted by people who already believed that
government regulation, taxes, labor unions, etc. were bad
things.'[28]

New Economy proselytisers argued that Silicon Valley entrepreneurs were 'near divine figures who should not be restricted
in any way'. Steve Jobs and Bill Gates were a new breed of
businessmen – cool rulers whose creative and business acumen
chimed with a renewed faith in neoliberalism, or what Frank
calls 'market populism', namely the increasing conviction 'that
laissez-faire, free-market capitalism was the quintessence of
human freedom; that markets expressed the popular will in a
manner that government could never do; and that business
would inevitably and rightfully triumph over its enemies – the

welfare and regulatory state, organized labour, and social critics'.[29]

Such ideas had been expressed by polemicists for neoliberalism, such as Friedrich Hayek and Robert Nozick, decades earlier; but the association of their anti-state, anti-government ideas with the desirable products of Silicon Valley and the near-miraculous powers of its leading entrepreneurs strengthened the case.

Faith in the New Economy induced investors into buying Silicon Valley stocks. Internet-based companies were envisaged as the future of commerce, leading to excessive market speculation. Valuations of dotcom start-ups were based on projected earnings and profits that would not occur for years, even on the – sometimes fanciful – assumption that their business models would work. But investors threw caution to the wind and poured money into digital businesses irrespective of how well they were currently doing.

For instance, when the web browser Netscape went public on 9 August 1995 – the date often cited as the start of the dotcom bubble – its stock rose from $28 to $75 in hours, even though the company wasn't profitable. Between 1995 and 2000, the technology-dominated Nasdaq index rose from under 1,000 to an all-time high of 5,132.52 on 10 March 2000. By the end of 2001, though, a majority of publicly traded dotcom companies had folded, and trillions of dollars of investment capital evaporated. Dotcom businesses once supposed to be sure things, such as Pets.com, Kozmo and eToys, collapsed, while Amazon and eBay, among others, held on.

In this context, Apple's launch of the iPod was a risky venture. It came as investors in the New Economy were getting queasy, and as the United States reeled from 9/11. But the iPod delivered something new, and proved – to put it mildly – to be worth investing in. It seamlessly combined two things: the sense of maximum freedom for the consumer to play the music she wanted where and when she wanted; and the optimising of market domination, and thus profits, by the manufacturer. For all the breathless paeans by iPod fans such as Dylan Jones about how they were able to curate recorded music eclectically to suit their own tastes, what is often overlooked is that the iPod was also designed according to a neoliberal business model. Two years after it was launched, Apple launched iTunes, its own online music store. Instead of downloading music from their own digitised collection on their personal computer, iPod users increasingly bought it from iTunes. As Steve Jobs put it, Apple then owned 'the whole widget', because there was vertical integration between the hardware (iPod) and software (iTunes).

At the time, the iTunes store seemed benign to record companies and musicians terrified at what kids were doing with the new digital tools. Digital natives seemed particularly adept at freeloading music by copying it from friends or accomplices online. MP3 players at the turn of the millennium were largely stuffed with music ripped from CDs and files taken by rather dubious means from the secret corners of the web. One of those dubious means was Napster, a service that relied on piracy. It was a peer-to-peer service, in the sense that you needed an accomplice online to share a song with you and the technical savvy to download it from the internet. Given that, at the turn of the millennium, dial-up modems that shared their connections with home phone lines were commonplace, this was no mean feat. It was a laborious process to download one four-minute song illegally, be it Dre and Snoop's 'Nuthin' but a "G" Thang' or Metallica's 'Seek and Destroy'. Sure, the music was free, but the cost in time exorbitant.

Napster was seen as taking money from the mouths of musicians. In 2000, both Dre and Metallica sued Napster alleging infringement of their copyrighted music. At the time, it was quite possible to use Apple's iTunes program to play illegally shared music on one's iPod, or CDs that one had borrowed from friends and ripped into digital files. But when iTunes was launched as a digital store in 2003, it could posture as a new sheriff bringing law and order to the Wild West of music sharing. 'Consumers don't want to be treated like criminals and artists don't want their valuable work stolen', Steve Jobs said in his announcement keynote. 'The iTunes Music Store offers a groundbreaking solution for both.'[30]

Customers ostensibly terrified at being taken to court for illegally downloading, say, Missy Elliot's 2001 'Get Ur Freak On' were appeased. Moreover, the record industry and musicians were mollified. Because Apple charged for songs that were bought from the iTunes store and transferred some of the proceeds to the artists, it seemed as if the old business model of paying for creative content had been restored. No matter that Apple decided the price point and the size of their cut of sales. Effectively, what Jobs and Apple did was to replace bigger bricks-and-mortar retailers with a digital store that worked as a near monopoly, with minimal overheads. Record companies at the time seemed grateful to get a cut of a new digital business they didn't quite understand. Steve Jobs effectively bought up the music industry cheap.

If only the investors who got burned so badly in the dotcom crash had had the foresight to put their money into Apple rather than, say, WorldCom and Global Crossing. In 2007, Apple launched the iPhone. Unlike iPods, it had no scroll wheel. There were no buttons to dial the phone. Instead, the iPhone employed a touchscreen. At the time it seemed to have miraculous powers. You could use wireless technology (Wi-Fi) to surf the internet; check your email; and access the iTunes store, where you could preview, buy and download songs, TV shows and videos. The iPod was soon to become obsolete, supplanted by a new fetish object by means of which Apple controlled the widget as never before.

The attempts made by iTunes at predictive analytics never matched the sophistication of, say, Netflix data mining. When iTunes 8 was launched in 2008, it offered a so-called 'Genius' facility, which could automatically generate a playlist of songs from the user's library that 'go great together';[31] but this seemed a crude facility – no match for the predictive analytics being developed by music streaming services such as Pandora, Songza and – most importantly – Spotify. The last of these – which had more than 200 million monthly users by 2019, and whose stakeholders included record companies – curated playlists algorithmically, including a weekly playlist including music from a user's favourite artists; but it also recommended artists based on listening history. Spotify, headlines proclaimed, knows your tastes better than you do yourself; iTunes, not so much.

The appeal of iTunes lay first in its being legal, and second in its capacity to offer a way to store media, particularly music, that had hitherto been inconceivable. Houses filled with CDs and LPs could be cleared out, and vast music collections stored on small devices. But iTunes turned out to be a way-station between such physical libraries and what has succeeded it: streaming services. The advent of streaming meant that buying music and other media content to own was no longer necessary. First, owning physical artefacts became redundant, then owning digital artefacts became redundant – and the latter undercut the iTunes stores' business model. If you can stream anything you want from the cloud for a monthly fee, buying and owning an album or a film in digital form loses its rationale. What's more, its pretensions to be a one-stop shop for media made the app cumbersome to use. Today iTunes still persists, but as what some call a heritage app – the digital equivalent of LPs, cassettes or VHS tapes, sustained by nostalgia for old technology. Apple now offers a service called Apple Music, which serves the same streaming market that replaced MP3 players such as the iPod.

In a matter of a few years, the iPod strut was replaced by the smartphone walk, or what detractors called the dumb-walk – head down, arms outstretched, pace glacial, and absorption in a hand-held screen apparently total. Kittler was right: the technology that seemed to extend our prosthetic reach in the world has facilitated our domination. Heads bowed in prayerful contemplation before our profane gods, we differ from our devout ancestors only in that we worship alone.

Virilio developed the concept of 'dromology' (from the Greek *dromos*, 'race') to denote the 'science (or logic) of speed'.[32]

He argued that our cult of speed, facilitated by technological innovation, would be our undoing. 'The more speed increases, the faster freedom decreases', he wrote.[33]

It would be folly to extrapolate from this change in human behaviour into the breakdown of society. The Japanese mobile giant NTT Docomo once produced a simulation to show what would happen if everyone did the dumb-walk across Tokyo's most busy crossing, the Shibuya. There would be more than 400 collisions every time the lights changed, the simulation predicted, and most likely just 36 per cent of people would get across. In reality, nothing like that number of collisions occurs. Miraculously, apparently absorbed dumb-walkers seem to notice oncoming pedestrians, and swerve without colliding.[34]

But the moral of this story is not only that, in Japan at least, social civility hasn't yet been destroyed by technological innovation, but that the medium yet again is the message. What matters is the fact that we dumb-walk, not what is absorbing our attention when we do so. Marshall McLuhan never had an iPhone, but he understood what was important about it. Alone yet not quite lonely, we skip across the Shibuya, avoiding eye contact, never committing the faux pas of colliding with others, checking our Twitter feed and listening to Taylor Swift, all the while looking for a Wi-Fi hotspot to minimise our data consumption. 'The supple, well adapted man', wrote McLuhan long ago, 'is the one who has learned to hop into the meat grinder while humming a hit parade tune.'[35]

Often, we are so beguiled by these technological innovations and changes they produce in human behaviour, as well as improvements in consumer satisfaction, that we disdain to think about the exploitation of the workers who made these changes possible. 'There is no document of civilization which is not at the same time a document of barbarism', wrote Walter Benjamin.[36] But, when it came to Silicon Valley and the New Economy, the document of barbarism was wiped in favour of another narrative, in which entrepreneurs posture as rebels against an old establishment.

In 1984, Steve Jobs and Apple marketed the first Apple Mac as if they were on the side of the rebels against Big Brother. In doing so, Jobs not only brilliantly implied that Apple's chief business competitor, IBM, held values more akin to those of Soviet Russia than freedom-loving Americans, but encouraged us to equate in our minds what would become part of the most sophisticated surveillance technology ever deployed on humans with a revolution against tyranny and in favour of freedom.

After the Cold War ended, Silicon Valley's leading entrepreneurs, realising that the New Economy in general and the internet in particular were being greeted with public enthusiasm, capitalised on that good-will to pose as different from businessmen of yore. A new generation of dressed-down, ostensibly cool entrepreneurs like Jobs, Bill Gates, and Ben Cohen and Jerry Greenfield – of Ben & Jerry's fame – projected to the world traits like charisma, vision, intuition and communication skills that helped to associate their products with the younger, hipper and ostensibly more radical demographics of digital natives.

But it wasn't just the image that these companies projected to their consumers that mattered. Inside enterprises such as Apple, Microsoft, Ben & Jerry's and later Facebook, Google and Twitter, another revolution was being effected. The bosses were, or at least affected to be, approachable. They didn't wear ties, but did on occasion wear flip-flops as office footwear. The formal trappings of bureaucratic authority (keys to the executive washrooms and inner sanctums to which only VPs and above were admitted) were superseded by democratic beanbags in break-out zones and bonding with your boss over the office's foosball table. While customers of these companies are misdirected into supposing that new technology liberates, all the while having their data plundered and monetised for profit by strangers, internally their workers are duped into thinking that they and their bosses are equals, and their businesses unalloyed forces for good. That magic trick was pulled off partly because of two things: workers, especially white-collar workers, felt unfulfilled in traditionally bureaucratic enterprises; and, from the 1960s onwards, the quest for personal authenticity and self-fulfilment had become, if not imperative, then compellingly desirable. Silicon Valley appeared to blur the line between work and play, flatten hierarchies, and promise personal creative fulfilment on a scale and of an intensity that would have seemed impossible decades earlier. Thus, the likes of Jobs, Gates, Sundar Pichai, Jack Dorsey, Sheryl Sandberg and Mark Zuckerberg headed new tech companies that combined entrepreneurial acumen and business creativity with instilling a sense that their workers could be part of visionary projects.

As a result, much of Silicon Valley can be seen as extolling a profane liberation theology whereby there is no need for bosses to exercise authoritarian control, since control has been internalised by workers who share their bosses' vision, and who themselves dream of becoming visionaries in their own right. All this happened while working hours grew longer and managers received share options, giving them an interest in minimising costs – which meant that real wages fell. Those stock options wouldn't pay for themselves; hence the outsourcing of production from Cupertino to Chengdu, and the exploitation of Chinese workers, even as New Economy bosses postured as anti-elitist. We had gone through the looking glass. Capitalism itself had become revolutionary.

To make sense of these paradoxes, we should consider one of the profoundest analyses of the functioning of enterprises in the post-modern, neoliberal era: *The New Spirit of Capitalism*, by French sociologists Luc Boltanski and Eve Chiapello, published in 1999. Boltanski and Chiapello's compelling suggestion is that capitalism drew on the very subversive forces that were aimed at destroying it. Their analysis explains why, for instance, Steve Jobs owes a debt to the countercultural hippie figure Stewart Brand: without the counterculture's lifeblood, capitalism would not be in such rude health.

Boltanski and Chiapello understand capitalism as a virus to which it would be absurd to ascribe moral qualities. They describe it as a system driven by 'the need for the unlimited accumulation of capital by formally peaceful means'.[37] For them, capitalism is and always has been fundamentally absurd and amoral. Under capitalism, they wrote, 'Wage-earners have lost ownership of the fruits of their labour and the possibility of pursuing a working life free of subordination. As for capitalists, they find themselves yoked to an interminable, insatiable process, which is utterly abstract and dissociated from the satisfaction of consumption needs, even of a luxury kind.'[38] Both wage-earners and capitalists need to be convinced to take their irksome roles in this system, to enter willingly into what the sociologist Max Weber called the iron cage of capitalism. So what is needed is a justification of that system – or what they call the 'spirit of capitalism'.

They suppose there have been three spirits of capitalism, each suited to the demands of sustaining it during different eras. The first spirit of capitalism is the one that Weber recognised in the nineteenth century, whose hero was the Promethean bourgeois entrepreneur, who risked, speculated and innovated at work, but at home was distinguished by his determination to save, personal parsimony, and austere attachment to the family. In *The Protestant Ethic and the Spirit of Capitalism*, Weber argued that the values of hard work and progress were seen as endowed with moral and spiritual significance, and the refusal to waste money meant that a large proportion of the proceeds of capitalism could be reinvested in nascent businesses.

The second spirit of capitalism, Boltanski and Chiapello argue, existed from about 1930 to 1960. Instead of the nineteenth-century entrepreneurial hero, the second spirit's hero was the director of the large, centralised, bureaucratic corporation. In France, in particular, the spirit that sustained capitalism during this time involved long-term planning and rational organisation, fixed career structures, self-realisation linked to security, and a common interest in satisfying consumers and overcoming scarcity.

But *les évènements* in France in 1968 exorcised this second spirit of capitalism. In France in that year, two critiques of capitalism – the first artistic, and spearheaded by anti-bourgeois philosophers, filmmakers and other subversive figures; the second social, and represented by trade unions – came together in mass revolt against a Gaullist regime that, protestors argued, held an oppressive capitalist system in place. Student uprisings in Paris triggered the largest general strike in world history. Capitalism looked for a moment as if it was trapped by a pincer movement.

The New Spirit of Capitalism starts from a sense of discombobulation. How could capitalism and the liberal state not just survive 1968, but emerge even stronger from that great upheaval? As the Gaullist government teetered, capitalism had to adapt to survive. Boltanski and Chiapello's analysis is that capitalism responded to 1968 by giving its opponents something of what they demanded. They divide the indignation against capitalism into two forms: artistic and social. The first, artistic critique involves the demand for liberation and the rejection of inauthenticity. The second, social critique involves a refusal of egoism and a response to suffering. Both forms of critique have shadowed capitalism since its inception. An artistic critique originated in the nineteenth century in response to a bourgeoisie that owned land, women and factories, and – as Boltanski and Chiapello put it – was 'rooted in possessions, obsessed with preserving their goods, endlessly concerned about reproducing, exploiting and increasing them, and thereby condemned to meticulous forethought, rational management of space and time, and a quasi-obsessive pursuit of production for production's sake'.[39] Artistic critique pitted against this bourgeois norm an antinomian, rebellious figure called the dandy. This slacker figure, beloved of countercultural French literary bad-boys from Charles Baudelaire to Michel Houellebecq, hadn't got the memo about how one ought to live under capitalism. The dandy disdained production, apart from the important task of self-production, and freed himself from all attachments, especially those to do with owning things – except, presumably, for absinthe, lilac gloves and stout shoes for aimless, economically inexplicable *dérives* around Paris.

A social critique, by contrast, arose from the indignation of those who were excluded from the material fruits of growing wealth, detested the egoism of the bourgeoisie, and loathed the atomisation of social and working life caused by capitalism. In France, as in other advanced countries, it was organised labour and leftist parties that strongly developed this social critique.

On the face of it, this taxonomy may seem too vague, and too rooted in France's particular history, to be able to make sense of struggles around the world against capitalism, and for recognition by those unheard, oppressed or excluded under the norms of the megalothymic state that accords recognition to a minority of the population. But I suspect it is more generally applicable in helping us to understand how capitalism mutated to overcome its foes, and thereby survive.

The social critique was neutralised because workers were bought off. In his essay 'Workers in a Repressive Society of Seductions: Parisian Metallurgists in May–June 1968', French historian Michael Seidman argued that strikers returned to work because they were offered increased pay, enabling them to buy more desirable consumer durables, and improvements to their working conditions.[40] French workers now entered an era in which demands for such goods largely replaced any lingering revolutionary yearnings, and proved to have much greater popular resonance than workers' control. After 1968, French communism declined, and organised labour never again flexed its muscles quite as it did during the heady days of May 1968.

But while the social critique of capitalism dwindled into irrelevance as a result, the artistic critique grew in power and significance. The new spirit of capitalism that emerged after 1968 drew on libertarian and romantic currents of the late 1960s and on the Gallic philosophers who theorised them. Deleuze and Guattari proselytised for the revolutionary force of desire. They also produced the most telling metaphor of the post-modern age – the rhizome – suggesting that the rhizomatic structure or network better comprehended how society did and should work than the metaphor of the tree. The rhetorical force of this metaphor is to indict hierarchies – not least the dynastic transmission of wealth and privilege.

What seemed like a nutty idea in the early 1970s has become ubiquitous, not least thanks to the rhizomatic structure of the internet. Boltanski and Chiapello even joke at one point that Deleuze and Guattari could be taken for management gurus rather than anti-establishment philosophers. It was the libertarian and romantic currents of the late 1960s that, in their challenge to bourgeois norms, had inspired a new form of capitalism. Among those currents were the struggles for the rights of women, homosexuals and people of colour. As in architecture, the shift from modernism to post-modernism involved an abandonment of a single utopian vision – indeed, even of a belief in progress, and certainly progress conceived in the grandiose manner of Le Corbusier or Mies van der Rohe – so that the rise of identity politics, and the backlash against it, undermined a grand narrative of human progress in favour of many micro-narratives of struggles against oppression, or the denial of recognition.

What Boltanski and Chiapello call artistic critique – the struggles for authenticity, recognition and liberty – became central to capitalism's survival. They became its spirit. The most successful businesses, notably those of Silicon Valley, affected to be havens of authenticity and liberty.

To dramatise the change in the spirit of capitalism before and after 1968, Boltanski and Chiapello compared management literature from the 1960s with that of the 1990s. They found that the former sought to solve problems of running huge corporations by giving limited autonomy to managers without loss of overall control. Feared above all was any survival of patriarchal or familial taints among employers. By contrast, the literature of the 1990s rejected anything that smacked of hierarchy or top-down control as uneconomic in terms of transaction costs and repugnant in its moral overtones. The central organisational figure of the contemporary world had thus become the network, and the new hero of capitalism was the network extender. And the network extender was a soulmate of Zygmunt Bauman's liquid modern – one who is always at work forging connections, a human rhizome sending out sprouts everywhere; uprooted and anxious, yes, but also light and mobile, tolerant of difference, informal and friendly.

Lean in, urged Sheryl Sandberg, Facebook's chief operating officer – especially if you're a woman. 'I understand the paradox of advising women to change the world by adhering to its biased rules and expectations', Sandberg wrote. 'I know it is not a perfect answer but a means to a desirable end.'[41] But that desirable end, the goal of personal fulfilment, was touted by her and by others as something that one could achieve, more than ever, by becoming more like a cool boss; or, to put it another way, by emulating Sheryl Sandberg.

The network also replaced the arboreal metaphor in another way. We are uprooted from all that held us in place before – community, pensions, homes, cars, jobs. We have a less rigid relationship to property and ownership. We don't need to own a car, because we can hire one by the hour. We don't need working contracts, because that would constrain us to work for the Man when we want to work for ourselves. The network model that was supposed to be liberating perhaps is so – but it also provides a smokescreen beneath which were smuggled in zero-hours contracts, companies like Uber that disdained to offer employment rights to their workers, and the emergence of a new exploited class called the precariat. The new spirit of capitalism helped the amoral virus to thrive in hitherto unimaginable ways.

What became lost above all in the rise of this new justificatory spirit of capitalism, and the supposedly anti-hierarchical notion of the network, was social class. Marxism relied on this hierarchical, arboreal concept in accounting for social division and capitalistic exploitation. But, like Marxism, class was purportedly obsolete. Social exclusion became the preferred term to account for the oppressed or excluded. It was as if the problem were not how capitalism systematically exploited workers, but that there were some in society who remained outside the network. The corollary was obvious: what needed to be done was not the overthrow of capitalism, but the extension of its network so that all fell within its grasp.

III

In 2001, Greece joined the Eurozone and dispensed with the drachma; but only after its government had cooked the books to hide its levels of debt. To get into the elite Eurozone club, the Greeks needed to meet the terms of the 1992 Maastricht Treaty, the founding document of the European Union. That treaty demanded that Eurozone countries have a rate of inflation below 3.9 per cent and a government deficit below 3 per cent of gross national product. In 1991, Greece's inflation rate stood at 20 per cent, and its deficit at 11.4 per cent. Even in 1999, when the euro was launched, Greece failed to meet the criteria. But two years later, it did – by cooking the books in ways so shameless that the guys in the count room of the Tangiers casino in Las Vegas would have been amazed.

Consider railways. The Greek railway system had more employees than passengers, leading a minister to remark that it would be cheaper to send everyone by taxi. Its debts exceeded €1 billion, but managers hid the truth by issuing shares that the government would buy, and the resulting transaction did not appear on balance sheets. On paper, in 2001 the Greek government claimed the country's deficit was 1.5 per cent, but the real deficit was 8.3 per cent. Only by 2004 did the true extent of Greek indebtedness reveal itself. Instead of addressing the debt problem, Greek governments in the first decade of the new millennium borrowed more to cover the deficit.

But it would be unfair to blame Greek mismanagement alone. Banks queued to lend money to Greece, believing that there was no risk of default because its new currency, the euro, was underpinned by the strength of economically more-robust EU member states, chiefly Germany. Greece was able to borrow at interest rates as low as those offered to Germany. Every Eurozone country, for this purpose, was Germany.

But not for long. When the financial crisis hit in 2008, Greece was running double-digit fiscal deficits and had debts worth nearly 130 per cent of the country's GDP. It got further into debt thanks to being a member of the Eurozone, and failed to address its underlying structural problems. For the Greek people, the results were catastrophic.

Greece typified a new world of debt, both personal and state-wide, that arose in the neoliberal era. 'In the last forty years', wrote economics journalist Philip Coggan in his 2011 book *Paper Promises: Money, Debt and the New World Order*, 'the world has been more successful at creating claims on wealth than it has at creating wealth itself.'[42] In August 1971, President Richard Nixon suspended the convertibility of the US dollar into gold, ending the Bretton Woods system established after World War II. That system allowed central banks to redeem dollar holdings at a rate of $35 an ounce. But Nixon, fearing a run on US gold reserves, brought it to an end.

In severing the link between paper debts and bullion, Nixon enabled indebtedness to spiral. The United States at the beginning of the 1970s, for instance, though it had borrowed huge sums to finance war in Vietnam, had a debt burden scarcely larger than its national output. By 2010, that burden – including the liabilities of government, businesses and individuals – was three times the size of its gross domestic product. What had long been an economic fact of life for developing countries had hit the advanced West. The UK's debt ratio was 4.5:1 in 2010; those of Ireland and Iceland were even bigger.[43]

It has become easier than ever to acquire debt. The first credit card was introduced in 1950; but by the last decade of the twentieth century, credit cards were widely used, and many of their customers often outspent their earnings and were unable to pay off their outstanding monthly balances. It was not just advanced Western countries that became more able to generate claims on wealth than wealth itself, but their increasingly indebted citizens. For instance, private debt in the United States during the decade up to 2008 grew more than three times faster than the public debt. Of America's homes with mortgages, 22 per cent had debt exceeding the value of the house.[44] Student debt in the United States was described in 2019 as a $1.5 trillion crisis. Family debt has become a substitute for wages and salaries, which have increasingly lagged behind the cost of living.[45]

But, despite the increase in indebtedness, debt in the neoliberal era remains a cause of shame. In a 1981 interview, Margaret Thatcher said: 'My policies are based not on some economics theory, but on things I and millions like me were brought up with: an honest day's work for an honest day's pay; live within your means; put by a nest egg for a rainy day; pay your bills on time; support the police.'[46] But increasingly few of these millions were living within their means or saving money; instead, they were borrowing to stay afloat. In 1971, Barclaycard offered the only credit card in the UK, and credit-card debt was only £32 million; by 2019, there were thousands of credit cards, and debts stood at £72.4 billion. If this figure was added to overdrafts and personal loans, the total nationwide level of debt in the UK was £225 billion in 2019.[47] Hardly anyone in Britain was living within their means – not just because, in post-modern times, we demand everything immediately all the time, but because salaries had fallen behind the cost of living.

Debt is a means of control, argued David Graeber. There is no better way to justify unequal power relations than 'by reframing them in the language of debt . . . because it immediately makes it seem that it's the victim who's doing something wrong'.[48]

Since the 1971 Nixon Shock, rentier capitalism has thrived. Rentiers, unlike traditional capitalists, make money from the ownership of existing assets – and one of the most valuable assets is debt. They therefore have an interest in governments, businesses and even you remaining deep in debt, the better to profit from it. Such rents are a safer bet than profits derived from traditional capitalist production. Profits are uncertain, partly because they are sensitive to local conditions. It's much safer to invest in property in New York or London, buying and flipping real estate for an eye-watering profit.

Furthermore, reduced capital gains tax encourages rentier capitalism. In the UK, for instance, as late as 2020, standard capital gains tax was 20 per cent, while income tax was 40 per cent for those earning salaries between £50,001 and £150,000. If you add to this the ease of moving capital gains to tax havens, where rentiers boost their wealth while avoiding taxes, it seems obvious why rentier capitalism has thrived in the past half-century, even if it has meant that governments, corporations and the rest of us struggle under huge debts.

Rentier capitalism, like the amoral virus Boltanski and Chiapello imagined capitalism in general to be, has mutated to thrive during the post-modern, neoliberal era. The advent of private equity in the late 1980s, and its rise throughout the 1990s and beyond, has been predicated on the business model of creating debt and profiting from it. Private equity firms will pay small amounts of cash to buy a business, and then borrow large sums to pay for the purchase, often in cahoots with junk-bond underwriters. This is what is called a leveraged buyout. But here's the twist: instead of shouldering the debt burden them-selves, private equity firms load it onto the firm they have purchased. What this means in practice is that the users of assets repay the debt. If the targeted firm is a railway company, that debt may well be repaid by higher train fares; if it's a football club, through higher gate receipts; if it's a housing association, through higher rents.

The leveraged buyout originated in 1982, when a group led by former US Treasury secretary William Simon bought Gibson Greetings, the country's third-largest greeting card business, by leveraging $1 million of their own money, with loans of $79 million. Eighteen months later, they sold the company for $290 million, and Simon pocketed $66 million on an investment of $330,000. In 1989, the private equity firm Kohlberg, Kravis, Roberts & Co. succeeded in the hostile leveraged buyout of RJR Nabisco, the food and tobacco giant responsible for inflicting Oreos and Camels on the world. Soon after the deal was signed, KKR began selling off the firm to meet interest payments, as well as axing an estimated 2,600 jobs and saddling consumers with paying off the debt (Ritz crackers reportedly rose in price by more than 30 per cent); meanwhile, Nabisco's ousted top executives 'pulled the rip cords on their golden parachutes', as Hope Lampert put it in *True Greed: What Really Happened in the Battle for RJR Nabisco*.[49] Chief executive F. Ross Johnson's parachute alone was worth $53 million. But what's important is that this hostile leveraged buyout served as a model for making money from indebting other people. 'Hoisted onto the auction block, RJR Nabisco became a vast prism through which scores of Wall Streeters beheld their reflected glories', wrote Bryan Burrough and John Helyar in *Barbarians at the Gate: The Fall of RJR Nabisco*.[50]

Since 1989, the barbarians have moved from the gates to unexpected areas. Even public assets funded by taxpayers have been subject to leveraged buyouts, which, as economist Ann Pettifor put it, has involved capitalists 'parasitically squeezing' rents from care homes, railways, health services, prisons, and electricity and water companies.[51]

The rise of this form of capitalism was spurred by neoliberalism – by the Nixon Shock, as well as Reagan and Thatcher's liberalisation of finance and the opening up of capital markets – and has encouraged further indebtedness even in rich countries like the United States and the UK. Neoliberal governments created the circumstances for indebting their citizens, argues Ann Pettifor. 'Led by Presidents Nixon and Reagan in the US and Margaret Thatcher in the UK, and then by their successors – and implemented by respected central bankers – these changes empowered the financial markets. Politicians and central bankers abrogated their roles as guardians of national finances and handed over crucial powers to the invisible and unaccountable finance sector.'[52]

Worse yet, the biggest capital gains are made by creditors who lend to risky speculative ventures, while profit from productive sectors is likely to be lower. The liberalised financial system therefore has a vested interest in saddling individuals with debt and economic instability. The biggest rewards to creditors come from the misery of others.

Virtual money is not new. What is new, argued Graeber, is the political end to which virtual credit was put after 1971. 'Insofar as overarching grand cosmic institutions have been created that might be considered in any way parallel to the divine kings of the ancient Middle East or the religious author-ities of the Middle Ages, they have not been created to protect debtors, but to enforce the rights of creditors.'[53] Neoliberalis-ation, David Harvey once argued, might be considered as either a utopian project to reorganise international capitalism, or a political project to restore the power of economic elites. He argued that it was the latter, and his case is strengthened by considering what has happened since 1971. The response of the International Monetary Fund, as well as of the European Central Bank and the Federal Reserve, to the economic crisis of 2008 was to minimise the suffering of the banks. The US Fed-eral Reserve, the Bank of England and the European Central Bank loaned banks money at virtually no cost. Banks were then encouraged to buy government bonds, which paid much higher rates of interest. The public was effectively subsidising banks, while millions suffered unemployment and bankruptcy. The novelist and Marxist economist Benjamin Kunkel wrote:

A far simpler and more effective monetary policy would have been for the government to print a new batch of money, distrib-ute an equal amount to everyone, then sit back and watch as stagnant economies were stirred to life by the spending and debts were paid down and eroded by temporarily higher infla-tion. The inconceivability of such a policy is a mark not of any impracticability, but of the capture of governments by a financial oligarchy.[54]

While banks were bailed out with public money, many tax-payers struggled to make monthly payments on outstanding credit-card balances, were hit with penalty fees, and quickly fell into default. Such defaults rose after the global financial crisis of 2008.

In Greece, debt ballooned to 177 per cent of GDP after 2008. Two years later, frozen out of bond markets, the country was bankrupt. Nobody confused Greece with Germany anymore; the Greek government asked for a financial bailout from the EU and the International Monetary Fund. Successive loan packages came at the price of drastic austerity measures, including higher taxes, reduced public expenditure, and cuts to salaries and pensions. In 2013 unemployment peaked at 27.5 per cent – but for those under twenty-five it was 58 per cent.[55]

In January 2015, an economist called Yanis Varoufakis became Greece's minister of finance, tasked with leading nego-tiations with Greece's creditors. He joined a government led by a coalition of radical leftist groups called Syriza, which was committed to overturning neoliberal reforms of pensions and social security and to renegotiating Greece's role within the European Union. His was, to put it mildly, an interesting appointment. In 2011, he published *The Global Minotaur*, his analysis of the 2008 financial crisis, arguing that America had since 1971 become a debtor nation.[56] While the Cretan minotaur of Greek myth satisfied its hunger with sacrificial offerings of youths and maidens, the United States received flows of capital from the world's surplus nations (pre-eminently from China). These flows were converted into demand that kept the world economy in business.

Varoufakis called this process a global surplus recycling mechanism. But this GSRM was unsustainable. The Cretan minotaur was slain at the heart of its labyrinth by the Greek hero Theseus; the global minotaur, by contrast, destroyed itself. After 2008, the ability of the United States to consume vast quantities of imports decreased, and investing in Wall Street became a much less inviting prospect.

Varoufakis's appointment was made even more intriguing by his perspective on Germany, bankroller-in-chief of Greek debt. Germany presides over an EU system of fixed exchange rates that thwarts any means of recycling surpluses towards deficit countries. Germany made too much and consumed too little, Varoufakis argued; it created stagnation outside its borders to ensure the security of its surplus. Greece became a victim of a Eurozone system that was never designed to deal with the eventuality of a member country going bankrupt and defaulting on its debts. But in 2010, that is what Greece was threatened with, in spectacular fashion.

Varoufakis's speciality as an academic had been game theory, and he applied this in his negotiations as finance minister with his country's creditors in 2015. He considered that the so-called troika of Greece's creditors – namely Germany, the IMF and the ECB – had to believe that Syriza was prepared to default on loans that were becoming due, or leave the euro. His sense was that the EU would not countenance either option, and would roll over loans that were coming due. After all, he had argued that the bailout of 2010 was designed to save the French and German banks as much as to put Greece on the economic straight and narrow. Instead of defaulting on its debts, Greece was being encouraged to get deeper into the red.

Many in Germany did not see the issue that way. For them, Greece was a welfare scrounger who needed to shape up. 'We Germans can pay off our debts because we get up and go to work!' went a headline in Germany's mass-circulation *Bild* newspaper. Perhaps, it was implied, the Greeks should try that option. Others argued that Greece's lethargic growth was to do with inflexible working practices and lavish benefits payments. Varoufakis disagreed with both diagnoses, arguing that Greece's problems were due to 'the way most of Europe was falling under the spell of German surpluses'.[57]

But after only six months in office – and despite a referendum in June that rejected the conditions of another EU bailout – Varoufakis resigned, chiefly because his boss, Prime Minister

Alexis Tsipras, decided to compromise and accept another EU bailout. Tsipras, in the words of Paul Mason, effectively decided that 'staying in power as a dented shield against austerity was preferable to handing power back to a bunch of political mafiosi backed by a mob of baying rich-kid fashionistas'.[58] Varoufakis returned to academia. But the shield has hardly protected the Greek working class: its austerity-straitened citizens will be repaying the debts for decades. Greece, like the rest of us, remains perilously in the red: in 2018, the country's debt stood at 181.2 per cent of GDP.[59]

But it doesn't have to be this way. David Graeber called for a cancellation to outstanding consumer and government debts.[60] By contrast, Pettifor argues that there is nothing wrong with debt, nor with credit. 'Credit-based monetary systems are a great civilisational advance – developed over time to enable societies to undertake transactions and put unique human abilities to work. Like sanitation or the water supply, monetary systems are a great public good.' But, in the hands of barbarians, these are not great public goods, but evils. 'Credit creation is an extraordinary and relatively effortless power that has been captured by the rentier class, for the self-serving interests of the 1 per cent.' Those 1 per cent, Pettifor argues, are the rich, who rely not on income but on assets.[61]

What is needed, she argues, is to make it tougher for capital to flow overseas – a reform that would make it more likely that billionaire rentiers would pay taxes. The creation of credit should be supervised by governments and central banks. Reducing the bias in tax systems that favours debt over equity financing would also help reduce incentives for excessive borrowing.

What has happened since 1971 is the rise of a neoliberal system in which the barbarians have seized power. 'Politicians and central bankers abrogated their roles as guardians of national finances and handed over crucial powers to the invisible and unaccountable finance sector. Today, the global economy is the servant of these financial masters. The money-changers have taken over the temple. In doing so, they have generated a vast credit bubble of "easy money" whose counterpart is debt.'⁶²

The rich – the 1 per cent Pettifor cited – have benefited from falling labour costs and from the fall of prices for such goods as coffee, copper and cocoa, which the poorest countries in the world depend upon for their income. The poor, whether in London or overseas, have been forced to borrow to compensate for their declining incomes, while the rich have no such debt burdens; rather, they have debt assets. Neoliberalism was supposed to involve a trickle-down effect, improving the lot of the poor while further enriching the wealthy. But it never happened.

Afterword:
Ghost Modernism

Up the road from where I live in north London, there are two little council estates with a mixture of flats, houses, bungalows, sheltered accommodation and communal gardens. For many years the Belvoir and Highcroft estates scarcely impinged on my consciousness, even as I daily walked through them with my daughter on the way to and from school. Apart, that is, from two things.

The names of the streets intrigued me, because many were named after women, which is very unusual – particularly in the 1980s, when these estates were built: Daisy Dobbings Walk, Edith Cavell Close, Jessie Blythe Lane, Louise Aumonier Walk, Florence Cantwell Walk, Cathering Griffiths Court, Barbara Rudolf Court, Edith Turbeville Court, Mary Kingsley Court, Miriam Price Court, Marie Stopes Court, Mary Lloyd Gardens.

Who were these women? Edith Cavell was the World War I nurse who cared for soldiers irrespective of which side they fought on, and whose statue near Trafalgar Square bears the words she spoke the night before she was shot by a German firing squad: 'Patriotism is not enough. I must have no hatred or bitterness towards anyone.'[1] Marie Lloyd was a Hoxton-born musical hall star famous for her rendition of 'My Old Man', a song she first performed in 1919 about a working-class couple doing a moonlight flit because they can't afford the rent – a song with renewed resonance today, in a London where average rents are more than £2,000 per month and rising.

As for Marie Stopes, she was a palaeobotanist and eugenicist who pioneered birth-control clinics, one of the first of which is nearby, at 61 Marlborough Road. Stopes's own 'Pro-Race' cervical caps were dispensed from that clinic to women whom she judged should not conceive. 'Are these puny-faced, gaunt, blotchy, ill-balanced, feeble, ungainly, withered children the young of an imperial race?' she wrote, while in 1922 she called on MPs to sign a declaration calling on the Ministry of Health to give such information 'as will curtail the C3 [the unskilled working class] and increase the A1'.[2]

Jessie Blythe, Catherine Griffiths and Florence Cantwell were mayors of Islington. Blythe, the first woman to hold that office, said once: 'I certainly will not forget those in the back streets – I hope I shall never do that' – as if she worried that the glamour of an office hitherto wielded only by men would corrupt her.[3] Emily Heartwell Close commemorates a woman described as 'tenant for life' in the London Metropolitan Archives. She was one of those women, perhaps, whom Marie Stopes thought should not breed, but whom Jessie Blythe sought to keep in her heart. I've not been able to find out about the other women named.

Only recently has it occurred to me that the naming of these streets and courts is post-modern history of a kind that puts forgotten and celebrated women from history on the same level. In life, the racist Marie Stopes, the spy Edith Cavell and the pioneering mayor Jessie Blythe may have had very little in common; now, by giving their names to these humble closes and courts, they are equals. The most neglected of these women live on, their names spoken and written every day.

At the same time, they remind me of how the post-modern princess, Diana, was memorialised a few miles away in Hyde Park in 2004 with a fountain and water course – the seemingly post-modern female antidote to phallic monuments to men, such as the nearby Albert Memorial. The woman who designed that fountain, landscape architect Kathryn Gustafson, told me once: 'Hyde Park is one of the most important parks in the world and I thought it would be wholly inappropriate to impede or penetrate those views.'[4] These women-named streets, too, are low-rise and anything but intrusive.

But the other thing that impinged on my consciousness about this estate was the colour scheme. The bright yellow metal window frames for conservatories, royal blue front doors, green metal trellises and red hand rails date from an era when, it seemed to me, architects weren't building a land fit for heroes, but for toddlers. In those days – the early years of Margaret Thatcher's government – playgrounds were painted in jaunty primary colours. But so were public buildings, from James Stirling's Clore Galleries at Tate Britain, with their green-framed windows, to the poppy-red façade of China Wharf in Southwark.

The colour-coding of the new architecture that I was dimly aware of in London when I moved there in the 1980s was laughably childish. Many of these primary-coloured buildings favoured portholes for windows and triangular pediments. It seemed vaguely insulting – as if council tenants were being offered houses made from toy bricks; as if architecture was designed not for phallically challenged patriarchs, but for a population that was to be infantilised by means of their built environment. This may have been neoliberalism in action, but it was also post-modernism in embryo. All the values and distinctions that once had been solid were melting: this childish architecture was preparing Britain for a time when it was acceptable for grown-ups to read Harry Potter novels in public, even though they were written for children.

Parts of this infantilised architecture haven't aged well. Just as brutalist concrete weathers badly in England's unfortunate climate, so the red handrails of the Highcroft estate have become discoloured. What was supposed to be a jaunty antidote to modernist solemnity has become sad, like a cake left out in the rain.

While researching this book, I found out something sadder still about Belvoir and Highcroft. Built during the 1980s, they were the last of the London Borough of Islington's new-build estates – symbols of the end of almost a century of public housing provision in London. The sell-off of council houses to tenants, combined with cuts to local authority budgets, under Margaret Thatcher's governments has meant that new social housing has become a rarity. These two estates were the last hurrahs of a tradition of local authority housing, ironically expressed in the architectural language that was the lingua franca of Thatcherite deregulation and yuppie triumphalism.

Since then, London has become a playground for real-estate speculators. For example, from the room where I'm writing this I can see high-rise glass towers being built above Finsbury Park tube station. This is City North, a vast new development where flats priced at up to £850,000 are advertised overseas, the better to attract the speculative investors who have already put much of London's property beyond the reach of its citizens, adding to the inequality and poverty in the capital. Just yards away, there has been a rise in rough sleepers under the railway bridge. Defenders of the project have made much of the fact that some of City North will be 'affordable'. What that means was defined by Boris Johnson when he was London mayor as 80 per cent of market rate. Only 47 of City North's 308 apartments are classed as 'affordable', though 80 per cent of £850,000 is still way beyond the means of most Londoners.[5]

The neoliberal values that shrank the state and co-opted a style of architecture called post-modernism to provide its primary-coloured fig leaf are thriving. I'm not sure which is worse – these neoliberal values or the debasement of language in the implicit suggestion that only 261 of those apartments are unaffordable.

All this makes the revival of post-modern architecture of the 1980s rather hard to take. The artist Pablo Bronstein organised tours of London's iconic post-modern buildings in 2006, and eulogised something I missed – namely the architectural movement's Thatcherite erotics. 'How it must have seduced after those winters of discontent, race riots and rainy council-house esplanades', he wrote. Bronstein has a point: what seduced was a playful, decadent kind of architecture that didn't just quote and pastiche past styles, but also erased history for the financiers who thrived as Thatcher rolled back the state, celebrating their success in apartments with what he called 'Playdoh pediments, Lego walls and cheap multicultural facings'.[6]

In 2017, another champion of post-modern revivalism, the young London-based designer Adam Nathaniel Furman, set up a Postmodern Society on Facebook to celebrate what his peers disdain. 'It's got a bad name from the late corporate stuff that the next generation turned into a straw man to demolish', he told the *Guardian*. 'But at its heart, it is a truly sensuous kind of architecture that celebrates pluralism and embraces the chaotic, complex, global nature of the world.'[7]

That sensuousness is expressed in Furman's own work. Robert Venturi once challenged the 'less is more' ethos of minimalism and modernism with his own maxim: 'Less is a bore.' In 2017, Furman put on an exhibition at the former London home of that architectural-appropriation artist, Sir John Soane, called 'The Roman Singularity'. It consisted of a 3D-printed city, celebrating, as the blurb put it, 'Rome as the pilgrimage site for the world's imagination: the spatial equivalent of the internet, a place in which all of history, art and style is simultaneous and coextensive, merging into one a-historical and liberating atmosphere of storied objects.'[8]

Furman's post-modern revivalism was also showcased in the same year in a series of patterned gateways he installed in a square behind London's Kings Cross. Giddy with colour, dense with historical references, and occupied as often as not by toddlers in swimwear running through them after sporting in Granary Square's fountains, these gateways were Furman's reappropriation of post-modern principles for a new era. To decorate his gateways, Furman used different kinds of tiles – some hand-made from Istanbul, created in traditional Iznik fashion; others digitally printed; and yet others hard-wearing coloured tiles of the kind used in sports centres. The designs quoted the Ishtar Gate of Babylon, the Safavid façades of Isfahan's Naqsh-e Jahan Square, Sinan's Ottoman mosques, the majolica cloisters of Santa Chiara in Naples, the gothic terracotta of New York's Woolworth building, and the red-glazed ceramics of tube stations.

And yet, for all that, it struck me as poignant that Furman's gateways were not just colourful and seductive, but portals to something fearful. Granary Square is an example of the neo-liberal surveillance state in action. It may look like a public square, but it is instead what social geographer Bradley L. Garrett calls a pseudo-public space. Just as council houses were sold off without replacement in the 1980s, so many large squares, parks and thoroughfares that appear to be public in cities such as London are in fact owned and controlled by developers and their private backers, because local authorities cannot afford to maintain such spaces themselves.

Neoliberalism, often with post-modernism as its cultural handmaiden, has presided over this erasure of the commons. As visitors enjoyed Furman's joyful gateways in Granary Square, they were very likely having their images captured by means of facial recognition software in security cameras. The private owners of the square, Argent, issued a statement saying: 'These cameras use a number of detection and tracking methods, including facial recognition, but also have sophisticated systems in place to protect the privacy of the general public.'[9] University of Essex researchers found that police trials of facial recognition technology to search for suspects had an 81 per cent error rate. If you're a person of colour, you may not feel reassured, though, by research that suggests that, the darker your skin tone, the more likely you are to be misidentified by facial recognition software.[10]

Neoliberalism – rolling back the frontiers of the state, extending corporate control over our lives, and using technology, by turns, to dominate, titillate and exclude the masses – is thriving. It once used post-modern architecture to provide its façades, but no longer. Pablo Bronstein, considering the ruins of London's post-modern architecture, wrote: 'Designed to inspire us with the glamour of finance, the conspicuousness of their effort now looks gauche and, embarrassed, we have discarded them . . . they have been abandoned by the very ideology they helped to victory.'[11] Post-modernism, which once plundered history, had become a negligible moment in it.

In 2011 the Victoria and Albert Museum seemed to put the nail in post-modernism's coffin with an exhibition treating it as just another historical movement that had come and gone. In 2017 John Outram's colourful Post-Modern Pumping Station on London's Isle of Dogs was Grade II* listed, as was James Stirling's No. 1 Poultry, in the City. The revolution had become national heritage.[12]

But there is a problem with this revivalism. Post-modernism is not just a style of architecture that served neoliberal business before being cast off, only to be brought back from the dead and colonised by the heritage industry – although it is all of those things. Post-modernism is not only ghost modernism, haunting us with its fading primary colours and now-abject playfulness. Its spirit still thrives, and it shows no signs of rolling over. It lives among us, expressed in post-truth politics, gender theory, the overturning of high art's values. Digital technology and social media have hardly made post-modernism obsolete; rather, they have given it new life.

Many critics have supposed otherwise. For them, post-modernism is dead. The only question is when. In 2007, Brian McHale asked: 'What Was Postmodernism?', and the journal *Twentieth Century Literature* published an issue titled 'After Postmodernism'.[13] For some, 9/11 marks the end of post-modernism.

In 'The Death of Postmodernism and Beyond', written in 2006, philosopher Alan Kirby looked at a course module entitled 'Postmodern Fictions':

Most of the undergraduates who will take 'Postmodern Fictions' this year will have been born in 1985 or after, and all but one of the module's primary texts were written before their lifetime. Far from being 'contemporary', these texts were published in another world, before the students were born: *The French Lieutenant's Woman, Nights at the Circus, If on a Winter's Night a Traveller, Do Androids Dream of Electric Sheep?* (and *Blade Runner*), *White Noise*: this is Mum and Dad's culture. Some of the texts ('The Library of Babel') were written even before their parents were born. Replace this cache with other postmodern stalwarts – *Beloved, Flaubert's Parrot, Waterland, The Crying of Lot 49, Pale Fire, Slaughterhouse 5, Lanark, Neuromancer,* anything by B.S. Johnson – and the same applies. It's all about as contemporary as The Smiths, as hip as shoulder pads, as happening as Betamax video recorders. These are texts which are just coming to grips with the existence of rock music and television; they mostly do not dream even of the possibility of the technology and communications media – mobile phones, email, the internet, computers in every house powerful enough to put a man on the moon – which today's undergraduates take for granted.[14]

Perhaps, if post-modernism is dead, it was the 2008 global financial crisis that killed it. That crisis seemed to catalyse political struggles that don't fall under the post-modern banner. Socialism seemed to make a return, thanks to the likes of Alain Badiou, who published his own pseudo-Maoist Little Red Book, and Žižek, the protestors of Zucotti Park, and the Syriza and Podemos movements. At the same time, fourth-wave feminism, which would culminate in the MeToo campaign, arrived on the scene. The aftermath of the global crash, though, involved not a revaluation of our values, but the continuation of an economic dogma whereby money continues to have no relation to value. In 'Crisis Theory and the Falling Rate of Profit', David Harvey argues: 'When the Federal Reserve adds trillions to the money supply through quantitative easing this has no necessary relation to value creation. Most of it seems to have ended up in the stock market to boost the asset values that are so important to the rich and powerful.'[15]

In the same year as the crash, the cryptocurrency Bitcoin was launched – seemingly the most post-modern of currencies, since it depends on no central bank or single administrator. It is plebeian in precisely the way Perry Anderson used the term to characterise the post-modern. But its anarchic philosophy has never been realised – rather, its post-modern dream has been confounded by neoliberal reality. Its subversion of the existing order has been co-opted by that order. Indeed, the story of Bitcoin is the story of how anarchic post-modern playfulness or subversion can be bought up and exploited by the powers it seeks to overthrow.

The first Bitcoin transaction took place in 2009. Since then, fortunes have been amassed. In December 2017, for instance, Nakamoto's fortune was worth over $19 billion, making him/her/them possibly the forty-fourth-richest person in the world (if indeed he/she/they is a person); and fortunes have been lost since early 2018, when Bitcoin crashed. In January 2021, though, Bitcoin revived spectacularly, its price rising from $5,000 the previous March to above $37,000. As a result of Bitcoin's resurgence, the combined value of all cryptocurrencies surpassed the value of payments for the giants of the credit card industry, Mastercard and Visa, in early 2021.[16]

Power over the Bitcoin network is now concentrated in the hands of those few whose computer power and maths skills are sufficient to mine for Bitcoins (mining involves using costly software to solve maths problems, and miners help keep the Bitcoin network secure by approving transactions). Just as the anarchist vision of a decentralised, uncensored, free internet foundered with its commercialisation, so Bitcoin has been taken over by those whom economist Nouriel Roubini calls 'charlatans and swindlers' – or, to put it another way, by neoliberalism rampant.[17]

What each of these obituarists of post-modernism seems to have forgotten is that post-modernism is plural. Post-modern architecture may be fit only for the heritage industry. Post-modern literature may be as cutting-edge as dad dancing. But post-modernism still offers the best way of explaining how neoliberalism functions today. What has gone is the playful, reckless spirit of post-modernism, its cheeky rebuffs to modernism and its pleasure in blowing raspberries at the guardians of semiotic sobriety. What remains is post-modernism's darker side. What was civilised has now become barbarism.

The digital world enables us to access everything immediately, all the time, everywhere, and at the same time establishes a new surveillance society that works differently, yet is more elegantly totalitarian and oppressive than anything described by Orwell or Jeremy Bentham. 'Confession obtained by force has been replaced by voluntary disclosure', wrote Byung-Chul Han. 'Smartphones have been substituted for torture chambers.' Well, not quite. Torture chambers still exist – it's just that we in the neoliberal West have outsourced them (thanks, rendition flights) so that we can pretend they don't exist. Through the use of 'big data', neoliberalism has tapped into the psychic realm and exploited it, with the result that, as Han colourfully puts it, 'individuals degrade into the genital organs of capital'.[18]

This is illustrated in an episode of the dystopian TV series *Black Mirror*, which dramatised a none-too-implausible future in which every human encounter is ranked by participants out of five on their phone, and where your own personal ranking determines such things as which cars or apartments you can rent. 'Nosedive' was a pitch-perfect satire of the Sisyphean labour of social media in which our heroine, Lacie (Bryce Dallas Howard, channelling a candy-coloured Stepford wife and nauseating omni-niceness), desperately wants to improve her ranking above 4.5 to join the elite.

Black Mirror asked questions that possess us in the post-modern era. Are we nice enough? Are we interesting enough? Why don't trolls like us? How can we blind ourselves to others' suffering? And, if we aren't nice or interesting, can we use technology to make ourselves seem that way to improve our social capital? This is a world described by the sociologist Zygmunt Bauman in *Liquid Love* – a world terrified of the perils of non-disclosure. The fear of silence and the exclusion it implies make us anxious that our ingeniously assembled security will fall apart.

And, while not Orwellian, we networked moderns have our own Newspeak. Freedom, for instance, means coercion. Microsoft's early ad slogan was 'Where do you want to go today?', evoking a world of boundless possibility. That boundlessness was a lie. We had just freed ourselves from the disciplinary panopticon – then threw ourselves into a new and even more efficient panopticon – and one that needs no watchman, since even the diabolical geniuses of neoliberalism, Mark Zuckerberg and Jeff Bezos, don't have to play Big Brother. They have persuaded us to play that role ourselves.

Perhaps we never really wanted to be free. Maybe, Byun-Chul Han muses, freedom is an intolerable burden, and so we invented God in order to be guilty and in debt to something. And then, having killed God, we put our faith in capitalism. Like God, only more efficiently, capitalism makes us feel guilty for our failings and encourages us to be deep in immobilising debt. Han, though, weakens his case by exaggerating it. He attacks Naomi Klein for suggesting that self-created economic catastrophe offers neoliberal capitalism an opportunity to exploit and subdue us more effectively. That, to me, sounds pretty much like what has happened since the 2008 economic crash, since which we've been working harder for less money. Han demurs: 'Neoliberal politics is SmartPolitics: it seeks to please and fulfil, not repress.'[19] The truth, though, is that torture chambers, the gig economy and the precariat, as much as the examples of the SmartPolitics he cites (Facebook and iPhones, in particular), are our political reality: the pleasing and fulfilling of Han's psychopolitics, paradoxically, exist alongside Klein's shock doctrine. Both help keep us docile.

What remains is irony. Once irony was a rebel yell; now it is spiritually corrupting, the voice of the damned of neoliberalism.

When David Foster Wallace wrote about post-modern irony, he yearned for something better. Post-modern irony became a measure of hip sophistication and literary savvy. It became not liberating, but enslaving. It became the song of the prisoner who's come to love his cage.

I decided to walk up to the post-modern council estates of Islington to look at them properly. Armed with a book called *Post-Modern Buildings in Britain* and notes from local history websites, I learned that post-modern architecture originated in the United States and combined aspects of that country's traditions with the knowing irony of pop art.[20] It arose in London with the '1980s revival of the British economy', with major urban projects and striking imagery for commercial and residential developments in Docklands and elsewhere. How do these little estates fit into these grand narratives, when, for one thing, that economic revival came at a time when public expenditure was being slashed?

The authors cited a bold and playful post-modernist design, restrained in its gestures, suited to its domestic function and suburban setting. I noticed things that had passed me by before – the influence of James Stirling's Neue Staatsgalerie, Stuttgart, in the striped stair turrets, swooping parapets, triangular-headed lintels and yellow metal conservatories; the allusion to Charles Rennie Mackintosh in the design of gridded windows. I doffed my cap to Islington council's already cash-strapped architects' department for managing such flourishes. And yet, at the same time, I worried that post-modernism at such moments seems wrapped up in itself – an exclusive game for the cognoscenti to win by displaying insider knowledge.

Local details, I read, were quoted to witty effect. Is wit, I wondered, what we want from our homes? The Y-tracery glazing of some of the houses on Highcroft estate, I read, nods towards St Mary's Church to the south. But who is that nod for? In the south of the borough, for instance, the 1980s Catherine Griffiths Close used square tiles, thereby quoting the tiles of Tecton's Finsbury Health Centre opposite – a modernist classic designed by Berthold Lubetkin. I used to walk down Catherine Griffiths Close for decades on my way to work, never once noticing, still less appreciating, this wit and irony.

What I did appreciate, though, as I walked around Belvoir and Highcroft estates, was something else. The broad curves of the terraces and stairs on Hillrise Close were designed to accommodate the turning circles of residents' wheelchairs and mobility scooters. On Edith Cavell Close is a roughly symmetrical group of four L-plan bungalows; each has one bedroom and a terrace, and each is designed for wheelchair access. In this way, the architects anticipated the provisions of the Disability Discrimination Act of 1995.[21] That, I thought as I walked home, is worth treasuring. We need in our culture not more irony and wit, but more thoughtfulness and kindness. I'm not at all sure that the values of post-modern architecture have much to do with those virtues, but here in a little corner of London, they thrive despite the cruelty and rapaciousness of neoliberalism all around.

Acknowledgements

This book isn't entirely my fault. Leo Hollis, my editor at Verso, came up with the idea for it and prevented me making even more mistakes than remain in it. I was long put off writing about post-modernism because I didn't want to spend more time than necessary thinking about its ugly buildings and smugly self-referential novels, still less among theorists who win literary awards for bad writing and who are so often to clarity of expression and intellectual plausibility what Boris Johnson is to haircare.

I'm very grateful too to the women and men I interviewed, including Jenny Holzer, Salman Rushdie, David Graeber, Zygmunt Bauman, Daniel Dennett, Richard Rorty, Sophie Calle, Ted Sarandos, Stephen King, and Santiago Sierra among them. I'm also thankful that editors at the *Guardian* and the *Spectator* allowed me to write about some of the themes I address in the book without complaining as much as I would have done had I been in their shoes.

Most of all, though, I'm indebted to people closer to home – to my wife, Kay Holmes, and daughter, Juliet Jeffries. They read several manuscript versions of the book and spared it from becoming as inscrutable and pretentious as much po-mo thought often is. Kay proofed the manuscript, and Juliet gave me new perspectives on the themes of the book. You should be grateful: if they hadn't got involved, this book would have been much, much worse than it is.

Notes

Introduction

1. Stuart Jeffries, 'Jenny Holzer: Drawn to the Dark Side', *Guardian*, 4 June 2012.
2. Byung-Chul Han, *Psychopolitics: Neoliberalism and the New Technologies of Power* (London: Verso, 2017), p. 14.
3. David Harvey, *A Brief History of Neoliberalism* (Oxford: Oxford University Press, 2005), p. 42.
4. Dan Graham, 'Signs', *Artforum* 19: 8 (April 1981), pp. 38–9. Emphasis in original.
5. Roland Barthes, *Image Music Text* (London: Fontana, 1977), p. 146.
6. Michel Foucault, *Language, Counter-Memory, Practice* (Ithaca, NY: Cornell University Press, 1980), p. 113ff.
7. Barthes, *Image Music Text*, p. 147.
8. Jacques Derrida, *Memoirs for Paul de Man* (New York: Columbia University Press, 1989), p. 73.
9. See Byrne's essay in the V&A's exhibition catalogue. Glenn Anderson and Jane Pavitt, *Postmodernism: Style and Subversion, 1970–1990* (New York: Harry N. Abrams, 2011), p. 287.
10. Le Corbusier, *L'art décoratif d'aujourd'hui* (Paris: Flammarion, 1996 [1925]), p. 98.
11. Adolf Loos, *Ornament and Crime* (London: Penguin, 2019), p. 167.
12. Charles Jencks, *The Language of Post-Modern Architecture* (London: Academy Editions, 1984), p. 9.
13. Michael Kimmelman, 'Towers of Dreams: One Ended in Nightmare', *New York Times*, 25 January 2012.
14. Åsa Berggren, 'Rethinking Waste: A Study of the Concept and Handling of Waste and Waste Space through the Case of

Pruitt-Igoe', Department of Architecture, Chalmers University of Technology, Gothenburg, Sweden, 2013.

15. *The Pruitt-Igoe Myth*, Unicorn Stencil Doc Films, available at vimeo.com.

16. Jencks, *Language of Post-Modern Architecture*, p. 9.

17. From George Orwell's review of F. A. Hayek, *The Road to Serfdom* and K. Zilliacus, *The Mirror of the Past*, in the *Observer*, 9 April 1944.

18. All quotes from Unicorn Stencil Doc Films, *The Pruitt-Igoe Myth*.

19. Rowan Moore, 'Pruitt-Igoe: Death of the American Urban Dream', *Observer*, 26 February 2012.

20. Fredric Jameson, *Postmodernism: Or, The Cultural Logic of Late Capitalism* (Durham, NC: Duke University Press, 1991), p. 43.

21. Ludwig Wittgenstein, *Philosophical Investigations*, transl. G. E. M. Anscombe, P. M. S. Hacker and Joachim Schulte (Chichester: Wiley-Blackwell, 2009), p. 36.

22. Daniel C. Dennett, 'Dennett on Wieseltier v. Pinker in the *New Republic*', 10 September, 2013, at edge.org.

23. Gilles Deleuze and Félix Guattari, *A Thousand Plateaus* (London: Bloomsbury, 2019), pp. 1–27.

24. The Post-Modern Generator was created in 1996 by Andrew C. Bulhak of Monash University. It is a computer program that produces imitations of post-modernist writing. Not only can the Generator help students produce post-modern essays (though they really shouldn't), its results are more readable than certain books that, for the public good, I won't be citing. To see examples and generate post-modern gibberish of your own, visit elsewhere .org/pomo. 'It is a literally infinite source of randomly generated, syntactically correct nonsense, distinguishable from the real thing only in being more fun to read', reported zoologist Richard Dawkins in his paper 'Postmodernism Disrobed', *Nature* 394 (9 July 1998), pp. 141–3.

25. Dick Hebdige, *Hiding in the Light: On Images and Things* (London: Routledge, 1988), pp. 181–2.

26. Philip Damico, 'A Chronology of Postmodernism', 2017, at themetamodernist.com.

27. All quotations from 'Notes on Camp', in *A Susan Sontag Reader* (London: Penguin, 1983).

1. Shock Doctrines, 1972

1. David Harvey, *A Brief History of Neoliberalism* (Oxford: Oxford University Press, 2005), p. 10.

2. David Graeber, *Debt: The First 5,000 Years* (New York: Melville House, 2014), p. 697.
3. Antonio Gramsci, *The Gramsci Reader: Selected Writings 1916–35*, ed. David Forgacs (New York: New York University Press, 2000), p. 290.
4. Jason Hickel, 'A Short History of Neoliberalism (and How We Can Fix It)', 9 April 2012, at zcomm.org.
5. Barry Eichengreen, *Exorbitant Privilege: The Rise and Fall of the Dollar and the Future of the International Monetary System* (Oxford: Oxford University Press, 2011), p. 3.
6. Paul A. Volcker and Toyoo Gyohten, *Changing Fortunes: The World's Money and the Threat to American Leaders* (New York: Crown, 1992), p. 80.
7. Robert Nozick, *Anarchy, State, and Utopia* (New York: Basic, 2013), p. ix.
8. David Graeber, 'On the Phenomenon of Bullshit Jobs', 2013, at atlasofplaces.com.
9. David Graeber, *Bullshit Jobs: A Theory* (New York: Simon & Schuster, 2019), p. xxi.
10. Daniel H. Pink, *A Whole New Mind: Why Right-Brainers Will Rule the Future* (London: Penguin, 2005), introduction.
11. Barry Schwartz, *The Paradox of Choice* (London: HarperCollins, 2009), p. 19.
12. See 'UK Manufacturing Statistics', at themanufacturer.com.
13. David Harvey, *The Condition of Postmodernity* (London: Blackwell, 1990), p. 147.
14. Ibid., p. 240.
15. Frances Cairncross, *The Death of Distance: How the Communications Revolution Is Changing Our Lives* (Cambridge, MA: Harvard Business School Press, 1997).
16. See Mike Savage, Fiona Devine, Niall Cunningham et al., 'A New Model of Social Class? Findings from the BBC's Great British Class Survey Experiment', *Sociology* 47: 2 (2 April 2013).
17. Nozick, *Anarchy, State, and Utopia*, pp. 333–4.
18. Bruce Palling, 'Obituary: Julio Gallo', *Independent*, 5 May 1993.
19. See Steve Edwards, *Martha Rosler: The Bowery in Two Inadequate Descriptive Systems* (Cambridge, MA: MIT Press, 2012).
20. Each system undermines the other's self-consciously feeble attempts at portraying the social reality of skid row. Bouncing between a general lexicon of alcoholism and a visual vernacular borrowed from the likes of Depression-era social reformist documentarian Walker Evans, Rosler pokes fun at the mannerism that

inevitably accompanies mediation. Cassie Packard, 'Martha Rosler Tackles the Problem of Representation', 16 October 2014, at hyperallergic.com.

21. Susan Sontag, 'The Image-World', in *A Susan Sontag Reader* (London: Penguin, 1983).

22. Fiona Macdonald, 'Don McCullin: The Photos We Can't Look Away From', BBC Online, 13 February 2019 at bbc.com.

23. Included in Allan Sekula, *Photography against the Grain: Essays and Photo Works, 1973–1983* (London: Mack, 2016).

24. Roland Barthes, *Camera Lucida* (New York: Vintage, 1993), pp. 23–4.

25. Ibid., p. 27.

26. Susan Sontag, *On Photography* (London: Penguin, 2014), p. 20.

27. See Allan Sekula, 'Dismantling Modernism, Reinventing Documentary (Notes on the Politics of Representation)', *Massachusetts Review* 19: 4 (Winter 1978).

28. Cassie Packard, 'Martha Rosler Tackles the Problem of Representation'.

29. Quoted at 'Martha Rosler: Semiotics of the Kitchen', 1975, at moma.org.

30. Quoted in Gilles Deleuze and Félix Guattari, *Anti-Oedipus* (London: Athlone, 1990), pp. 284–5.

31. Ibid., p. 341.

32. Gilles Deleuze and Claire Parnet, *Dialogues II* (New York: Columbia University Press, 2007), p. 40.

33. See R. D. Laing, 'Section III: Normal Alienation from Experience', in *The Politics of Experience and the Bird of Paradise* (London: Penguin, 1990).

34. Deleuze and Guattari, *Anti-Oedipus*, p. 293.

35. Rob Weatherill, *The Anti-Oedipus Complex: Lacan, Critical Theory and Postmodernism* (Milton Park: Taylor & Francis, 2017).

36. Deleuze and Guattari, *Anti-Oedipus*, p. xiv.

37. Ibid., p. 116.

2. Disappearing Acts, 1975

1. Robert Nozick, *Anarchy, State, and Utopia* (New York: Basic, 2013), pp. 42–5.

2. See Hannah Booth's reminiscence of the concert, 'During the Gig, David Bowie Told the Crowd He Was Retiring. People Were Crying', *Guardian*, 27 May 2018.

3. Simon Critchley, *On Bowie* (London: Serpent's Tail, 2016), p. 30.

4. BBC Two, *David Bowie: Finding Fame*, broadcast 8 February 2019. See Stuart Jeffries, 'David Bowie: Finding Fame Review – A Pretty Tough Watch for Fans', *Guardian*, 9 February 2019.
5. Critchley, *On Bowie*, p. 24.
6. Quoted in Glenn Collins, 'A Portraitist's Romp through Art History', *New York Times*, 1 February 1990.
7. Judith Williamson, 'Images of "Woman"', *Screen* 24: 6 (November–December 1983).
8. Laura Mulvey, 'A Phantasmagoria of the Female Body: The Work of Cindy Sherman', *New Left Review* 1:188 (July–August 1991).
9. Ibid.
10. Ibid.
11. Quoted in Eva Respini, *Cindy Sherman* (New York: Museum of Modern Art, 2012), p. 30.
12. Mulvey, 'Phantasmagoria of the Female Body'.
13. Quoted in Betsy Berne, 'Studio: Cindy Sherman' (interview), Tate, 1 June 2003, at tate.org.uk.
14. *Arena*, 'Cindy Sherman: Nobody's Here but Me', BBC, 24 April 1994.
15. Mulvey, 'Phantasmagoria of the Female Body'.
16. Ibid.
17. See Erving Goffman, *The Presentation of Self in Everyday Life* (New York: Doubleday, 1956).
18. Nathan Jurgenson, 'The Selfie and the Self: In Defence of Duckface', Verso blog, 16 May 2019, at versobooks.com. See also Jurgenson's *The Social Photo: On Photography and Social Media* (London: Verso, 2019).
19. Quoted in Diana Kendall, *Sociology in Our Times: The Essentials* (Boston, MA: Cengage Learning, 2006), p. 91.
20. See Alice Newell-Hanson, 'Ayano Sudo's Creepy Photographs of Japan's Kawaii Culture', *i-D*, 23 October 2015.
21. Williamson, 'Images of "Woman"'.
22. Sara Suleri, *Meatless Days* (London: Penguin, 2018).
23. Kwame Anthony Appiah, *In My Father's House: Africa in the Philosophy of Culture* (Oxford: Oxford University Press, 1993), pp. 137–58.
24. Kwame Anthony Appiah, *The Lies That Bind: Rethinking Identity* (London: Profile, 2018), p. 96.
25. Edward Said, *Orientalism* (London: Penguin, 1994 [1978]), p. 108.
26. See Roger Ebert, 'Lost in the Emptiness' (review of *The Passenger*), rogerebert.com, 10 November 2005.
27. Theodore Price, 'Michelangelo Antonioni: The Truth about *The Passenger*', *Senses of Cinema* 74 (March 2015).

28. John J. O'Connor, 'Television', *New York Times*, 8 January 1973.
29. Umberto Eco, 'De Interpretatione, or the Difficulty of Being Marco Polo', *Film Quarterly* 30: 4 (1977).
30. Susan Sontag, *A Susan Sontag Reader* (London: Penguin, 1983), pp. 362–3.
31. Gideon Bachmann, 'Antonioni after China: Art versus Science', *Film Quarterly* 28: 4 (Summer 1975), p. 26ff.
32. Jean Baudrillard, *Simulacra and Simulation* (Ann Arbor, MI: University of Michigan Press, 1994), p. 95.

3. No Future, 1979

1. Jenny Turner, 'Sid after a Hamster, Vicious because He Wasn't', *London Review of Books* 13: 24 (19 December 1991).
2. Ivan Chtcheglov, *Formerly for a New Urbanism* (Seattle: Oblivion Books, 2016), available online at bopsecrets.org/si/Chtcheglov.htm.
3. Quoted in Julien Temple's film, *The Great Rock 'n' Roll Swindle* (1980).
4. See Richard Cabut and Andrew Gallix, *Punk Is Dead: Modernity Killed Every Night* (Alresford: John Hunt, 2017).
5. Dick Hebdige, *Subculture: The Meaning of Style* (Abingdon: Taylor & Francis, 2002), p. 47.
6. 'Shirt Worn by Sid Vicious on Sale for £10,000', *Telegraph*, 25 May 2010.
7. Simon Reynolds, 'Myths and Depths: Greil Marcus Talks to Simon Reynolds (Part 3)', *Los Angeles Review of Books*, 11 May 2012.
8. Quoted in Jonathan Brown, 'Never Mind Four-Letter Words . . . Here's the Sex Pistols: When Television Met Punk Rock', *Independent*, 1 December 2006.
9. See Dick Hebdige, 'Mistaken Identities: Why John Paul Ritchie Didn't Do It His Way', in Dick Hebdige, *Hiding in the Light: On Images and Things* (London: Routledge, 1988).
10. See 'Punk (1979)', 8 September 2014, at greilmarcus.net.
11. See Slavoj Žižek, *The Sublime Object of Ideology* (London: Verso, 1989).
12. Quoted in Hannah Ellis-Peterson, 'Punk Is a McDonald's Brand: Malcolm McLaren's Son on Burning £5m of Items', *Guardian*, 24 November 2016.
13. Quoted in 'Employment (Young Persons)', Hansard 932 (24 May 1977), at hansard.parliament.uk.
14. See Chris Horrie, '"Epoch-Making" Poster Was Clever Fake', BBC News Online, 16 March 2000.

15. Anne Perkins, 'Margaret Thatcher Obituary', *Guardian*, 8 April 2013.
16. Quoted in David Harvey, *A Brief History of Neoliberalism* (Oxford: Oxford University Press, 2005), p. 59.
17. Brian Towers, 'Running the Gauntlet: British Trade Unions under Thatcher, 1979–1988', *Industrial and Labor Relations Review* 42: 2 (January 1989), p. 163.
18. See Nicholas Crafts, 'British Relative Economic Decline Revisited: The Role of Competition', *Explorations in Economic History* 49: 1 (January 2012); John Cassidy, 'The Economic Case for and against Thatcherism', *New Yorker*, 9 April 2013.
19. Harvey, *Brief History of Neoliberalism*, p. 59.
20. Quoted in David Smith, *Something Will Turn Up: Britain's Economy, Past, Present and Future* (London: Profile, 2015).
21. Quoted in 'Housing Bill', Hansard 976 (15 January 1980), cc1443–575, at api.parliament.uk.
22. See Lynsey Hanley, *Estates: An Intimate History* (London: Granta, 2012), quoted in Jamie Robertson, 'How the Big Bang Changed the City of London for Ever', BBC News Online, 27 October 2016, at bbc.co.uk.
23. Quoted in Richard Benson, *The Wit and Wisdom of Margaret Thatcher: And Other Tory Legends* (Chichester: Summersdale, 2010). See also Pru Cox, John Whitley and Peter Brierley, 'Financial Pressures in the UK Household Sector: Evidence from the British Household Panel Survey', Bank of England *Quarterly Bulletin*, Winter 2002 – pdf available at bankofengland.co.uk.
24. Quoted in Benson, *Wit and Wisdom of Margaret Thatcher*.
25. See Cox, Whitley and Brierley, 'Financial Pressures in the UK Household Sector'.
26. 'Margaret Thatcher: A Life in Quotes', *Guardian*, 8 April 2013.
27. Perkins, 'Margaret Thatcher Obituary'.
28. 'Tony Blair: "My Job Was to Build on Some Thatcher Policies"', BBC News Online, 8 April 2013, at bbc.co.uk.
29. Jean-François Lyotard, *The Postmodern Condition: A Report on Knowledge* (Manchester: Manchester University Press, 1986), p. 6.
30. Ibid.
31. Quoted in Gerd Hohendorf, 'Wilhelm von Humboldt', *Prospects: Quarterly Review of Comparative Education* 23: 3–4 (1993), pp. 613–23.
32. Ibid., p. 34.
33. Ibid., p. 6.
34. Ibid., p. 5.

35. Julian Nida-Rümelin, 'Die Universität zwischen Humboldt und McKinsey: Perspektiven wissenschaftlicher Bildung', *Vierteljahrsschrift für wissenschaftliche Pädagogik* 82: 5 (2006).
36. Lyotard, *Postmodern Condition*, p. 45.
37. Cassidy, 'Economic Case for and against Thatcherism'.
38. Lyotard, *Postmodern Condition*, p. 37.
39. Ibid., p. 4.
40. Ibid., pp. 46, 45.
41. Richard Rorty, *Philosophy and the Mirror of Nature* (Princeton, NJ: Princeton University Press, 1979).
42. Lyotard, *Postmodern Condition*, p. 18.
43. Ibid., p. 60.
44. Jürgen Habermas, *Legitimation Crisis* (London: Polity, 1992), p. 58.
45. Ibid., p. 62.

4. Living for the City, 1981

1. Benjamin Elisha Sawe, 'Why Was There So Much Crime in New York in the 1970s?', *World Atlas*, 27 February 2018, at worldatlas.com.
2. See *Daily News* front page, 'Ford to City: Drop Dead – Vows He'll Veto Any Bail-Out', 30 October 1975 – reproduced at gettyimages.co.uk.
3. Bret Easton Ellis, *American Psycho* (New York: Vintage, 1991), p. 4.
4. Denise Scott Brown, Steve Izenour and Robert Venturi, *Learning from Las Vegas* (Cambridge, MA: MIT Press, 1977).
5. Ibid. p. 87.
6. Quoted in Henry Grabar, 'The Architect Who Wanted More', *Slate*, 21 September 2018, at slate.com.
7. Brown, Izenour and Venturi, *Learning from Las Vegas*, p. 3.
8. Paul Goldberger, 'What Happens in Vegas', *New Yorker*, 27 September 2010.
9. Jean Baudrillard, *For a Critique of the Political Economy of the Sign* (Candor, NY: Telos, 1981).
10. Nelson George, *Hip Hop America* (London: Penguin, 2005), p. 10.
11. Marshall Berman, *All That Is Solid Melts into Air* (London: Verso, 1983), p. 292.
12. Ibid., p. 295.
13. Ibid.
14. Jane Jacobs, *The Death and Life of Great American Cities* (New York: Vintage, 2016).

15. Robert Kanigel, *Eyes on the Street: The Life of Jane Jacobs* (New York: Knopf Doubleday, 2016), p. 234.
16. Berman, *All That Is Solid Melts into Air*, p. 298.
17. See Robert Caro, *The Power Broker: Robert Moses and the Fall of New York* (New York: Knopf, 1974).
18. Ibid., p. 893.
19. Joe Flood, 'Why the Bronx Burned', *New York Post*, 16 May 2010. See also Joe Flood, *The Fires: How a Computer Formula, Big Ideas, and the Best of Intentions Burned Down New York City – and Determined the Future of Cities* (New York: Riverhead, 2011).
20. See Marc Ambinder, 'The Fires This Time: Joe Flood on Managing New York City' (interview), *Atlantic*, 13 May 2010.
21. Douglas Kinnard, *The War Managers* (Annapolis, MD: Naval Institute, 2014), p. 75.
22. Flood, 'Why the Bronx Burned'.
23. Ibid.
24. Hebdige, *Subculture: The Meaning of Style* (Abingdon: Taylor & Francis, 2001), p. 104.
25. See John F. Szwed, *The Real Old School in Crossovers: Essays on Race, Music, and American Culture* (Philadelphia, PA: University of Pennsylvania Press, 2005).
26. Nelson George, *Hip Hop America*, p. 18.
27. Claude Lévi-Strauss, *The Savage Mind* (Chicago, IL: University of Chicago Press, 1966), p. 17.
28. See Julia Kristeva, 'World, Dialogue and Novel', in *The Kristeva Reader*, ed. Toril Moi (New York: Columbia University Press, 1986), p. 37.
29. Nelson George, *Hip Hop America*, p. 95.
30. Quoted at 'All Posts Tagged: Lee Quinones', at brooklynstreetart .com.
31. Olivia Laing, 'Race, Power, Money – The Art of Jean-Michel Basquiat', *Guardian*, 8 September 2017.
32. Ibid.
33. George L. Kelling and James Q. Wilson, 'Broken Windows: The Police and Neighbourhood Safety', *Atlantic Monthly*, March 1982.
34. Quoted in Forrest Wickman, 'Ed Koch's Legacy in Hip-Hop', *Slate*, 1 February 2013.
35. Kim Phillips-Fein, *Fear City: New York's Fiscal Crisis and the Rise of Austerity Politics* (New York: Metropolitan, 2017).
36. Constance L. Hays, 'Transit Agency Says New York Subways Are Free of Graffiti', *New York Times*, 10 May 1989.
37. Mike Davis, *City of Quartz: Excavating the Future in Los Angeles* (London: Verso, 1990), p. 224.

38. Easton Ellis, *American Psycho*, p. 4.
39. Justin Jeffers, 'A Complete Guide to the Men's Fashion in American Psycho', *Business Insider*, 25 September 2013.
40. Pablo Bronstein, *Postmodern Architecture in London* (London: Koenig Books, 2008), p. 58.
41. Quoted in Jonathan Glancey, 'Life after Carbuncles', *Guardian*, 17 May 2004.
42. Quoted in Jack Self, 'Mies's Mansion House Square: The Best Building London Never Had?', *Guardian*, 11 February 2017.
43. Ibid.
44. See Bradley L. Garrett, *Explore Everything: Place-Hacking the City* (London: Verso, 2013).
45. Quoted in Oliver Wainwright, 'Cheeky, Cartoonish . . . and under Threat: Why Our Postmodern Buildings Must Be Saved', *Guardian*, 22 November 2017.
46. Charles Jencks, *The New Paradigm in Architecture: The Language of Post-modernism* (New Haven, CT: Yale University Press, 2002), p. 175ff; Bradley L. Garrett, 'These Squares Are Our Squares: Be Angry about the Privatisation of Public Space', *Guardian*, 25 July 2017.
47. Jencks, *New Paradigm in Architecture*, p. 178.
48. T. S. Eliot, *The Waste Land*, ll. 61–4.
49. Umberto Eco, *Travels in Hyperreality* (London: Picador, 1986), pp. 43–5.
50. Umberto Eco, 'Postmodernism, Irony and the Enjoyable', postscript to *The Name of the Rose*, quoted in Charles Jencks, *The Post-Modern Reader* (London: Wiley, 1992), p. 22.
51. Iain Sinclair, *Lights Out for the Territory* (London: Granta, 2003), pp. 40–1.
52. Pablo Bronstein, *Postmodern Architecture in London*, p. 7.
53. Ibid., p. 24.
54. Michael Lewis, *Liar's Poker* (New York: W. W. Norton, 2010), p. 11.
55. Quoted in David Teather, 'Paul Reichmann Obituary', *Guardian*, 28 October 2013.
56. Bronstein, *Postmodern Architecture in London*, p. 60.
57. See full speech, 'A Speech by HRH the Prince of Wales at the Corporation of London Planning and Communication Committee's Annual Dinner, Mansion House, London', 1 December 1987, at princeofwales.gov.uk.
58. Glancey, 'Life after Carbuncles'.
59. Léon Krier, *The Architecture of Community* (Washington, DC: Island, 2009), p. 327.

60. Quoted in Leon Krier, *Leon Krier: Architecture and Urban Design 1967–1992*, ed. Richard Economakis (London: Academy Editions, 1992), p. 13.

61. Rahul Razdan, 'The Truman Show, the New Urbanism Movement, and the Lessons for Large Metros', *Forbes*, 4 February 2020.

62. Quoted in Jenny Diski, 'Thank You, Disney', *London Review of Books* 22: 16 (24 August 2000).

63. Ibid.

64. Ibid.

65. Andrew Ross, *The Celebration Chronicles: Life, Liberty, and the Pursuit of Property Value in Disney's New Town* (London: Verso, 2000), p. 270.

66. Ibid.

67. Ibid.

68. See reviews of Douglas Frantz and Catherine Collins, *Celebration, USA: Living in Disney's Brave New Town* (New York: Henry Holt, 1999), at amazon.com.

69. See full speech, 'A Speech by HRH the Prince of Wales at the 150th Anniversary of the Royal Institute of British Architects (RIBA), Royal Gala Evening at Hampton Court Palace', 30 May 1984, at princeofwales.gov.uk.

70. Quoted in 'Architects vs Prince Charles: If the Column Goes, We Go', *Art Newspaper*, 6 May 2015.

5. We Are Living in a Material World, 1983

1. Quoted in Rozalia Jovanovic, 'Sophie Calle's Controversial "Address Book" Will Be Published as a Book for the First Time', *New York Observer*, 8 August 2012.

2. Stuart Jeffries, 'Sophie Calle: Stalker, Stripper, Sleeper, Spy', *Guardian*, 23 September 2009.

3. Erving Goffman, *The Presentation of Self in Everyday Life* (New York: Doubleday, 1959), p. 22.

4. From Sophie Calle, *The Address Book* (Los Angeles: Siglio, 2012). Quoted in Jovanovic, 'Sophie Calle's Controversial "Address Book" Will Be Published as a Book for the First Time'.

5. Ibid.

6. Olivier Laurent, 'Protecting Privacy, Limiting Street Photography', *New York Times*, 23 April 2013.

7. Sophie Calle and Jean Baudrillard, *Suite Vénitienne* (Toronto: Bay, 1988), p. 10.

8. Ibid., p. 21.

9. Fisun Güner, 'She's Lost Control', *New Statesman*, 29 October 2009.

10. Arthur Schopenhauer, *The World as Will and Representation*, vol. 1 (Mineola, NY: Dover, 1969), p. 196.

11. Jean-Paul Sartre, *Being and Nothingness* (New York: Simon & Schuster, 1992), p. 567.

12. Quoted in Stuart Jeffries, 'Take a Walk on the Wild Side' – review of Edmund White's *The Flâneur*, *Guardian*, 17 February 2001.

13. Guy Debord, 'Definitions', t*Internationale Situationiste* 1, June 1958, quoted at cddc.vt.edu.

14. Quoted in Brendan Martin, *Paul Auster's Postmodernity* (London: Routledge, 2007), p. 198.

15. Quoted in Ananada Pellerin, 'Sophie Calle: Talking to Strangers', *Dazed*, 21 October 2009.

16. Jean Baudrillard, 'Please Follow Me', in Steve Redhead, ed., *The Jean Baudrillard Reader* (New York: Columbia University Press, 2008), p. 74ff.

17. Jeffries, 'Sophie Calle: Stalker, Stripper, Sleeper'.

18. Umberto Eco, 'La bustina di Minerva', *Espresso*, 30 September 1994. Quoted in Stephen Monteiro, ed., *The Screen Media Reader: Culture, Theory, Practice* (New York: Bloomsbury, 2017), p. 63.

19. See Steven Levy, *Insanely Great: The Life and Times of Macintosh, the Computer that Changed Everything* (London: Penguin, 2000), p. 180ff.

20. Quoted in Jodi Dean, *Publicity's Secret: How Technoculture Capitalises on Democracy* (Ithaca, NY: Cornell University Press, 2018), p. 84.

21. 'Harris Poll Finds Mixed Attitude on High-Tech', *Computerworld*, 12 December 1983.

22. David Burnham, 'The Computer, the Consumer and Privacy', *New York Times*, 4 March 1984.

23. David Sheff, 'Playboy Interview: Steve Jobs', *Playboy*, February 1985.

24. Burnham, 'The Computer, the Consumer and Privacy'.

25. Ibid.

26. See John Markoff, 'Apple's Visionary Redefined Digital Age', *New York Times*, 5 October 2011.

27. Quoted in Carole Cadwalladr, 'Stewart Brand's Whole Earth Catalog, the Book that Changed the World', *Observer*, 5 May 2013.

28. Marshall McLuhan, *Understanding Media: The Extensions of Man* (Cambridge, MA: MIT, 1994), p. 19.

29. Quoted in Cadwalladr, 'Stewart Brand's Whole Earth Catalog'.
30. Ibid.
31. Byung-Chul Han, *Psychopolitics: Neoliberalism and the New Technologies of Power* (London: Verso, 2017), p. 15.
32. Alan Deutschman, *The Second Coming of Steve Jobs* (London: Penguin, 2000).
33. Quoted in Edward Rothstein, 'A Crunchy-Granola Path from Macramé and LSD to Wikipedia and Google', *New York Times*, 25 September 2006.
34. Rebecca Solnit, 'Poison Apples', *Harper's*, December 2014.
35. The full script of *Reservoir Dogs* can be found at imsdb.com.
36. Quoted in Jeff Dawson, 'The Making of *Reservoir Dogs*', *Empire*, 13 November 2017.
37. Quoted in Austin Scaggs, 'Madonna Looks Back', *Rolling Stone*, 29 October 2009.
38. Georges-Claude Guilbert, *Madonna as Postmodern Myth: How One Star's Self-Construction Rewrites Sex, Gender, Hollywood and the American Dream* (Jefferson, NC: McFarland, 2015), p. 1.
39. Ibid.
40. J. Randy Taraborrelli, *Madonna: An Intimate Biography* (New York: Simon & Schuster, 2002), p. 92.
41. Edgar Morin, *The Stars* (New York: Grove, 1980), p. 90.
42. Zoë Heller, 'Book Review: Kids, I Tasted the Honey: *Sex* – Madonna', *Independent*, 24 October 1992.
43. Adam Sexton, *Desperately Seeking Madonna: In Search of the Meaning of the World's Most Famous Woman* (New York: Delta, 1993), p. 286.
44. Quoted in Alexandra Pollard, 'Madonna Was Right: There Are Rules if You Are a Girl', *Guardian*, 12 December 2016.

6. The Great Acceptance, 1986

1. Quoted in Ingrid Sioschy, 'Koons, High and Low', *Vanity Fair*, 3 October 2007.
2. Quoted in Stuart Jeffries, 'Gilbert Adair Obituary', *Guardian*, 5 December 2011.
3. Roberta Smith, 'A Bunny Balloon Sheds Its Steel Skin', *New York Times*, 23 November 2007.
4. David Harvey, *The Condition of Postmodernity* (London: Blackwell, 1990), p. 298.
5. See Owen Gleiberman, 'Film Review: "The Price of Everything"', *Variety*, 1 April 2018.

6. Fredric Jameson, *The Cultural Turn: Selected Writings on the Postmodern 1983–1998* (London: Verso, 1998), p. 135.
7. See Sophie Howarth, 'Marcel Duchamp: *Fountain*, 1917, Replica 1964', April 2000, at tate.org.uk.
8. Roberta Smith, 'Art: 4 Young East Villagers at Sonnabend Gallery', *New York Times*, 24 October 1986.
9. Herbert Marcuse, *One-Dimensional Man: Studies in the Ideology of Advanced Industrial Society* (London: Routledge, 2002), pp. 66–7.
10. Jonathan Jones, 'Jeff Koons' Louis Vuitton Bags: A Joyous Art History Lesson', *Guardian*, 12 April 2017.
11. Marcuse, *One-Dimensional Man*, p. 64.
12. Luc Boltanski and Eve Chiapello, *The New Spirit of Capitalism* (London: Verso, 2018).
13. Jeff Koons and Norman Rosenthal, *Jeff Koons: Conversations with Norman Rosenthal* (London: Thames & Hudson, 2014), p. 10.
14. Norman Rosenthal and Alexander Sturgis, *Jeff Koons at the Ashmolean*, exhibition catalogue (Oxford: Ashmolean Museum, 2019), p. 58.
15. Laura Cumming, 'Jeff Koons at the Ashmolean Review – A Master of Deflection', *Observer*, 10 February 2019.
16. bell hooks, 'Cool Cynicism: Pulp Fiction', in bell hooks, *Reel to Real: Race, Sex and Class at the Movies* (London: Routledge, 2009), p. 59.
17. James Wood, 'You're Saying a Foot Massage Don't Mean Nothin', and I'm Saying It Does', *Guardian*, 12 November 1994.
18. hooks, 'Cool Cynicism', p. 63.
19. Quoted in Paul O' Callaghan, '10 Great Films That Influenced Quentin Tarantino', 27 March 2017, bfi.org.uk.
20. Bret Easton Ellis, 'The Gonzo Vision of Quentin Tarantino', *New York Times*, 12 October 2015.
21. Quoted in Peter Debruge, 'Quentin Tarantino: The Great Recycler', *Variety*, 7 October 2013.
22. hooks, 'Cool Cynicism', p. 62.
23. A pdf of the whole *Pulp Fiction* screenplay is on Roger Avary's website, at avary.com.
24. Robert Kolker, *A Cinema of Loneliness: Penn, Stone, Kubrick, Scorsese, Spielberg, Altman* (Oxford: Oxford University Press, 2011), p. 265.
25. Ibid., p. 250.
26. hooks, 'Cool Cynicism', p. 61.
27. Michael Z. Newman, 'Say *"Pulp Fiction"* One More Goddamn

Time: Quotation Culture and an Internet-Age Classic', *New Review of Film and Television Studies* 12: 2 (21 November 2013).

28. Daniel Bell, *The Coming of Post-Industrial Society* (New York: Basic, 1973).

29. Quoted in Rowan Moore, 'Pompidou Centre: A 70s French Radical That's Never Gone Out of Fashion', *Observer*, 8 January 2017.

30. Quoted in Nicholas Wroe, 'Richard Rogers: "The Street Is Where Society Comes into Itself" ', *Guardian*, 11 July 2013.

31. Quoted in Moore, 'Pompidou Centre: A 70s French Radical'.

32. Max Horkheimer and Theodor Adorno, *Dialectic of Enlightenment* (London: Verso, 1997), pp. 140–1.

33. Quoted in Elaine Woo, 'Gae Aulenti Obituary', *Washington Post*, 5 November 2012.

34. Quoted in Stanley Meisler, 'All Aboard for the Opening of Paris Art Museum', *Los Angeles Times*, 2 December 1986.

35. Pierre Bourdieu, *Distinction: A Social Critique of the Judgment of Taste* (Cambridge, MA: Harvard University Press, 1984) – for example, p. 273.

36. Patricia Mainardi, 'Postmodern History at the Musée d'Orsay', *October* 41 (Summer 1987).

37. Ibid.

38. Ibid.

39. Paul Lewis, 'What's Doing in; Paris', *New York Times*, 19 April 1987.

40. Mainardi, 'Postmodern History at the Musée d'Orsay'.

41. Woo, 'Gae Aulenti Obituary'.

42. Fredric Jameson, *Postmodernism: Or, The Cultural Logic of Late Capitalism* (Durham, NC: Duke University Press, 1991), p. x.

7. Breaking Binaries, 1989

1. Francis Fukuyama, 'The End of History?', *National Interest*, Summer 1989, p. 17.

2. Francis Fukuyama, *The End of History and the Last Man* (London: Penguin, 2012).

3. Fukuyama, 'End of History?'.

4. Quoted in Evan Goldstein, 'What Follows the End of History? Identity Politics', *Chronicle of Higher Education*, 27 August 2018.

5. Samuel P. Huntington, *The Clash of Civilizations and the Remaking of World Order* (New York: Simon & Schuster, 2007), p. 54.

6. Ibid., p. 183.
7. Peter Sloterdijk, *In the World Interior of Capital* (London: Polity, 2013), p. 217.
8. Quoted in Goldstein, 'What Follows the End of History?'.
9. Fredric Jameson, *Postmodernism: Or, The Cultural Logic of Late Capitalism* (Durham, NC: Duke University Press, 1991), pp. 305–6.
10. Perry Anderson, *The Origins of Postmodernity* (London: Verso, 2006), pp. 112–13.
11. Ibid., p. 113.
12. Jürgen Habermas, 'Modernity: An Unfinished Project?', reproduced in Charles Jencks, ed., *The Post-Modern Reader* (London: Wiley, 1992), p. 162.
13. Jürgen Habermas, 'Modern and Postmodern Architecture', in John Forrester, ed., *Critical Theory and Public Life* (Cambridge, MA: MIT Press, 1985), p. 328.
14. Anderson, *Origins of Postmodernity*, pp. 44, 46.
15. Alex Callinicos, *Against Postmodernism: A Marxist Critique* (London: Polity, 1991).
16. Terry Eagleton, *The Illusions of Postmodernism* (London: Blackwell, 1996), pp. 134–5.
17. Ibid., p. 27.
18. Richard Rorty, 'Pragmatism, Relativism and Irrationalism', *Proceedings and Addresses of the American Philosophical Association* 53: 6 (1980), p. 727.
19. Quoted in 'Chomsky on Postmodernism', at tinyurl.com/49uyr8h4.
20. Daniel Dennett, 'Postmodernism and Truth', *Proceedings of the World Congress of Philosophy* 8 (2000), pp. 93–103.
21. Ibid.
22. Ibid.
23. Michel Foucault, 'Truth and Power', in Michael Patrick Lynch, ed., *The Nature of Truth: Classic and Contemporary Perspectives* (Cambridge, MA: MIT Press, 2001), p. 317.
24. Richard Rorty, *Contingency, Irony and Solidarity* (Cambridge: Cambridge University Press, 1991), p. 178. Emphasis in original.
25. Ibid., p. xv. Rorty writes there that he is borrowing this conception of cruelty from fellow philosopher Judith Shklar.
26. Bernard Williams, *Truth and Truthfulness* (Princeton, NJ: Princeton University Press, 2002).
27. Stuart Jeffries, 'The Quest for Truth', *Guardian*, 30 November 2002.
28. George Orwell, *As I Please: 1943–1945*, Sonia Orwell and Ian Angus, eds, (Jaffrey, NH: Nonpareil Books, 2004), p. 88.

29. George Orwell, 'Looking Back on the Spanish War', in Sonia Orwell and Ian Angus, eds, *My Country Right or Left 1940–1943, Collected Essays, Journalism and Letters of George Orwell*, Vol. 2 (San Diego, CA: Harcourt Brace Jovanovich, 1968), pp. 258–9.

30. George Orwell, *Nineteen Eighty-Four* (London: Penguin, 1975), p. 159.

31. Rorty, *Contingency, Irony and Solidarity*, p. 73.

32. Ibid.

33. Eagleton, *Illusions of Postmodernism*, p. 24.

34. Quoted in Stuart Jeffries, 'The Effect of the Whip: The Frankfurt School and the Oppression of Women', Verso Online, 29 September 2017, at versobooks.com.

35. Simone de Beauvoir, *The Second Sex* (London: Everyman Library, 1993), p. 281.

36. Judith Butler, *Gender Trouble: Feminism and the Subversion of Identity* (London: Routledge, 2011), p. 33.

37. Judith Butler, 'The Backlash against "Gender Ideology" Must Stop', *New Statesman*, 21 February 2019. Emphases in original.

38. Ibid.

39. Kwame Anthony Appiah, *The Lies That Bind: Rethinking Identity* (London: Profile, 2018), p. 15.

40. Butler, *Gender Trouble*, p. 6.

41. Judith Butler, *Bodies That Matter: On the Discursive Limits of Sex* (New York: Routledge, 1993), p. 125.

42. Martha C. Nussbaum, 'The Professor of Parody: The Hip Defeatism of Judith Butler', *New Republic*, 22 February 1999.

43. 'Cis' is the Latin prefix meaning 'on this side of' – the opposite of 'trans', which means 'on the other side of'.

44. Quoted in Robert R. Reilly, 'Pope Francis vs Gender Ideology', *Catholic World Report*, 13 August 2016.

45. Quoted in 'Pope Francis: Human Ecology Begins with Accepting the Body', Catholic News Agency, 26 June 2018, at catholicnewsagency.com.

46. Butler, 'Backlash against "Gender Ideology" Must Stop'.

47. Eve Kosofsky Sedgwick, *Epistemology of the Closet* (Berkeley, CA: University of California Press, 1990), p. 22.

48. Appiah, *Lies That Bind*, p. 217.

49. Quoted in Nussbaum, 'Professor of Parody'.

50. Ibid.

51. Ibid.

52. Catharine MacKinnon, *Are Women Human? And Other International Dialogues* (Cambridge, MA: Harvard University Press, 2006), p. 62.

53. Quoted in Kenan Malik, *From Fatwa to Jihad: How the World Changed – The Satanic Verses to Charlie Hebdo* (New York: Atlantic, 2017), p. 8.

54. Stuart Jeffries, 'Salman Rushdie: The Fatwa, Islamic Fundamentalism and Joseph Anton', *Guardian*, 12 September 2012.

55. Salman Rushdie, *The Satanic Verses* (London: Random House, 2011), p. 340.

56. Stuart Jeffries, 'Everybody Needs to Get Thicker Skins' (interview with Salman Rushdie), *Guardian*, 11 July 2008.

57. Ibid.

58. Robert Towers, 'Not Quite Pakistan', *New York Times*, 13 November 1983.

59. Salman Rushdie, *Salman Rushdie: Critical Essays: v. 1*, ed. Mohit Kumar Ray and Rama Kundu (New York: Atlantic, 2006), p. 140.

60. Quoted in Kenan Malik, *From Fatwa to Jihad*, p. 2.

61. Jeffries, 'Salman Rushdie'.

62. Salman Rushdie, *Joseph Anton: A Memoir* (New York: Random House, 2012), p. 177.

63. Quoted in Malik, *From Fatwa to Jihad*, pp. xiv–xv.

64. Jeffries, 'Salman Rushdie'.

65. Quoted in Appiah, *Lies That Bind*, p. 55.

66. Malik, *From Fatwa to Jihad*, p. xxv.

67. Salman Rushdie, 'The New Empire within Britain', *New Society*, 9 December 1982.

68. Hanif Kureishi, *My Son the Fanatic*, vol. 1 (Munich: Hueber Verlag, 2008), p. 13.

69. Peter Sloterdijk, *You Must Change Your Life* (London: Wiley, 2014), p. 4ff.

70. Rushdie, *Joseph Anton*, p. 345.

71. Jeffries, 'Salman Rushdie'.

72. Ibid.

73. Jeffries, 'Everybody Needs to Get Thicker Skins'.

74. Shlomo Sand, *The End of the French Intellectual: From Zola to Houellebecq* (London: Verso, 2018), p. 3.

75. Full script quoted at subslikescript.com.

8. Just Deserts, 1992

1. Jean Baudrillard, *Simulacra and Simulation* (Ann Arbor, MI: University of Michigan Press, 1994), p. 1. Emphases in original.

2. Christopher Norris, 'Lost in the Funhouse: Baudrillard and the Politics of Postmodernism', in Roy Boyne and Ali Rattans, eds, *Postmodernism and Society* (London: Macmillan, 1990), p. 119.
3. Jean Baudrillard, *The Gulf War Did Not Take Place* (Bloomington, IN: Indiana University Press, 1995), p. 28.
4. Christopher Norris, *Uncritical Theory: Postmodernism, Intellectuals and the Gulf War* (Amherst, MA: University of Massachusetts Press, 1992), p. 110.
5. Theodor Adorno, *Minima Moralia: Notes on Damaged Life* (London: Verso, 2005), p. 113.
6. See Steve Connor, 'The War in Truth', lecture delivered at 'Postmodernism and Truth' colloquium, University of Sunderland, November 1993, available at stevenconnor.com.
7. Jean Baudrillard, *The Intelligence of Evil: Or, The Lucidity Pact* (London: A&C Black, 2013), p. 18.
8. Baudrillard, *Gulf War Did Not Take Place*, p. 30.
9. Sven Lindqvist, *A History of Bombing* (London: Granta, 2002).
10. Jean Baudrillard, *America* (London: Verso, 2010), pp. 109–10.
11. Ibid., p. xiii.
12. Ibid., p. 28.
13. Mark Poster, ed., *Jean Baudrillard: Selected Writings* (Redwood City, CA: Stanford University Press, 1989), p. 8.
14. Umberto Eco, *Travels in Hyperreality* (London: Picador, 1986), p. 44.
15. Ibid., p. 45.
16. Poster, *Jean Baudrillard: Selected Writings*, p. 175.
17. Douglas Kellner, *Jean Baudrillard: From Marxism to Postmodernism and Beyond* (London: Polity, 1989), p. 170.
18. Baudrillard, *America*, p. 28.
19. Ibid., p. 72.
20. Ibid., p. 138.
21. *Casino*, dir. Martin Scorsese – full screenplay at dailyscript.com.
22. Ibid.
23. Harry Pettit, 'The Text Turns 25: British Programmer Neil Papworth, Who Sent the First SMS in 1992, Recreates His Pioneering "Merry Christmas" Message with Emoji', *Daily Mail*, 30 November 2017.
24. Zygmunt Bauman, *Liquid Love: On the Frailty of Human Bonds* (London: Polity, 2003), pp. 59–60.
25. Luc Boltanski and Eve Chiapello, *The New Spirit of Capitalism* (London: Verso, 2018).
26. Daisy Buchanan, 'Wondering Why That Millennial Won't Take Your Phone Call? Here's Why', *Guardian*, 26 August 2016.
27. Baudrillard, *America*, p. 50.

28. Ibid., pp. 47, 48.
29. Ibid., p. 47.
30. Slavoj Žižek, *In Defence of Lost Causes* (London: Verso, 2017), p. 203.
31. Bauman, *Liquid Love*, p. 75.
32. See Stuart Jeffries, 'Sock Puppets, Twitterjacking and the Art of Digital Fakery', *Guardian*, 29 September 2011.
33. Eco, *Travels in Hyperreality*, pp. 30–1.

9. That's Entertainment, 1997

1. Chris Kraus, *I Love Dick* (Cambridge, MA: MIT Press), p. 266.
2. Ibid., p. 44.
3. Ibid. p. 43.
4. Elaine Blair, 'Chris Kraus: Female Anti-Hero', *New Yorker*, 14 November 2016.
5. Ibid.
6. Ibid.
7. Kraus, *I Love Dick*, p. 71.
8. Ibid., p. 72.
9. Quoted in Elle Hunt, 'Chris Kraus: *I Love Dick* Was Written "in a Delirium"', *Guardian*, 30 May 2017.
10. Philomena Epps, 'Chris Kraus on Her Radical 1997 Novel *I Love Dick*', *Dazed*, 31 May 2016.
11. Quoted in Hunt, 'Chris Kraus: *I Love Dick* Was Written "in a Delirium"'.
12. Andrew Morton, *Diana: Her True Story – in Her Own Words* (London: Simon & Schuster, 2017), p. 59.
13. Benjamin Kentish, 'Princess Diana Calls Wedding to Prince Charles "Worst Day of My Life" in New Tapes', *Independent*, 28 July 2017.
14. Zygmunt Bauman, *Liquid Love: On the Frailty of Human Bonds* (London: Polity, 2003), p. 183.
15. Transcript of BBC *Panorama* interview with Martin Bashir, at bbc.co.uk.
16. Ibid.
17. Charles Taylor, *A Secular Age* (Cambridge, MA: Harvard University Press, 2009), p. 300.
18. Hilary Mantel, 'The Princess Myth', *Guardian*, 26 August 1997.
19. Ibid.
20. Blair, 'Chris Kraus: Female Anti-Hero'.
21. Epps, 'Chris Kraus on Her Radical 1997 Novel *I Love Dick*'.
22. Quoted in Hunt, 'Chris Kraus: *I Love Dick* Was Written "in a Delirium"'.

23. Kraus, *I Love Dick*, p. 268.
24. Nellie Eden, 'Chris Kraus: When Classic Turns Cult', *i-D*, 12 June 2017.
25. David Foster Wallace, 'E Unibus Pluram: Television and US Fiction', in *A Supposedly Fun Thing I'll Never Do Again* (London: Abacus, 1998), p. 68ff.
26. Ibid., p. 68.
27. David Foster Wallace, *Infinite Jest* (New York: Back Bay Books, 2006).
28. David Lipsky, *Although of Course You End Up Becoming Yourself: A Road Trip with David Foster Wallace* (New York: Crown, 2010), p. 79.
29. Neil Postman, 'Foreword', in *Amusing Ourselves to Death: Public Discourse in the Age of Show Business* (London: Penguin, 2005).
30. Raymond Williams, *Television: Technology and Cultural Form* (London: Psychology, 2003), p. 151.
31. Ibid., pp. 86, 93. Emphasis in original.
32. Stuart Jeffries, 'Netflix's Ted Sarandos: The "Evil Genius" behind a TV Revolution', *Guardian*, 30 December 2013.
33. Eli Pariser, *The Filter Bubble: What the Internet Is Hiding from You* (New York: Viking, 2011), p. 5.
34. Quoted in Tom Vanderbilt, 'The Science behind the Netflix Algorithms That Decide What You'll Watch Next', *Wired*, 7 August 2013.
35. Lipsky, *Although of Course You End Up Becoming Yourself*, p. 87.
36. Wallace, 'E Unibus Pluram'.
37. Don DeLillo, *White Noise* (New York: Viking, 1985), pp. 12–13.
38. Judith Williamson, *Decoding Advertisements* (London: Boyars, 1978), p. 45.
39. Ibid., p. 53.
40. Max Horkheimer and Theodor Adorno, *Dialectic of Enlightenment* (London: Verso, 1997), p. 167.
41. Quoted in Wallace, 'E Unibus Pluram'.
42. Robert D. Putnam, *Bowling Alone: The Collapse and Revival of American Community* (London: Simon & Schuster, 2000).
43. Quoted in Wallace, 'E Unibus Pluram', p. 67.
44. Ibid., p. 63.
45. Lipsky, *Although of Course You End Up Becoming Yourself*, p. 86.
46. Steven Poole, 'Bang, Bang, You're Dead: How *Grand Theft Auto* Stole Hollywood's Thunder', *Guardian*, 9 March 2012.
47. Ibid.

48. Quoted in Lawrence Kutner and Cheryl Olson, *Grand Theft Childhood: The Surprising Truth about Violent Video Games and What Parents Can Do* (London: Simon & Schuster, 2008), p. 168.
49. Quoted in Associated Press, '*Grand Theft Auto* Player Convicted', *Wired*, 10 August 2005.
50. Cassie Rodenberg, '*Grand Theft Auto* V Makes It Cool to Pick Up – Even Kill – Prostitutes', *Guardian*, 27 December 2013.
51. Quoted in Steven Poole, 'Play the Game', *Guardian*, 3 November 1999.
52. Douglas E. Jones, 'I, Avatar: Constructions of Self and Place in *Second Life* and the Technological Imagination', *Gnovis* 6 (2006).
53. Mark Twain, *The Adventures of Tom Sawyer* (Hartford, CT: American, 1881), p. 32.
54. Horkheimer and Adorno, *Dialectic of Enlightenment*, p. 137.
55. See Steven Poole, 'Working for the Man', 28 October 2008, at stevenpoole.net.
56. Ibid.
57. Espen Aarseth, 'I Fought the Law: Transgressive Play and the Implied Player', Proceedings of the DiGRA International Conference: Situated Play, University of Tokyo, September 2007, vol. 4, at digra.org.

10. All That Is Solid Melts into Air, 2001

1. Rebecca Allison, '9/11 Wicked but a Work of Art, Says Damien Hirst', *Guardian*, 11 September 2002.
2. Quoted in Anthony Tommasini, 'Music; The Devil Made Him Do It', *New York Times*, 30 September 2001.
3. Quoted in Stuart Jeffries, 'Provocative? Me?', *Guardian*, 11 October 2002.
4. Quoted in Stuart Jeffries, 'Dark Rider', *Guardian*, 18 September 2004.
5. Hari Kunzru, 'Postmodernism: From the Cutting Edge to the Museum', *Guardian*, 15 September 2011.
6. Quoted in Eric Randall, 'The "Death of Irony," and Its Many Reincarnations', *Atlantic*, 9 September 2011.
7. Quoted in Glenn Kessler, 'Trump's Outrageous Claim that "Thousands" of New Jersey Muslims Celebrated the 9/11 Attacks', *Washington Post*, 22 November 2015.
8. Ibid.
9. Ibid.

10. Quoted in Tom McCarthy, 'Jersey City: Trump's Claims Residents Cheered on 9/11 Are "Absolutely Not True"', *Guardian*, 24 November 2015.
11. See Matthew d'Ancona, *Post Truth: The New War on Truth and How to Fight Back* (London: Ebury, 2017), Chapter 4.
12. Aaron Blake, 'Kellyanne Conway Says Donald Trump's Team Has "Alternative Facts", Which Pretty Much Says It All', *Washington Post*, 22 January 2017.
13. 'President Bush Addresses the Nation', *Washington Post*, 20 September 2001.
14. Shirley Williams, 'The Seeds of Iraq's Future Terror', *Guardian*, 28 October 2003.
15. Kunzru, 'Postmodernism'.
16. Marshall McLuhan, *Understanding Media: The Extensions of Man* (London: Blackwell, 2001), p. 32.
17. Slavoj Žižek, *Welcome to the Desert of the Real* (London: Verso, 2002), p. 15ff.
18. Ibid., p. 15.
19. See Ive's introduction to Dieter Rams, *As Little Design as Possible* (London: Phaidon, 2014).
20. Ibid.
21. Dylan Jones, *iPod, Therefore I Am* (London: Bloomsbury, 2008), quoted in Mick Grown, 'Play That funky Music, White Boy', *Daily Telegraph*, 27 July 2005.
22. McLuhan, *Understanding Media*, p. 8.
23. Quoted in Stuart Jeffries, 'Friedrich Kittler and the Rise of the Machine', *Guardian*, 28 December 2011.
24. Paul Virilio, *Speed and Politics: An Essay on Dromology* (New York: Columbia University Press, 1986), p. 48.
25. Paul Virilio, *L'Accident Original* (Paris: Galilée, 2005), p. 27.
26. Rich Karlgaard, 'Bet on the Hares', *Forbes*, 22 August 1999.
27. Thomas Frank, *One Market under God: Extreme Capitalism, Market Populism, and the End of Economic Democracy* (New York: Doubleday, 2000).
28. Quoted in Wen Stephenson, 'Email Interview: Thomas Frank', PBS, 24 January 2002, at pbs.org.
29. Quoted in ibid.
30. Quoted in 'Apple Launches the iTunes Music Store', press release, 28 April 2003, at apple.com.
31. Apple Newsroom press release, 'Apple Announces iTunes 8', 9 September 2008, at apple.com.
32. Paul Virilio, *Speed and Politics*.
33. Ibid., p. 158.

34. Alex Marshall, 'Japan Enters the Era of Smartphones and "Dumbwalking"', BBC Online, 14 July 2014, at bbc.co.uk.
35. Marshall McLuhan, *The Mechanical Bride: Folklore of Industrial Man* (Boston, MA: Beacon, 1967), p. 128.
36. Walter Benjamin, 'Theses on the Philosophy of History', in *Illuminations: Essays and Reflections* (New York: Schocken, 2007 [1968]), p. 248.
37. Luc Boltanski and Eve Chiapello, *The New Spirit of Capitalism* (London: Verso, 2018), p. 4.
38. Ibid., p. 7.
39. Ibid., p. 38.
40. Michael Seidman, 'Workers in a Repressive Society of Seductions: Parisian Metallurgists in May–June 1968', *French Historical Studies* 18: 1 (Spring 1993).
41. Sheryl Sandberg, *Lean In: Women, Work and the Will to Lead* (New York: Knopf, 2013), p. 6.
42. Philip Coggan, *Paper Promises: Money, Debt and the New World Order* (London: Allen Lane, 2011), pp. 134–5.
43. Robert Chote, Rowena Crawford, Carl Emmerson and Gemma Tetlove, 'Public Spending under Labour', Institute for Fiscal Studies, Election Briefing Note, 2010, pdf available at ifs.org.uk.
44. Richard Vague, 'The Private Debt Crisis', *Democracy Journal*, Autumn 2016.
45. Zack Friedman, 'Student Loan Debt Statistics in 2019: A $1.5 Trillion Crisis', *Forbes*, 25 February 2019.
46. Quoted in Nicholas Watt, 'Cameron Harks Back to Thatcher on Taxation', *Guardian*, 19 May 2008.
47. 'Regulating the Credit Card Market: Why We Need a Cap on Costs', End the Debt Trap Campaign briefing, July 2019, pdf available at jubileedebt.org.uk.
48. David Graeber, *Debt: The First 5,000 Years* (New York: Melville House, 2011), p. 5.
49. Hope Lampert, *True Greed: What Really Happened in the Battle for RJR Nabisco* (New York: New American Library, 1990), p. 234.
50. Bryan Burrough and John Helyar, *Barbarians at the Gate: The Fall of RJR Nabisco* (New York: HarperCollins, 2009), p. 514.
51. Ann Pettifor, 'Vultures Are Circling Our Fragile Economies – We Must Not Let Them Feast', *openDemocracy*, 16 June 2020, at opendemocracy.net.
52. Ann Pettifor, 'Coming Soon: The New Poor', *New Statesman*, 1 September 2003.
53. Graeber, *Debt: The First 5,000 Years*, p. 368.

54. Benjamin Kunkel, *Utopia or Bust: A Guide to the Present Crisis* (London: Verso, 2014), p. 126.
55. David Molloy, 'End of Greek Bailouts Offers Little Hope to Young', BBC Online, 18 August 2018, at bbc.co.uk.
56. Yanis Varoufakis, *The Global Minotaur: America, the True Origins of the Financial Crisis and the Future of the World Economy* (London: Zed, 2011).
57. Andrew Anthony, 'Yanis Varoufakis: "If I'm Convicted of High Treason, It Would Be Interesting"', *Observer*, 23 August 2015.
58. Paul Mason, '*Adults in the Room* by Yanis Varoufakis Review – One of the Greatest Political Memoirs Ever?', *Guardian*, 3 May 2017.
59. European Commission, 'European Commission Staff Working Document: Country Report Greece 2020', pdf at ec.europa.eu.
60. Graeber, *Debt: The First 5,000 Years*, p. 391.
61. Pettifor, 'Vultures Are Circling'.
62. Pettifor, 'Coming Soon: The New Poor'.

Afterword

1. Quoted in Catherine Butcher, *Edith Cavell: Faith before the Firing Squad* (Oxford: Monarch, 2015), p. 19.
2. Quoted in William Garrett, *Marie Stopes: Feminist, Eroticist, Eugenicist* (Morrisville, NC: Lulu.com, 2008), p. 113.
3. Quoted in Charlotte Hopkins, '1937: Jessie Blythe Lane', at layersoflondon.com.
4. Stuart Jeffries, 'I Still Love my Diana Fountain', *Guardian*, 12 October 2004.
5. Lucas Cumiskey, '"Gentrification": Boris Johnson and City North Blasted for Rough Sleeping and Anti-Social Behaviour under Stroud Green Bridge', *Islington Gazette*, 6 June 2009.
6. Bronstein, *Postmodern Architecture in London* from p. 362, pp. 5–6.
7. Quoted in Oliver Wainwright, 'Cheeky, Cartoonish . . . and under Threat: Why Our Postmodern Buildings Must Be Saved', *Guardian*, 22 November 2017.
8. See Adam Nathaniel Furman: 'The Roman Singularity', at soane .org.
9. Quoted in Zoe Kleinman, 'King's Cross Developer Defends Use of Facial Recognition', BBC Online, 12 August 2019, at bbc.co.uk.
10. See Stuart Jeffries, 'Invisibility Cloaks and 3D Masks: How to Thwart the Facial Recognition Cameras', *Guardian*, 14 August 2019.

11. Pablo Bronstein, *Postmodern Architecture in London* (London: Koenig, 2008), p. 9.

12. Richard Waite, 'John Outram's Po-Mo Pumping Station Given Grade II* Listing', *Architects' Journal*, 21 June 2017.

13. Brian McHale, 'What Was Postmodernism?', *Electronic Book Review*, 20 December 2007; 'After Postmodernism: Form and History in Contemporary American Fiction', *Twentieth Century Literature* 53: 3 (Fall 2007).

14. Alan Kirby, 'The Death of Postmodernism and Beyond', *Philosophy Now*, 2006, at philosophynow.org.

15. David Harvey, 'Crisis Theory and the Falling Rate of Profit', in Turan Subasat, ed., *The Great Meltdown of 2008: Systemic, Conjunctural or Policy-Created?* (Northampton, MA: Edward Elgar, 2016) – pdf of essay available at thenextrecession.files .wordpress.com.

16. See Anthony Cuthbertson, 'Cryptocurrency Market Tops $1 Trillion for First Time as Bitcoin Price Hits New Record High', *Independent*, 7 January 2021.

17. Quoted in Angela Monaghan, 'Bitcoin Biggest Bubble in History, Says Economist Who Predicted 2008 Crash', *Guardian*, 2 February 2018.

18. Byung-Chul Han, *Psychopolitics: Neoliberalism and the New Technologies of Power* (London: Verso, 2017), p. 4.

19. Ibid., p. 36.

20. Elain Harwood and Geraint Franklin, *Post-Modern Buildings in Britain* (London: Batsford, 2017).

21. See 'Disability Discrimination Act 1995', at legislation.gov.uk.

Index